This is number two hundred and twenty-seven in the
second numbered series of the
Miegunyah Volumes
made possible by the
Miegunyah Fund
established by bequests
under the wills of
Sir Russell and Lady Grimwade.

'Miegunyah' was Russell Grimwade's home
from 1911 to 1955
and Mab Grimwade's home
from 1911 to 1973.

THE LAST TOUR

THE LAST TOUR

Paul and Eslanda Robeson's visit to Australia and New Zealand

ANN CURTHOYS

Melbourne University Publishing acknowledges the traditional owners of the unceded land on which we work, learn and live: the Wurundjeri Woiwurrung peoples of the Kulin Nation. We pay respect to elders past, present and future, and acknowledge the importance of Indigenous knowledge.

THE MIEGUNYAH PRESS
An imprint of Melbourne University Publishing Limited
Level 1, 715 Swanston Street, Carlton, Victoria 3053, Australia
mup-contact@unimelb.edu.au
www.mup.com.au

First published 2025

Cover design by Pfisterer + Freeman
Typeset in 11¾pt Whitman Text by Cannon Typesetting
Printed in Malaysia by Papercraft

A catalogue record for this book is available from the National Library of Australia

9780522879896 (paperback)
9780522879902 (ebook)

To my mother, Barbara Curthoys (1924–2000),
and John, Ned, Shino and Leo

Contents

Abbreviations

AAF	Aboriginal-Australian Fellowship
ABC	Australian Broadcasting Commission ('Corporation' from 1983)
ACTU	Australian Council of Trade Unions
ALP	Australian Labor Party
APC	Australian Peace Council
ASIO	Australian Security and Intelligence Organisation
BWIU	Building Workers' Industrial Union (Australia)
CICD	Congress for International Cooperation and Disarmament (Melbourne) ('Campaign' from c.1987)
CPA	Communist Party of Australia
CPNZ	Communist Party of New Zealand
CPUSA	Communist Party of the United States of America
CRC	Civil Rights Congress (USA)
DNZB	Dictionary of New Zealand Biography
EYL	Eureka Youth League (Australia)
FCAATSI	Federal Council for the Advancement of Aborigines and Torres Strait Islanders
HMV	His Master's Voice
HUAC	House Un-American Activities Committee
ILWU	International Longshore and Warehouse Union (USA)
LSE	London School of Economics
NAACP	National Association for the Advancement of Colored People (USA)

NFSA	National Film and Sound Archive (Australia)
NZBC	New Zealand Broadcasting Corporation
QCAATSI	Queensland Council for the Advancement of Aborigines and Torres Strait Islanders
UAW	Union of Australian Women
USSR	Union of Soviet Socialist Republics
WPC	World Peace Council
WWF	Waterside Workers' Federation (Australia)

Introduction

On Wednesday 9 November 1960, a very tall and imposing African American man in his early sixties, dressed in a formal suit and large coat rather too warm for the late spring weather, arrived at the construction site of what would become the Sydney Opera House.

On the shores of Sydney's imposing and beautiful harbour, at a prominent spot named Bennelong Point, the foundations were being laid by a range of workers in the building trades—construction workers, carpenters, plumbers, electricians and many more. Their most powerful union, the Building Workers' Industrial Union (BWIU), had invited this man, Paul Robeson, to sing to them in their lunch hour, and he had readily accepted. Famous as a singer and actor, known for his powerful bass-baritone voice, stunning stage presence and controversial pro-communist and pro-Soviet politics, he was on a concert tour of Australia and New Zealand. Sydney was his sixth stop, after Brisbane, Auckland, Wellington, Christchurch and Dunedin.

Paul's wife, Eslanda Robeson, had another appointment: at Vine House in the city, she was speaking to several hundred women about a range of topics, including Africa, the United Nations and the US civil rights movement.

Nor were the tour sponsors present, and their insistence that if he sang to the workers it must be unaccompanied so as not to undermine the sale of concert tickets meant that his usual accompanist, Larry Brown, was not there either.

With him that day were Pat Clancy from the BWIU, who as secretary of the NSW branch of the union had written Paul the letter of invitation to sing; Bill Morrow, a leading figure in the local Peace Council who was coordinating Paul's extra-concert activities in Sydney; and Miriam Hampson, from the radical New Theatre, who afterwards would take him to a harbourside restaurant for lunch.

After a tour of the site conducted by the manager, Paul stood near a microphone, said some words of welcome, cupped his hand to his ear, and sang. He began with a well-loved spiritual, 'Water Boy', evoking the call for water of thirsty enslaved workers on cotton plantations in the southern United States—'Water boy, where are you hidin'?' Next was 'Joe Hill', a song composed in 1936 by Earl Robinson with lyrics by Alfred Hayes. Joe Hill was a Swedish-born American labour activist, songwriter and member of the Industrial Workers of the World who had been unjustly convicted and executed for a murder it seems he had not committed. The song contains the much-loved line, in response to a question from the singer who has thought Hill long dead, '"I never died," says he'. Third and last came his most famous song, 'Ol' Man River', from the smash-hit musical *Show Boat*, with its evocation of the life of the riverside dockworker—'You and me, we sweat and strain/ Body all achin' and racked with pain/ Tote that barge and lift that bail!/ Show a little grit and you lands in jail'[1]—and its haunting refrain about the river, 'He just keeps rollin' along'. When Paul finished singing, the workers, arrayed on scaffolding and building materials, cheered and clapped and got him to sign their work gloves. As American scholar Shana Redmond writes in her book traversing the world for traces and memories of Robeson, 'he sang that Opera House into being'.[2]

This event is now part of Australian cultural legend and popular memory. Paul's performance marked a remarkable event in a specific place at a particular time, and it reappears in more detail later in this book. Yet it also reminds us of large cultural and political themes that cross geographical, national and temporal boundaries. It occurred late in a year that had witnessed many flashpoint events around the world on questions of decolonisation, race relations, peace and disarmament, all issues close to the Robesons' hearts. Think of Harold Macmillan's

'Winds of Change' speech in January and February; the African American lunch counter sit-in in Greensboro in the United States, also in February; and the Sharpeville massacre in apartheid South Africa in March. It was a year that saw a range of African countries, including Cameroon, the Republic of Congo, Somalia, the Republic of Côte d'Ivoire, Senegal and Nigeria, gain their independence, and the introduction of many newly independent countries into the United Nations.

There were other major events, too, such as the Soviet shooting-down in May of an American U-2 plane spying over Soviet territory, derailing plans for summit meetings on nuclear disarmament. In October, with relations between the United States and the Union of Soviet Socialist Republics (USSR) at a particularly low ebb, numerous heads of state attended the General Assembly of the United Nations and passed the Declaration on the Granting of Independence to Colonial Countries and Peoples. One of the most reported events at that historic meeting was Soviet premier Nikita Khrushchev's protest against a speech concerning Soviet suppression in Eastern Europe by pounding his shoe on the desk. Khrushchev's angry and unorthodox behaviour occurred on 12 October 1960, coincidentally the day Paul and Eslanda Robeson arrived in Sydney at the start of their Australian and New Zealand tour. A focus on Paul and Eslanda's tour in such a tumultuous year in world history—a year in which the themes of decolonisation, peace, and Cold War conflicts over communism are clearly evident—enables us to explore both African American and Australian and New Zealand cultural, musical and political history.

Having grown up in a communist family in the 1950s and early 1960s, one of my preoccupations as a historian has been to better understand the Cold War.[3] I first became interested in the Robesons' tour of Australia and New Zealand, which occurred in the later years of the Cold War, when completing my earlier research into the Australian Freedom Ride of 1965. The Freedom Ride, in which I participated as a nineteen-year-old student, was a two-week journey through country towns in New South Wales by a busload of a little over thirty students from the University of Sydney. Led by Charles Perkins, one of the country's first Aboriginal university students, the 'freedom riders' protested in several towns against racial discrimination in public facilities such as swimming pools, council halls, cinemas and, most egregiously of all, returned servicemen's clubs that excluded Aboriginal veterans. Through the research for my book *Freedom Ride: A Freedom Rider Remembers*, which appeared in 2002, I became aware that for at least some of the freedom riders, attendance at a Paul Robeson concert in their early teens had been an influence on their understanding of racial discrimination and Aboriginal rights. I had not attended a Robeson concert myself as the city of Newcastle, located on the Australian coast 200 kilometres north of Sydney, where I grew up, was not on Paul's itinerary. Newcastle was an industrialised, working-class city with a strong coalmining hinterland; its many Welsh and other British immigrants would have welcomed a Robeson concert, but it was not to be. Nevertheless, *The Last Tour* touches on part of my own history, as I was well aware as a teenager of my mother's love of Robeson records.

Intrigued by the question of just what influence Paul Robeson's concert tour had on the emergence of a strong Aboriginal protest movement, I decided to explore the visit further. There was little existing scholarship when I started, apart from a useful four-page account (along with some excellent and very detailed endnotes) in Martin Duberman's monumental 1989 biography of Paul Robeson.[4] I was interested not only in the Robesons themselves but also in their visit, which I saw as an ideal vantage point, given its occurrence at such a pivotal time, for investigating more closely the slow transition from the Cold War era of the late 1940s and the 1950s to the sixties era of the New Left, new social movements and the demand for Aboriginal rights.[5] As my research progressed, I became interested in Eslanda's life and achievements, too, and realised that the story of her tour also needed to be told. There was nothing at all on Eslanda's tour until Barbara Ransby's biography appeared in 2013 with a valuable one-page description.[6] I wanted to know more about her conduct as manager of the extra-concert side of the tour, her media interviews and her public talks.

Paul and Eslanda Robeson: Their lives in brief

Despite a rapidly expanding international scholarship, many people today have little knowledge of Paul and Eslanda Robeson, so effective was the Cold War suppression of Paul's career and memory. The following few paragraphs may help us meet them as they were when they came to Australia and New Zealand. This summary, like *The Last Tour* as a whole, draws on the extensive scholarship on Paul and the growing one on Eslanda. In Paul's case, I have found invaluable Duberman's major biography, *Paul Robeson*, which traces Paul's public and private life in immense detail. Also helpful are the biographies by Gerald Horne, Jordan Goodman, Jeff Sparrow and Paul Robeson Jnr, and the studies of Robeson's voice and music by musicologist Grant Olwage.[7] While less has been written about Eslanda, she figures in Ransby's excellent biography, Duberman's biography of Paul, and other work.[8]

Paul Robeson lived a rich and varied life. He was born in 1898. His mother died when he was six and he was brought up by his father, William, an African American pastor who as a fifteen-year-old in 1860 had escaped slavery. Paul's church background influenced him deeply as a speaker and especially as a singer of spirituals. He was one of the first African Americans to attend Rutgers University, and as a student became a famous college footballer, the best of his generation.

While in hospital with a football injury, he met Eslanda Cardoza Goode, who came from an educated middle-class African American family that included, as the 'Cardoza' in her name indicates, Sephardic Jewish ancestry. For many African American women, she was truly an agenda setter. Having gained her degree in chemistry at Columbia University in 1917, she was working in the surgical pathology department at New York City's Presbyterian Hospital, the first African American to do so.

Paul and Eslanda married in 1921 and, despite some difficult patches in their marriage, would stay together until her death in 1965. Although he graduated from Rutgers with a law degree in 1919, Paul never practised law. Instead, he became a stage actor and then a singer, after an impromptu singing performance he gave when acting in Eugene O'Neill's *The Emperor Jones* attracted attention. In the 1920s he began singing spirituals in solo concert performance to much acclaim, and after a period of combining her work as a pathologist with supporting Paul's emerging career, Eslanda gave up her hospital position and became his full-time manager.[9] She also took the first steps towards her lifelong career as a writer and journalist, at first by writing plays and a novel (these were never published).

Paul's fame as a singer and actor rose rapidly from the late 1920s through live performance, records and radio; there were many half-hour radio programs devoted solely to playing his songs. He was well known for singing spirituals and especially for the song 'Ol' Man River', from the musical *Show Boat*.

With Paul's enormous success in Europe, the couple moved to London in 1928 with their baby son, Paul Robeson Jnr, known as Pauli. Two years later, Eslanda's desire to be a recognised writer was realised when she published *Paul Robeson, Negro*. A biography of Paul, who was then only thirty-two, it was written in response to people wanting to know more about this suddenly famous singing and acting star, and sought to emphasise an African American success story.[10] It told the story of his life from childhood through the Harlem years and on to his huge success on the stage and as a singer.

Paul's fame grew even more through the 1930s, when he performed and sang leading roles in a series of movies set in Africa. Of these, the best known and most popular in Australia and New Zealand was *Sanders of the River*, which he later came to denounce as expressing imperialist and colonialist ideology. While living in London in the 1930s, both Paul and Eslanda undertook further studies: Paul, a brilliant linguist, learned several languages, and Eslanda enrolled at the London School of Economics (LSE) to undertake graduate anthropology courses on Africa.

In the middle 1930s Paul became more politically engaged, especially after he and Eslanda visited the Soviet Union in 1934 at the invitation of filmmaker Sergei Eisenstein, who wanted him to star in a movie on the Haitian revolution of 1791–1804. Paul loved what he saw in Moscow, met many like-minded people, and would often remark that this was when he first felt he'd been treated as a full human being: 'Here for the first time in my life, I walk in full human dignity.'[11] To his great detriment later on, he would never waver from his support for the Soviet Union.

Two other events enhanced Paul's turn to socialist politics and support for an international working class. One was his meeting with a group of Welsh miners, working-class men whose collective singing he loved, which led him to stay emotionally connected with Wales for the rest of his life. The other was the Spanish Civil War—a conflict between the elected Republican government and right-wing forces led by General Francisco Franco—with Paul firmly on the side of the Republicans. In January 1938 he visited Spain, where he spoke and sang to members of the International Brigade and other Republican forces.[12]

Eslanda, meanwhile, continued to develop her knowledge and understanding of Africa. Critical of much existing scholarship, which she saw as conducted too often by privileged British white men who regarded African people and cultures as uncivilised and primitive, she wanted to understand Africa from her standpoint as an African American. In 1936, without Paul but with their son, Pauli, she visited South Africa and Uganda. Her book *African Journey*, published nine years later, significantly enhanced her standing as a writer.[13]

Paul and Eslanda returned to the United States to live in 1939, and during World War II Paul's fame continued to increase as he performed in support of the war effort and made many recordings, most notably the song 'Ballad for Americans', an inclusive patriotic song that became exceptionally popular. After the war, however, everything changed. With the onset of the Cold War in 1946, Paul's politics, especially his support for the Soviet Union, became anathema in the United States. In the heated anti-communist climate of the late 1940s and the 1950s, performance venues and recording studios were closed to him. Not wanting someone with Paul's fame speaking adversely of the United States abroad, the US authorities in 1950 revoked both his and Eslanda's passports.

While Paul had limited opportunities to perform or record in the United States, Eslanda was able to continue as a writer and journalist.

Her third and last book, *American Argument* (1949), co-written with Pearl Buck, a white American southerner brought up in China, staged a wide-ranging and sometimes heated conversation between Eslanda and Pearl.[14] While they agreed on many issues, such as the state of American politics and the importance of women's political activism, they disagreed strongly about the Soviet Union, with Pearl highly critical and Eslanda a strong defender. Eslanda continued to write throughout the 1950s as an accredited journalist at the United Nations for the Associated Negro Press, an international news agency for Black American newspapers, covering a wide range of stories concerning African Americans, Africa and the African diaspora.

Paul also turned to writing. His book *Here I Stand* appeared early in 1958 and signalled his desire to again be heard as a singer, a musical theorist and an activist for African Americans' civil rights. He also read extensively about music and song and developed plans to write a book on the universality of music.

Eventually, in June 1958, as the Cold War eased and after a sustained international campaign on Paul's behalf, the US Supreme Court found the State Department had no right to withhold his (or, indeed, Eslanda's) passport on the basis of his political views. On regaining their passports, they immediately left the United States and based themselves again in England, where they had spent such productive and congenial years in the 1930s. For Paul, the next two-and-a-half years saw a frenzy of touring, performing and public speaking.

Finally, two New Zealand entrepreneurs made an offer for a commercial concert tour of Australia and New Zealand that was too good to refuse. The resulting tour was accompanied, everywhere they went, by public lectures, meetings and social events involving both Robesons. They arrived in Sydney on 12 October 1960 and, after touring both countries, left Perth on 4 December.

A surprising tour

The tour was a financial success, but it would be the Robesons' last. A few months after his return home to London, while visiting Moscow,

Paul attempted suicide. Suffering from exhaustion and depression, he underwent treatment in Moscow and the United Kingdom for almost three years and returned to the United States in December 1963. He retired from public life and never toured again.

The fact that Paul attempted suicide so soon after the Australasian tour ended has for some Robeson scholars cast a shadow over the tour as a whole.[15] Horne goes so far as to say that Paul 'may have been better served by skipping the Australian-New Zealand tour', not only because of the lengthy travel involved—undesirable for a man with health problems—but also because 'what he saw there hardly improved his mood'.[16]

Here I present a rather different account, based on new archival sources. While the Robesons' open attachment to and praise for the Soviet Union in the tense Cold War atmosphere of the times could have damaged the concert tour seriously through media hostility or blackout or perhaps simply a loss of audience, this is not what happened. Paul's concerts were loved by their capacity audiences and warmly praised by music critics, Eslanda's public lectures were well attended, and the couple's frequently stated and reported concern with questions of race, colonialism and Indigenous peoples' rights generated discussion. Paul's undeniable stature as a singer and performer enabled him to reach out not only to those in the peace movement and the trade unions who thought as he did, but also more widely to people who thought differently but loved his voice, his music, his songs, his movies and his recitations. Media coverage of Eslanda was uniformly positive, and while there was some hostility to Paul, especially when he first arrived in Sydney, most reporting was warm and respectful.

This book is a tour history—a genre that provides an opportunity to add not only to our knowledge of touring celebrity figures, but also to gain insight into the places and people who saw, heard or met them. As pop culture historian Kit Macfarlane suggests, 'It's easy to see the problems of another society in an international visitor, but all too rarely do we pay enough attention to the reflections of ourselves these visitors provide.'[17] My history of the Robesons' antipodean tour strives for a multi-perspectival and transnational approach.[18] This tour reminds us that the Cold War, the decolonisation of Africa and

Asia, and the emerging civil rights movements in the United States, Australia and New Zealand were all occurring at the same time.

Following Paula and Eslanda and those they met has led my exploration along several thematic pathways—music and performance, the peace movement, trade unions and workers' movements, the Aboriginal and Māori protest movements, and the fears and hopes accompanying the decolonisation of Africa and Asia; and, through Eslanda, feminism and journalism. It was, in a remarkable way, several tours rolled into one.

The musical tour

Central to the tour was a series of twenty concerts performed in nine cities. As Chapter 4 discusses in detail, the concert programmes drew on songs Paul had sung over his long career and were chosen and juxtaposed to illustrate his ideas about the universality of music and the connections between classical and folk music. Important at these concerts were recitations, notably the final monologue from Shakespeare's *Othello*, Langston Hughes' anti-segregationist poem 'Freedom Train', and William Blake's anthem 'Jerusalem'. Subsequent chapters discuss in depth both audience responses to and newspaper music reviewers' comments on the concerts. Media interviews were an important aspect of the tour, many of them delving into Paul's musical ideas at some length and demonstrating to readers, listeners and viewers that for Paul, despite everything that had happened to him and the many causes for which he fought, music remained profoundly important for humanity.

The peace tour

Operating alongside the concert tour, the visit had a political side. Both Paul and Eslanda expressed their political opinions freely in media interviews and public talks. They spoke about imperialism, decolonisation, the need for peace and disarmament, the struggle for racial equality and, in Eslanda's case, women's rights, responsibilities and struggles. They took time to meet and speak to people interested in, and sympathetic to, their politics, who included communists, ex-communists and other socialists, and activists in peace, women's and Aboriginal rights organisations.

From their point of view, when setting out at the beginning of the tour, the cornerstone of the political side was to be the peace movement—specifically the communist-dominated peace councils in each city, all of which were affiliated to the World Peace Council (WPC), to which Paul belonged. Their insistence was based in part on their political commitment to the pro-Soviet strand of the worldwide peace movement, and in part on a desire to limit the number of organised meetings with supporters by dealing with a single organisation in each city. This strategy worked to an extent, ensuring well-attended meetings with supporters in nearly every city (I have found no mention of one in Dunedin), but it had its limitations. The peace movement in 1960 in both countries was undergoing notable change in response to worldwide alarm at the proliferation of nuclear weapons. New non-communist strands such as the Campaign for Nuclear Disarmament, especially active in New Zealand, and the Congress for International Cooperation and Disarmament (CICD), based in Melbourne, were beginning to displace the peace councils. The result was that in some cities the peace councils provided a narrower pathway to like-minded people than the Robesons would have hoped and expected.

The workers tour

In addition to the twenty commercial concerts, Paul gave seven informal concert performances to large groups of workers—two to railway workers, four to waterside workers, and one to building workers. In both Australia and New Zealand, the best publicly remembered moments from the tour are those where there is a surviving recording of Paul singing to one of these large groups of workers. In New Zealand, that event occurred when he spoke and sang at the Addington Railway Workshops in Christchurch, an audio recording subsequently being circulated and later providing the basis for a well-known and occasionally repeated radio program on Radio New Zealand (RNZ).[19]

In Australia, best remembered are the news films recording Paul speaking and singing to the workers on the Opera House construction site in Sydney. There are other occasions that made a huge impression at the time, especially Paul singing to waterside workers in Wellington, Sydney, Melbourne and Adelaide, but at which no such recordings were made; for these, I have relied on oral histories and printed accounts in trade union newspapers.

That these occasions where Paul sang informally to large groups of workers made such an impression at the time is a clue not only to his own preference for singing to workers, but also to the importance of unionism in 1960 for these all-male transport and building workers. The ease with which he could slip between a formal evening or matinee concert with a well-dressed paying audience to a lunchtime meeting with large groups of workers in work clothes and stout boots tells us a lot about him, but also about the nature of class in Australia and New Zealand at the time. Though unionism would soon face long-term challenges leading to declining union membership, in 1960 the tour reveals glimpses into some strong and confident trade unions with broad cultural concerns and influence.

The Indigenous and anti-colonialism tour

Paul and Eslanda's relationship with Aboriginal and Māori people, organisations and issues is a complex and important one. For the Robesons, the situation of Aboriginal and Māori people and their struggles for recognition and equality were a distinguishing feature of each country, different from any other country they knew, and a source of curiosity. They expressed an interest in meeting Aboriginal and Māori people, and in Paul's case in learning about Aboriginal and Māori music, from the tour's beginning through to the end. There were important times of connection, such as meeting Māori in Auckland and Aboriginal people in Brisbane, Sydney and Perth, and I explore these in the relevant chapters. Yet there were also cities where such meetings were rare or non-existent, and it is clear that the peace councils they relied on were not always the best way to meet

Indigenous people. Nevertheless, Paul's comments in Australia on the situation of Aboriginal people became a defining feature of the tour, explored here especially in chapters 8, 9 and 14.

An important feature of both Paul's and Eslanda's commentary on questions of race is that they drew connections between civil rights struggles in the United States and the wider struggles of 'coloured' and colonised peoples everywhere. In the United States in the 1940s and 1950s, they had been among those African American activists who made these links, most notably through Paul's role in the Council on African Affairs, which Penny Von Eschen examines in her 1997 book *Race Against Empire: Black Americans and Anti-Colonialism, 1937–1957.*[20] This strand in the civil rights movement, Von Eschen argues, had been crushed in the 1950s as the Cold War came to define a 'free' United States and its allies against the unfree, authoritarian and expansionist Soviet Union, in the process casting colonialism and anti-colonialism as less important movements that were in danger of being manipulated by the Soviet Union for its own purposes. Paul's own suppression in the 1950s had been driven, Von Eschen argues, by a fear that his anti-imperialism and anti-colonialism would undermine the American project of casting itself as the leader of the free world. Suppressed Paul certainly had been during the 1950s, but his comments in the Australian and New Zealand tour in 1960 show that he continued to link the different struggles that people of colour were waging around the world.

The feminism tour

While Paul did not have much to say about women's rights or gender equality, Eslanda made up for it, frequently drawing attention to the importance of women's political activism. Her well-attended public lectures were hosted in New Zealand mainly by the local branches of the United Nations Association, to which she belonged, and in Australia by the Union of Australian Women (UAW).[21] Although she did not describe herself as a feminist—few socialist women (including my mother) at the time did, seeing feminism as a bourgeois middle-class women's movement and not for them—in current uses of the term she certainly was one. In her lectures and interviews, she consistently emphasised the vital role of women in the struggle for peace, for independence in Africa, and for civil rights in the United States.

It is time, then, to get on with the story. *The Last Tour* is structured through chronology and place. It begins with a chapter exploring Australian and New Zealand engagements with Paul Robeson's singing and movies in the 1920s and 1930s. Two chapters follow investigating the impact of World War II and the Cold War from 1946 to 1958 on Paul's career and on the access Australians and New Zealanders had to him as a performer and political figure. Chapter 4 looks at how the tour came about, the musical, commercial and political planning that took place, and the role of Eslanda as Paul's manager. The tour proper takes up chapters 5 to 14, proceeding in order as Paul and Eslanda move from one city to another, starting in Australia, then moving to New Zealand, and returning to Australia. Though Eslanda appears in every chapter, Chapter 11 is devoted specifically to her independent contribution as a public speaker and in media interviews. The book ends in Chapter 15 with a discussion of how the tour, and Paul and Eslanda generally, have been remembered since.

My hope is that this book contributes both to our knowledge of Paul and Eslanda as a couple engaging with their times, and to our understanding of Australia's and New Zealand's cultural and political history within an international and cosmopolitan frame of reference. I hope also that it is not only enjoyable to read but also helps readers feel something of the hope, inspiration and renewed energy for present challenges that those who encountered them so strongly felt in 1960.

1

Australia and New Zealand Love Paul Robeson, 1925–1939

When Paul Robeson visited Australia and New Zealand in 1960, he expressed amazement at the way people knew and loved particular songs from his records. Very often they asked him to sing songs he had not sung for many years, and he had to remind himself of the words. The familiarity with his songs of people so far away from his life in Europe and North America may have surprised Paul, but Australians and New Zealanders had been listening to him on record and radio since the late 1920s and seeing and hearing him on film since the 1930s.

Even before hearing him on radio, buying his records and seeing him in movies, some Australians and New Zealanders first heard about Robeson as a stage actor. He had begun his acting career to much acclaim in New York in May 1924 in the role of Brutus Jones in *The Emperor Jones*, a play by Eugene O'Neill in which an African American man escapes prison in the United States and flees to an island in the West Indies, where he becomes a tyrannical emperor; again he must flee to escape revolution, and as he flees is confronted by a phantasmagoria of images from his own and his people's past, including the galley of a slave ship, slave auctions and prison experiences.

While little information about the New York production of *The Emperor Jones* reached Australia and New Zealand, it would be a different story when the play opened in London in September 1925 to near-universal praise for Robeson's performance.[1] It was common practice for newspapers in both Australia and New Zealand to report on British cultural life, especially the London stage, and they printed several stories about Paul's performance in *The Emperor Jones*. The *Daily Telegraph* in Sydney had a story from a special correspondent headed 'Great Negro actor in new play' that outlined in some detail the plot of the play and Paul's performance and remarked that 'thanks to the genius of O'Neill and the magnificent performance of Mr Robeson, the play was an artistic and popular triumph. Mr Robeson is a gigantic young negro, 6ft 3in [190 centimetres] in height, with a bearing of extraordinary dignity and the richest and most resonant speaking voice I have ever heard.'[2] The London correspondent for the *Sydney Morning Herald*, Martyn M Threlfall, described both the play and Robeson's performance as 'extraordinary'. Characterising him as 'a negro actor of genius' with a voice that was mellow, rich and deep, he evoked the play and concluded that 'London will not forget the Emperor or Paul Robeson for a long time'.[3]

Spirituals, other songs, and solo concerts

At the same time as Paul was making his name as a stage actor in the United States and the United Kingdom he was becoming known as a singer of spirituals, beginning with a concert in Boston in November 1924.[4] Sung by enslaved African Americans, spirituals had first reached wider audiences in the United States and beyond, including Australia and New Zealand, through the tours and performances of the Fisk Jubilee Singers in the nineteenth century. In the 1880s, the group had made an extensive and successful tour lasting almost three-and-a-half years of the Australian colonies, including visits to Aboriginal communities at the Maloga Mission on the Murray River in August 1886.[5] The Fisk Singers also introduced spirituals to New Zealand, leaving behind them familiarity with and love of songs such as 'Steal Away' and 'Swing Low, Sweet Chariot', sung in some nonconformist churches.[6] In New Zealand the singers met Māori community leaders and members; on one occasion, at a dinner of about 300 people in Greymouth, Māori performed a haka for them and they in response sang several songs.[7] A wide range of audiences heard and appreciated their singing, and the Fisk Singers and their successors influenced the development of Aboriginal and Māori singing groups for decades afterwards. As cultural studies researcher Nicole Anae shows, as late as the 1930s Indigenous singing groups in both countries were still including in their repertoire songs they had learned from the Fisk Jubilee Singers.[8]

Spirituals took on a new significance in the twentieth century when WEB Du Bois, a major African American thinker and close friend of Paul Robeson, discussed them in his groundbreaking and influential book *The Souls of Black Folk* (1903). The songs, he wrote, were 'half-forgotten' outside the American South until the Fisk Jubilee Singers 'sang the slave songs so deeply into the world's heart that it can never wholly forget them again'.[9]

A decade later, African American singers began experimenting with a new style of performance of the spirituals that Paul would make his own. In a break from the collective concert performances pioneered by the Fisk Jubilee Singers, solo concert performances were coming into vogue. One of the earliest examples of a spiritual written in art-song form for a solo recital by a trained singer was 'Deep River', published in 1916 by Harry T Burleigh, an African American classical baritone singer.[10] When Paul turned to singing spirituals in a solo concert format with his debut concert in Boston in November 1924, he was inspired and influenced not only by Burleigh but also by African American musicians Roland Hayes and Lawrence Brown, who had been performing Black-authored music in concerts since 1919.[11] Hayes influenced Robeson in programming, arranging and performing spirituals in vocal recitals, while as Robeson's accompanist Brown would have an even greater influence over a long period of time.[12] Through their jointly carefully crafted performances, Brown helped Robeson's spirituals to become recognised as a legitimate artistic form.[13] He would be Paul's accompanist for thirty-five years, including on the tour of Australia and New Zealand in 1960.

Paul and Lawrence Brown's musical partnership began when they performed spirituals together at a series of concerts in April and May 1925 at the Greenwich Village Theatre.[14] At the first concert, Paul sang twelve spirituals that he would retain throughout his career. Brown, generally known as 'Larry', was his accompanist and arranged eight of the twelve songs; according to music historian Grant Olwage, his contribution to Robeson's performance was enormous. Over thirty-five years later, Paul would sing three of these songs in Australia and New Zealand—'Deep River', 'Go Down, Moses' and 'We Are Climbing Jacob's Ladder'. 'Deep River' is a song of longing for a place of peace. Beginning and ending with the refrain 'Deep river, my home is over Jordan/ Deep river, Lord, I want to cross over into campground', in between it twice asks the listener: 'Oh, don't you want to go to that gospel feast/ That promised land where all is peace?' 'Go Down, Moses' is also a deeply religious song, evoking the story of Moses from the book of Exodus. The singer urges Moses to go down and tell the Pharoah to 'let my people go', and the refrain 'Let my people go' can be taken as a demand for liberation from slavery. 'We Are Climbing Jacob's Ladder' calls on another biblical story, that of Jacob, the son of Isaac and grandson of Abraham, who dreams of a ladder leading from earth to heaven. It calls on the 'soldiers of the Cross', the Christians, to serve Jesus and to reach higher and higher.

Paul's turn towards singing spirituals in concert performances for a wide range of audiences was part of the Harlem Renaissance of the 1920s—that upsurge in African American contributions to a wide range of creative arts, especially music, literature and drama. In March 1925, just before the first of Paul and Larry's concerts in Greenwich, Alain Locke, an African American philosopher at Howard University, edited an edition of *Survey Graphic* magazine showcasing African American artistic creativity. In his introduction, Locke emphasised the rise of African American race pride and a cosmopolitan consciousness of the role of African Americans in advancing African people worldwide. He comments that 'As with the Jew, persecution is making the Negro international' and foresaw an important role for African Americans in the 'future development of Africa'.[15] Locke's idea of the New Negro was discussed in Australian newspapers, the South Australian *Chronicle*, for example, reporting in May 1925 on Locke's issue of *Survey Graphic*, which it thought demonstrated 'the spirit of a racial awakening' in Harlem, and the role of Harlem in focusing African Americans 'culturally and spiritually'.[16] In one essay in his collection, 'The Negro spirituals', Locke urged Black artists to rework and transform African American spirituals, 'the most characteristic product of Negro genius as yet in America'.[17] As scholar Shane Vogel writes, 'While WEB Du Bois famously emphasized the spirituals as a record of a Black past in *The Souls of Black Folk* ... Locke emphasized them as a ground for a Black Future.'[18] By the end of the year, Australian newspapers were noting the emergence of the new art-concert style of spirituals sponsored by Burleigh and Hayes.[19]

Already familiar with spirituals from the Fisk Jubilee Singers and others, listeners in Australia and New Zealand were ready for the emergence of this new form of solo concert performance in which Paul Robeson would excel, but it would be some time before they heard African Americans singing art spirituals in person. In 1924, a successor group to the Fisk Jubilee Singers known as the Dixie Jubilee Singers toured New Zealand, their repertoire including many original Fisk songs, such as 'Steal Away', 'Roll Jordan Roll' and 'Swing Low, Sweet Chariot', and some non-spiritual African American songs, such as 'Carry Me Back to Old Virginny'.[20] That same year, a white American mezzo-soprano named Edna Thomas toured Australia performing solo spirituals, signifying that art-song spirituals had become so popular that both Black and white singers were including them in their concert programmes.[21] Thomas's performance, which emphasised her whiteness, was a long way from the vision of Du Bois and Locke of spirituals as demonstrating the creativity of African American people. Billed as 'The Lady from Louisiana', she performed dressed in a crinoline suggestive of the Old South and told Australian and New Zealand reporters that she had learned her songs from her 'black mammy, Ninna'.[22] She was wildly popular in Australia, returning in 1925 after touring New Zealand; by early 1926, her records were available.[23]

While Robeson was becoming known in the United States and the United Kingdom as a famous singer of spirituals, the song that made him world famous, including in Australia and New Zealand, was not a spiritual. 'Ol' Man River' was composed by Jerome Kern with lyrics by Oscar Hammerstein II for the stage musical *Show Boat*, first performed on Broadway in December 1927. In part a romance and a family story, it is set on a boat that travels along the Mississippi River, stopping at towns and presenting theatrical performances. Its characters include not only the family, the performers and the stagehands but also the dockworkers, one of whom, named Joe, leads a Black ensemble. The musical produced several classic songs, the most famous of which was 'Ol' Man River', composed to be sung by Joe; it situates the struggle of African Americans against the unceasing flow of the river. It begins with the voices of African Americans working the boats along the Mississippi ('Here we all work while the white folk play/ Pullin' them boats from the dawn till sunset') and expresses their desire to go away from the Mississippi and instead to the River Jordan ('That's the old stream that I long to cross'). In fact, they keep working ('You and me, we sweat and strain/ Body all achin' and racked with pain') and the Mississippi keeps flowing ('Ol' man river, he just keeps rollin' along').

The stage musical was an enormous success and many applauded it for taking the art form into new, more serious territory. From the start, Kern and Hammerstein intended for Robeson to sing 'Ol' Man River', but Paul was unavailable for the musical's opening run. He was very much there, however, for the London production in May 1928, which was a huge hit. British newspapers published numerous stories explaining who Robeson was, some of which were adapted for and reprinted in Australian and New Zealand newspapers.[24] Some Australian papers had their own reporters, such as Gerald Marr Thompson, a former music critic for the *Sydney Morning Herald* who in retirement still contributed occasional articles to the paper when he visited England. Thompson reported in October on the success of the play and especially Robeson's performance, commenting that 'the pathos of the oft-repeated melody, "Old Man River", is now being hummed in the London streets'.[25] Both Australian and New Zealand newspapers reported the song's popularity, describing it as the bestseller of 1928.[26]

The success of *Show Boat* led to new concert engagements for Larry and Paul. When they performed several extraordinarily successful concerts of spiritual songs at Drury Lane in London in July 1928, the enthusiasm of the English reviews spilled over into the Australian and New Zealand press. In an article describing the concerts, the Melbourne *Age* in October 1928 commented that only a few weeks earlier no-one would have predicted that 'a negro singer would, single-handed, crowd the great spaces of Drury-lane Theatre with several audiences come to hear him sing this one class of song'. But that, it went on, 'is what has happened'; the theatre, with 3000 seats, had sold out twice. The article went on to list Robeson's many accomplishments—university graduate, actor, and a man of 'herculean stature'.[27] The *Auckland Star* on 16 August 1928 ran a story headed 'Critic captivated by Negro genius' and subtitled 'Vast audience sits spellbound while Paul Robeson sings'.[28] Many other newspapers in both Australia and New Zealand reported the near-frenzy of admiration that ensued from the Drury Lane concerts.[29]

Now based in London, Paul went from one outstanding success to another. Less than two years after reading about *Show Boat* and the Drury Lane concerts, Australians and New Zealanders learned of his performances as the title character in Shakespeare's *Othello* in a production at the Savoy Theatre. Opening on 19 May 1930, the play attracted attention and controversy and mixed reviews, but for Robeson himself, considerable acclaim.[30] In one newspaper article, Stephen Roberts, professor of history at the University of Sydney, listed 'the theatrical art of Paul Robeson' as an example of the African American cultural revival.[31] Robeson would appear twice more in *Othello* productions, one in the United States in 1942–43, and the other in the United Kingdom at Stratford-upon-Avon in 1959; taken together, these three productions changed thereafter the way the play was performed and assumptions about who should perform the role of Othello.[32] It became identified with Paul throughout his life, and he often included in his concerts Othello's final speech, given as the character commits suicide after killing Desdemona in a jealous rage and learning she had not, after all, been unfaithful to him. It begins, strikingly, with Othello saying, 'I have done the state some service, and they know it', and then asks whoever will tell his story to

> Speak of me as I am; nothing extenuate,
> Nor set down aught in malice. Then must you speak
> Of one that loved not wisely but too well.

Always to much acclaim, Paul would recite this monologue frequently in Australia and New Zealand, both at commercial concerts and when speaking and singing more informally to workers.

Records, tours and radio

By the late 1920s, Australians and New Zealanders were not only reading about Paul's success as a singer in London but were also able to hear for themselves, through phonograph records, him singing both spiritual and secular songs. By the mid-1920s, one-third of Australian households owned a gramophone and the records played on them were either imported or produced by the local Australian branches of multinational gramophone companies.[33] Robeson began recording spirituals with His Master's Voice (HMV) in late 1925, and by 1926 news of these records was being reported in Australia and New Zealand.[34] Robeson records were occasionally mentioned in the press through 1927 and 1928, but it was really in 1929 that they seem to have become freely available.[35] A music critic who signed themselves as 'AHT' enthused in the Brisbane *Telegraph* in January 1929 about Robeson's recent two 10-inch HMV records of 'negro songs' and spirituals and said they were 'the first of Robeson's that have come to Australia' and would be on sale at all record shops shortly. They would cost 4 shillings each, making them at the higher end of the market.[36] Several more Paul Robeson records featuring spirituals and other songs appeared that year, notably a Gramophone Company record marketed as 'plantation songs', including 'Old Folks at Home', 'Away Down South in Dixie,' 'Carry Me Back to Old Virginny' and

'My Old Kentucky Home'. These were old Southern songs and, as one newspaper commented, the 'popularity of these songs never seems to flag, and in this record, Paul Robeson gives a really thrilling and moving performance'.[37] More records became available when in June 1929 the record of *Show Boat* including 'Ol' Man River' went on sale in Australia and New Zealand.[38]

By September, more Robeson records were on sale, including one featuring 'Water Boy', a song he would sing frequently on the Australian and New Zealand tour as he had throughout his singing career. This was a folk song composed by American songwriter Jacques Wolfe in the style of African American spirituals and subsequently arranged and popularised in the 1920s as a jazz song by Avery Robinson, expressing the call by a thirsty labourer on a chain gang for the water carrier to bring him water.[39] It begins, 'Water boy, where are you hidin'?', continues with 'If you don't come I will tell your mammy', and then has the rhythms of a prison gang breaking rocks: 'There ain't no hammer/ That's on-a this mountain/ That ring-a like mine boy/ That ring-a like mine.'

Through the 1920s and 1930s the Australian and New Zealand reception of spirituals crossed the high culture/popular culture divide, being both praised by musical critics and widely available on radio and gramophone records. The *Brisbane Courier* observed on 1 January 1930: 'Robeson's records have had phenomenal popularity, due to [his] splendid bass voice, sincere artistry, and interesting personality.'[40]

Another musical form closely associated with African American performers had a more mixed reception. Australians first heard of jazz in their newspapers in 1917; the first local band emerged in 1918, and from then on it rapidly grew in popularity. Visits by African American jazz performers began in 1923 with the arrival of the Royal Southern Singers, an African American group who performed a mix of jazz tunes and spirituals.[41] As its popularity increased in both countries, jazz also gained in the United States a somewhat negative reputation associated with improper conduct in questionable venues, uninhibited dancing and, notably, Black and white people dancing together. As Alwyn Williams argues in his PhD thesis, many Black intellectuals at first distanced themselves from jazz, fearing it would 'perpetuate the idea prevalent among whites that blacks were lascivious and primitive', and much preferred the spiritual, 'loaded with dignity and religious yearning', that was also popular with white Americans and Europeans.[42]

In Australia, the idea that jazz was an inferior and sexually and racially dangerous form of music began to take hold among music critics and social commentators. When *The Age*, one of Melbourne's leading newspapers, welcomed Edna Thomas's plantation songs and spirituals in 1924, for example, it commented that they were 'a great relief from the harsh jazz exhibitions, the usual offering of her countrymen'.[43] To a concern about the moral influence of African American jazz was added strong opposition by the Australian Musicians' Union (AMU) to American jazz band visits, fearing that local players were being displaced and angry that American musicians' unions had excluded Australian bands and solo musicians from touring in the United States.[44] The conservative Australian Government began refusing to admit African American jazz bands, excluding two in 1923 and several more in the following years.[45] In 1928, as historian Deirdre O'Connell has explored in detail, it admitted Sonny Clay and his jazz band The Colored Idea, probably because they were presented by their promoters as theatre rather than jazz performers. The band conducted successful concerts in Sydney and Melbourne in early 1928, but its members' social interactions in Melbourne in March with young white women were seen as a scandal, and in a moral panic the band was deported.[46]

From then on, the government screened visiting 'coloured theatrical performers or vaudeville artists' more rigorously, to the delight of the AMU and many who were devoted to the White Australia policy.[47] The iniquitous 'character test' operated from the early 1920s. Designed especially to exclude jazz performers, it seems to have constrained but not eliminated visits by African American performers in other musical genres. As author Bill Egan shows, Australian audiences occasionally saw African American performers in these years, such as baritone Bob Parrish, whose concert repertoire included 'Ol' Man River'.[48] Most notably, in August 1937, Nina Mae McKinney, one of Robeson's co-stars in *Sanders of the River*, arrived in Australia for a tour with her revue *Hello Harlem!* and would stay for several months after the revue ended.

There remained uncertainty among musical entrepreneurs whether the new 'character test' applied to all, or only jazz-playing, African American performers. Though the racially discriminatory policy was surely inhibiting bringing African American performers to Australia, it does not seem to have applied to singers of spirituals. In August 1929 the Kentucky Jubilee Singers, a group of 'eight coloured singers of spirituals and plantation songs', toured without incident.[49] I have found no speculation that the ban would affect Robeson, should he have wished to tour Australia.

From early 1929, Australians and New Zealanders could also hear Robeson on radio. The first radio broadcast in New Zealand occurred in Dunedin in 1922 and in Australia in 1923. In both countries there was in the early years a combination of government-owned and privately owned stations, a blend of the British system, where the BBC had a monopoly, and the American system, where radio stations were privately owned. This system persisted in Australia, while in New Zealand nearly all stations became government-owned. Music would be a feature on all kinds of radio. For several years it consisted of broadcasted live studio concerts, but from about 1926 radio broadcasters began to play gramophone records.[50] Newspapers began to print radio programs, which in Australia from June 1929 indicate that the stations were scheduling programs, usually lasting half an hour, devoted entirely to Paul Robeson's songs.[51] Radio programs appeared from May 1929 in New Zealand noting various Robeson time slots, usually much shorter than was common in Australia, such as a nine-minute slot entitled 'Paul Robeson, Plantation Songs', on the Masterton program.[52] Given the accessibility of radio, it seems likely that for many people this is how they heard and knew Robeson's voice.

Fame in the 1930s

Two books would help spread Paul Robeson's fame in the early 1930s. One was Eslanda's biography, *Paul Robeson, Negro*, the first of her three books; it was published in England by Victor Gollancz on 20 May 1930, the day after Paul began his run in England playing Othello. At the time, Eslanda wanted to become a writer, and the sudden fame of her husband, with people wanting to know more about him, gave her a subject.

In her account of Paul's life, she gave attention to the importance of the church and of a vividly described Harlem in African American life, and contrasted racial discrimination and segregation in the United States with what she saw as a lack of it in England.[53] Yet at the time of writing the marriage was rocky, coming close to divorce, and though in the end they stayed together, things were never the same. The result was a book of apparently loving praise with an undertone of criticism, such as that Paul was lazy and flirtatious. Some commentators found Eslanda's habit of referring to herself in the third person odd and distracting, and I would agree. Though Paul was only thirty-two, leading some to suggest he was rather young for a biography, most reviewers thought his international acclaim and fame as a singer and actor made the biography worthwhile.

The book was available in Australia and New Zealand but there were few reviews; one in the Sydney *Sun* liked it for its frankness 'tinged with wifely adoration' and thought it 'a very strong plea for the advancement of the negroes'.[54] In the United States, as scholar Robert Shaffer notes, several leading African American intellectuals praised the book and its subject. Langston Hughes thought ordinary black folk were proud of Paul's achievements, while WEB Du Bois considered that although Paul was made 'a little too perfect', the triumph of a 'fine black man' was fascinating and unusual.[55] Paul Robeson Jnr writes in his biography of his father that Paul did not see his representation as perfect at all, and was so angered by the book for harping on his faults, displaying him as immature and lazy and amplifying Eslanda's own role in his success, that he never entirely forgave her.[56]

The other book contributing to Paul's fame was written by the well-known New York drama critic Alexander Woollcott, a white American who wrote for the culturally influential *New Yorker* magazine. His best-selling collection of essays and anecdotes, *While Rome Burns* (1934), which was said to have sold a quarter of a million copies,[57] included a chapter, 'Colossal Bronze', about his friendship with Robeson, with a particular focus on how 'Ol' Man River' came to be composed and written especially for him. He writes: 'of the countless people I have known in my wanderings over the world [Paul Robeson] is one of the few of whom I would say that they have greatness ... Paul Robeson strikes me as having been made out of the original stuff of the world'.[58] This comment was much quoted thereafter, starting, it seems, with 'SEN', the reviewer for the *Sydney Mail* in 1935.[59] Woollcott's comments were not forgotten: when the Robesons came to Australia in 1960, several newspaper commentators referred to his view of Paul, especially the idea of him as a great man.[60]

One indicator of Robeson's fame in Australia in the 1930s is the way in which promising Aboriginal singers of that era would be dubbed 'Australia's Paul Robeson'. In Aboriginal communities in the 1930s, there was a growing culture of musical performance for both Aboriginal and non-Aboriginal audiences, including at commemorative events such as the opening of the Sydney Harbour Bridge in 1932 and a re-enactment of the First Fleet landing for the sesquicentennial celebrations in 1938. These performers combined a range of singing and playing styles and, as Anae shows, Indigenous singing groups in both Australia and New Zealand in the 1930s included in their repertoire songs they had learned from the Fisk Jubilee Singers.[61]

One of the most common musical styles in Aboriginal communities was the gum-leaf bands that emerged on Aboriginal missions in the south-east of the country in the 1930s, and in the west of the country in the Mt Margaret Native Minstrels.[62] These bands, consisting of Aboriginal musicians and singers performing for a wide variety of audiences, sang minstrel songs such as 'Swanee River' and 'Old Folks at Home', along with Australian folk songs and Christian hymns.[63] Yorta Yorta man Jimmy Little Snr, father of the famous Aboriginal singer Jimmy Little, led the vaudeville entertainment at the Cumeroogunga Mission, on the NSW side of the Murray River, which formed the border with Victoria; the repertoire included songs learned from the Fisk Jubilee Singers.[64]

In Victoria, Ted Mullett, a performer in the Lake Tyers Concert Party in the 1930s, was sometimes dubbed 'Australia's Paul Robeson'.[65] Aboriginal singers were well known in the north, too; a report of one performance during Christmas celebrations in Darwin in 1937 referred to 'a blind native who is known locally as the "Paul Robeson" of the compound'.[66] This tradition would continue into the post-war period, when promising young Aboriginal singer Harold Blair would also be described as 'Australia's Paul Robeson', signifying a mix of being Black with a wonderful voice, and musically gifted.[67]

Movies

Paul Robeson was also becoming known to Australians and New Zealanders through movies, especially 'the talkies', which cinemas began to screen in 1929. Through the 1930s, in addition to movie theatres in the main cities, there was a network across the country of small, wooden-seated picture theatres and community halls in country towns, the movies brought there by travelling showmen. In both city and country Robeson's movies were popular, and very often they led to a surge of interest in his records. Two American movies starring Paul, *The Emperor Jones* in 1933 and *Show Boat* in 1936, were widely screened and both became hugely popular, especially *Show Boat*, which became one of the most popular movies ever screened in Australia. As in the United States and the United Kingdom, audiences loved the mix of serious romantic drama and well-known popular songs.

Popular, too, were Robeson's 'African' movies of the 1930s. Like many films in this era, these movies, mainly British productions, featured white heroes in desert settings and extolled the benefits of British colonialism. Yet they also had African characters and some of them contained extensive ethnographic footage shot in Africa. Robeson was a huge figure in several of these movies, the best loved in Australia and New Zealand being *Sanders of the River* (1935). Directed by Hungarian-born, London-based director Zoltan Korda, it was set in colonial Nigeria and was a major commercial success. The Sanders of the title is a British administrator, and Bosambo, the role played by Robeson, is the educated and literate chief of the Ochori tribe who becomes Sanders' ally in the struggle against gunrunners and slavers. When Bosambo's wife, played by Nina Mae McKinney, is kidnapped by a rival tribe led by King Mofolaba, Bosambo is captured when he comes to her aid and Sanders arrives just in time to save both their lives—McKinney's character is saved, that is to say, not by the charismatic African husband played by Robeson but by a white saviour, the colonial administrator. The movie has several songs sung by Robeson, most notably 'The Canoe Song', a Congo melody arranged with new lyrics in which Bosambo sings Sanders' praises as a just and even-handed administrator: 'Sandy the strong/ Sandy the wise/ Righter of wrong/ Hater of lies'. The song has a stirring chorus: 'So each for all/ We stand or fall/ And all for each/ Until we reach/the journey's end'. Australian audiences also loved a rather bloodthirsty battle song that Paul sings several times in the movie, its lyrics including 'Off, off into battle/ Make the war drums rattle/ Mow them down like cattle/ Onward, on, on into battle/ Bite them into the dust, into the dust/ Charge, cheer, shoot, spear, smash, smite, slash, fight, and slay'.

Sanders of the River began its antipodean run in August 1935 and reviewers in both Australia and New Zealand immediately loved it. The *New Zealand Herald* gave an enthusiastic review and noted that the audience had applauded the film at the end of its screening in the Regent Theatre in Auckland, while the *Labor Daily* in Sydney praised Robeson in the role of Mosambo for using 'his fine voice to perfection in his war-stirring songs, and again in leading the canoes down the rapids ahead of "Sandi"'.[68] Over the next eighteen months the movie was shown around both countries to appreciative audiences. It was still screening in Australia in January 1937 when, in the small northern town of Darwin, an Aboriginal audience rose to its feet and with chants, clapping and stamping joined in when Robeson sang the war songs.[69]

While Paul himself rejected and intensely disliked the movie, regarding it as praising British colonialism (which it did), it was easily his best remembered in Australia and, to a lesser degree,

New Zealand, when he finally arrived there in 1960. Audiences appear to have loved its dramatic storyline, Robeson's presence and singing, the stirring songs composed by Mischa Spoliansky, and the scenes of African tribes in conflict. In his last interview in Sydney, Paul, having become aware of the popularity of *Sanders of the River* in Australia, would take steps to set the record straight on his own feelings about the movie. He recounted how some African students had challenged him on appearing in such a film, which 'shows Africans as children, needing European guidance', leading him to view the film again and to see that they were right: 'I had unwittingly helped create a symbol of imperialism.' The artist cannot live in a vacuum and 'must choose which cause he is going to serve'.[70] Even after this disclaimer, Australian journalists would refer to *Sanders of the River*, one telling him that he had seen it when he was a young boy and the only thing he remembered about it was Paul Robeson.[71]

The appearance of four more African movies starring Robeson—*Song of Freedom* in 1936 and *Big Fella*, *Jericho* and *King Solomon's Mines*, all in 1937—further increased antipodean knowledge of him and his wonderful singing voice. Paul sang in all these movies, and even people who did not see them may well have heard and enjoyed the songs on radio.[72] Songs from *Big Fella*, for example, were broadcast on Australian radio in what was then dubbed a 'film broadcast' on 19 September 1937.[73] The movies brought Robeson's fame to new heights. As movie reporter Mary Olivier commented in *The Queenslander* in 1938, people had liked hearing his voice on gramophone records but knew little about him until the success of his movies. She pointed out: 'In the last two years Paul Robeson has risen to extraordinary screen prominence, the more amazing because he is the first coloured actor to gain world-wide recognition in films, the only coloured man ever to reach stardom.'[74]

Two of the movies were British films directed by J Elder Wills, and in both Robeson played a dockworker. In *Song of Freedom*, his character, John Zinga, becomes a singing star and subsequently discovers he is a descendant of Queen Zinga of Casanga (an African island), whose local people ultimately accept him. In *Big Fella*, his character helps find a lost English boy who has disappeared from a vessel in the port of Marseilles. In this movie, in which, incidentally, Eslanda appears as a cafe proprietor, some songs, such as 'Ma Curly Headed Baby', were old favourites that Paul had sung in concerts, while others were written especially for him.[75]

Paul also sang in *King Solomon's Mines*, a popular British movie directed by Robert Stevenson that was based on the 1885 novel by H Rider Haggard—one of the first African adventure novels to feature European encounters with hitherto unknown African kingdoms. Paul's character is Umbopa, a Zulu man who helps a group of adventurers led by Allan Quartermain; they are searching for the missing father of one of their party, who had been looking for the fabled King Solomon's mines, believed to contain a treasure trove of diamonds. When the party reaches Kukuanaland, Umbopa reveals that he is the lost heir to the throne and, together with local dissidents and the group of explorers, he overthrows the false King Twala. In the movie, Robeson sings several songs by Spoliansky, namely 'Walk! Walk!', 'Climbin' Up' and 'Kukuwana'. Although many background scenes were filmed in southern Africa, near Pietemaritzburg in Natal, Robeson and the other actors were filmed in London.

Perhaps the most striking of these movies to a modern audience is *Jericho* (1937), a British film directed by Thornton Freeland—a white American who made movies both in the United States and Britain. *Jericho* shares the Orientalist fascination of the era with desert settings, but its portrayal of race relations is distinctive and less clearly colonialist than other films of the period. It is the story of an educated African American who, through a series of events during World War I, escapes to Africa, where he remains and thrives. As the film opens, Robeson's character, Jericho Jackson, is an army corporal with medical training on a ship transporting African American soldiers to France. When the ship is torpedoed, he saves many lives but accidentally kills an obstructive officer in the process. At the American base in Bordeaux he is subsequently convicted of murder and disobeying orders, but escapes by boat to North Africa where he joins the Tuareg people, among whom he heals the sick, marries and has a child, and eventually becomes their leader.[76] Although not shown extensively in the United States, *Jericho* was widely exhibited in Britain and the Commonwealth, including in Australia and New Zealand, where it received enthusiastic reviews.[77]

While Australia's film industry was small in the 1930s, there were some movies produced in the style of Paul's African movies but situated in an Australian context. One of these was Charles Chauvel's *Uncivilised* (1936), in which the white ruler of an Aboriginal tribe kidnaps Beatrice Lynn, a white female author investigating the tribe; after many adventures, the author falls in love with her kidnapper.[78] Using footage of spectacular scenery in north Queensland, the film also featured Aboriginal performers, mostly from Palm Island but also including Bill Onus, a Wiradjuri and Yorta Yorta man then living in Sydney, who would three years later join and become a leading figure in the Aborigines Progressive Association. The *Sydney Morning Herald* film critic expressed the view that had the film been of the same high quality as the scenery, 'Mr Chauvel would have fathered a new *Sanders of the River*'; as it was, 'The aborigines in *Uncivilised* are responsible for whatever success the film attains.'[79] That *Sanders of the River* was seen as the benchmark of good entertainment hints at just how popular this movie was in Australia in the 1930s.

'The artist must take sides': Fame and politics in the 1930s

Through the 1930s, Paul's politics were taking a sharp turn to the socialist left and he was becoming increasingly outspoken on political matters. The political positions he developed at this time, some of them covered in the Australian and New Zealand press, would strongly influence the views he would later express during his tour.[80] There were several dimensions to this political turn, including connection with British workers, admiration for the Soviet Union, condemnation of the rise of fascism in Germany, support for the beleaguered Republican government in Spain, and championing African nations' independence. Paul and Eslanda were becoming socialists who were strongly critical of imperialism and colonialism.

Wales

Paul's greater interest in the labour movement and socialist politics seems to have begun in Wales. During the Australian and New Zealand tour he often spoke about his special affinity with and love for Wales, a connection that had begun over thirty years earlier. In 1929 in Pontypridd near Cardiff, where he was performing in *Show Boat*, he encountered a group of unemployed Welsh miners from the Rhondda Valley singing as they walked to London as part of a 'national hunger march' organised by the National Unemployed Workers' Movement, led by the Communist Party of Great Britain.[81]

Captivated by their singing, Paul immediately joined them. Fifty years later, one of the miners present recalled how stunned they had been; as author and activist Jeff Sparrow writes, they saw 'a huge African-American stranger in formal attire incongruous next to the half-starved Welshmen in their rough-hewn clothes and mining boots'.[82] After the march, he sang 'Ol' Man River' and some spirituals, and donated enough money for them to take the train back to Wales.

Many times afterwards Paul visited mining towns and sang in Wales, and the reception was so warm and positive that he always regarded it as a kind of home away from home. He would later tell audiences in Australia and New Zealand that he could knock on any door in Wales and would be invited in and offered a cup of tea.

The Soviet Union, 1934 and after

One of the key turning points in the lives of Paul and Eslanda was their visit to the Soviet Union in 1934 at the invitation of the esteemed Soviet film director Sergei Eisenstein. Eisenstein had made *Battleship Potemkin* in 1925 and continued to make films in the Soviet Union through the latter 1920s. In 1931, he began thinking about making a film on Toussaint Louverture, the Haitian revolutionary leader, to be titled *Black Majesty*. As his close friend the English journalist Marie Seton recalled in a biography she wrote twenty-one years later, Eisenstein wanted to 'reflect the developing genius of the

Negro people', who had attracted his warm interest on a visit to America a few years earlier.[83] As a famous African American actor, Robeson seemed ideal for the role of Louverture, and Eisenstein was delighted when Paul agreed to come to Moscow to discuss the project. Both he and Eslanda had been interested in Russia for some years. Eslanda's family was fascinated by the country, her mother having had an abiding interest in its culture and her two older brothers having already visited it.[84] Paul had begun learning the language in 1931 and quickly became very proficient; he began introducing Russian songs into his concerts and commenting publicly on the affinity between Russian and African American music.[85]

When Paul and Eslanda arrived in Moscow accompanied by Seton, Paul and Eisenstein hit it off immediately. They had a lot in common, having been born in the same year and having both come to fame at the age of twenty-seven in 1925.[86] They sat up, Seton recalled, half the night 'discussing the evolution of languages; then they turned to music as the expression of comparative cultural development and played the African and Siamese records which Paul Robeson had brought as a present for Eisenstein'.[87] They found a common interest in stadial theory, whereby humanity progresses through various stages—an indication, perhaps, of the growing influence of Marxism on Robeson's thought. There followed a fourteen-day visit, with Eisenstein and Paul constant companions and having many long conversations. One evening, Seton writes, they 'began to discuss the aboriginal tongues of Australia and the dialects of Africa and China'.[88] The Robesons enjoyed a round of parties, receptions and film showings. One of the people they met was Herbert Marshall, a British theatre and film director then working in Russia, who was able to introduce Paul to leading figures in Soviet theatre and who would later become a close friend and colleague in London.[89]

Already well known in Russia as a singer, Paul was treated as a celebrity and invited to perform in an opera and sing Negro spirituals on radio and at government social events. The Soviet authorities used his rendition of 'Sometimes I Feel Like a Motherless Child' on the soundtrack of a short film about racism and labour exploitation in the American sugar industry.[90] He sang to workers at a ball-bearing plant that employed many foreign and American workers.[91] Paul and Eslanda's friend and leading member of the US Communist Party (CPUSA) William L Patterson serendipitously met with them in Moscow in early 1935, and their several long conversations strongly influenced Paul's turn to a more revolutionary politics.[92]

On leaving Moscow, Paul and Eslanda went to Leningrad (now St Petersburg), where they spent time with African American singer Marian Anderson, who had performed a concert there on 7 January.[93] Robeson and Anderson had a great deal in common: they were close in age and were both pioneers in bringing spirituals to a wide international audience. As scholar Sharon Vriend-Robinette writes, they both 'rose to prominence from limited means. Each had lived in Europe. Both used and popularized spirituals in an attempt to educate their audiences and to connect with an African American understanding of life and liberty.'[94] Their paths, however, would diverge politically, as we shall see.

When he left Moscow, Paul agreed to return to make *Black Majesty* with Eisenstein. With various competing pressures on each of them, however—Eisenstein to get a film made quickly and Paul with his many concerts and political engagements—the two men could not find a mutual time and the film was never made.[95] Nevertheless, their meeting made, in Seton's words, 'an indelible impression' on both of them. For Paul, his visit to the Soviet Union was a transformative experience. His politics became increasingly radical and socialist as he came to see the Soviet system as free of the racial hierarchy and oppression that marked his experience of the United States. As he would often say, he felt that for the first time in his life he had been treated not through the prism of race but simply as a human being. He commented to Julia Dorn from the radical theatre journal *New Theatre*, 'In Soviet Russia I breathe freely for the first time in my life. It is clear, whether a Negro is politically a Communist or not, that of all the nations in the world, the modern Russians are our best friends.'[96] This freer breathing generated a profound romantic affiliation with Russia and the Soviet Union for the rest of his public life that nothing would shift.[97] Like many others on the political far left, he refused to believe negative reports of the Soviet Union, seeing them as disinformation spread by that nation's enemies. The excitement and validation he received during this visit would create a loyalty that later events would not dislodge and the public expression of which would damage him politically, commercially and professionally.

Though Eisenstein's film was never made, Paul did star in March 1936 as the Haitian revolutionary leader in *Toussaint Louverture*, a play written by CLR James, a Trinidadian writer and political activist based in London.[98] It was performed in London on several Sunday evenings, to poor reviews.[99] Yet Paul and James formed a friendship out of the experience, and James later said of Paul that he was a great man.[100] 'He was the most magnificent human being I have ever known or ever heard of,' James said in an interview. 'A man of tremendous powers, a man of remarkable gifts. A man who had achieved a great deal but was one of the simplest and one of the most gentle human beings.'[101]

As a fluent speaker of Russian and a prominent supporter, Paul received a warm welcome in the Soviet Union when he undertook a triumphal concert tour there in December 1936 and January 1937. This visit involved concerts in widely dispersed parts of the country—Moscow, then Leningrad in the far north, followed by Kiev (now Kyiv) and Odessa in the south.[102] While in Moscow in early 1937 he saw at the Bolshoi a performance by the Uzbek National Theatre that combined the music of 'Mussorgsky, Tchaikovsky, Prokofiev, Shostakovich' with that of the Uzbeks, stemming 'from an old and proud civilisation'. He was struck not only by the musical performance but also by the fact that Joseph Stalin was in the audience.[103] On this visit, Paul would meet and observe the presence of Indigenous and peasant people in modern Soviet society—observations that would give rise to his thinking about Indigenous people and modernity that would have great significance during his Australian and New Zealand tour.

In her biography of Robeson, Seton describes this 1936 visit and summarises Paul's understanding of these people who a generation before had no written language and who had now 'built theatres where their own actors played in dramas in their own languages'.

Seton quotes (without attribution) Robeson as saying, 'I saw with my own eyes that people are not "backward" because of colour, but because they are kept back.'[104] A few months later, he applied his thinking about Indigenous people and modern society to Australia. In April 1937, the Melbourne *Argus*, along with many other newspapers, printed a story from Australian Associated Press (AAP) mentioning Paul's interest in visiting Australia and reporting views he had recently expressed about Australia's record on matters of race. This interview provided Paul with his first known opportunity to talk about the achievements of Aboriginal people. It is hard to know his sources of information, but they may have included a book by pro-Aboriginal activist and writer Mary Bennett entitled *The Australian Aboriginal as a Human Being*, which had been published in London in 1930, or perhaps the work of anthropologists such as Alfred Radcliffe-Browne and AP Elkin. Now, he questioned the commonly held notion that Aboriginal people were 'backward', a theme he would return to during the tour more than two decades later. Any people, he said, can be lifted, 'no matter how low their social position'; and in questioning the idea that Aboriginal people were 'low' he remarked: 'It must be remembered that the boomerang introduced a new mathematical principle.'[105] In this last comment, he was expressing a common view among those who had become interested in the principles of flight as aviation records continued to be made and broken. As O'Connell points out, Americans were especially fascinated by the boomerang, which they saw as straddling the modern and the ancient, and indeed, she says, 'Black and White Americans' knowledge of Aboriginal culture could be summed up in a single word—"boomerang".' During the 1920s and 1930s, when aviation adventures and exploits were all the rage, American magazines 'celebrated the boomerang as the perfect marriage of a propeller and wing'.[106]

Eslanda shared Paul's views on the Soviet Union and on much else. Though his affairs with other women made their relationship strained at times, he and Eslanda had a common political vision. They both admired and supported the Soviet Union to the full. They made no public comments about Stalin's forced collectivisation policies that were in place during the 1930s and led to famine and the loss of millions of lives. As biographer Martin Duberman puts it, 'Apparently the Robesons had still heard nothing, or chose not to credit the few rumors that might have come their way.'[107]

It is a measure of both Paul and Eslanda's love for the Soviet Union that during this 1936–37 tour they settled their son, Pauli, in Moscow in the care of Eslanda's mother, known as Ma Goode, so that he could attend school and experience life in what they saw as a non-racist country. Pauli and Ma Goode would live in Russia for almost two years.[108] From their son in mid-1937 they would learn something of Stalin's purges, then reaching a peak, for Pauli's schoolmates were talking about their parents' fears and in some cases disappearances. Perhaps troubled, Paul told his son they must not judge, as 'only the Russians themselves could decide'.[109] Later, with Pauli back in London but aware of the staged nature of Stalin's third purge trial and the killing of someone the family knew, Paul said to his son that he was aware that terrible things had been done, that innocent people had been sacrificed, and that sometimes 'great injustices may be inflicted on the minority when the majority is in the pursuit of a great and just cause'.[110] His loyalty to the Soviet Union was so deep, however, that he never gave even such limited acknowledgements in public.

Africa

As well as supporting the Soviet Union, Paul and Eslanda strove for an end to racism and colonialism, and favoured socialism and opposed capitalism. Africa in particular meant a lot to both of them. London was a centre of African diaspora study, scholarship and activism, attracting, as historian James Smethurst puts it, 'Black US artists, intellectuals, activists, and merchant sailors'.[111] In this environment, Paul had developed connections with the West African Students' Union alongside future African leaders such as Jomo Kenyatta (who had, in addition, been an extra in *Sanders of the River*). In 1937 he helped found, and funded generously, the International Committee on African Affairs (from 1941 the Council on African Affairs), an organisation based in the United States that sought the decolonisation of Africa and the Caribbean alongside the liberation of African Americans.[112]

Eslanda had even more direct connections with Africa. Not long before Paul's Soviet concert tour of 1936–37 and the relocation of young Pauli in Moscow, she spent several months in Africa as part of her doctoral study in anthropology at LSE. Increasingly restive at the way LSE taught African anthropology, she had begun a PhD on cattle farming in Uganda and in 1936 undertook fieldwork there, taking young Pauli with her. In South Africa, Tanganyika and Uganda, she found that because of her unusual status as an educated African American woman and the wife of a famous man, she was able to meet a wide variety of people, from senior white government officials and academics to African leaders and ordinary Africans.[113] She would later publish a book entitled *African Journey*, based on her visit in 1936.

Spain

The Spanish Civil War was especially important in Paul Robeson's turn to the left, as it was for many others. Increasingly famous as a public speaker, on 24 June 1937 he made a huge impression at a mass rally at the Albert Hall in London sponsored by prominent figures such as WH Auden, EM Forster, Sean O'Casey, HG Wells and Virginia Woolf, held to raise financial aid for Basque child refugees from the war.[114] In what became his most well-known and influential speech, he stressed how important it was for artists and scientists and others to take a political stand: 'Every artist, every scientist, every writer must decide *NOW* where he stands. He has no alternative. There is no standing above the conflict on Olympian heights.' The artist, he continued, must 'elect to fight for freedom or for slavery'. He then turned from third person to first: 'I have made my choice. I had no alternative … I stand with you in unalterable support of the government of Spain.'[115] His speech on this occasion about the obligations of artists to stand up for what they believe in was striking at the time and has been much remembered and quoted since.[116] Then, on 20 December 1937, he sang to 9000 people, again in the Albert Hall, in support of the same cause. It was at this concert that he first famously changed the words of 'Ol' Man River' from 'I'm tired of livin' and scared of dyin'' to 'I must keep fightin' until I'm dying', thus rendering it a call for action rather than an expression of acquiescence.[117] Soon after, he visited Spain where he broadcast to the nation and sang to soldiers on the Republican side.[118]

Not only was Paul speaking out more directly on political issues, but his growing attachment to socialist politics was also influencing his choice of songs. In the 1920s his concerts had consisted of spirituals and secular folk songs such as 'Water Boy', songs by African American composers such as 'Li'l Gal' and 'Down de Lovah's Lane', and songs by white composers such as 'Ma Curly Headed Baby' and 'Mah Lindy Lou'. Through the 1930s he broadened his repertoire, sometimes with songs from his films, such as 'Lord God of Abraham' from *Proud Valley* and 'I Still Suits Me', written for *Show Boat*, and sometimes with songs from classical composers, including Beethoven, Mozart and Schumann. He added English recital songs such as 'Oh, No, John!', which remained in his repertoire throughout his career, and Russian songs including 'Song of the Volga Boatmen', which he first recorded in 1938.[119] This last song had been made famous in Australia and New Zealand by Russian opera singer Feodor Chaliapin during his highly successful tour there in 1926; a recent biography of Chaliapin describes the song as 'incredibly popular with the public dying to hear it performed by the talented artist', and thirty-four years later Paul would include it in his Australian and New Zealand concert tour programme.[120] He also added to his repertoire some more politically radical songs such as 'The Peat-Bog Soldiers'; militant African American folk songs such as 'No More Auction Block for Me'; and 'Chee Lai', a Chinese revolutionary song composed in 1935 that would after the 1949 revolution become the Chinese national anthem.[121]

A visit?

Robeson was so popular in Australia and New Zealand that there was frequent speculation that he might visit and tour. In September 1936, the Melbourne *Argus* reported that, according to two visiting 'negro variety artists' named Tom Brooking and Sam Van (soon to appear in a review entitled *Carnival Time* at the Tivoli in Sydney), Paul Robeson, 'the famous negro singer', would probably visit Australia the following year.[122] In 1937, Nina Mae McKinney, who was in Australia with her *Hello Harlem!* revue, was frequently asked by reporters for information about Robeson, to which she responded that he was 'keenly interested' in her visit and had told her that 'he hoped to visit the country soon'.[123]

In April 1937, along with many other newspapers, *The Argus* printed a story from AAP mentioning Robeson's plans to visit, and reporting views he had recently expressed about Australia's record on matters of race. In addition to the comments on Aboriginal peoples' achievements mentioned earlier, in this interview he criticised the White Australia policy, saying that it 'must lead to an explosion sooner or later'. He called on the Australian labour movement to shift the debate, commenting: 'The people cannot be divided by race or colour. Only economic differences are fundamental.'[124] Reactions to his comments varied, but perhaps the response from the Brisbane-based *Sunday Mail* is indicative of the feelings of many: it defended the White Australia policy as an economic, not a racial, policy (as was commonly done at the time) but then went on to say, 'Mr Robeson makes a sincere and dignified plea for his race and colour. If we cannot accept his argument, his visit will be none the less welcome … It will not limit our appreciation of a golden voice.'[125] In these newspaper discussions in 1936 and 1937 of a possible Robeson visit, no-one mentioned the 'character test' used to screen and exclude 'coloured' performers that had operated since the early 1920s.

Though Paul was too busy to visit Australia in 1938, newspaper commentators remained hopeful, several remarking in August that year that he was planning to visit Australia in 1939.[126] In March 1939, *The Argus* reported that he had postponed his tour of Australia 'because of film contracts conflicting with the dates that had been decided'.[127] He had in fact been persuaded to return to movie acting in order to make *The Proud Valley*, which would feature him as an unemployed African American who worked in the Welsh mines and became involved in the miners' struggles.[128] His decision to take the role was influenced by the fact that the scriptwriters were Herbert Marshall, whom Paul had met in Moscow in 1934, and his wife, Fredda Brilliant (of whom more in the next chapter). Just as Europe was going into war in early September 1939, shooting began. In later years, Paul would say that of all his films, this was his favourite. Although *The Argus* thought Robeson might come to Australia in 1940, when filmmaking was completed, it didn't turn out that way.[129] After spending twelve years in London, for many of which Paul was at the height of his fame as a singer and stage and screen actor, he and Eslanda decided to return to the United States. Paul wanted to reconnect with American audiences and engage more closely with African American struggles and people. He had visited there earlier in the year and told the *Sunday Worker* that 'it is now time for me to return to the place of my origin' and to support the struggles of 'my people'.[130] As soon as shooting for *The Proud Valley* ended, he and Eslanda returned on 30 September 1939.[131] War would engulf the United States just over two years later.

For the next decade, there was no further talk of Paul visiting Australia or New Zealand for a commercial tour. As we shall see, when two invitations to visit Australia came in 1950, they would be for political rather than commercial purposes.

2

'He simply electrifies you'

Wartime Fame and a Cold War Tragedy

DURING WORLD WAR II, Paul Robeson remained well known and popular in Australia and New Zealand. His Welsh movie, *Proud Valley*, screened for several years, as did his Hollywood movie *Tales of Manhattan* (1942), an anthology film also starring Charles Boyer, Rita Hayworth, Ginger Rogers, Henry Fonda, Edward G Robinson and Charles Laughton. Although Australians and New Zealanders seem to have liked both movies, Paul loved *Proud Valley* but hated *Tales of Manhattan* for its portrayal of African Americans as demeaning and stereotyped. He wanted to stop it from screening anywhere and vowed not to deal again with Hollywood until it changed its ways. As it turned out, he never made another movie.

It was not only movies that kept Robeson in the public eye in Australia and New Zealand. News about him continued to appear in Australian and New Zealand newspapers during the war, and he remained extremely popular on radio as well, with regular programs devoted to selections of his songs. On one occasion, in 1942, he participated in a radio program on the US Government–sponsored international radio service Voice of America that was broadcast to New Zealand. It was the first in a series called *Answering New Zealand*, which typically featured distinguished New Zealanders and Americans answering questions about the United States sent in by New Zealanders.[1] Along with Robeson on the panel on this occasion were Walter Nash, New Zealand's minister to the United States and later to become prime minister; Eleanor Roosevelt, wife of the US president; and George Palmer, the superintendent in charge of maintaining the Statue of Liberty. Paul would later meet Prime Minister Nash in New Zealand, in October 1960.

While Paul thrived as a singer, and with his portrayal of Othello on stage in a Broadway production in 1942–43 an enormous success,[2] Eslanda was doing well, too. On her return to the United States in 1939, she transferred her enrolment from LSE to the Hartford Seminary Foundation in Connecticut, and while she did not complete her doctorate, she did write *African Journey*, based on the research she had undertaken in Africa in 1936.[3] It is a highly readable travel book, partly because her liminal position meant she had been able to talk to an unusually wide range of people. The book combines a number of different voices—those of the anthropologist, the political and social activist, the tourist, and the African American seeking to understand her African inheritance.[4] It has a strong critique of colonialism, but this arises quite gently from her narration of the ideas and circumstances of the people she sees and encounters. She is very enthusiastic about African people and Africa's future: 'I find myself continually impressed with the ambition, energy, and capacity for work of the African.'[5]

African Journey was warmly reviewed in Australia, as it was in both the African American and white American press.[6] Reviewers were intrigued by its originality as an African American view of Africa, and reviews often had titles such as 'An American Negro in Africa'.[7] There were few newspaper reviews in New Zealand, though *The Press* in Christchurch reprinted John Latouche's praising review from the American *Saturday Review of Literature*. In Australia, by contrast, the book was reviewed in most major newspapers around the country, under titles rather similar to those in America, examples including 'The dark continent through a Negro's eyes' and 'A Negro looks at Africa'.[8] Australian newspaper reviewers generally were reading *African Journey* as affording welcome new insights into political and economic developments in Africa, which for Australians was an insufficiently understood continent. The Adelaide *Advertiser* was especially warm: 'Mrs Robeson reveals herself in this book as a woman of fine intelligence, wide knowledge and deep and warm sympathy for, and understanding of, the underdog, particularly the unfortunates of her own race.'[9] 'FB' in *The Argus* said 'this informative, well-written book reflects a fine human being, a fighter of great courage with a keen mind and a big heart. *African Journey* ... is well worth reading'.[10] Russell Braddock in Sydney's *Daily Telegraph* was especially struck by Eslanda's account of the dangerous conditions and low pay of African workers in the goldmining industry in South Africa.[11] In addition to the reviews, several newspapers reported that South African officials had asked booksellers not to sell the book, given its criticisms of that country.[12]

Australians' emotional connections with the Robesons during the war and afterwards were enhanced by the fact that about 100,000 African American soldiers, constituting 10 per cent of the total of about a million American troops, were passing through Australia during the war, often on recreation leave. Despite some anxiety over their possible treatment, given Australia's well-deserved reputation for racism, the African American soldiers were generally given a warm reception. As scholar Clare Corbould has shown, African American newspapers that had for three decades been critical of the White Australia policy and of the treatment of Indigenous people—who were seen as exploited workers similar to colonised peoples around the world—now commented on the surprising welcome Australians gave African American soldiers during the war years.[13] Paul Robeson would comment a few years later on the paradox of this warm response to African Americans on the one hand and the White Australia policy on the other. One part of the explanation is that Australians have long directed their racial anxieties primarily at those staying or seeking to stay permanently rather than at visitors. African American soldiers were not only short-term visitors but were also allies in a major war.[14]

From war to Cold War

In September 1945, when I was born and the war was ending, Paul Robeson was one of the best known African Americans in the world.

In October 1945, he was awarded the prestigious National Association for the Advancement of Colored People (NAACP) Spingarn Medal for outstanding cultural and political achievements, and that same year Howard University granted him an honorary degree.

Six months later, Australian and New Zealand newspapers began to speculate excitedly that now, at last, he might be able to visit.[15] These speculations came to nothing as Paul had other priorities both in the United States and abroad. More generally, there was in the early Cold War years something of a drought in overseas touring visitors for a variety of reasons, including distance, tax arrangements, and insufficient entrepreneurial connections.[16] One notable exception was the tour of Australia in July and August 1946 by baritone Todd Duncan. A classically trained opera singer who had made his name in the role of Porgy in the stage versions of *Porgy and Bess*, Duncan was also a professor of music at Howard University. He would have been familiar to some Australians also for his role in the 1943 movie *Syncopation*, a musical directed by William Dieterle.[17] Before he left the United States, Duncan commented to friends that he was happy to come to the 'wilds of Australia' while his friends were going to the 'ruins of Europe'.[18] His decision paid off, and his visit was a huge success. At one of his many Melbourne concerts he sang 'Ol' Man River', Robeson's signature song, which had also helped make its lyricist, Oscar Hammerstein II, famous—with Hammerstein himself, along with his Australian-born wife, Dorothy, in the audience.[19]

Before and during the tour, the Australian press often compared Duncan to Robeson in a manner that honoured and favoured them both. A long article in *The Argus* in October 1946 drawing attention to the rise of attacks on and beatings and lynchings of African Americans in the southern United States was accompanied by large photographs of both Duncan and Robeson as 'Negro crusaders'.[20] As newspapers reported extensively, during his visit Duncan met in Melbourne a young Aboriginal man named Harold Blair, who had attracted attention in 1945 when singing on radio in *Australia's Amateur Hour* and was training, with financial assistance from left-wing trade unions, for a Diploma of Music at the Melba Conservatorium in

Melbourne.[21] In some newspaper coverage, Blair was being hailed as a future 'Paul Robeson of Australia'.[22] It would be partly as a result of Duncan's encouragement that Blair left Australia in September 1949 for the United States to study singing, though financial constraints meant he did not in fact study at Howard University in Duncan's own department, or at the Juilliard School of Music in New York, both of which Duncan had promised.[23] He did, however, gain wider experience, singing at New York's Town Hall on 8 March 1951, and is well-remembered today as Australia's first successful Aboriginal opera singer.[24]

While Duncan was delighting Australian audiences with 'Ol' Man River' and other songs, Paul Robeson was taking a different path, one that would lead him away from a commercial concert tour of Australia or New Zealand. He was becoming deeply involved in US radical and anti-racism politics in an increasingly embittered Cold War context. So much had questions of racial equality come to the forefront of his thinking that he announced at a press conference in St Louis, Missouri, in January 1947 that he intended to abandon the theatre and concert stage for two years in order to speak out against race hatred and prejudice.[25] In fact, he stopped stage acting for twelve years but continued to perform as a singer, often in support of political causes.[26] Especially important in his wide range of political activities in these early post-war years was the Council on African Affairs, which he had chaired since 1941. It campaigned strongly throughout the war and after for an end to colonialism in Africa.[27]

In these activities he cooperated closely with communists such as Max Yergan (who later became a leading anti-communist and opponent of Robeson's) in the Council on African Affairs and William Patterson in the Civil Rights Congress (CRC). Indeed, Paul may himself have been a member of the CPUSA; many years later, 88-year-old former party chairman Gus Hall claimed that he had been, though there were few voices in support of Hall's claim.[28] Whether he was actually a member or not hardly matters; what is clear is that he was very close to the CPUSA at this time and worked hard to defend communists from threats of imprisonment. For this cooperation he would pay dearly.

The country was entering a period of anti-communist repression and hysteria that would profoundly affect Paul's life and career. For his political activities, often in association with communists, he was cited in April 1947, along with nearly 1000 others, by the House Committee on Un-American Activities as 'supporting the Communist Party and its front organisations'.[29]

He could, however, still draw a huge crowd, both in the United States and outside it. One of the largest would include Rona Bailey, a pakeha New Zealander who would become one of his political hosts in New Zealand in 1960. In late May 1947, Paul gave three concerts in the Panama Canal Zone hosted by the United Public Workers of America, which was seeking to organise Black Panamanian workers. Two were held in the Colón Arena and another in Panama City's national stadium.

The opening concert attracted 10,000 people and his concert programme included folk songs, classical pieces by Mendelssohn and Mussorgsky, spirituals, and an excerpt from *Othello*. For encores, he sang 'Water Boy', 'Deep River', 'Let My People Go', 'Scandalize My Name' and 'The House I Live In'.[30] The first three of these were among his favourite spirituals. 'Scandalize My Name' was another spiritual that he had been singing for twenty years, but now with a direct implication for the present. It tells of people who speak negatively about the singer behind the singer's back, and perhaps Paul now chose to sing it in protest against the denigration of his name he was then experiencing. 'The House I Live In' was a World War II song expressing love for the people of America. It expresses admiration of America for its freedom and democracy, praising not only American heroes such as Abraham Lincoln, Thomas Jefferson and George Washington, but also ordinary Americans—'The worker and the farmer, the sailor on the sea', along with 'my neighbours, white and black' and 'the people who just came here, or from generations back'.

Though the concert was primarily for Black Panamanian workers, it so happened that a few travelling pakeha New Zealanders were also there, their ship having stopped in Panama for repairs. Rona Bailey was a physical education official and instructor who was bound for Europe, where she would attend the 1st World Festival of Youth and Students in Prague, to be held from 25 July to 20 August, and visit Hungary and Yugoslavia. She recalled these events many years later. Wandering the streets of Colón, she saw an advertisement for a Robeson concert hosted by the Silver Dollar Union of Workers, the 'Silver Dollar' signifying an all-Black union. She located the union, who helped her attend the concert 'in the huge open-air arena in Colon on a wonderful balmy night'; Robeson was in 'full throated voice'. She evoked the scene: 'the arena was packed and everyone in the brightest of clothing, screaming and yelling. There were huge crowds outside trying desperately to get in and at half time Robeson insisted the gates be opened and crowds more flooded in for nothing, sitting on the banks.' As a finale, Robeson 'spoke about the indignities which black people suffered all over the world, calling on them to rise up and fight and then he gave the famous speech of Othello which starts "I have done the State some service and they know it".' It was, she reflected, 'quite extraordinarily moving to be part of this huge black audience and know that he was speaking directly to them'.[31] Robeson's impression on her as a singer and a politically admirable man never left her and, as we shall see in Chapter 15, she more than anyone else would help to keep his memory alive in New Zealand.

Despite growing harassment and cancellation of venue bookings in 1947 and 1948, Paul was still a popular public figure and his presence at an event continued to guarantee a large turnout. Throughout 1948 he used this popularity to assist Henry Wallace for the American Progressive Party campaign for president, appearing at many well-attended rallies for him around the country. Unionists were still attending Paul's concerts in large numbers, as they did in Hawaii in March 1948 when he conducted a week-long fundraising tour as a guest of the International Longshore and Warehouse Union (ILWU).[32] The ILWU's leader, Australian-born Harry Bridges, was a good friend, Robeson having publicly saluted him as a courageous leader in 1943 and written personally to President Franklin D Roosevelt in 1945 opposing threats to deport Bridges on political grounds.[33] It was on Bridges' initiative that Paul had in 1943 been made a lifetime honorary member of the ILWU, a membership he would frequently refer to on his Australian tour.[34] The two had met again when Paul visited the US West Coast in 1946 on behalf of the National Negro Congress.[35] As Robeson would later explain, it was Bridges who told him about Australia and its strong trade union traditions.

Less sympathetic to Robeson's political stance was another Australian, Robert Gordon Menzies, who during an overseas trip to the United States of America in October 1948 attended a huge rally of 20,000 for Wallace in Madison Square Garden and heard Robeson sing. A deeply conservative and anti-communist politician, founder of the Liberal Party of Australia in 1944, and in 1948 still leader of the Opposition in the federal parliament, Menzies would have attended the rally in an inquiring spirit rather than as a Wallace supporter, but he may well also have been interested to see and hear Robeson.[36] He would have welcomed the election result far more than Bridges or Robeson did, for in November 1948 Harry S Truman was elected and Wallace received a low vote. A year later, in November 1949, the conservative National Party defeated the governing Labour Party in New Zealand, ending its fourteen years in power. The following month, in December 1949, the Australian Labor government would also lose an election and a conservative government headed by Menzies would be in place. The political tide in all three countries was continuing to turn away from the united-front politics of the 1940s and towards Cold War hostilities.

The year 1949 would prove a tumultuous and in many ways catastrophic one for Paul Robeson, the events of which would delay for over a decade Australians' and New Zealanders' chance of hearing him in live performance, speaking on political issues or welcoming him to their country. As the year opened, Robeson found his planned tour of the United States in tatters after mass cancelling of bookings by venue managers either vehemently opposed to his politics or afraid in such a hostile climate of being classed as communist sympathisers themselves. Instead, he planned a British tour that would include not only musical performances but also political speeches on a range of issues.

It began well, for Britain did not follow the United States in excluding Robeson from public performance. Arriving in London on 17 February, Robeson made several political appearances, including at a conference sponsored by the Coordinating Committee of Colonial Peoples and organised by YM Dadoo, an Indian leader of the African National Congress, and VK Krishna Menon, future defence minister of India; there, Robeson gave a powerful speech condemning the introduction the previous year in South Africa of a government policy of apartheid.[37] (In response, the South African Government banned the playing of his records on radio.[38]) His association with the Coordinating Committee of Colonial Peoples arose from his close connections to India from the 1930s onwards. It also demonstrates his abiding concern with colonialism and his continuing connection of African American struggles with those of colonised peoples worldwide.[39]

The concert tour then began, consisting of around twenty performances in Britain alone, including two packed-out concerts at the Albert Hall in early April. One of the thousands who heard him there, and then attended ten days later the much-lower-priced concert at the Harringay Stadium in North London, was a thrilled young Australian. Nance Macmillan (later known as Nancy Wills) was an aspiring playwright and member of the Communist Party of Australia (CPA) who had followed Robeson's career with interest since she was fourteen. Now, at twenty-eight, she was visiting London (indeed, she had arrived the same day as Robeson) and working temporarily as a receptionist in a small hotel near the House of Commons.[40] To her delight, she met Paul socially in London through Fredda Brilliant, a well-known Polish-born sculptor she had met in Melbourne in 1947.

Born in Lodz in 1903, Brilliant had migrated to Melbourne with her family in 1924 before moving to New York in the late 1920s, then Moscow, and finally London in 1937. Her visit to Melbourne in 1947 to see her family, during which she mounted an exhibition of her sculptures and gave interviews to the local papers, had made quite an impact.[41]

Brilliant and her husband, Herbert Marshall, were good friends of the Robesons and had worked with Paul on *The Proud Valley* and the play *Plant in the Sun*.[42] Meeting again in London, Nance and Fredda got on well, and when Fredda and Herbert left London in April 1949 for a trip to Germany before attending the upcoming peace conference in Paris, Nance house-sat their apartment in Hampstead.[43] Her brief social contact with Paul in London and later in Paris would prove to be one of the defining moments of her life, and she would become a major advocate for him in Australia.

Macmillan made good use of her social contact with Robeson to interview him in April 1949 for *Tribune*, the CPA newspaper. When she asked him if he could come to Australia, he replied that he could perhaps come when he went to Hawaii at the end of the summer. 'I'd sure like to,' he said. 'Harry Bridges', he added, 'has told me lots about your country, and I like what I read of the fine spirit of the Australian working class. I've also liked those Australians I've met. Tell me some more about your country—your people and your traditions.' Some aspects of Australia, though, troubled him, and after talking more about the civil rights struggles going on right then in the United States, he paused and asked Macmillan, 'What's the strength of your White Australia policy anyway?' African Americans had spoken to him warmly of their time in Australia during World War II, and it seemed to him that the country's racial immigration policy was at odds with 'the attitude of the people'. The conversation then turned to the peace movement. The Soviet Union was firmly committed to peace, Robeson observed to Macmillan, not least because huge armaments, 'the paraphernalia of war and defence', hindered economic development.[44]

A turning point: The Paris peace congress, April 1949

Shortly before the interview with Macmillan, Robeson had finally decided to appear at the forthcoming peace conference in Paris as he wished above all to return to the United States for the forthcoming trials of members of the CPUSA. Owing presumably to his late acceptance he was not on the program, and not a formal delegate or observer.[45] It would prove to be a fateful decision. The conference, formally titled the World Congress of Partisans for Peace, was aligned to the world communist movement headed by the Soviet Union, despite the fact that many people who wanted peace had originally held hopes that the congress could bridge the divide between East and West in preventing further war. In a post-war world afraid of further war, and especially of the threat of nuclear war, many people worldwide wanted peace and the Soviet Union sought to build on this mood to achieve a world peace movement friendly to it. The Soviet-based Communist Information Bureau (Cominform) had resolved at its inaugural meeting in September 1947 that peace 'should now become the pivot of the entire activity of the Communist Parties', and in that spirit communists worldwide strongly supported the meeting in Paris, the first large post-war peace conference.[46]

For Paul, the fact that the planned Paris peace conference was friendly towards the Soviet Union was a plus. Some of his friends, however, were concerned about his decision to attend. Harry Belafonte, also a singer and political activist and a lifelong admirer of Robeson's, recalls in his memoir, *My Song*, attending a dinner at the Robesons' home in New York where the guests discussed whether Paul should appear in Paris.[47] 'At a long table set off by two huge silver candelabras,' Belafonte remembers, around which were eight or ten guests, including the poet Langston Hughes and WEB Du Bois, 'there was some serious discussion of whether Robeson ought to have accepted now that the Cold War had truly begun … I remember a couple of his guests arguing about the wisdom of his going.'[48] Now, in mid-April, as the conference opening approached, and after some uncertainty, Robeson was committed to attending.

In the days before the conference opened on Wednesday 20 April, national delegations from all over the world converged on Paris. Some of them were huge, numbering hundreds (the British delegation involved 400 delegates and 100 additional individual attendees); there would be nearly 2000 delegates from seventy-two countries.[49] One of the smallest was from New Zealand, where two students, Kenneth J Hollyman and ST Scoones, both studying in Paris, were delegates representing their student body at Victoria College, Wellington.[50] A little larger, but still small, was the Australian delegation; with only eight weeks between the announcement of the conference and its opening session, there was neither the time nor the funding to come from so far away. In the circumstances, it fell to journalist and communist Rupert Lockwood, based in London as a foreign correspondent for *Tribune* and representative of the CPA in Europe, to scrabble together a delegation. He drew on left-wing and mainly communist Australians visiting or living in London, many of whom were writers, artists, teachers or students. Not in the delegation but very much part of the circle of far left Australian artists and art students living in London at the time was Bernard Smith, a student on a British Council scholarship at the Courtauld Institute of Art who would later become a leading and indeed foundational figure in the study of Australian art history.[51] 'We were part', he would later write of these London-based Australians of the late 1940s, 'of that exodus of the restless who wanted to get to Europe after the war, to savour a culture older than ours.'[52]

This Australian delegation of seven included Rupert Lockwood, Noel Counihan, Stephen Murray-Smith (accompanied by his wife, Nita, who was not a delegate), Bert Williams, Daphne Gollan, Blanche Chidzey and Nance Macmillan.[53] To attend as a delegate, as distinct from an individual invitee, each of them had to be accredited by an organisation such as a trade union or a cultural or social association, leading to some urgent letters back home in the weeks before the conference. As Counihan wrote to his wife on 9 April, though a small group they wanted to be recognised as a separate national delegation 'rather than be submerged in and subject to the large British delegation'.[54] Counihan was, nevertheless, somewhat embarrassed and scornful of Australia's tiny delegation, describing it to his wife as 'insignificant, poor in personnel, and reflecting the lack of appreciation in Australia … of the profound, historic importance of this Congress'.[55]

The leader of the delegation, Lockwood, represented several unions—the Seamen's Union, the Ironworkers, and the Waterside Workers.[56] Bert Williams had been senior vice-president of the Eureka Youth League in New South Wales and one of its delegates at the founding congress in London of the World Federation of Democratic Youth; that congress had elected him to be one of its three full-time secretaries, and in that role he was now based in Paris.[57] Counihan was a Melbourne-based artist and member of the CPA who had recently arrived in London as a jumping-off point for a proposed three-year stay in Europe to advance his art education; he would represent the Sydney-based Studio of Realist Art and a range of trade unions and left-wing cultural organisations such as New Theatre in Sydney and Melbourne and Unity Theatre in Brisbane.[58] Murray-Smith, a former student radical from Melbourne who was now teaching in London, represented Melbourne's Australia-Soviet House.[59] Daphne Gollan represented the New Housewives' Association, a communist-dominated organisation that had broken away in 1946 from the longer-standing Federated Association of Australian Housewives. She had been secretary of its NSW branch before leaving Sydney the year before with her husband, Bob Gollan, who was taking up a scholarship to study for a PhD at LSE under the supervision of Harold Laski and would later become a leading Australian labour historian.[60] Bernard Smith, the Gollans' friend and lodger at their Earls Court apartment, later commented with an artist's eye on Good Friday, 15 April 1949, that 'Daphne Gollan was preparing to attend the Paris Peace Conference for which Picasso had created his Peace Dove: a formidable bird that looked more like a pigeon'.[61] Macmillan represented the Victorian branch of the Clerks' Union (as did Counihan), while her friend Blanche Chidzey, a science teacher living in London, represented both Australia-Soviet House in Melbourne and the Christian Social Order Movement of Australia, a socialist Christian organisation formed in 1943 that had been especially active in the context of post-war reconstruction.[62]

At last, on 20 April 1949, the Paris peace conference opened. Counihan represented Australia on the presidium, which gave him an excellent vantage point from which to sketch the speakers. He was rather overwhelmed by the congress, finding it, he wrote two days later, 'so vast, so representative, so full of the unexpected and so constantly adding to itself, so talented, so heroic, and so powerful as to be beyond my powers of description'.[63] It was indeed a huge event, *Tribune* reporting excitedly that 500,000 people attended its final rally for peace—100,000 inside the giant Stade Buffalo and 400,000 outside.[64]

Thirty years later, in her memoir, *Shades of Red*, Macmillan described Robeson's arrival and speech:

> When, on the third day, Paul Robeson arrived at the Salle Pleyel, the huge concert hall where the Congress was being held, the audience rose to its feet and he was cheered and clapped, and clapped and cheered. This man, 'ce géant noir', his songs, his fight for his people's right to equality, his identification with the working people of the whole world, and the price he had paid for his devotion to their cause, was known to the people of the whole world.

Macmillan then summarised his speech:

> He spoke very briefly, apologised that he had to be back in New York tomorrow, but that, the night before, in London he had met with the Co-Ordinating Committee of Colonial Peoples, and Dr Dadoo, President of the South African Indian Congress; two thousand people were present, and they had asked him to address this Congress and say, in their name, that they did not want war, that nine hundred million coloured people would not go to war with the Soviet Union![65]

After the speech, Paul sang several songs. Some of them evoked revolutionary struggle, such as 'The Four Insurgent Generals', a revolutionary song from the Spanish Civil War, and 'Joe Hill'. He also sang 'Chee Lai', which had begun as 'March of the Volunteers', first performed for a popular Chinese film, *Lovers in Troubled Times* (1935). In its opening lines it urged the Chinese people to resist Japanese invasion.[66] Paul had learned of the song in 1941 in New York and had recorded it, first in Chinese and then in English, with the original lyricist Tian Han, conductor Liu Liangmo and Paul himself collaborating in the translation. He had sung it many times since, and now, as he sang it in Paris, the Chinese communist forces were in a winning position and three days later would capture Nanjing.[67] Paul also sang 'Ol' Man River',[68] which was, according to Counihan, a new version 'in which the last verses express his desire for world peace'.[69]

Like everyone else, the Australian delegation was delighted and moved to hear Paul Robeson speak and sing. As Counihan wrote to his family, 'Paul Robeson came and delivered a wonderful speech and sang for us so movingly that many of the people present were in tears ... I was only a few feet from Robeson when he sang.'[70] Macmillan concurred; as she wrote a year later, 'We were moved to tears to hear him sing the songs of protest now so uniquely his: "Water Boy", "Joe Hill" and "Old [sic] Man River".'[71]

While the Australians present found the Paris conference exhilarating and inspiring, for Paul it was a disaster. His speech, or at least the reported versions of it, would accelerate the destruction of his good name and further undermine his ability to perform in the United States.[72] He was reported as having said, 'It is unthinkable that American Negroes would go to war on behalf of those who have oppressed us for generations against a country [the Soviet Union] which in one generation has raised our people to the full dignity of mankind.'[73] As biographer Jordan Goodman shows in detail, it is clear that Robeson was talking about colonised Black people in general rather than African Americans specifically. Robeson himself said in an interview a little later that what he said had been distorted; when he referred to 'Negroes', he had been thinking not only of African Americans but also of West Indians and Africans who had no stake in a war against the Soviet Union. He had, after all, been talking about peace.[74] However, he was understood as having said African Americans specifically would refuse to fight against the Soviet Union, and on this basis almost everyone who commented publicly fiercely denounced him. As Duberman puts it, 'The white press rushed to inveigh against him as a traitor; the black leadership hurried to deny he spoke for anyone but himself.'[75]

Particularly hurtful for Robeson was the energy with which the Black leadership condemned him, fearing that any association with communism and the Soviet Union would threaten the civil rights cause. The apparent suggestion that African Americans would not fight in a war with the Soviet Union was particularly worrying for civil rights leaders at this time, since African Americans had only recently won desegregation of the military based on their proven loyalty to the United States of America in World War II. During the election, Truman, in order to attract the Black vote away from Wallace for whom it was initially high, had promised desegregation of the armed forces, and he had delivered on 26 July 1948.[76] Even a well-known African American pacifist like Bayard Rustin, a proponent of non-violent protest who had co-founded the Congress of Racial Equality in 1942, refused to support Robeson, calling together a meeting of Black leaders to develop a strategy for telling the American public that they were united in disagreeing with Robeson, and that he was not speaking for them.[77]

Some of the furore over the Paris speech reached Australia. Newspapers reported Robeson's speech, some noting the angry rebuttal from Walter White, the secretary of the NAACP.[78] White had said that while he acknowledged that many African Americans would be glad that Robeson had spoken out if it led white Americans to realise how determined African Americans were to 'break the shackles which race prejudice fastens upon them', he also insisted that in the event of any conflict between the United States and another nation, African Americans would meet the responsibilities imposed on all Americans.[79]

Australians also had direct access to one individual African American response to the Paris speech. In July, Todd Duncan, who was now on his second and last Australian tour, talked to several newspapers about Robeson. Although a long-time friend of Paul's, Duncan joined the general condemnation of the Paris speech. In an interview in Melbourne, after discussing the history of spirituals, he said of Robeson that while he had 'long admired and respected him as a brilliant and sincere man', he disagreed with his Paris speech and 'his sweeping statement that the negroes of America would not fight in a war against the Soviet'.[80]

Paul was now isolated from the most vocal African American leaders of the time.

Robeson in Moscow, 1949

Robeson's European tour, meanwhile, continued. He was one of the Soviet Union's staunchest allies in the West and was received as such when he visited Moscow on 4 June for the celebration of the 150th anniversary of Alexander Pushkin's birth.[81] Cultural studies scholars Lisa Merrill and Theresa Saxon draw our attention to the fact that Pushkin's great-grandfather was African and that the famous poet acknowledged his African as well as his Russian ancestry, suggesting that Pushkin's fame and African connection contributed to Russian acceptance of African American performers like Robeson.[82]

Although Paul was very popular in Moscow, events on this visit tested his loyalty and have remained prominent in Robeson scholarship ever since. He had met and considered as friends two prominent Soviet Jews who had visited the United States in 1943 as members of the Soviet-initiated Jewish Anti-Fascist Committee (JAC). One was JAC chairman Solomon Mikhoels and the other was JAC member Itzik Feffer; both had spoken in New York on 8 July 1943 at the largest pro-Soviet rally ever held in the United States. Along with a range of famous people, including Charlie Chaplin and Marc Chagall, Paul had given a speech of welcome and had sung 'The Prayer of Rabbi Levi Isaac of Berditchev', sometimes referred to as the 'Hassidic Chant'.[83] Now, six years later, he hoped to reconnect with Mikhoels and Feffer, but soon found that the situation of Soviet Jews had changed radically in just a few years. Whereas the JAC had been valuable to the Allied war effort, the Soviet Union was by 1949 in the midst of a government-instigated anti-Semitic campaign. Robeson may not have been aware of the situation when he arrived in Moscow but, as Duberman records, he grew uneasy at being unable to locate his Jewish friends. He could not find Mikhoels (who had in fact been executed in January 1948) but after persistent questioning of officials did meet with Feffer in a hotel room.

Our knowledge of what happened there comes from Paul's son, Paul Robeson Jnr, who says his father told him what happened but ordered him not to repeat it during his father's lifetime.[84] Feffer indicated through gestures that the room was bugged, and through notes and gestures told Paul that the secret police had murdered Mikhoels and arrested many prominent Jewish figures. He also indicated that he, Feffer, expected soon to be executed as well (as indeed he was three years later, on 12 August 1952, along with a dozen or more other Yiddish writers in an event that would become known as the Night of the Murdered Poets).[85] With this awful knowledge, Robeson concluded his last Moscow concert on 14 June with a pointed reference to his great joy in having met Feffer again and sang as an encore 'Zog Nit Keynmol' or 'The Song of the Warsaw Ghetto', in the original Yiddish, dedicating it to Mikhoels.[86] The audience was transfixed and, Paul Robeson Jnr writes, 'erupted with sustained waves of ovation'.[87]

Paul continued, however, to say publicly that there was no anti-Semitism in the Soviet Union, a silence that has proved troubling for his admirers.[88] Where communists around the world tended to disbelieve stories of Russian atrocities as simply Western propaganda, Robeson on this occasion was learning of them firsthand. This episode reveals, in my view, just how strong was his loyalty to the Soviet Union. As historian Maxim Matusevich suggests, Robeson simply could not incorporate what he was now learning into his understanding of the Soviet Union, which to him remained a beacon of hope for anti-colonial and anti-racism movements internationally.[89] His loyalty was shared by many Western socialists, both those who had visited the Soviet Union and those who had not.

For the Robesons, who shared a love of Russian culture and in Paul's case loved and spoke fluently the Russian language, their loyalty was multilayered and ran deep. There were, of course, specific dimensions in Robeson's case to his unwavering support for the Soviet Union. The first was that in 1934 he had experienced the Soviet Union as a place without racism; he was treated there, he often said, not as a Black man but just a man, and saw the Soviet Union as a symbol of what Black and colonised peoples could achieve in the future. The second was that when he loved the Soviet Union, it loved him back. The legendary concerts in Moscow in 1949 and 1958, where mass audiences expressed their love for him so emotionally, would have been balm to the soul of someone who had experienced the exclusions and calumny that Robeson had in his home country. As academic Kate Baldwin puts it, 'Robeson's relationship with the Soviet Union permitted him a status, a sense of self-worth … and international agency unrealizable at the time in the United States.'[90]

Conflict in New York

When Paul returned to New York a few weeks later, two major events occurred on the same day, 19 June 1949. In the evening, he spoke about his Paris speech and associated matters at a 'Welcome Home' rally in Harlem, New York, organised by the Council on African Affairs. In Duberman's judgement, this speech was 'one of the most powerful polemics of his career'.[91] Australians had access to the full text of it in a locally printed pamphlet, 'Paul Robeson calls on the American people to fight for freedom and peace'.[92] In it, Paul attacked the Black leadership that had deserted him, saying, 'How Sojourner Truth, Harriet Tubman, Frederick Douglass must be turning in their graves at this spectacle of a craven, fawning, despicable leadership.' He insisted on his love for America and his internationalism and said that African Americans should not 'die in vain any more on foreign battlefields for Wall Street … If we must die, let it be in Mississippi or Georgia. Let it be wherever we are lynched and deprived of our rights as human beings.'[93] He also hinted at his continuing desire to sing directly to workers, something he would do regularly in both Australia and New Zealand. In response to the cancellation of his concert venues, he responded, 'Well, they can have their concerts! I'll go back to their cities to sing for the people whom I love, for the Negro and white workers whose freedom will insure my freedom.'[94]

Earlier in the day, racism had marred Paul and Eslanda's son's wedding to a white Jewish woman (Marilyn Greenberg) when total strangers attended and booed in opposition to an interracial marriage. Australian readers of *Tribune* learned of this event when it republished Eslanda's poetic essay on what had happened. The verbal abuse at what should have been a happy family time had been followed, she writes, by 'postcards, letters and telegrams from strangers who dare not sign their names, wishing us evil'. She thanked those who wished her son well and notified her enemies that she would 'fight them every step of the way until we achieve the equality as American citizens which is guaranteed by our Constitution'.[95]

Soon after their son's wedding, Eslanda's third book was published—and this one made clear her own attachment to the Soviet Union. Titled *American Argument*, it was an edited conversation between Eslanda and the popular writer Pearl Buck, with an overall narration by Buck. Eslanda and Buck were friends and Buck had through her husband, a publisher, been involved in editing *African Journey*. *American Argument* rests on a comparison and contrast between the lives of the two women, Eslanda's as a widely travelled, educated African American woman, and Buck's as a white southerner brought up in China. As noted in the introduction, they disagree strongly about the Soviet Union, which Buck opposes and Eslanda supports. When Buck asks her what she thinks of the Soviets' one-party system, Eslanda responds, as supporters of the Soviet Union so often did, that it is no worse than 'our own celebrated two parties, which act as one on many important issues, and which have a fit when a third party is suggested'.[96] Eslanda insists that the Bolsheviks had no choice but to 'remove' their opponents, talking at this point specifically of the intellectuals.[97] Buck replies that while she agrees with Eslanda that 'there should not be oppressors and tyrants', 'we can deal with them in other ways than by death'.[98] Eslanda, however, is unmoved by Buck's arguments. The book was favourably reviewed in both Australia and the United States, though less so than had been the case for *African Journey*.[99]

The Australian peace movement invites Paul to visit and speak

Paul Robeson was fast becoming a symbol of the Cold War in ways that affected attempts to entice him to Australia. One outcome of the Paris peace conference was the formation of the World Committee of Partisans for Peace, composed almost entirely of communists, to which were soon affiliated national peace councils around the world.[100]

By 1949, having experienced major defeats in the trade unions and facing possible illegalisation, Australian communists were glad to be able to turn to the peace movement as a top priority. It was, after all, an attractive cause, and despite their Soviet alignment, the national peace councils could attract non-communists, especially some left-leaning activist Christians, who wanted to help prevent the outbreak of nuclear war.[101]

The Australian Peace Council (APC), formed on 1 July 1949, followed the international pattern, its executive including three ministers of religion (the reverends Alfred Dickie, Frank Hartley and Victor James), Australian Labor Party (ALP) member Jim Cairns, Heather Wakefield from the Student Christian Movement and one communist, John Rodgers. Dickie, Hartley and James were known as the 'peace parsons'; all three combined Christian and socialist ideals and were prepared to work openly with communists throughout the 1950s. As historian Malcolm Saunders and political scientist Ralph Summy note, despite the fact that the membership was quite diverse, the CPA was the driving force, doing most of the organising and providing the first three national organising secretaries—Ian Turner, Alec Robertson and Stephen Murray-Smith.[102] The aims of the council included mobilising public support for the fledgling United Nations, fostering support for the idea of peaceful coexistence, banning atomic weapons, and opposing war propaganda and race hatred.[103]

When the world learned at the end of August 1949 that the Soviet Union had successfully tested its first atom bomb, it was clear that another world war could well become a nuclear war. Only a week after the Soviet test, on 7 September, the fledgling APC held its inaugural meeting in Melbourne Town Hall, attended by 3000 people. In the months following, the APC established branches in every state except Tasmania.[104] The national executive planned a much larger conference with international speakers for April 1950, to focus on opposition to the use of atomic weapons. It would be known as the Melbourne Peace Conference and one of its supporters was Senator Bill Morrow. Morrow is important to our story, for he would become a key person in the political aspects of the Australian leg of the Robesons' tour in 1960.

An experienced trade union leader and an avowed socialist, he had been elected to the Senate for the ALP in 1946 for a six-year term. His socialist politics put him at the far left of the ALP's political spectrum; even when Labor had been in government, he had spoken out against some of its decisions, such as its military intervention to end the coal strike in 1949.[105] Now, in Opposition, he remained a strong supporter of the developing peace movement.

It soon became clear that Paul Robeson was one of the international speakers sought by the APC, as he was by many of its counterparts around the world. Robeson, however, was having a hard time at home in the United States. Infamously, in late August 1949 vigilante anti-communists violently held up his scheduled performance organised by the CRC at Peekskill, outside New York; after the rescheduled performance a week later, the same groups savagely attacked departing concertgoers while police stood by.[106] For communists and their supporters around the world, the assaults at Peekskill became iconic instances of a general pattern of attacks on communists everywhere. Australians were aware of these events not only through mainstream newspapers, which reported them widely, but also through *Tribune* and a pamphlet containing the American Civil Liberties Union's detailed report, 'Violence in Peekskill'.[107] A 78 rpm record of the concert and its aftermath somehow reached Australia; I remember as a child hearing my mother play it.[108] Robeson had truly become for communists an emblem of defiance in the face of adversity, and one of the communist world's most prominent speakers for peace.

The Cold War was intensifying in Australia, as it was in the United States. After the federal election in December 1949, the newly elected conservative coalition government headed by Menzies immediately condemned the proposed Melbourne Peace Conference, especially the involvement of Morrow.[109] Undaunted, the APC announced on 4 February that it had invited three overseas speakers, including Robeson—without, it seems, attempting to gain acceptances before making the announcement.[110] It sent a cablegram to Robeson signed by leading trade unionists and cultural figures, saying how welcome a visit would be.[111] The other two invited dignitaries were Madame Sun

Yat-Sen, wife of the Chinese president, and the dean of Canterbury, Dr Hewlett Johnson, known as the 'Red Dean' for his support for the Soviet Union and as a frequent speaker at international events. When Johnson accepted, the conservative government was asked in federal parliament on 16 March whether it would grant him a visa; Minister for Immigration Harold Holt replied that assuming he had a British passport, he would be allowed to attend.[112] At this stage, being British and white overrode political considerations.

Neither Paul Robeson nor Madame Sun Yat-sen accepted the invitation. Paul replied that he was too deeply committed to working for peace in America to be able to visit Australia at that time.[113]

In the end, the Peace Conference sessions, held from 16 to 19 April 1950, were packed. As labour historian Robin Gollan notes, the dean of Canterbury was a genuine drawcard who attracted large crowds, though he also attracted extensive negative press commentary that would increase on his subsequent extended tour of Australia.[114] Communist activist Ralph Gibson recalled in his memoir going to the Exhibition Building in Melbourne, along with at least 10,000 others, to hear Johnson speak on the theme that the Soviet Union wanted peace, not war.[115] The conference programme stated there would be a recorded goodwill message from Robeson to conclude the proceedings, but in fact he was unable to send such a message.[116]

No sooner had the APC's April conference ended than three days later, on 22 April, there was another conference in Melbourne involving many of the same people that would lead to a second attempt to attract Robeson to Australia. This second conference, titled the Conference for Democratic Rights, was concerned with the government's forthcoming Communist Party Dissolution Bill, which those on the left feared would be designed to outlaw the CPA. Organised by the Democratic Rights Council, whose membership overlapped significantly with that of the APC, the Conference for Democratic Rights was chaired by Dickie.[117] The charter of freedom developed by the conference would, Dickie said in his opening address, outline 'the rights and liberties of the Australian people as a basis for a nation-wide campaign in defence of freedom' and would oppose the proposed legislation.[118]

After speeches on a wide range of topics, the conference unanimously adopted an Australian Charter of Freedom that said Australians had always fought for freedom, 'against convict slavery, against colonial subjection, against militarism, fascism, and all forms of tyranny'. It included sections on freedom of speech, publication and organisation; freedom of science and culture; freedom of the person; and freedom from racial or religious persecution.[119]

The section on freedom from racial or religious persecution is of particular interest here, especially as evidence of racial inequality and injustice would interest and trouble Paul and Eslanda Robeson when they came to Australia in 1960. The section sought first to 'combat religious and racial hatred and especially to destroy the cancer of anti-Semitism, condemned by history as a fascist device to divide and confuse the people'. Then, it demanded for Aboriginal people, 'our deeply wronged forerunners in this country', the 'strict preservation of their remaining tribal lands, the immediate abolition of inhuman practices such as flogging and chaining by the neck, and the guarantee to them in practice of full economic, social and political rights'.[120] The conference agreed it should hold an 'Assembly of Human Rights' just before the next sitting of parliament.

Although Robeson had not toured internationally since the events at Peekskill in August 1949 and was refusing nearly all of the many overseas speaking invitations he received, he did accept one. This was from the British National Peace Council, which was hosting a meeting of the WPC in London at the end of May 1950. While the US State Department was already considering ways to prevent Robeson from speaking abroad, it had not yet taken away his passport, and he was able to attend. As proof of his continuing popularity in Britain, when he spoke and sang the following evening, 1 June, at a peace demonstration in Lincoln's Inn Fields, possibly 20,000 attended.[121] To rapturous applause, he sang Chinese, Russian and American songs and told the huge audience that Americans would never support fascism.[122] One of those who heard him was a young Australian writer, Dymphna Cusack, whose novel *Come In Spinner* would soon appear with great success and who was for a while living in London, as had many Australian writers over the decades. She wrote evocatively about the concert to her 71-year-old friend (Stella) Miles Franklin, an Australian author who had herself lived in London for many years and had been well-known ever since the publication fifty years earlier of her first novel, *My Brilliant Career*, now regarded as an Australian classic.[123]

> Old, old, gardens between the Temple (*Law Courts*) along Chancery Lane. A perfect evening warm and bright—the plane trees thick and full of birds—an enormous crowd packed into the gardens and the closed street. And Robeson! Such a personality! You can't describe the effect of his voice both speaking and singing. He simply electrifies you. He spoke and sang a number of songs and the crowd went wild and the whole of respectable Lincoln's Inn Courts and Chambers leant out and waved and shouted. I felt it was worth a trip overseas just for that single evening.[124]

Neither Cusack nor her 20,000 fellow audience members, nor possibly Robeson himself, were aware that this would be his last performance outside North America for eight years.

Soon after he returned to New York, Paul received a second invitation to visit and speak in Australia. Just a few days after the Charter of Freedom conference had ended on 22 April, Prime Minister Menzies had introduced, on 27 April 1950, the anti-communist bill the peace movement had been expecting. The Communist Party Dissolution Bill outlawed and dissolved the CPA, provided for other organisations thought to be substantially communist to be declared illegal and their members declared ineligible for employment by the Commonwealth or any Commonwealth authority, and prevented key trade unions from having 'declared' persons as officials. Their worst fears now realised, the Democratic Rights Council and the APC began jointly organising the People's Assembly of Human Rights. They invited two international speakers, one of them Paul Robeson, to attend.[125]

This second invitation arrived just as Robeson was desperately fighting against the imminent loss of his passport, and thus his freedom to travel abroad. With so much happening at home, it was not the time for physically taxing speaking engagements in distant and unknown places. The *Argus* newspaper reported that he had declined, with his spokeswoman, Louise Patterson (organisational director of the Council on African Affairs), citing nervous exhaustion.[126] When columnist Frank Doherty asked in the same newspaper a few days later, on 22 June, whether this second rejection was a result of Robeson's dislike of the White Australia policy and the current anti-communist legislation, Nance Macmillan responded in a letter to the editor that it was not, and that Robeson was indeed exhausted.[127]

At the time she wrote her letter, Paul was writing to her, giving the true reason he could not come.[128] It was neither political disapproval nor exhaustion, but rather commitment to fighting for peace and against injustice in the United States. His letter sent words of greeting to 'the Australian Defenders of peace' and expressing his 'deep affection for the Australian people'. However, he wrote, he could not come owing to his 'commitments in connection with the growing peace movement in the United States' and his involvement in defending African Americans from continuing injustice. He referred to particular African Americans on death row—the seven youth from Martinsville, Virginia, and Willie McGee of Mississippi—who would 'die within a month unless the outraged conscience of American and world humanity will save them'. This very day, he wrote, the FBI had picked up Haywood Patterson, one of the so-called Scottsboro Boys, who had for three years been a fugitive 'from the barbarous Alabama prison-keepers who made his life a living hell'.[129] He mentions others in gaol or in danger of gaol for their 'alleged contempt of our notorious Un-American Activities Committee'—Howard Fast, George Marshall (chairman of the CRC), Eugene Dennis (secretary of the CPUSA). The letter is signed 'Paul Robeson, Chairman, Council on African Affairs', and concludes with a note that he deeply regretted that it was impracticable to send a recording of his message.[130]

Just two days before Robeson wrote this letter, President Truman had announced his decision that the United States would provide military support to Korea against communist forces in the north. The day after, 28 June 1950, in a speech to a CRC rally of 18,000 people at Madison Square Garden, Robeson condemned Truman's decision in support of 'a corrupt clique of politicians south of the 38th parallel'.[131] The place for African American people to fight for their freedom, he said, as he had said many times earlier, 'is here at home—in Georgia, Mississippi, Alabama and Texas—in the Chicago ghetto, and right here in New York's Stuyvesant Town'.[132] As Duberman points out, the US authorities had long wanted to muzzle Robeson for his outspoken critique of US racial and foreign policy; now his opposition to US military involvement in Korea was the last straw. They decided to prevent him from leaving the country again.[133] In early August, the State Department revoked his passport and ordered immigration and customs officials to prevent him from leaving the country; soon afterwards, Eslanda Robeson lost her passport as well.[134]

To the organisers' great disappointment, Paul Robeson would not be coming to Australia to speak at the People's Assembly for Human Rights or, indeed, at any similar event. When he did arrive with Eslanda fully ten years later, he would be a changed man, it would be a commercial rather than a political tour (though it would develop decidedly political aspects), and Australian society would have changed dramatically.

3

'Let Robeson Sing'

The Robesons, Australia and New Zealand during the Cold War Years, 1950–1958

THROUGH THE 1950S, Paul Robeson became a symbol of struggle and resistance for the left internationally. In the Soviet bloc, he was seen as a friend. He shared the International Peace Prize with Pablo Picasso at the Second World Congress in Defence of Peace in Warsaw in October 1950,[1] and was awarded in 1952 the Soviet Government awarded him the International Stalin Prize for Strengthening Peace Among Peoples, worth £11,000, given to people internationally who opposed war.[2]

He remained popular also in much of Western Europe; in Paris on 14 July 1951, he was one of four people whose pictures were carried by the crowd in the Bastille Day parade.[3] In 1953, he had to turn down invitations from England to perform Othello and from Wales to sing at the National Eisteddfod.[4] It was a very different story in the United States, where he was rapidly transformed from heroic popular figure to one of the most vilified African Americans in the country.[5]

In Australia and New Zealand, he was neither shunned as much as in the United States nor celebrated as much as in Europe. While his musical presence sharply declined as there were no new records or movies to maintain his celebrity and few radio broadcasts, many people still had his records and some of his films continued to screen around the country. For socialists and communists in Australia, who were in an increasingly unpopular and embattled political position themselves, he was an inspiration, a revered figure of defiance and integrity in the face of intense opposition and denigration.

The Cold War in the United States, Australia and New Zealand

The US experience of the Cold War has been well documented, interpreted and reinterpreted. Put briefly, the late 1940s and the 1950s were marked by a US Government determination to destroy the Communist Party and to render silent anyone who espoused ideas that could in any way be called communist. With the Soviet Union now considered an enemy rather than an ally, any sign of approval of or allegiance to the Soviet Union was regarded as highly dangerous and had to be expunged from American politics and culture.

It was no small matter to achieve these aims, as communism had developed a minor but significant following during the Depression years of the 1930s and the Soviet Union had been an American ally in wartime from 1941 to 1945. Methods used to suppress communism and communists included banning of the CPUSA, public humiliation of individuals through the House Un-American Activities Committee (HUAC), and exclusion of anyone suspected of communist ideas from a vast range of employment opportunities. For Paul Robeson, the Cold War years meant that he could rarely perform in the United States as nearly all venues were closed to him, and his exclusion from mainstream newspapers, radio, television and film. His near-erasure was swift and thorough; in October 1950, for example, the mayor of Boston barred the display of an image of Robeson, probably still the most famous African American in the world, in a touring exhibition of portraits of famous Black people.[6] The result was that while older Americans remembered him, younger people were scarcely aware of his existence. The emerging civil rights movement was careful to keep a distance from him, not wanting to be tarred with the communist brush as Paul and Eslanda had been.

The Australian and the New Zealand Cold War echoed that of the United States in some ways—notably in the determination of conservative governments to eliminate communists from national prominence and influence—but they also differed in certain major respects. There were few counterparts to the HUAC and other show trials that were such a feature of the United States in the late 1940s and much of the 1950s, and only a few gaolings of communists for subversion, all in Australia. One of those few was William Fardon Burns who, as the official publisher of the CPA newspaper, *Tribune*, was found guilty of sedition for publishing a series of articles expressing opinions like Paul's. In June 1950, *Tribune* opposed Australia's participation in the war in Korea on the grounds that the aggression had been initiated by South Korea rather than North Korea and that American action in Korea risked a third world war; it summed up its view with the slogan 'Not a Man, Not a Plane, Not a Gun for the Aggressive Imperialist War on Korea and Malaya'.[7] Burns, a waterside worker, served a little over half of his six-month sentence in 1951, and in 1960 would be delighted to hear Robeson speak to a mass meeting of waterside workers in Sydney.[8] Others who were gaoled included Lance Sharkey, who served thirteen months in prison in 1950 for saying, 'if Soviet forces in pursuit of aggressors entered Australia, Australian workers would welcome them'.[9]

Yet if the situation was less extreme than in the United States, there were significant similarities. In Australia, the Menzies-led coalition government set out to ban the CPA. As we saw in the previous chapter, there was strong opposition in 1950 to the Australian Government's proposed legislation. The People's Assembly for Human Rights to which Paul had been invited to speak went ahead without him in September 1950 and was well attended and supported by leading figures in the trade unions, peace committees and civil liberties organisations.[10] Despite public opposition, the *Communist Party Dissolution Act* was passed by parliament in October 1950; it was subsequently found by the High Court to be unconstitutional. The government then called a referendum in September 1951 to amend the Constitution and thus render the Act legal. Like most Australian referenda, this one failed, and the CPA remained legal. From then on, the government relied heavily on the Australian Security and

Intelligence Organisation (ASIO) to watch communist activity closely, ensure communists were not employed in government positions, and infiltrate communist organisations. I grew up in a household where my parents always assumed their phone was tapped and their meetings were likely attended by ASIO spies. In New Zealand, the government established the Security Intelligence Service in 1956, charging it with excluding communists from public service employment.

Suppressing communism was not only a matter of government policy—the mass media and popular attitudes also strongly opposed communism and especially the Soviet Union. The communist party in both countries continually lost members and community support. Nevertheless, the CPA remained a force in certain respects that would become relevant when the Robesons visited in 1960. It retained its presence on international bodies sympathetic to communism and especially to the Soviet Union, such as the WPC, the Women's International Democratic Federation, and the World Federation of Trade Unions. At the same time, it developed a close relationship with the new communist regime in China, which held party schools to teach Marxist and Maoist ideas to several CPA delegations for periods lasting from several months to several years.[11] Within Australia, the CPA continued to retain several important areas of strength and influence. One was the trade union movement, where, despite losing control in the early 1950s of some major unions such as the Federated Ironworkers' Association of Australia, communist officials remained powerful in key unions such as the Waterside Workers' Federation (WWF) and the BWIU, both of which would be important in welcoming Paul to Australia in 1960. The Communist Party of New Zealand (CPNZ) was weaker but it, too, had some influence in key trade unions.

The peace movement gathered strength throughout the 1950s as it campaigned against nuclear weapons and for mutual coexistence. It confronted a considerable amount of war talk; from 25 June 1950 until 27 July 1953, during which time 17,000 Australian military personnel fought with the United States on the side of South Korea, Prime Minister Menzies spoke often of the real possibility of a third world war.[12] The CPA and the peace movement took the opposite view. In opposition to the spectre of such a war, and closely following Soviet policy, the CPA reaffirmed at its sixteenth party congress in August 1951 its view that peace was the most pressing issue of all.[13] Communist attention to the peace movement led the ALP, anxious to avoid any association with communists, in May 1950 to prohibit its members from participating in the movement.[14] Nevertheless, the peace movement did attract a range of supporters, including a group of Protestant clergy who established the Peace Quest Forum, leading to two major peace conferences, one in Melbourne in 1952 and the other in Sydney in 1953.[15] The APC sponsored its own Australian Assembly for Peace conference in Sydney in September 1956, and invited Paul to speak; he had, however, yet another application for return of his passport rejected, and could not accept.[16]

With few opportunities to perform, Paul devoted himself to issues of racial struggle and liberation both at home and abroad. He was an active chairman of the Council on African Affairs, which had a close relationship with the African National Congress and the South African Indian Congress, and famously narrated for the Council an anti-apartheid documentary entitled *South Africa Uncensored* in 1951. While some leading African American figures and organisations continued to disparage and exclude him, notably the NAACP, he turned to other forms of activism for African American civil rights.[17] With WEB Du Bois, now eighty-two, he established a new journal, *Freedom*, aimed at an African American readership. From its first appearance in December 1950, *Freedom* supported a range of causes, including the labour movement, world peace and anti-colonialism. In collaboration with Lloyd L Brown, Paul wrote a column for it and supported its fundraising campaigns.[18] At the same time, Eslanda joined a largely communist African American women's organisation, Sojourners for Truth and Justice, which issued 'a call to Negro women' in September 1951.[19]

Paul also supported the Civil Rights Congress, a controversial and vigorous communist-led organisation headed by William L Patterson. The CRC strongly believed that a focus on Jim Crow laws and deprivation of Black people's rights would be an embarrassment for the United States abroad and might hasten overdue reform, a judgement proved prescient when the American civil rights movement a decade later adopted these same tactics. In its campaigns on specific cases of racist repression it attracted the support of well-known people, including English author Jessica Mitford, who became a leading East Bay figure in California; crime writer Dashiell Hammett, who went to gaol as a result of being a trustee of the CRC's bail fund; and African American entertainers like Josephine Baker and Lena Horne.[20] Most notably, Paul became a leading figure in the CRC's 'We Charge Genocide' petition of December 1951, submitting it to the UN Secretariat in New York at the same time as Patterson submitted it to the UN General Assembly in Paris.[21] Presented only eleven months after the 1948 UN Genocide Convention went into effect, the petition argued that lynching and other forms of assault on the lives and livelihood of African Americans from 1945 to 1951, especially the frenzied attacks on returning Black American veterans, amounted to genocide.[22] Eslanda and other leading Sojourners signed the petition and in April 1952 formed links with the African National Congress Women's League, much to the delight of the latter.[23] By September 1952, however, the Sojourners for Truth and Justice had folded, as did many leftist organisations in the context of McCarthyism. Within a few years, the much larger CRC and the Council on African Affairs had also collapsed.[24]

Eslanda's life took a new turn when, in 1952, she became a journalist. The *New World Review*, an American communist-allied journal reporting on the Soviet Union, China and global protest movements, appointed her as a correspondent and then as an editorial consultant on African American and colonial issues. This position gave her press credentials and a desk in the UN press room, from which vantage point she was able to extend her knowledge of and connections to global politics, and to report on the United Nations itself.[25] She also wrote for several Black publications, including the *Pittsburgh Courier* and the *California Eagle*, for the Associated Negro Press news service, and for Paul's journal, *Freedom*, until it folded in 1955.[26]

As a journalist, Eslanda reported on a range of heated debates concerning the United Nations, such as whether the UN should admit the People's Republic of China, and what UN policy should be on French colonialism in Algeria and Cameroon. She wanted women to play a larger role in the United Nations and reported in July 1953 on the annual meeting of the UN Commission on the Status of Women.[27] Some of her writings brought her to the attention of the authorities seeking to crush communism and pro-Soviet advocacy within the United States. The US Committee on Government Operations' Permanent Subcommittee on Investigations, headed by Senator Joseph McCarthy himself, interviewed her on 7 July 1953. When McCarthy ordered Eslanda to answer queries arising from her 1945 book, *African Journey*, in which she had expressed strong support for the Soviet Union, her defiant and confident responses led to some praise from the Black press.[28]

Connections

In Australia and New Zealand, although knowledge of Paul Robeson lessened dramatically during the 1950s, he did not disappear from notice altogether. Some of his movies were still in circulation, especially *Sanders of the River*, which continued to screen around Australia in cinemas and from late 1956 was occasionally shown on television.[29] *Jericho*, too, was still available for screening.[30]

While Paul's recordings were not as easily acquired as they had once been, they were still available, and there were occasional newspaper advertisements for them, such as one for a 10-inch record 'with a selection of his most popular songs' available at Morgan's Book Shop and Record Lounge in Sydney in April 1956.[31] While that record was based on songs recorded before Paul fell out of favour in 1950, there was one highly valued and hard-to-get Robeson record of more recent origin. This was the recording, first sold in 1953, of the Peace Arch concert held in Canada in May 1952. When he was banned in January 1952 from entering Canada, for which no passport was necessary, Paul sang at the US/Canadian border to 30,000 people. He stood on a makeshift stage in Peace Arch Park in Blaine, Washington State, just 30 centimetres from the border, while the audience gathered on the Canadian side. Robeson later wrote: 'I shall always remember that concert on May 18, 1952, when 30,000 Canadians came from many miles away to hear me, to demonstrate their friendship and to protest against all barriers to cultural exchange.'[32] The concert would be repeated each year to somewhat smaller crowds for the next three years.[33] Some Australians were present at these concerts; during the third one, in August 1954, for instance, members of the Australian sporting team in Vancouver for the Empire Games were invited by the organisers, the International Union of Mine, Mill and Smelter Workers, to travel down to Blaine to hear him.[34]

Mostly, though, Australians heard the Peace Arch concerts on the record made from the first one. Along with some speeches, it consisted of spirituals (including 'Every Time I Feel the Spirit' and 'No More Auction Block for Me'), traditional folk songs ('Loch Lomond', 'Oh, No, John!' and 'L'Amour de Moi'), and more recently composed songs (notably 'Ol' Man River', 'Joe Hill', 'Over the Mountains' and 'Ma Curly Headed Baby').[35] Organisers of the Canadian border concerts sent a copy to 'a fan in Australia' in 1955, and there seem to have been several copies available locally that were much prized and played.[36] In 1957 the CPA bookshop in Sydney, Current Book Distributors, advised that it had ordered twenty-four copies of 'the record known as Concert on the Canadian Border' and advised customers to place an order soon, since orders would be filled in 'strict priority of payments received'.[37] The record seems to have become very popular with left-wing Australians for decades afterwards. In an interview many years later, Mary Okello in Brisbane recalled as a child hearing a family friend playing Robeson records, including one of Paul's border concerts with Canada.[38]

The connection with the WWF was especially strong. In November 1955, it and other left-wing trade unions helped maintain interest in Paul Robeson in Australia when they screened a recent film, *The Song of the Rivers*, featuring him singing its theme song. Directed by Dutch socialist documentary filmmaker Joris Ivens, the film was made on the initiative of the third World Trade Union Congress, held in Vienna in October 1953. Ivens and Robeson were friends. The two men had a great deal in common, having both been born in 1898, been involved in the international avant-garde art world in the 1920s, and aligned themselves with the Soviet Union during the 1930s. As film historian Charles Musser writes, the two men shared 'the vision of a new socialist utopia in which conflicts of classes, races and nations would be overcome'.[39] Both had had their passports withheld by their government for political reasons, though Ivens for a shorter time than Robeson. Now, in 1954, based in different continents, the two worked together on *The Song of the Rivers*. The film depicted the lives of workers along six major rivers—Amazon, Ganges, Mississippi, Nile, Volga and Yangtze—and its advertising poster was painted by Picasso.[40] For the English, French and German versions of the film, Robeson sang an English translation of its theme song, composed by Dmitri Shostakovich with lyrics in German by Bertolt Brecht.[41] Unable to hire a studio, he sang the song at his brother's home in Harlem with his son as sound engineer, and it was not until the film was completed that he learned who the composer and lyricist were.[42]

The film was scarcely available in the United States, and Robeson himself was unable to see it for some time, but it was hugely popular in Western Europe and elsewhere with its theme of the unity of working-class humanity.[43] Though it did not receive commercial screening in Australia, left-wing trade unions welcomed it. Ivens was familiar to the Australian left, having eight years earlier made *Indonesia Calling* (1946), featuring Australian waterside workers' support for the Indonesian independence movement in September 1945.[44] Recalling that 'great documentary', the *Maritime Worker*—the journal of the WWF—now drew its readers' attention to *The Song of the Rivers*.[45] Distributed by Quality Films, it was shown at the Sydney Trade Union Club on 20 November 1955,[46] and the BWIU screened it a few days later, on 25 November, at its celebration of the tenth anniversary of the establishment of the World Federation of Trade Unions.[47]

The passport campaign

While Paul's political activities within the United States were not well known in Australia and New Zealand, some Australians and New Zealanders remained aware of him through newspaper reporting of his struggle to regain his passport. From 1950 to 1958, Paul presented a string of applications for its return, all of which were unsuccessful. He was not alone, though the length of time his passport was withheld was unusually long. Other African American political leaders who found their ability to travel overseas curtailed in the 1950s included the ageing great and revered WEB Du Bois, while others, like Louis Armstrong, were closely monitored.[48] In contrast, those the government could trust not to say the wrong thing found their way eased. Marian Anderson's tour of Japan in 1953 is just one example, as Katie A Callam, Makiko Kimoto, Misako Ohta and Carol J Oja point out in their in-depth study.[49] Robeson and Anderson, despite their shared musical interests and talents, had gone on very different paths in the late 1930s, when Paul became a socialist, a fervent supporter of the Soviet Union, and an outspoken critic of racism and segregationist policies in the United States, while Anderson did not and remained quite reserved publicly on political matters. The result in the 1950s was that while Paul struggled for years to regain his passport and thus his right to travel and perform internationally, Anderson was able to tour freely and extensively.[50]

As the US State Department continued to reject his applications for return of his passport, Paul began to appear in American and Australian newspapers as a tragic figure, a talented man who had lost his career by backing the wrong side in the Cold War. The idea that his story was tragic appeared in an article published pseudonymously in the NAACP magazine *The Crisis* in 1951, and newspaper and journal articles would repeat it many times afterwards. When Paul's passport was again denied in August 1952, the Sydney-based *Sunday Herald* featured an article from its New York office headed 'America's fallen idol', which contrasted his earlier fame with the continued cancellation of venues where he was scheduled to speak or perform.[51] The unidentified writer, who had talked with Robeson in a two-hour interview, emphasises that his story is a tragedy, the 'story of a courageous, intelligent man whose passionate hatred of race prejudice has driven him into the camp of almost any group that shares his hatred'. Even this view, a softer one than some of the more strident attacks on Robeson as a traitor, seems to have originated with the US authorities. Historian Penny Von Eschen points out that the idea for the 'tragic' angle on Robeson seems to have come initially from a US Government official based in Accra, Gold Coast (now part of Ghana), who suggested to the State Department that this would be a gentle but effective way to undermine Robeson's high reputation in Africa.[52]

In Australia, Nance Macmillan, now living in Brisbane, remained an important source of information about Paul's passport struggles. She alerted *Tribune* readers in 1953 to the fact that 9 April was his birthday, during which he would receive, as he did each year, greetings from all around the world, and she urged them to write to Washington demanding return of his passport.[53] There were in fact a range of letters sent from Australia to the United States supporting Robeson's case. One was from the 'Democratic Discussion Group' in Woollahra, Sydney, which sent a protest letter direct to President Dwight Eisenhower, plus a copy to Paul. The letter to the president read:

> We emphatically protest against the detention in the USA of Paul Robeson, the greatest American singer of all time. We in Australia would like nothing better than for Paul Robeson to visit our shores, to sing to us in person. Where is the America of democratic and liberal tradition? Why are you afraid to allow your best-loved citizen this elementary human right? In any case, we already know his life story. You make a singer into a hero by robbing us of the right to listen to his songs. Is this your intention? If not, then let Paul Robeson come and go as he pleases, and we hope he pleases to visit us.

On the copy to Paul, the letter added: 'You are a most precious member of progressive humanity for whom the love of the people is reserved. Your steadfast courage is a challenge and your art an inspiration … We pledge you our determination to continue protesting against your detention until your right to travel is restored.'[54]

Live performances and film aimed to encourage further action and letter-writing in support of Paul. In May and June 1953, two performances of a narrative musical play called *The Paul Robeson Story* were presented in Redfern, Sydney, with about seventy people attending each time. The musical was written and arranged by W Brown—a *Tribune* journalist—and presented by Bert Keesing of the Australasian Book Society. Interspersed with narration of phases of Paul's life were played on record a series of songs: 'St Louis Blues' (life before he became a singer), 'Ol' Man River' (from *Show Boat*), 'Ah Still Suits Me' (more *Show Boat*), 'Soviet Land' (his visits to the Soviet Union in the 1930s), 'Canoe Song' (from *Sanders of the River*) and songs such as 'Joe Hill', 'Peat Bog Soldiers' and 'Ballad for Americans'. A recital of the poem 'Freedom Train' represented the violence at Peekskill and Paul's struggle to regain his passport.[55] After each performance, the organisers screened *Jericho* (1937), the only full-length film featuring Robeson available in Australia on 16mm at the time. On both occasions, those present called on the US Government to restore Paul's passport so that he could travel outside the United States.[56] The CPA rented copies of the script and a set of records to its branches so they could hold similar events.

Supporters and admirers around the world wanted to hear Paul sing, act and speak, and an international campaign for the return of his passport emerged. In May 1954, the Provisional Committee to Restore Paul Robeson's Passport launched a campaign in New York seeking support from around the world. The response was encouraging, especially in Britain, where the campaign was called 'Let Robeson Sing'.[57] In Australia, *Tribune* immediately reported the campaign launch and advised Australians to send messages of support to the New York committee.[58] Soon after, the Victorian branch of the Australian Tramway and Motor Omnibus Employees' Association sent a protest direct to the US Embassy in Melbourne.[59] The seafarers on the SS *Denman* cabled Robeson a message of support.[60] When he was again denied his passport in July 1954, the Australian mainstream press reported it[61] and communist-led unions took up his cause, the *Maritime Worker* publishing a cartoon on 13 July headed 'Robeson, a prisoner!' The accompanying story recounted his many achievements and urged readers to protest directly to President Eisenhower in Washington, DC.[62]

In August 1954, two more Robeson evenings in Sydney not only supported the passport campaign but provided something of a reminder to their audiences of Robeson's cultural achievements. At these events there were screenings of *Jericho* and of an eight-minute extract from *Song of Freedom* (1936) in which Robeson sang a song entitled 'The Black Emperor'. Several recordings were played: Robeson singing 'Ballad for Americans', the recording of the incidents at Peekskill in 1949, and a speech he made at a celebratory event for the London *Daily Worker*.[63] The NSW Realist Film Association cabled President Eisenhower urging the return of Robeson's passport.[64]

These Robeson evenings and other activities helped keep his situation before Australian supporters. In October 1954, Macmillan suggested in *Tribune* that Australians send a petition to the US State Department and to the New York–based Provisional Committee to Restore Paul Robeson's Passport, and informed *Tribune* readers of a letter she had received from Robeson thanking Australians who supported the committee and commenting, 'All my best to my many friends in Australia. I'll get over there one day soon.'[65] When he arrived in Australia, Paul would several times comment publicly on the importance of the letters he had received from Australians supporting his passport applications.

When the US Court of Appeals ruled in June 1955 that the State Department did not have the right to arbitrarily deny passports to American citizens, *Tribune* reported it in detail and expressed the hope that Robeson would finally be granted his passport and be able to travel.[66] But Paul's passport struggle would continue, as the State Department remained determined he did *not* regain it. After yet another of his requests for its restoration was rejected in August 1955, the international campaign for him to regain his passport gathered momentum.[67] In October a conference of Scottish trade unionists in Glasgow launched a nationwide petition to President Eisenhower.[68] A public meeting in Manchester on 11 March 1956 attracted prominent sponsors and was attended by 500 people, leading to the formation of a national Paul Robeson committee and an accelerated campaign.[69] In Australia, *Tribune* continued to report Paul's failed attempts to secure a passport and the strength of the 'Let Robeson Sing' campaign.[70]

While Paul struggled to regain his passport and both he and Eslanda faced public hearings in the United States designed to locate and destroy communism, Australia was going through its own series of political crises. The defection in April of Vladimir Petrov, third secretary in the Soviet Embassy in Canberra and agent of the Russian secret police (operating as part of the Ministry of Internal Affairs, or MVD), prompted one of the key events of the Australian Cold War: the holding by the Menzies government of the Royal Commission on Espionage, which lasted from May 1954 to March 1955. After ten months and 119 witnesses, in August 1955 it concluded that while there had indeed been espionage as Petrov indicated, the MVD had had no success in gaining access to information concerning security and defence. The commission recommended no prosecutions of Australian citizens.[71] The Soviet Embassy, however, which had been closed when Petrov defected, would remain closed for several more years, reopening only on 13 March 1959.

Having survived the royal commission, CPA members learned a year later about Nikita Khrushchev's secret speech, which he delivered to a closed session of the 20th Congress of the Communist Party of the Soviet Union in February 1956. It denounced Stalin, who had died two years earlier, for his use of mass terror in the Great Purge of the mid-1930s.[72] Khrushchev also accused Stalin of a 'cult of the personality', glorifying his leadership, and of purging the leading officers of the Red Army; deporting entire nationality groups, including the Karachay, Kalmyk, Chechen, Ingush and Balkar peoples; and, before his death, attempting a purge of Jewish doctors in fabricated accusations of conspiracy known as the doctors' plot.[73] The speech was published by the *New York Times* on 5 June, leading to reverberations, especially in communist parties, around the world.

It is hard to know exactly how the Robesons responded to the secret speech, as they made little or no comment. Paul must have been shocked, having extolled Stalin as a great man when he died in March 1953. On that occasion, Paul had recalled attending a concert in Moscow in 1937 where Stalin was present and commented that he was a man 'who was wise and good—the world and especially the socialist world was fortunate indeed to have his daily guidance'. In the development of national minorities, he thought, 'Stalin had played and was playing a most decisive role'.[74] Now, only three years later, Stalin's terror campaigns against citizens, the military, party members and national minorities were known to the world. Martin Duberman thinks Paul accepted that the charges were true but saw them, as the CPA did, as a temporary derailment.[75] When subpoenaed to appear before the HUAC on 12 June 1956 for hearings on 'Unauthorized Use of United States Passports', he answered forthrightly and acutely except when questioned about his support for the Soviet Union. Then, Jordan Goodman points out, he suddenly became evasive, responding to questions by saying he did not know or could not remember. With only a week having passed since publication of the speech, he had not yet articulated a response.[76]

Khrushchev's speech had a major impact in Australia and New Zealand, weakening the communist party in both countries significantly. The party that would so strongly support the Robesons' visit a few years later was not as large or as influential as the one they would have met a decade earlier. In New Zealand, the party had reached its maximum membership of around 2000 during World War II, with numbers falling dramatically thereafter, especially after first the speech and then the Soviet invasion of Hungary later in 1956. Key intellectuals and trade unionists had departed, leaving the party severely diminished.[77]

There was a similar pattern in Australia, though the party survived better than it had in New Zealand. At first, Australian communists found the revelations in the speech, as writer and former CPA member Len Fox records, 'shattering' and 'unbelievable' yet 'obviously authentic'.[78] Having hitherto seen allegations against the Soviet Union of dictatorship, purges and terror as fictions created by the capitalist press, they now had to deal with the fact that the allegations were true. At first the party leadership tried to prevent members' access to the secret speech, then for a brief period *Tribune* and the Melbourne-based

Guardian published letters critical of the party's secrecy; but by late 1956, as historian Stuart Macintyre records in detail, the leadership closed down party discussion. Members who circulated copies of the report were expelled, and those who questioned Stalinism were attacked as 'revisionists'.[79] The CPA now spoke of Stalin's 'mistakes' and took the view that these had been reversed under the new Soviet leadership. Many of the party's leading intellectuals, including Helen Palmer, Stephen Murray-Smith, Ian Turner, Robin Gollan and David Martin, left the CPA in this period. More party members left in response to the Soviet invasion of Hungary in November 1956. Some dissidents stayed, hoping to reform the party from within; some of these would leave later over a variety of issues.

The 'Let Robeson Sing' campaign, meanwhile, gathered strength. An all-day Robeson celebration in Britain on 26 May 1957 was supported by notable figures such as Leonard Woolf, Julian Huxley, Benjamin Britten and Kingsley Amis. To Robeson's joy, British Actors' Equity voted for a resolution that he should be allowed to perform in Britain.[80] In the evening, he sang by transatlantic phone circuit to a packed audience of around 1000 people at St Pancras Town Hall in London. The event was a technological breakthrough at the time, the cable enabling transatlantic telephone calls being less than a year old and never before used for a concert-hall performance.[81]

As the international campaign grew, the State Department stood firm. After yet another hearing on his passport on 29 May 1957, the US authorities again refused Robeson permission to travel internationally, except to places not requiring a passport, like Alaska, Hawaii, Puerto Rico, American Samoa, Bermuda, Mexico and many parts of the Caribbean.[82] In response, the campaign intensified. Welsh miners who had been present at the St Pancras event arranged for a similar concert in the tiny town of Porthcawl, with Paul singing on the telephone. It was held on 5 October 1957 and over 5000 people attended. Robeson sang 'All Through the Night', 'Didn't My Lord Deliver Daniel?' and 'All Men Are Brothers' and was received so rapturously the concert is still remembered warmly today.[83] He wrote about it soon afterwards: 'I cannot say how deeply I was moved on this occasion, for here was an audience that had adopted me as kin and though they were unseen by me I never felt closer to them.'[84]

Around this time, Paul's records were again becoming available. In Australia and New Zealand they were returning to record shops, ensuring that music lovers and political activists could establish or replenish their Robeson record collections.[85] Coronet, a Sydney-based record company that released material licensed from international labels, produced in 1957 a new 12-inch LP, using older recordings by Columbia, called *Paul Robeson's Favourites*, with songs including 'Ol' Man River', 'Ma Curly Headed Baby', 'Water Boy' and 'Go Down, Moses'.[86] Also newly available was a three-record version of *Othello* as performed on Broadway in 1942–43 with Robeson in the title role. Coronet also produced a 45 rpm disc called *Ol' Man River*, which featured 'Ol' Man River', 'Ma Curly Headed Baby', 'I Still Suits Me' and 'Wagon Wheels'.

Paul was reappearing on radio, especially the Australian Broadcasting Commission (ABC) and New Zealand Broadcasting Corporation (NZBC). In a letter to the ABC radio listeners' journal, *ABC Weekly*, Nancy Short praised announcer Russ Tyson for 'having the courage to play a Paul Robeson record on April 14 [1958] and for having paid tribute to this wonderful man on his sixtieth birthday'.[87] Short is referring to the long-running *Hospital Half-Hour* presented by Tyson, which had begun in 1939 and would last until 1975, and centred on requests made by listeners at a particular hospital each session. Given the likely advanced age of many of those making the requests, one can imagine that they knew Robeson's records and movies from the 1930s and 1940s. Short's letter suggests that Robeson had been missing from the program and was now reappearing. In both Australia and New Zealand, his name resurfaced in radio listings in newspapers.

Paul re-emerges

It was clear that the worst of the ostracism and exclusion was over. As Cold War tensions eased, Paul found venues in the United States opening to him after seven long years of rejection. He sang in concerts in October 1957 to 10,000 people in Los Angeles and San Francisco,[88] and took steps to enhance his public profile and especially his connections with other African Americans that had suffered at the height of the Cold War. However, despite the Robesons' longstanding and firm commitment to racial justice within the United States and internationally, the new generation of African American leaders saw both Paul and Eslanda as a liability and kept them at a distance from the emerging new civil rights movement.[89] Paul was not, for example, invited to speak or sing at the Prayer Pilgrimage for Freedom in Washington, DC, on 17 May 1957, an event celebrating the third anniversary of the pathbreaking *Brown v. Board of Education* decision outlawing segregation in schools, and one that marked the emergence of Martin Luther King Jnr as a civil rights leader.[90] Despite the snub, Paul and Eslanda attended along with 30,000 others; when they sat far in the background under a large tree, many people came up to Paul to pay their respects.[91]

His visibility both in the United States and internationally increased when, early in 1958, *Here I Stand*, a manifesto-autobiography written by Paul with Lloyd L Brown, was published by independent Harlem publisher Othello Associates. The book, planned in 1952 and completed in late 1957, primarily addressed an African American audience. Though white American publications ignored the book, the African American press reviewed it widely and it sold well, a clear indication that Robeson was starting to come back into favour, at least with African Americans. It was also well reviewed in the United Kingdom, Japan and India.[92] In Australia, it was covered extensively by *Tribune* and some mainstream papers.[93] Martin Long reviewed it favourably and presciently for the *Sydney Morning Herald* in November, saying it exemplified the comment by Alexander Woollcott that Paul was 'a man touched by destiny'. While his 'avowed fellow-travelling with Communism confused his followers and enabled his enemies to silence him for nearly nine years', recent developments meant that 'Robeson may find the tide running his way again'.[94]

The book includes a detailed account of Paul's emerging political consciousness, important to which was his 'discovery' of Africa and

Africans. In England he had come to know many Africans, including students who later became leaders of African independence movements, and seafarers in the ports of London, Liverpool and Cardiff; and he had begun to study African languages and culture. Paul also outlines his relationship to the Soviet Union, which he saw as a place without racial discrimination and a supporter of anti-colonial and liberation movements. Visiting Spain during the Spanish Civil War, he says, changed his life, especially when he met the men of the Lincoln Battalion, part of the International Brigade. The book also outlines Robeson's view of the necessity for African American activism, understood as part of a worldwide struggle for Black people's liberation, and for united and determined action now rather than later. This was a critique of those, Black and white, who favoured gradual reform; its view that the time was *now* prefigures King's more famous critique of those who say 'wait' in his 'Letter from Birmingham Jail' in 1963. *Here I Stand* remains in print and today is widely discussed and cited.

Paul's reputation remained high outside the United States, with his birthday being celebrated in many parts of the world. Altogether twenty-seven countries celebrated his sixtieth birthday on 9 April 1958, with especially notable events occurring in London, Mexico City, Cape Town, East Berlin, Tokyo, Peking and Moscow.[95] In India, Nehru's daughter, Indira Gandhi, sponsored an all-India 'Paul Robeson Day' for the occasion.[96] The celebrations were huge, involving events in many major cities, and his signature song, 'Ol' Man River', was adapted into several South Asian languages, with the Mississippi becoming the Ganges.[97] In an article on the birthday celebrations in *The Worker* in late April 1958, Eslanda stressed the international support for Paul, noting that committees had been formed worldwide, including in Australia, and that Paul had received telephone calls and greetings from around the world, including from Sydney.[98]

Even in the United States, Paul was to some extent coming back into favour. He was able to resume commercial music recording, now with Vanguard, and with that label made some of his most outstanding recordings, including 'Shenandoah', 'Deep River', 'Water Boy' and 'All Through the Night'.[99] At concerts in California, Portland and Chicago he fostered a gentler image and received enthusiastic reviews, leading Black churches to open their doors to him. He was later to tell an Australian radio interviewer that one of the most satisfying concerts of his life took place in Oakland, California, in February 1958. It was a rainy day, there were 2000 people present and he was still unused to major concert performing, and he was delighted that it went well.[100]

The best-remembered concert from this time, however, was in New York. Reunited with his accompanist, Larry Brown, who would accompany him in Australia and New Zealand, Robeson appeared at Carnegie Hall on 9 May 1958 before a huge, mainly white audience, giving a notable performance that mixed songs with comments and reminiscences. A second concert followed on 23 May, for which organisers distributed tickets in Harlem, ensuring a significant Black audience.[101] A recording would become available in Australia more than two years later, in August 1960, not long before Paul and Eslanda arrived there.[102]

The Carnegie Hall concerts gave Paul an opportunity to put the musical theories he had developed during his lengthy period of isolation into practice. As writer, editor and composer Jonathan Karp explains, with his opportunities to perform limited, Paul had undertaken extensive ethnomusicological research and developed a theory to support his long-term interest in world folk culture and song. This was the theory, which he would refer to frequently in Australia and New Zealand, that folk music based on the pentatonic scale (a musical scale of five notes per octave that connects different musical traditions) was the foundation of music universally.[103] In Karp's words, 'what Robeson was aiming at was a conception of folk music as indicative of a precultural, tonal deep structure embedded in human nature and manifested in a primal form of undifferentiated music/speech'.[104] Now, at Carnegie Hall, he had an opportunity to put his ideas into practice.

Grant Olwage has discussed the Carnegie Hall programme in depth, and it is worth following him here as there would be some similarities between it and the two programmes Robeson and Brown would present in Australia and New Zealand. The recording of the Carnegie Hall concert contains twenty-two songs, and Olwage examines in detail the thirteen songs constituting the first half of the programme. Robeson often began his programmes with a simple song, in this case the English folk song 'Over the Mountains'. Next came the English national song 'Jerusalem', based on the poem by William Blake, which Paul had first recorded in London just before returning to the United States in September 1939. Then came an African American spiritual, 'There Is a Balm in Gilead', followed by a revolutionary Czech song, 'Svornost', arranged by Bedřich Smetana; Robeson sang the first verse in English and the rest in its original language. The first set finished with a lullaby by Schubert, 'Sleep, My Little One', and Beethoven's 'All Men Are Brothers'. The arrangement of songs was meant to convey Robeson's deep interest in the unity and diversity of humanity and drew on pieces he had been singing for up to three decades. The second set began with 'Going Home', a popular tune by Antonín Dvořák, and continued with another English folk song, 'Oh, No, John!', two songs by Modest Mussorgsky sung in Russian, one about a king and the other about an abandoned orphan, together expressing Robeson's familiarity with Russia; then a Russian song, 'Song of the Volga Boatmen', an unnamed Chinese folk song, and the 'Hassidic Chant of Levi Isaac'. 'Jacob's Ladder' was sung as an encore.[105] Through it all, Robeson was displaying impressive cosmopolitanism as well as drawing on different moments in his musical career, as he would do in his tour of Australia and New Zealand.

On 25 June 1958, the US Supreme Court ruled against the secretary of state, declaring he had no right to deny a passport on the basis of political beliefs.[106] Suddenly it was all over, and Paul and Eslanda were free to travel. They decided to move to London. Ron Tarrant, foreign correspondent in New York for the *Sydney Morning Herald*, interviewed Paul just before they left the United States for Britain on 10 July. Headlined 'Robeson on the way back', his story emphasised the power of Paul's voice, which, he said, enabled Paul to answer whatever queries there may be as to the quality of a voice that had for so long been rarely heard. Paul explained his plans to sing in Britain and Europe and told Tarrant he would eventually visit Australia, though he warned that 'there are many places I must see first'. The story ended with a quote from Robeson: 'I don't want people to get the wrong idea about me. I want to be a fine performer. I want to be a good representative of my people.'[107]

Two weeks after receiving their passports, Paul and Eslanda left the United States; they would not return for five-and-a-half years. While Australia and New Zealand were clearly not high on Paul's 'must go' list, a commercial tour of one or both countries was now a serious possibility for the first time since 1939.

4

'The World Is His Song'

Escape to England, and the Australian and New Zealand Tour Is Planned

When paul and eslanda left the United States on 10 July 1958, just two weeks after the return of their passports, there was huge press, radio and television coverage. At the airport in London 200 friends and fans, many carrying bouquets, welcomed them and they conducted a well-attended press conference. Both were full of gaiety and excitement.[1] They had decided to base themselves in London, where they had lived for twelve years in the late 1920s and through the 1930s.

Cedric Dover, an Indian Marxist anti-racist activist whom they knew from their time in London in the 1930s, described them as 'bubbling over' with joy. 'As we ride through the streets,' he wrote, 'Paul every now and again bursts into a chuckle of deep-throated but incredulous delight.'[2] Another old friend from the 1930s, Jawaharlal Nehru, now prime minister of India, was determined that Paul's return to the world outside the United States be properly celebrated, and his sister Vijaya Lakshmi Pandit organised a welcoming reception at the Indian Embassy in London.[3] Paul held a book signing of *Here I Stand* at Selfridges, and British politicians, Indian journalists, a Nigerian government minister and leading actors all dined with him in celebration of his arrival.[4] Eslanda reconnected with Claudia Jones, who was born in Trinidad then lived in the United States, where she was gaoled and then deported for her communist beliefs; Jones had since become deeply involved with the large West Indian community in London.[5]

Paul was hot property again, and in Britain media coverage was sympathetic and extensive. One of those who interviewed him on radio was Therese Denny, an Australian employed at the BBC; she asked if he regretted having lost his liberty as a result of his political beliefs. He replied that he did not, that he was proud of his contribution, and 'If you want freedom, you have to suffer some time'. He also indicated, though, that he would try to separate his art from his politics, emphasising that as a concert performer he came back as 'an artist, one who loves people'.[6] It was a theme he would reiterate frequently in Australia and New Zealand.

The warm welcomes continued. Composer Alan Bush wrote a song in Paul's honour entitled 'The World Is His Song', and so it now seemed.[7] Accompanied by Larry Brown, he sang to a packed audience of 7500 on 10 August at the Albert Hall.[8] This concert, which was extensively reviewed, included the songs for which he was best known, songs he would sing in Australia and New Zealand, including 'Every Time I Feel the Spirit', 'Ezekiel Saw de Wheel', 'I'll Hear the Trumpet Sound', 'Get On Board Little Children', 'L'Amour de Moi', 'Song of the Volga Boatmen', 'Joe Hill' and, of course, 'Ol' Man River'.[9] Most of those listed are spirituals, but 'L'Amour de Moi' is a fourteenth-century French love song set in a beautiful, tranquil garden; he had sung it in Moscow in 1949 and then at the first Peace Arch concert, and now, at the Albert Hall, he first spoke the words in English and then sang in French. Of the spirituals, we can note here that 'Get On Board Little Children', which he would later sing on television in Sydney, was a popular gospel song that had been in the repertoire of the Fisk Jubilee Singers. With its invitation to everyone, rich and poor, to get on board the gospel train, it can be read as a timeless call to join the faith. Some commentators recognise another possible meaning: a call for the oppressed to join an act of rebellion or escape.

In August 1958 Paul went to Moscow, where he received a tumultuous welcome and wide television coverage, followed by visits to Uzbekistan, Georgia, the Black Sea and Yalta.[10] Australian newspapers reported on the welcome in Moscow, and it may have been on this visit that he made the Russian records, one dated 1958, that Australian communist Margaret Mortimer brought home.[11] This record seems to have become known in Australia, a copy being donated to the organisers of a centennial celebration of Paul's life some forty years later.[12] Some of the songs were in English, others in Russian. One was a recording of a concert in which Paul introduces each song in Russian and the crowd applauds each song enthusiastically.

Many of the songs on this Russian record, such as 'Joe Hill', 'John Brown's Body', 'Ode to Joy', 'There Is a Balm in Gilead', 'We Are Climbing Jacob's Ladder' and 'Sometimes I Feel Like a Motherless Child', as well as a recitation of Othello's final speech, would be included on his Australian and New Zealand tour programmes.[13] 'Didn't My Lord Deliver Daniel?' was a Robeson favourite, with its expression of faith that God would deliver the enslaved person from slavery and its pointed refrain asking 'Why not every man?' 'There Is a Balm in Gilead' is another spiritual Paul sang frequently. Its title derives from the Hebrew Bible, where Jeremiah 8:22 asks, 'Is there no balm in Gilead? Is there no physician there?' The song lyrics say yes, there is in fact a balm in Gilead that can heal the wounded, and that balm is faith in Jesus: it can 'make the wounded whole' and 'heal the sin-sick soul'.

The Robesons, Africa and the Caribbean

Both Paul and Eslanda continued to develop their strong ties with African nations, diasporas and causes. In Paul's case, these ties were particularly strong with South Africa and the struggle against apartheid. Four thousand people heard him speak and sing at the evensong service at St Paul's Cathedral on 11 October to collect for the International Defence and Aid Fund. Established two years earlier by St Paul's canon John Collins, this fund sought to aid victims of apartheid, especially political prisoners, by paying for their legal defence, supporting their families, and publicising information about apartheid. Paul began with a passage from Isaiah 2:4 in the King James

Bible: '[And] they shall beat their swords into plowshares, and their spears into pruning hooks. Nation shall not lift up a sword against nation, neither shall they learn war any more.'[14] His reception was so warm that he commented that it was 'an historic moment in my life ... I am close to tears about it.'[15] One of those present was Geoffrey Hutton, London correspondent for the Melbourne newspaper *The Age*, who would later refer to the service glowingly in a story about Robeson's impending arrival in Melbourne in November 1960.[16]

Paul would give further concerts supporting African struggles. Twice he gave fundraising concerts on the occasion of African Freedom Day, which the First Conference of Independent African States in Accra, Ghana, had declared on 15 April 1958. The first concert occurred in April 1959 and the second on 20 April 1960 with the Welsh Cwmbach Male Choir at the Royal Festival Hall.[17]

Eslanda had perhaps an even stronger connection with African and Caribbean struggles. Even before recovering her passport, she had, in April 1958, covered a historic meeting in Port of Spain, Trinidad, where no passport was required. This was the first meeting of the federal parliament of the newly formed West Indies Federation, viewed by many as a step towards independence.[18] Her presence there had been noted in a *Sydney Morning Herald* report, though with much less emphasis on her attendance than on the role of Princess Margaret in opening the parliament.[19] Eslanda also delivered two lectures—one at the main public library on 'The Negro in world focus' and the other to a women's trade union group on global affairs and international solidarity—and participated in a forum hosted by the Women's League of the People's National Movement of Trinidad.[20] A few months after arriving in London, she made a trip to Ghana in December 1958 that she would refer to frequently in her Australian and New Zealand talks and speeches. In her report for *New World Review* on the All-African Peoples' Conference held there from 5 to 13 December 1958, she wrote that although she was disappointed at the tiny number of women delegates (there were only eight women out of hundreds of delegates), she was pleased that 'Africans plan to assert, as from now, a new African personality in world affairs and at world forums'.[21]

Alongside their hectic schedules, both Robesons had through 1958 and 1959 some serious medical problems. Soon after her return to London, Eslanda was admitted to hospital with uterine cancer.[22] As her biographer, Barbara Ransby, describes in detail, she had had breast cancer in 1956 or a little earlier, for which she had been treated, and had had a mastectomy. Then, early in 1958, she was diagnosed with cervical cancer and uterine cancer and again had painful and prolonged treatment.[23] In January 1959 she went to the Soviet Union for radiotherapy, involving painful radium and gamma ray treatments, staying in hospital for five weeks. Paul was also hospitalised in Moscow early in 1959 suffering from dizziness—the effects of a bout of influenza and general exhaustion.[24] Towards the end of the year, in November, Eslanda was admitted to hospital in London in 'screaming pain', suffering from an ulcer caused by the radiation treatment earlier in the year.[25] For some time, their poor health made extensive overseas tours unlikely.

When he recovered, Paul attended a meeting of the WPC in Moscow in February 1959 where he established an important connection with the Australian peace movement and specifically with seventy-year-old Bill Morrow, an Australian member of the WPC Bureau. Morrow's term as an Australian senator had ended in 1953; having become unpopular in the ALP for his socialist views and public dissent from party policy (such as its support for the conservative government's Communist Party Dissolution Bill in 1950), he had lost preselection for another term.[26] In his retirement he devoted himself to the peace movement, especially the WPC, and at this meeting received the Joliot-Curie Silver Medal awarded by the Council for his services to peace. In conversation, Paul told Morrow that he might come to Australia in 1960, and indeed plans for such a visit emerged just a few months later.[27]

Despite his health problems, an exceptionally busy year followed for Paul—performances in *Othello,* a second visit to the Soviet Union, another UK tour, and extensive public speaking. His reputation grew as his records became more frequently available. Several were 45 rpm with two songs each side. In 1959 HMV produced *Paul Robeson: Negro*

Spirituals, another record simply titled *Paul Robeson*, and *Best Loved Songs*. Along with the earlier HMV record entitled *Canoe Song*, which appeared in 1957, these new records soon became available in both Australia and New Zealand. He was also reappearing on radio.[28]

The *Othello* run began on 7 April 1959 at the Shakespeare Memorial Theatre in Stratford-upon-Avon—with WEB Du Bois, now ninety-one, who had also lost his passport during the Cold War and had recently regained it, attending the opening night—and lasted until late November.[29] Gavin Edwards remembers seeing a performance: 'I have a vivid memory of his voice and of him standing in the middle of the stage with his arms raised and of his wonderful deep voice … A powerful memory.'[30] Paul's friend from anti-racism struggles in the United States in the early 1950s, Jessica Mitford, attended on 2 May, writing to her family back in America: 'Robeson was really magnificent, robed in white and gold cloak, and really heart-rending … The place packed, it's an enormous theatre and every inch taken by standees.'[31] Though far away, Australians also heard about Robeson's Othello; in April, Anthea Goddard, reporting for the *Sydney Morning Herald*, described his performance as 'achieving the high spot of his acting career, and fulfilling his greatest ambition, to play Othello at Stratford-on-Avon'. Goddard thought him an 'old man … heavy and almost clumsy' but whose voice, nevertheless, remained unchanged.[32] In July, the *Australian Women's Weekly* published a story, with a striking photo, about his return to the stage and described his Othello performance as having 'completely captured' the audience.[33]

Alongside his acting and singing career went many political appearances on questions of peace, including a huge disarmament rally of 10,000 people in Trafalgar Square on 28 June 1959.[34] Occasionally when travelling, speaking and performing he encountered Australians and New Zealanders, to whom he would frequently express an interest in visiting. From July 1959 these comments were meant seriously, for negotiations concerning a possible tour of Australia and New Zealand between one of his future sponsors and his London agent had begun.[35] In August 1959, when he joined his son and daughter-in-law at the World Youth Festival in Vienna, he met Australian Irene Gale and her husband, New Zealander Jim Gale, who were both working at the city's International Institute for Peace.[36] He told them he hoped to visit Australia and New Zealand the following year, and they were delighted.[37] Irene remembers that they met him at a reception:

> The reception was also for a Cuban poet who had also just been allowed to travel by his own government, Nicolás Guillén. They had last seen each other at the Spanish Civil War and warmly hugged each other. Paul said he would sing for Nicolás and asked what he would like to hear. Nicolás immediately said, 'The Four Insurgent Generals' and so Paul sang it for him, followed by 'Ol' Man River' and some others. It was all very moving and followed by some short speeches from a range of people.[38]

Importantly, the improvement in both Paul's and Eslanda's health during the later part of 1959 and in 1960 was such that a long tour was now possible.[39]

The concert tour of Australia and New Zealand takes shape

Paul's concert tour to Australia and New Zealand occurred at an auspicious time. For the previous six years, African American entertainers had been making increasingly successful visits to both countries. Two notable events in 1954 paved the way. The Musicians' Union lifted its ban on African American jazz singers, and Lee Gordon, an American who had migrated to Australia at the age of thirty, emerged as an entrepreneur able to forge links between African American jazz and other performers and Australian audiences. Starting in July 1954 with Ella Fitzgerald, followed by Louis Armstrong in October that year and Nat King Cole in January 1955, Gordon and his business partners brought African American and other American stars to Australia for a series of 'Big Shows'.[40]

There were other visiting African American performers, too, such as, in 1955, drummer Michael Silva, members of the Norma Miller Dancers in *Coloured Rhapsody*, and soprano Mattiwilda Dobbs, sponsored by the ABC in 1955 and 1959.[41] Gordon brought Nat King Cole again in 1956 and 1957, Lionel Hampton in 1957 and Sammy Davis Jr in 1959.[42] One of Robeson's greatest admirers, Harry Belafonte, toured Australia under Gordon's auspices in August 1960. Most of these artists, notably Cole, Armstrong and Belafonte, toured New Zealand as well.

These were all locally sponsored tours; in the 1950s, the goodwill ambassador programs sponsored by the US State Department as a way of counteracting international perceptions of the United States as a racist nation were not directed at Australia or New Zealand but rather at Asian, African and communist nations.[43]

Belafonte's tour was a huge success, with concerts consistently packed out.[44] He was widely interviewed by print, radio and television media; on television he spoke strongly against nuclear testing and for African American civil rights.[45] Before and throughout his tour, he displayed a special interest in Aboriginal people. In a pre-tour interview with Larry Foley in New York for the *Australian Women's Weekly*, he expressed his desire to meet with Aboriginal people when he came to Australia. Foley thought Belafonte a superb showman and drew attention to his activism: 'under the sleek skin of the entertainer beats the passionate heart of the social reformer'. Belafonte was interested in Aboriginal folk songs. 'I'm taking a tape-machine,' he told Foley, 'and hope to record authentic Australian folk-singing by your natives that perhaps I can adapt for myself.'[46] In a television interview soon after he arrived in Australia, Belafonte again spoke of his optimism that change was coming in America concerning civil rights, and of his interest in learning more about Australian music and folk culture.[47] As an aside, it's worth noting that Belafonte, who died in April 2023, continued to learn from and about Aboriginal people in his subsequent tours.[48]

The successful offer for Paul to do a concert tour in Australia came not from from Lee Gordon but from two New Zealand entrepreneurs. One was Robert James Kerridge, the owner of the largest chain of cinemas in New Zealand, who had sponsored many overseas performers, including all the visiting Soviet bloc performers.[49] The other was Dan O'Connor, born in Auckland in 1894, who since World War II had been based in Sydney. He had much experience of working closely with the British Council to bring British theatre companies and individual performers to both Australia and New Zealand.[50] Kerridge and O'Connor made a generous offer to Paul for twenty concert performances. Paul would probably have preferred to go to Ghana, as Duberman suggests, given its attraction as the first African nation to achieve independence from colonial rule, and given the rise of independence movements throughout Africa.[51] The offer from Australia and New Zealand, however, proved in a financial sense too good to refuse. Perhaps the introduction of commercial jet flights in 1959, bringing both countries 'closer' to Europe than ever before, also influenced Paul and Eslanda's decision to accept.

The arrangement with Kerridge and O'Connor was unusual in that it appears to be the only time the two entrepreneurs worked together on a tour of this kind.[52] The contract, drafted in June and finally signed in early October, was a payment of £20,000 for twenty concerts within a seven-week period from the date of the first concert. The concerts would last for a minimum of two hours and there would be no consecutive concerts, no more than three concerts per week, and no broadcasting or telecasting of the concerts.[53] Plans were made for Robeson to sing eight concerts in New Zealand and twelve in Australia, starting in Brisbane on 15 October and ending in Perth on 2 December, with the New Zealand part of the tour occurring in between.[54] The citizens of Darwin tried unsuccessfully to be included.[55]

The concert programmes

Paul Robeson prepared two different programmes for his Australian and New Zealand concert tour. Both contained a mix of Negro spirituals, folk songs from around the world, popular songs and songs by classical European composers who drew on folk music in some way. They encapsulated his political and musical journey from the 1920s to 1960 and exemplified his views on the connections between distinct kinds of music, especially between folk and classical music. Throughout the tour, the now 67-year-old Larry Brown would accompany him and, in order to break the programme into three parts, Janetta McStay would provide two pianoforte interludes. McStay was a distinguished New Zealand–based concert pianist who had played for the NZBC and the New Zealand Symphony Orchestra and toured with many international performers. The printed programmes for each country were slightly different in arrangement, but all gave biographical details of Robeson, Brown and McStay, as well as the lyrics of all the songs, complete with details of their composers and/or arrangers.

For Programme 1, Robeson sang in the first set the spiritual 'We Are Climbing Jacob's Ladder', which he had first performed with Brown's accompaniment in New York in April 1925. He followed this with three songs by classical European composers—'Art Thou Troubled?' (Handel), 'Ode to Joy' (Beethoven's Ninth Symphony) and 'Cradle Song' (Schubert). After a piano interlude by McStay, he then sang 'The Orphan' and 'A Doll's Lullaby' (both by Mussorgsky) and three spirituals, all arranged by Brown—'Every Time I Feel the Spirit', 'Swing Low, Sweet Chariot' (a favourite Fisk Jubilee Singers song) and 'Joshua Fit de Battle ob Jericho'. All three look to Jordan, the river and the land, for salvation. 'Every Time I Feel the Spirit' has the lines 'Jordan River chilly and col'/ Chills de body but not de soul', while 'Swing Low, Sweet Chariot' is notable for its image of looking over Jordan and seeing a band of angels 'Comin' for to carry me home'. Ending the sequence is 'Joshua Fit de Battle ob Jericho', a spiritual telling of Joshua leading the Israelites to bring down the walls of Jericho, the most important city in the Jordan Valley, so they could enter the Promised Land, with its stirring refrain, 'An' de walls come tumblin' down'.

After another interval and three piano solos by McStay came five more songs, the first being folk songs and the last a political song. They were, in order, 'The Volga Boatmen's Song' (a Russian folk song), 'I Drew My Ship' (an English folk song), 'Water Boy', 'Eriskay Love Lilt' (a Scottish folk song) and ending with 'The Purest Kind of a Guy'. 'I Drew My Ship', originally collected in 1893, was an unusual choice for Robeson. It tells the story of a sailor who has been drowned at sea whose lover mistakenly thinks she hears him come into the harbour and goes down to meet him.[56] 'Eriskay Love Lilt' was another traditional folk song that had often been recorded, including by Paul himself in 1938.[57] It, too, is a song about a sailor and his love, but this time the sailor sings of the importance of his love when he is lonely at sea, when 'black the night or wild the sea'. In contrast, 'The Purest Kind of a Guy' was a political song composed by Marc Blitzstein that Paul had recorded, along with 'Joe Hill', with Columbia Records in New York in 1942. The singer knows that a man is okay, 'the purest kind of a guy', not by whether he is 'Black or white or tan' but by 'How he says hello, how he says good-bye, how he winks his eye'.

At Kerridge's request, the concert programme ended with the final speech from *Othello*, as many of Paul's concerts over the years had done.[58] The speech thrilled audiences on many levels, one of which was its reminder of Paul's fame and stature as an actor in this most famous of plays.

Programme 2 had a similar structure but with different songs, with only the two Mussorgsky songs appearing in both programmes. Mussorgsky was a nineteenth-century Russian Romantic composer who sought to develop distinctly Russian music, inspired by Russian history and folk tales. His masterpiece was the opera *Boris Godunov*, based on the drama *Boris Godunov* by Alexander Pushkin and composed in two versions in the late 1860s and early 1870s; it remains the most popular Russian opera. The story concerns Boris Godunov, the Tsar of Russia from 1598 to 1605. To become Tsar, he had murdered the son of the previous Tsar, Ivan the Terrible. When a young monk leaves his monastery and, pretending to be the murdered son, raises an army to challenge Godunov, Godunov suffers guilt over the murder and dies. He is replaced by the pretender, who becomes Tsar Dimitri II. The people remain poor and oppressed. Paul had sung two songs from the role of Boris Godunov at the House of Cinema Workers in Moscow in 1934, and the workers had loved it.[59] As Marie Seton described it:

> The listeners could not believe their ears, so true to the Russian spirit was this voice ... They kissed him and hugged him. They wept, they laughed and called him all the loving names in the passion-charged

> Russian language, including the tenderest of all—Pavelushka—which means my dearest, beloved little Paul.[60]

Songs from *Boris Godunov* had remained a staple of Robeson's repertoire ever since.

The opening song of the second programme was a spiritual, 'Tramping', first arranged by Edward Boatner and recorded by Marian Anderson in 1930. Paul's programme used Boatner's arrangement and included the repeated refrain 'I'm tramping, tramping, tryna make heaven my home'. It was followed by 'L'Amour de Moi'. The first song in place of the Handel, Beethoven and Schubert songs on the first programme was 'A Mighty Fortress Is Our God' (JS Bach, based on a song composed by Martin Luther in the sixteenth century), followed by more spirituals, including 'There Is a Balm in Gilead', 'Didn't My Lord Deliver Daniel?', 'Steal Away' (another Fisk Jubilee Singers song) and 'Ezekiel Saw de Wheel'. 'Steal Away' was an especially popular spiritual, with its refrain 'Steal away, steal away, steal away to Jesus!/ Steal away, steal away home/ I ain't got long to stay here'). Paul and Larry had recorded 'Ezekiel Saw de Wheel' in 1927, only seven years after it was first recorded by the Biddle University Quartet. The song describes the vision of the prophet Ezekiel: 'Ezekiel saw de wheel/ Way up in the middle of de air/ One of these days about twelve o'clock/ Dis old world goin' to reel and rock'.

The second half of the programme began with 'Goin' Home' (from Dvořák's Ninth Symphony), then 'Oh! Rock Me Julie' (a spiritual that Robeson had first recorded in 1928). Then there was the short 'Song of the Fox', originally a piano piece composed for children by the Hungarian Béla Bartók in 1909; its simple words, though, in the version Robeson would sing have a harsher meaning. The owner of some chickens that Reynard the fox would like to eat tells the fox he would catch him, 'Put you in prison straight/ You'll be clapped in irons then/ You'll be clapped in irons then/ And you shan't be free again'. Next came 'The Castle of Dromore', an old Irish air whose English words are a lullaby, and ending with another spiritual, 'Oh! Didn't It Rain'.

In the Australian and New Zealand concerts, 'Joe Hill', like 'Ol' Man River', was saved for the encores. Paul would also sing as encores both 'The Song of the Warsaw Ghetto' and 'Hassidic Chant'.

Publicity and anticipation

News of the planned tour appears to have become public in August 1960, the same month the famous 1958 Carnegie Hall concert record became available in Australia, drawing further attention to Robeson.[61] Publicity for the tour began in mid-September, with newspapers drawing freely on the information supplied by the promoters. Wellington's *Evening Post*, for example, described Paul as 'Possessor of one of the greatest bass voices in living memory', a fighter in 'the struggle of the American Negro for equal rights and citizenship', an actor known especially for playing Othello, who had once been an outstanding football and basketball player. The *Post* reassured potential concertgoers that they need not worry about his voice—it had been wonderful in the famous recital at Carnegie Hall in New York on 9 May 1958, and his solo concerts in London in the past year 'were notable for scenes of extraordinary enthusiasm from capacity audiences'.[62]

In Australia, too, newspaper commentary was entirely positive. Papers that would usually have been savage in their denunciation of anyone who defended the Soviet Union treated Paul with respect and even, in some cases, liking and admiration.[63] The Queensland edition of *Truth* on Sunday 9 October had a full page on Robeson in preparation for his imminent visit. One story, 'Robeson ... Now for a new future', gave a brief biography and reassured its readers that his voice was unimpaired. There were photos of him in *Othello*, *The Emperor Jones*, *Show Boat* and *Sanders of the River* as well as a recent photo.[64] LR Swainson, a reporter for Sydney's *Sun-Herald* based in London, outlined some of Paul's life story, especially his rise to success during his time in Britain from the late 1920s to 1939, and noted that Eslanda, 'a singer who took up biology', would also be coming. Those who had deserted Paul when he lost his passport 'forgot the bigness of his heart, the generosity of his mind, his incomparable talents, and remember only his political naivety'. He had received a 'tumultuous reception' in Europe, and developed an unorthodox concert style that he would now bring to Australia.[65] Even the conservative Sydney paper the *Daily Telegraph* was sympathetic, saying that while people may disagree with his politics, few would question Robeson's sincerity.[66]

Developments in Australia and New Zealand as the tour loomed

Several developments in Australia and New Zealand would have an effect on the tour. Industrial relations were quite volatile, with ongoing strikes in both countries leading to invitations to Paul to speak to striking workers in Christchurch, Sydney and Melbourne. The political climate in New Zealand was unsettled, with the term of the Labour government led by Walter Nash coming to an end, putting the country in election mode throughout the Robesons' visit from 16 October to 3 November. Though a Labour government was still in place, there would be only limited government recognition of their visit. There would be no recognition at all at national level in Australia, with Robert Menzies heading a conservative government that in late 1960 was at the midpoint of its twenty-three years in power. Furthermore, five of the six Australian states had conservative governments, the exception being New South Wales, whose Labor government, like its conservative counterparts, ignored the visit. In two cities, however, Auckland and Sydney, the lord mayor would welcome both Paul and Eslanda to the city.

The question of nuclear disarmament was occupying major national and international attention, with the peace organisations able to attract greater support than before. The ALP was recovering from the intense conflicts, in part over the question of communism, that had torn it apart and led to a split in 1955. When a largely Catholic right-wing group left to form the Democratic Labor Party in 1955, the remaining ALP, especially in Victoria, eased its prohibitions on participation in the peace movement. Henceforth, within the peace movement, communists, the ALP, church groups and ex-communists could and did coexist.[67] Twelve months before the Robesons arrived, the Australian and New Zealand Congress for International Co-operation and Disarmament, held in Melbourne in November 1959, attracted well over 10,000 delegates. As Ralph Summy comments, it 'marked a watershed in the peace movement's postwar history'.[68] On request, Paul had supplied the organisers with a recorded message, which was played at the opening ceremony on 9 November 1959; activist John Ellis later described it as the most memorable part of the Congress, saying 'his message of hope and determination was overwhelming'.[69]

For the Robesons, these developments meant they would encounter an energetic peace movement in the early stages of the huge expansion and significant diversification it would experience during the 1960s.[70] Initiative was shifting from the Australian Peace Council to more independent peace organisations in each state, such as the CICD in Melbourne and the Association for International Cooperation and Disarmament in Sydney.[71] New organisations modelled on the British-initiated Campaign for Nuclear Disarmament, founded in February 1958, were emerging, especially in New Zealand. In an effort to maintain unity, the various peace committees around the country continued to adopt moderate policies and cautious programs.[72]

Paul and Eslanda's particular interest in meeting Indigenous people would be evident from the moment they touched down on Australian, and then New Zealand, soil. It is in Indigenous affairs that New Zealand and Australia differed most, though there were similarities. In both countries successive governments had pursued policies of assimilation and of inclusion of Indigenous peoples on terms set by the majority non-Indigenous population, and in both there was a strong pattern of Indigenous migration to the towns and cities, generating issues of housing, employment and education for these newly urban populations. Yet the two countries had quite different histories and reputations in settler–Indigenous relations: New Zealand was seen as having harmonious race relations while Australia was not. New Zealand, for example, had had since 1867 parliamentary seats reserved for Māori, resulting in much more visible leadership and recognisable spokespeople than was the case in Australia. Where the grassroots organisations seeking change and challenging government policies of assimilation in Australia had a largely non-Indigenous leadership in the 1950s, in New Zealand Māori drove them. The Māori Women's Welfare League, for example, formed in Wellington in September 1951 to promote 'fellowship and understanding between Māori and European women', was led by Māori women. It had 300 branches by 1956, and during the 1950s it participated in campaigning for improvement in Māori access to housing, health and education, especially in new urban areas. Scholars Aroha Harris and Mary Jane McCallum argue that the League maintained workable, 'though often strained' relationships with the Department of Māori Affairs, which wanted the League to assist it in its goal of assimilation. The League 'reworked state goals' to meet its own aspirations and assisted Māori women to enter the public sphere.[73]

In Australia, extensive practices of segregation, discrimination and exploitation of Indigenous people continued at both government and community levels. These practices ranged from discrimination in employment, including payment of low (if any) wages, to segregation in facilities such as clothing stores, swimming pools, hotels and hospitals. Education levels were extremely low, and Indigenous people had limited access to housing and health care. There was, however, a growing political movement seeking Aboriginal people's equality and freedom. These organisations frequently drew attention to the huge disparity between the situation of Aboriginal people and the human rights standards being established by international bodies such as the United Nations and the International Labour Organization. When they found resistance to change at state level and a federal government unwilling to act, insisting that, constitutionally, Aboriginal affairs were a state and not a federal issue, the organisations began in 1957 a decade-long campaign for a referendum to amend the Constitution to authorise Commonwealth involvement. They also formed the Federal Council for Aboriginal Advancement in February 1958 to coordinate Aboriginal organisations in each state.[74]

Getting ready

As the tour dates approached, activists on the left, especially those in or near the communist parties, became excited that Paul Robeson was coming.[75] They wanted to meet him personally, express their welcome and gratitude for supporting causes they believed in, hear him speak, and above all hear him sing. For their part, Paul and Eslanda saw the tour as not only a commercial enterprise but also a political opportunity. In each city they would talk privately with leaders of peace organisations, discussing both local and global issues.

Having met Paul in London the previous year, Bill Morrow for the APC became the primary point of contact between these supporters and the Robesons. Paul and Eslanda stipulated that all the extra-concert meetings and events were to be organised through the APC, and O'Connor was firm with Morrow that the events he was planning should not compete with the concerts.[76] When Morrow wrote to Eslanda on 30 September listing a range of proposed events, she became alarmed at how many he was suggesting; and just before they left London, she and Lili Williams, apparently her assistant, jointly wrote back to Morrow on 4 October saying, 'we have found time for only THREE extra private personal affairs'. In order not to jeopardise the commercial contract, these events were not to be advertised. Interestingly, in a letter written only six days before they left London, Eslanda seems not wholly certain of her own involvement, saying only, 'I am hoping to be able to accompany Mr Robeson' and if so, she was happy to speak to some of the people Morrow had suggested.[77] Eslanda's attempts to limit the number of these private events would prove only partly effective: in nearly every city there would be considerably more political and social events than those Eslanda and Lili had stipulated, not only for Paul but also for Eslanda herself.

While Eslanda was making these arrangements, Paul was undertaking a hectic schedule in Europe. For a man who had not long before been hospitalised with exhaustion, he seems to have pushed himself to the limit, making up for lost time. Earlier in the year he had undertaken a 32-city concert tour in the United Kingdom that was greeted with nearly unanimous praise.[78] His travels in the months preceding the Australian tour included visits to East Berlin in June (a photo of him with several children in Berlin appeared in the Christchurch newspaper *The Press*);[79] Vienna in August; Paris in early September for a festival celebrating the fortieth anniversary of the Communist Party newspaper; Budapest in September; and, with Eslanda, another visit to East Berlin for four days in early October. There, Paul received an honorary doctorate from Humboldt University and they were both awarded prizes by the East German peace movement. They were guests of honour at a folk concert attended by 5000 people, including the State Council chairman, Walter Ulbricht, who awarded Paul the Grand Star of Peoples' Friendship.[80]

Finally, on 10 October 1960, Eslanda, Paul and Larry Brown left London for the long flight to Australia and then New Zealand. Their departure was noted in the Australian press, *The Age* on its front page quoting Paul as saying his theme for the tour was 'the brotherhood of man'.[81] Between London and Sydney there would be seven stops—Frankfurt, Beirut, Karachi, Calcutta, Rangoon, Singapore and Darwin—before touching down on 12 October. Two of these stopovers would be overnight. After the long journey, they had a packed tour in front of them, lasting seven weeks in all, but they hoped it would be worth it financially, and perhaps in other ways as well.

5

Meeting the Robesons

Darwin, Sydney, Brisbane

Early in the morning of 12 October 1960, the Robesons' BOAC Comet flight from London to Australia touched down for the seventh time. This stopover was in Darwin, on the Australian north coast, and was the last stop before the flight's final destination in Sydney, 3150 kilometres further south-east. After five flights and two overnight stops, Paul, Eslanda and Larry Brown were surely exhausted. Even so, Paul found time to speak to a journalist and a small group of well-wishers, establishing from the beginning his interest in meeting and talking with people whenever he could.

The journalist was the esteemed Douglas Lockwood, who had a strong interest in racial issues, having won a prestigious Walkley Award two years before for a story concerning Ruth Daylight, an Aboriginal girl who had been taken from her home in Halls Creek in Western Australia to Canberra to meet the Queen Mother, and then returned to her poverty-stricken community.[1] After their conversation, he reported that racial equality was high on Robeson's agenda; the greatest need in the world, Robeson had said to him, was the freedom of the African people and the American 'Negroes'. Robeson also made it clear to Lockwood that he was 'still actively interested in Left Wing politics, and as angry as ever about his treatment by the American Government'.[2]

One of the topics Lockwood and Robeson discussed was the recent events at the Fifteenth Session of the UN General Assembly, which had begun three weeks earlier and was still going as they spoke. It would continue throughout the Robeson tour and beyond, and both Paul and Eslanda would make further comments during their visit on what was happening at the United Nations. This particular Assembly was notable for the unprecedented presence of many heads of state, including US president Dwight Eisenhower (whose presidency was drawing to a close) and Soviet premier Nikita Khrushchev. Also present were numerous representatives from newly independent African and Asian states, including key figures such as Gamal Abdel Nasser (United Arab Republic), Kwame Nkrumah (Ghana) and Jawaharlal Nehru (India), as well as Fidel Castro (Cuba) and leaders from European nations, including Harold Macmillan from the United Kingdom. Prime ministers John Diefenbaker from Canada, Robert Gordon Menzies from Australia and Walter Nash from New Zealand were also there.[3] China was still excluded, its UN place being taken not by the People's Republic of China (PRC) but by the nationalist government-in-exile based in Taiwan. It was not until 1971 that the situation would change and the PRC be admitted to the United Nations.

A key issue for the Assembly was that of nuclear disarmament. Hopes for progress had been high after Khrushchev and Eisenhower discussed the issue in September 1959, but those hopes were dashed after the incident on 1 May 1960 in which the Soviet Union shot down American U-2 pilot Francis Gary Powers, who was flying over USSR territory. Now, five months later, relations between Eisenhower and Khrushchev remained tense, especially on the question of disarmament. On behalf of five non-aligned nations seeking peaceful coexistence, Indian prime minister Nehru had proposed there be a summit between the United States and the Soviet Union alone. The Australian prime minister, Menzies, in his address to the Assembly on 5 October, opposed the Nehru proposal and instead sought to add France and Britain to the proposed summit, an amendment that humiliatingly received only five votes.[4] Talking to Lockwood, Paul had no hesitation in commenting on Australian politics; he appears to have been well-informed about Menzies' role and said he believed Khrushchev meant it when he said he wanted peace and that 'it would have been better if Mr Menzies had not said what he did at the UN'.

Paul also spoke at the airport for an hour with political supporters Des and Norma Robson, their son Matthew, and Norma's brother-in-law Johnny Banks; Des and Johnny would the following year help to revive the local branch of the CPA.[5] When they explained to Paul that plans for him to sing in Darwin had fallen through when they learned from the tour manager, Dan O'Connor, that the fee was £2000, Robeson laughed and said he didn't want £2000; if he had time after fulfilling his tour obligations, he would like to visit several places, look around, sing for the people in Darwin, and meet some Aboriginal people.[6] As Banks later wrote to *Tribune*, during their airport conversation Robeson 'showed a great interest in the Aborigines'.[7] This comment led to some fruitless attempts to bring Paul to Darwin; in reality, he had no extra time in his schedule.[8]

Sydney touchdown

Finally, at around midday on Wednesday 12 October, the Robesons and Brown arrived in Sydney, Australia's largest city with a population of well over two million and growing rapidly, a result of both a baby boom and large-scale European—especially British—immigration. At the eastern edge of a rapidly expanding suburban sprawl, the central business district was still fairly low rise, but this was about to change, with the city's first skyscraper, the AMP building at Circular Quay, under construction. Indeed, there was considerable building construction in Sydney in 1960, most notably at the site of the city's new Opera House, where Paul would memorably sing in November. Located on the country's eastern seaboard, the city has a magnificent harbour with an iconic bridge and an extensive network of ferries, as well as a long string of ocean beaches. It was becoming more accessible internationally with the acquisition by Sydney Airport of a new runway in 1959 to accommodate jet aircraft for the first time.

As Paul and Eslanda alighted, they were met and welcomed not only by their sponsor, O'Connor, but also by several hundred fans, some carrying banners for peace.[9] The Miners' Federation journal, *Common Cause*, reported that the crowd included trade union officials, peace bodies, women's organisations and 'Aboriginal women from La Perouse with flowers'.[10] According to the *Daily Telegraph*, Paul 'embraced the delegates from the Peace Council who rolled up with their banners, he shook hands with the wharfies'.[11] Bill Morrow led the noisy welcome, which lasted for fifteen minutes as the crowd cheered, sang and spoke words of welcome.[12] 'Good on you Paul … it's been a long time,' someone shouted. Paul explained that he had been planning to come twenty years earlier but World War II had broken out. He had waited 'nearly a generation to meet you … and now I have come … as a fighter for peace for the complete freedom of my own people, and for friendship between all the peoples of the earth'.[13]

Then followed an eventful twenty-minute media conference at the airport. It was not supposed to have happened at all; when O'Connor had suggested it, Harold Davison, the Robesons' agent in London, had consulted Eslanda and suggested to O'Connor that there be no press conference on arrival, pointing out that they would be tired after such a 'hectic journey' and would 'probably feel quite exhausted'.[14] Nevertheless, there *was* a press conference that afternoon, with results that had a significant impact on the tour itself and subsequent historical accounts. The reporting from this media conference varied enormously. To reconstruct it, I rely first on those varied reports, especially the most detailed one, which appeared in the Melbourne communist newspaper *The Guardian*; second on a two-minute excerpt from the Channel 7 television coverage; and especially on an audio recording made by one of the journalists present, Frank Proust, representing the *Sydney Morning Herald*.[15]

The *Herald* recording begins mid-sentence with Paul speaking of having wanted to come to Australia 'for many many a year'. He almost got here in 1939; later, he was unable to visit when they took his passport away. After all this time, he is 'extremely happy' to be here. Paul refers to the hundreds of letters he received over the years from people who liked his records and so forth, 'so I'm looking forward to the audiences'. He is also interested in meeting folks from the WPC, some of whom have just welcomed him, and other people who share his interests, especially from the trade union movement. In the Channel 7 excerpt, he emphasises the importance of the peace movement. He comments that during his visit to Spain during the Spanish Civil War he had seen 'fascism at its worst' and expresses both his pleasure at having been at the inaugural WPC conference in 1949 and his astonishment at those who resisted the peace movement.

The journalists are interested only in his politics. When asked why he has come, Paul replies, 'Well, why would Marian Anderson, or Leontyne Price, or Sammy Davis want to come?' (African American soprano Leontyne Price had visited in 1957, and both Anderson and Sammy Davis Jr would do so soon after, he in 1961 and she in 1962.) Why, he asks, would Australian artists want to go to America? The answer is, of course, that we all want to take our art to different places, he says, that is what we do. And he knows that Australians want to hear him, not only for his singing but also his movies.

Paul explains his political development. Because of the huge public success of *Show Boat* in Britain in 1928, he made his home and career there. His political views developed there, especially after he met the Welsh miners and shared in their struggles; for the first time, white people made him their friend. He made friends with Scottish workers, too, singing to 100,000 of them on May Day. He sang in Republican Spain to soldiers fighting against Franco, the fascist butcher. And ever since, he has, he says, stood with working men: 'Those waterfront guys I met this morning … they're in my corner and I'm in theirs.' So it is Britain, he comments, that you will have to blame for his socialist political views.

When asked about his loss of passport, he explains it was taken away by the US Government from 1950 to 1958; in addition, some Americans, like Senator Joseph McCarthy, did everything they could to stop him singing even inside the United States. He has never been able to sing on American television, or since 1950 perform Shakespeare on the stage. He insists that the passport ban was not just against him as an individual but was part of the struggle of the 'Negro' people. Later press accounts, and historians following them, have portrayed Paul's behaviour at this press conference as 'emotional' and angry. Yet when asked whether he is bitter about those years trapped in the United States unable to perform, he replies firmly no, and asks why would he be bitter? Since 1958 he has been travelling the world and getting a wonderful reception everywhere. By way of analogy, he explains that as a footballer, you don't feel bitter when someone knocks you down: 'I'd just knock somebody down and step on them—I wouldn't be bitter.' This was reported in *The Sun* as Paul saying he was not bitter at those who had taken his passport, though he would like to 'knock the whole lot of 'em down the stairs and walk right over 'em', much as he would have done in his youth if a player hurt him when playing football, emphasising this remark 'with a floor-shaking stomp of his big right foot'.[16]

When asked whether he thinks things are improving for the 'Negro' people, Paul replies yes, to a certain extent, but only as a result of the struggle of the Negro people themselves. He then tries to redirect attention to his presence as a concert singer:

> Look, I am here to give concerts. I'll sing all night long. I'll sing songs from America, Russia, China. Songs from Beethoven. I try to suggest that the music of all people is much the same, and people everywhere are much the same. The theme I want to suggest is 'all men are brothers'.[17]

He hopes that people will come to understand why he sings in about twelve different languages. He mentions that he is writing a book on music. And while he has strong opinions on political matters and is happy to answer questions about them, he is not going to do that on a concert platform. He is an entertainer, but also a man of ideas and convictions, with things to say: 'I have worked to be a public figure so I could speak out for my people and be heard.'

The journalists do not take up his invitation to talk about musical and performance issues. Rather, one asks why he doesn't live in the Soviet Union. This part of the press conference is missing from the audio recording but is mentioned in several press reports. He had been asked similar questions many times before. When asked at the HUAC in June 1956, he had answered, 'Because my father was a slave, and my people died to build this country, and I am going to stay here and have a part of it just like you.'[18] Now, in Sydney, he says he was born in America, English is his language, he is the son of a slave, and his fight is for his own people. He is at pains here to be friendly, and says, 'My fight takes me to many countries ... it has brought me here ... and I have come here to win friends.'[19]

The sense of a tense and angry press conference that one gets from some of the press reports does not fit with what we hear in the recording. The closest it comes to such an atmosphere is in the discussion of Hungary. Paul insists quite loudly that it was necessary for the Soviet Union to suppress a fascist revolution in Hungary; whoever stirred up the Hungarian people from outside knew that any uprising would be suppressed, and that is what happened. He comments that he has just been in Hungary (he had been to Budapest in September) and thinks that the people he met agreed the uprising had been a mistake and the current situation was quite healthy. He is expressing the views accepted by those in Western communist parties; those who disagreed and saw genuine protest in Hungary—not an externally motivated fascist uprising—had been leaving communist parties in large numbers.

Paul then tries to return to the fact he is in Australia as a singer, but the very next question is what he thinks about the White Australia policy. He sounds puzzled and asks, 'Is that the way you put it?', and the answer is yes, that is the vernacular description. He avoids discussing this issue, saying people will know his political views and he really is here to sing. He might discuss it a little later, but not now, when he has just arrived and is not ready to talk about a serious national policy knowing little of the country. The recorded interview ends with Paul saying he has no intention of retiring yet: 'today, I'm feeling fine'.

With that, the press conference was over. As *The Guardian* reported it, 'Robeson was on his feet, and pressmen were shaking his hand goodbye.' It all seemed productive and friendly. It had covered a lot of ground, though none of the journalists present had enough interest or musical knowledge to draw him out on his musical ideas and the nature of the concerts he would be performing.

With Paul's press conference over and an interview with Eslanda by the *Sydney Morning Herald* completed (to which we return in Chapter 11), they were free to go to the Hotel Australia and recover from their long flight.[20] The hotel had been for decades one of the city's finest, providing, as the *Dictionary of Sydney* puts it, 'high quality accommodation, dining and entertainment to some of the city's most distinguished visitors and residents'. With several dramatic entrances, a banqueting hall and a sweeping stairway 'set against an enfolding wall of black glass, incised with fantastic birds and foliage in silver', it had been the haunt of American servicemen during World War II and its ballroom had been the venue in April 1949 of the first successful television demonstration in Australia. By 1960, though, it was nearing the end of its life as a hotel (it would close in 1971 and be demolished in 1972) and may not have been quite as grand as in its heyday.[21]

The next day, Eslanda and Paul met with O'Connor as the manager of the concert tour, Bill Morrow representing the Peace Council and as the organiser of non-concert events, and Betty Bateman, head of publicity and public relations for the Elizabethan Theatre Trust. The Trust had been formed six years earlier to support the arts in Australia, and Bateman was involved as a result of Paul's eminence as a Shakespearean actor. She would remain in touch with Eslanda long after the tour was over.[22]

The day was dominated, though, by press coverage of the airport media conference. There was a positive story about Eslanda in the *Sydney Morning Herald*, drawing attention to her training as a chemist, her study of anthropology, her books *Paul Robeson, Negro*, *African Journey* and, with Pearl Buck, *American Argument*, and her work as a freelance correspondent at the United Nations.[23] Unsurprisingly, though, most attention was directed at Paul, and, predictably in this era of Cold War hostilities, reports varied. For some newspapers, the interesting point was that he had come to Australia to perform. The *Canberra Times* had a front-page photo of both Robesons and a brief account of their tour.[24] In a story headed '… He just keeps rollin' along', Robert Johnston in the Melbourne *Sun* described Paul as a 'likeable big fellow' and said he looked fit and his voice sounded as good as ever. *The Age* summarised his views fairly: 'Robeson declared his deep affection for Socialist countries and called for the emancipation of all coloured peoples. He spoke bitterly about his struggle to secure freedom for the Negro people, both in Africa and in the United States.'[25] *Tribune* thought 'Paul Robeson's 45-minute conference was a storm of sound and challenging ideas … of thunderous speech and the lightning flash of passionate conviction that all men are brothers, and that only struggle can win freedom and equality for black men and white'.[26] *The Sun* also reported that he had insisted on his right to express his political views: 'I'm here for a concert tour. I'll stand up there and sing all night for 'em if they want me. But I'm much more than an entertainer. Sitting here now, I'm not a singer, I'm Paul Robeson, American negro, and I'm entitled to state my views without fearing anyone.'[27]

The *Sydney Morning Herald* story on Paul, though headed 'Robeson bitterly critical of US', was even-handed in tone, and two of the paper's columnists were quite supportive.[28] The editor of the daily front-page 'Column 8' commented briefly that it was a pity the airport welcome had had such a strong political tinge as Paul was coming to Australia not as 'a political figure but as a great artist, who as singer, actor and film-star, has given pleasure to millions'.[29] Another column, signed by 'Onlooker', a few days later commented that while it was sad that Robeson was 'growing old, and bitter, and pre-occupied more with ideology than with his art', he had a 'just grievance' against the US Government that had withheld his passport: 'withholding of his passport for eight years was stupid and arbitrary'. This same columnist also reported their own 'cherished recollection' of seeing him perform the title role in *Othello* in London thirty years earlier, 'a great artist at the zenith of his powers'.[30]

Several newspapers, however, both in Sydney and elsewhere, focused on Paul's angry denunciations of the United States for withholding his passport for eight years and his comment that the

Hungarian rebellion two years previously had been a fascist revolt and not 'a revolution of the people'.[31] Several reported, misleadingly, that Paul had said if there were a war between Russia and the United States he would be on the side of Russia. They carried headlines such as 'He would side with the Soviet', 'Robeson here: I'd back Russia in a war' and 'Robeson lashes out at America, backs Soviet'.[32] Yet the recording makes it clear that Paul is talking about a war in which the Soviet Union was under a fascist attack: 'I was, am, and ever will be a great friend of the Soviet Union … I would stand with them against all the fascist attacks … and any war against the Soviet Union would be a fascist war … for I am an anti-fascist.' He does not mention the United States in this context. Ray Castle's column in the right-wing *Daily Telegraph* was especially hostile. Headed 'I wish he was still Bosambo', it contrasted admiration for Paul's singing with dislike of his politics.[33] It began: 'A wave of sadness crept over me yesterday as I saw an idol of 20 years crumble before my eyes in less than 30 minutes.' It portrays Paul as trying to divert the discussion towards politics and away from his singing, when the recording makes clear that the opposite is the case.

Castle's comment did not go unchallenged; in the letters pages two days later, communist and left-wing writer Len Fox commented scornfully on Castle's preference for seeing Negroes as 'contented toilers slaving for white pukka sahibs' rather than as 'men raising a militant voice for human dignity and brotherhood'. Castle was also quite wrong, Fox suggested, to say artists had no right to express political opinions; on the contrary, 'the artist has a right and a duty to take a stand on the great human issues of his day'. Finally, Fox continued, thank goodness 'the day of the Bosambos is gone'.[34] In the same issue, CW Steadman asked in a letter: 'What right have we to condemn Russia or any country for that matter, for its treatment of minorities when we hand out the type of treatment we have in the past to our own natives? … Let us clean up our own backyard before we criticise others for the state theirs is in.'[35]

But the damage was done. This was just what Robert Kerridge had feared might happen, having asked Paul through his London agent to avoid talking about politics at his press conferences: 'in the interests of the maximum success of his concert tour, I would suggest that it would be wise for Mr Robeson to avoid comment on political issues'.[36] As O'Connor wrote in a letter to Eslanda while the Robesons were in New Zealand, the reports from the press conference emphasising that Paul would side with the Soviet Union rather than the United States aroused resentment and consternation, especially 'in official circles and of course in the wealthy and rather snobbish section of concert patrons'.[37] O'Connor, Paul and Eslanda appear to have realised very quickly that negative publicity could endanger the concert tour through venue cancellations and reduced ticket sales. They would learn two weeks later from O'Connor that the concert in Hobart that was to have been hosted by the Department of Adult Education on 24 November had indeed been cancelled.[38] One of the most hostile of all reports had appeared in the Hobart *Mercury*, which probably influenced the concert host.[39] A Department of Adult Education sounds like an unusual host for a commercial music concert, but at the time its director, Englishman Kenneth Brooks, was ensuring that the department would play a major role in bringing cultural performance to Tasmania through arranging statewide tours of musicians and theatre companies.[40] The problem for the department was, as Brooks explained in a letter to O'Connor, that it was a government-funded body and its board was 'most reluctant to be associated officially with the presentation in Hobart'.[41] Yet the fallout in the end was not as bad as O'Connor and the Robesons feared. There were no other cancellations, and with Hobart cancelled there was time for a fourth concert in Melbourne.

News of Paul's press conference reached the United States, but so slowly that the Robesons had already completed their two-month visit and left Australia by the time it did. From 6 December 1960, a syndicated column by George Sokolsky, taken up in numerous newspapers, took Robeson to task in a rare mention of the Australian tour in the American press. Sokolsky was an ardent supporter of Senator McCarthy and had been directly involved during the 1950s in the processes surrounding the blacklisting of Hollywood performers, writers and producers. He deeply resented the softening of McCarthyism in the late 1950s and now took aim at Paul on the basis of his Sydney press conference. Sokolsky said Robeson 'chooses to spew hate against his own country' and complained that the US Government was doing nothing about it. He quoted Paul as having said in Sydney that if there was a war between Russia and America he would be on the side of the Soviet Union, 'who would win—and should win'. Sokolsky thought this 'pretty close to treason'. It had been better, he wrote, when the State Department was able to deny Robeson his passport, and he concluded that it was 'difficult to understand why a man who despises a country insists on being a citizen of it'.[42]

Even before news of the Hobart cancellation came through, Paul took care from this point onwards not to endanger the tour and adopted a gentler approach in subsequent interviews. There would be no shouting or stamping of feet at later press conferences, and there would be a focus on one-on-one (or, with Eslanda, joint) interviews. When invited to meet an interviewing panel in Brisbane for a Channel 7 program, *Meet the Press*, Paul refused. The channel's program chairman, Alan Underwood, said on Friday 14 October, 'In view of Mr Robeson's challenging statements, I personally invited him to appear.' Paul's reply was sharp: 'Nothing could be further from my mind than to play with any *Meet the Press*.'[43] Instead, he and Eslanda both made themselves freely available to individual press reporters. Paul spoke at some length with journalist Frank O'Neill in Sydney, leading to a very favourable profile in the *Sunday Mirror*, a tabloid newspaper that had been recently acquired by rising Australian newspaper magnate Rupert Murdoch, who was not yet the extreme right-wing media owner that he later became.[44] Robeson sang for O'Neill 'Ol Man River', and the story, headed 'A song to remember', was subtitled 'The rich, moving beauty of Paul Robeson's voice filled the hotel room'. O'Neill mentioned Robeson's many talents and said, 'the side of Robeson I saw was warm and humorous and erudite'. Paul mentioned politics only in reply to questions and wished mainly to talk about music and the beauty of sound. O'Neill concluded: 'I felt that I had heard music I shall not forget in a long time.'

Already a different Paul Robeson had come to the fore. The *Sunday Mirror* would play a vital role in publicising his support for Aboriginal people when he returned to Sydney three weeks later.

A warm reception in Brisbane

This first full day on Australian soil was not yet over. On Thursday 13 October, the Robeson party flew by Ansett-ANA Electra to Brisbane, leaving at 7 p.m. and arriving two hours later. The Brisbane Airport welcome was a happy and joyful family affair that included more than 100 men and women, and many children in pyjamas.[45] Jean Leary remembered going with her husband and sister-in-law to welcome him at the airport, and took a photo of Paul affectionately regarding her sister-in-law's baby.[46] Queensland Peace Committee executives—including its vice-president, Hector Chalmers, and its extremely efficient and effective secretary, his wife Norma Chalmers—led the welcome. The Queensland Peace Committee had been formed out of the preparatory committee for the 1959 Melbourne Peace Congress, and was closely tied to, and financially dependent upon, several trade unions affiliated to the Trades and Labor Council of Queensland. In keeping with developments in the Australian peace movement since the Melbourne Congress the previous November, both Hector, a businessman, and Norma were members of the ALP, Hector as a member of the state executive.[47] Their daughter, Janet, remembers meeting Paul at the airport and also the photograph of her father and Robeson walking arm in arm, Paul holding a bunch of flowers: 'one of the highlights of my life was meeting Paul Robeson'.[48]

Given the late hour, there was no press conference at the airport; but there were several separate interviews for press, radio and television the next day, Friday 14 October. All were held in Paul and Eslanda's suite in Lennon's Hotel. One interview led to a very favourable profile in the *Courier-Mail* that allowed the emphasis on music that Paul had unsuccessfully sought in Sydney. To the *Mail*, he emphasised that his concerts would seek to bridge the gap between classical and folk music, and indeed the connections between different kinds of music in general. Rock'n'roll, he explained, had its origins in Negro music.[49] The *Courier-Mail* also interviewed Eslanda, explaining in a story headed 'Chemist, student and writer, too' that she was an anthropologist, had trained as a medical chemist, had written 'two and a half books' and was an accredited freelance correspondent at the United Nations. Eslanda showed the reporter photos of her two grandchildren, David Paul and Susan, and both she and Paul showed them again to Marjorie Stapleton, an *Australian Women's Weekly* interviewer also present that afternoon.[50]

Both Paul and Eslanda were clearly bent on conveying a warmer, softer image than had emerged at the Sydney press conference. They succeeded; in her profile of them both, Stapleton commented that Eslanda was 'one of the most interesting women I have ever met', while Paul thanked the thousands of Australians who had written kind letters to him, especially when he had been ill in England two years earlier. They both stressed their love for children, Eslanda commenting that 'Wherever Paul goes, children cling to him', and Paul saying, 'When I sing to children, I pour out my love in a lullaby.' Paul also talked about the way singing derived originally from speaking, a favourite theme of his and one he demonstrated in his concerts with their frequent moves from spoken introductions to songs to speeches from *Othello*. 'First people spoke,' he said in this interview, and 'then, in moods of happiness or despair, they lilted the spoken word into song with intonations of prayer or rejoicing.' He gave as examples of 'speaking songs' some of his favourite concert songs—'Swing Low, Sweet Chariot', 'Go Down, Moses', 'Deep River', 'Nobody Knows the Trouble I've Seen'.

Another journalist to interview Robeson that day at Lennon's Hotel filed a sympathetic story under the heading 'Robeson talks politics'. 'It was', the unnamed journalist commented, 'worth a 32-year wait—that is how long it has taken entrepreneur DD O'Connor to bring Paul Robeson here.' Impressed by 'the huge, still youthful-looking singer' who at the end of the interview sang a few bars of 'Water Boy', the journalist revealed that Eslanda had warned him to 'Lay off politics or you might get it in the neck'. However, Paul was already again perfectly happy to talk about politics, and condemned Australia's refusal to recognise China: 'When I come back here—and I will—I hope you have got more sense over your foolish attitude towards Red China.' He also freely addressed Aboriginal issues: 'If you want to introduce politics,' he said in this interview, 'ask me what I think of your own country's treatment of its native people … I shall return to Australia to raise money for the indigenous peoples of your country—I won't call them blacks.' In this comment, he was much closer to current usage than the common language of the time. He was hoping, he said, after his concert the following night to meet Trades and Labor Council members and some Aboriginal people who planned to call on him. Paul would reiterate this promise—that he would return to Australia in support of Aboriginal rights—many times and with increasing frequency during his Australian tour.[51]

One of those who met Paul in Brisbane was Nancy Wills, formerly Nance Macmillan, who had been living with her husband, Geoff Wills, a musical instrument maker, in Brisbane since 1950. An ASIO agent reported that Nancy Wills took an active interest in Robeson's welfare while he was in Brisbane, but I have been able to find little additional information.[52] When Adrian Stevens asked her in an interview for the National Library Oral History program in 1987, when she was in her late sixties, what she and Robeson talked about when they met during his Brisbane visit in 1960, she replied that he had wanted to know a lot about Aboriginal people but she couldn't tell him much as 'there wasn't much to tell in 1960'. She had no other memories of their conversation but did recall that he met an Aboriginal social work student named Margaret Valadian that afternoon.[53]

In fact, Paul and Eslanda met several Aboriginal people in Brisbane, the first of whom was indeed, as Nancy remembered, Valadian, an Aboriginal student hoping to enrol in Social Studies at the University of Queensland. (She later did, becoming in 1965 one of the first two Aboriginal graduates in Australia; Charles Perkins, who had led the Australian Freedom Ride earlier that year, was the other.) A few days before Paul and Eslanda arrived in Brisbane, a local newspaper, *Truth*, had published a story entitled 'Margaret plans to meet

Paul', accompanied by Valadian's photo, in which she expressed her admiration for Paul as both a singer and a fighter for his people's rights. 'I want to talk to him about my people', she said. 'There are few of them left in Queensland who know the meaning behind old tribal customs. To the young ones, corroborees are ridiculous. They go to the pictures and sing hill-billies ... but they know nothing of opera, drama and ballet.' Valadian hoped Robeson could 'give me some suggestions that will help us combine the two cultures'.[54] Their meeting on 14 October was reported in the *Courier-Mail* along with a front-page photograph, with Valadian quoted as saying she was an admirer of Robeson's and had wanted to meet him.[55] She later attended his Brisbane concert and went backstage afterwards. 'He autographed a copy of a 45 rpm record for me', she recalled in 2008.[56]

Later, Paul and Eslanda would meet Aboriginal singer Sylvia Cairns, first at a garden party on Saturday held for Eslanda by the Union of Australian Women (UAW), and then at a cocktail party after the concert.[57] Only seven weeks earlier Cairns had met Harry Belafonte, leading to a striking photo of them both in the *Courier-Mail*.[58] As both a singer and a political activist, she was just the kind of person visiting celebrities such as Belafonte and Paul and Eslanda wanted to meet. She was a member of the Queensland Council for the Advancement of Aborigines and Torres Strait Islanders (QCAATSI), formed in 1958.[59] Although, like its counterparts around the country, the membership of QCAATSI was largely white—with a strong trade union component, some Christian church representatives, and both the CPA and ALP well represented—it did have Aboriginal members, including some who would become leaders in Aboriginal politics and culture in Queensland. Cairns was also an important figure in the UAW. A few months earlier, she had been one of the Queensland delegates to its second national conference, held in Sydney from 27 May to 2 June, where she had spoken strongly against the paternalism of Queensland state laws that prevented Aboriginal people from joining trade unions or receiving social services, and that allowed authorities to siphon off Aboriginal people's wages.[60] She had also proposed, in the words of an ASIO report, that 'the UAW adopt a policy of support for aboriginals, particularly for equal opportunity for schooling with white children'.[61] Her speech had been well received and had inspired the UAW to increase its support for Aboriginal struggles, the conference passing a resolution calling for recognition of Aboriginal people as completely equal citizens and their right to the collective ownership of tribal lands.[62] A Darwarbada woman, Cairns would subsequently become a noted writer of Aboriginal stories for children, collected in *Uncle Willie Mackenzie's Legends of the Goundirs* in 1967.[63]

The Brisbane concert

Robeson gave the first concert of the tour on the evening of Saturday 15 October to an enthusiastic capacity audience of 5000.[64] He sang the first of his two prepared concert programmes, which started with classical songs drawn from Handel, Beethoven and Schubert, moved on to Negro spirituals and folk songs, and concluded with the final speech from *Othello*.[65] Janetta McStay, who had recently arrived in the country after performing at the National Day celebrations in China on 1 October, played the interludes.[66] While the printed programmes, in conventional concert format, indicate which songs he sang, what Paul presented was something much more informal. As he would later explain to a journalist in Adelaide, 'It's not a concert, you know, it's an evening in which a guy's got to roam around the folk songs of the world, got to stop and be dramatic, be a real ham out there for a while as an actor and talk about things and make it a sort of family party.'[67]

The audience was enraptured, with many calls for encores, to which Robeson responded with, as *Truth* put it, 'a generosity almost unbelievable in a man whose voice must have been weary'.[68] The audience included a wide range of people: not only activists in women's, Aboriginal peace and trade union organisations, but also a wider range of people aware of his reputation as a singer and an actor. Florence Callaghan, a bedridden invalid living in Newcastle, over 700 kilometres south of Brisbane, was so desperate to hear him sing that she was taken on a special trip north to the concert.[69] Cairns attended with her friend Muriel Langford, also a member of QCAATSI, who was Welsh and had been a fan of Robeson's for a long time.[70]

Bob Anderson, a Ngugi man from Mulgumpin in Moreton Bay and an official in the BWIU, was on security duty. With several others he was on the lookout for threats to the occasion on the grounds of either politics or race. These voluntary security guards had a chance to hear some of the concert as those on duty took turns to stay outside to let latecomers in or come inside to hear Paul sing. Anderson thought Robeson a wonderful person—'what he did to unite people, building bridges between all people'—and especially loved his performance in *Sanders of the River*. He recalled in 2008:

> his voice always resonated, wonderful, wonderful. I can still hear him sing that song 'Lord Sandy': 'Sandy the wise, Sandy the strong'. It was the carriage of himself and his voice was wonderful. And he said in later years he regretted doing the [*Sanders of the River*] part for what it was, but at the time, I'm glad that he did.[71]

Also in the audience at Robeson's Brisbane concert was a group of Chinese trade unionists, whose presence was the main reason for the need for security. They were part of a delegation from the All-China Federation of Trade Unions and were visiting Australia at the invitation of the Australian Council of Trade Unions (ACTU). They would eventually have a successful three-week visit, meeting many Australian trade unionists and attending numerous work sites, but at this point they had just encountered a violent demonstration against them at Brisbane Airport.[72] Right-wing unionists had greeted them with placards reading 'Red Imperialists Go Home' and 'Free Chinese Slave-Labourers' and distributing leaflets on similar themes. In anticipation of further violence against the Chinese delegation there was a strong police presence at Robeson's concert, but no violence occurred.[73]

After the concert, a large group of supporters went to a cocktail party at the posh New Farm home of Ivy Scott, owner of Hoffman Tailoring, a men's tailoring shop. Those present had been chosen in consultation with Paul and Eslanda. One couple present was Phil O'Brien and his wife, Joyce; Phil was senior vice-president of the

Waterside Workers' Federation of Queensland. In an article in the *Maritime Worker* later, he said, 'Paul Robeson is the greatest living person I have had the pleasure to meet ... He promised his audience he would return to Brisbane—and all Brisbane people who heard and met him hope that day will not be far away.'[74] Phil recalled that when he was introduced to Paul, he 'gave me a hearty slap on the back and said, "I am also a fellow wharfie."' Paul was referring proudly to his lifetime membership of the ILWU in the United States. 'It was memorable for me', Phil wrote, 'to meet such a great man.'[75]

Brian Moynihan, then state secretary of the communist party's youth organisation, the Eureka Youth League, remembered attending the cocktail party and thought he was probably invited because Robeson had asked the organisers to invite young people and Moynihan was then in his early twenties. Like the others there, he shook hands with Robeson and chatted. Wally Stubbings, a waterside worker and union organiser, recalled the event in an interview with Sari Braithwaite in 2008, when he was ninety-five.[76] He thought that he and his wife may have been invited because they were foundation members of QCAATSI, and remembered that when Paul arrived, he 'talked of the struggle of his people'; Stubbings commented, 'I almost wept at his description.' He also recalled that 'after he [Paul Robeson] had moved around amongst the guests apparently somebody had told him that I was a member of the Communist Party and he took me aside and gave me a dressing down about the Aboriginal people, and the disgraceful position they were in.'[77]

It is clear that Paul had gained some strong impressions on the state of Aboriginal politics during his short stay in Brisbane. Stubbings' clear memory forty-eight years later of being reprimanded suggests that he, Stubbings, was a little stung, and it appears that white communists in Queensland subsequently stepped up their activism. In October 1960, when Paul and Eslanda visited, the Aboriginal rights movement was in fact growing, much to the consternation of the Queensland Department of Native Affairs (DNA). The critical attacks on DNA policy made by QCAATSI delegates at the annual Federal Council for the Advancement of Aborigines and Torres Strait Islanders

(FCAATSI) conference in Brisbane in April 1961 would so alarm DNA staff that they developed a plan using anti-communist sympathisers to destroy QCAATSI. Ironically, those infiltrating QCAATSI and who became foundational in setting up an alternative organisation more to the government's liking, named One People of Australia League (OPAL), included Muriel Langford, who had so keenly attended Robeson's concert. As former Queensland federal MP Elaine Darling's detailed account of the split makes clear, in the end, despite the destruction of QCAATSI, the Aboriginal movement in Queensland did not become the pawn of government policy the DNA hoped for. QCAATSI was re-formed into the Queensland Council for the Advancement of Aborigines (QCAA), and OPAL came to be led by some strong independent women, including Rita Huggins, the subject of her daughter Jackie Huggins' excellent biography, *Auntie Rita*.[78] Both sides of the split, Darling argues, flourished in their different ways and contributed to the success in Queensland of the 1967 referendum to alter the Constitution to allow the federal government a role in Aboriginal affairs.[79]

The Robesons had certainly taken on a punishing schedule. Friday had seen many press interviews and Saturday a garden party, a concert to 5000 people, and a cocktail after-party.[80] After all this, on Sunday they were again at Brisbane Airport for a 1.30 p.m. flight to New Zealand. A large group of well-wishers attended to see them off. Mary Okello, then a child, was there with her parents, John and Win Callaghan, both communists. Mary remembered Paul at the airport farewell as 'being very tall, and very black and having this deep deep deep booming voice', and Eslanda, 'his small small wife, also with a beautiful voice'. Her little sister Catharine, aged two, she recalled, rode on Paul's shoulders.[81]

Connie Healy was another of the well-wishers, along with her five-year-old son. She recalled in 2008 noticing that Paul was very concerned about critics' reports of his concerts, saying to Larry Brown, 'Have you got the critics' reports, you got the papers?' She was amazed that a man who had been around the world and knew he had a great voice was interested in what the Brisbane critics had to say.[82] In fact, he need not have worried: the press reports that Sunday were entirely favourable. *Truth* described Robeson as not only a musician but as 'one of the towering personalities of the stage' whose speech from *Othello* served to remind the audience that he was a great actor as well as a great singer,[83] while the *Sunday Mail* referred to his 'finely resonant voice' and 'his obvious sincerity whether in the presentation of his music or in the promulgation of his philosophy'.[84] In Monday's *Courier-Mail*, William Lovelock marvelled at his rich voice, especially when singing Negro spirituals.[85] Lovelock had been dean of the Faculty of Music at the University of London and then a founding director of the Queensland Conservatorium of Music, and was now a full-time composer and music critic.[86] Ten days later, on 26 October, there was a longer report in *The Bulletin* by 'DJM', who thought that 'this turbulent figure of the concert-halls remains one of the great artists of his time'.[87]

After a slightly rocky start with the Sydney Airport press conference, it looked like this would be a successful tour commercially and would have political significance as well. It would also be long remembered by those who met and heard the Robesons. When asked about the impact of the visit on her, Okello said it was just that she remembered having met Paul and Eslanda, 'which, you know, I'm going to cry … It's just always been an important memory … I was very sad when he died. Just somebody who I identified with … He inspired so many people, including me.'

6

'Captivated by Paul Robeson'

Music and Politics in New Zealand

AFTER THREE BUSY days in Australia, Paul and Eslanda arrived in another country entirely new to them. With a population of 2.4 million, it may have been smaller than Australia (population 10.3 million), but the pace did not slacken. With Larry Brown, they visited New Zealand's four largest cities, Paul gave eight formal concerts and sang and spoke to two mass union meetings, and Eslanda, sponsored by the United Nations Association, gave five public lectures. Paul would find in New Zealand many opportunities to talk in interviews about music and its importance to humanity. Here I focus mainly on Paul, his concerts and his ideas about music and humanity, while Chapter 7 considers the peace, workers and Indigenous aspects of the tour, and Chapter 11, Eslanda's lecture tour.

At each of the four cities the Robesons visited—Auckland, Wellington, Christchurch and Dunedin—they were met at the airport with a warm welcome. At Whenuapai Airport in Auckland on Sunday 16 October, around 300 well-wishers were there to greet them.[1] A Māori group from the Teachers' College welcomed them with Māori songs and a traditional welcome; a photo the next day in the *New Zealand Herald* showed Mrs KG Bidois doing with Paul a hongi—that is, a traditional Māori welcome in which those meeting press their noses together.[2]

As part of the welcome, the students performed a challenge, in which the hosts lay down an item—in this case a rakau, a challenge stick—that the visitors are invited to pick up to indicate that they come in peace. The students then gave the rakau to Eslanda, for whom it became a treasured possessions.[3] Paul said to the welcoming crowd that he had waited a long time to come and he would like to come again. He would, he said, like to bring a play like *Othello* to New Zealand.[4] He had arrived with a slight cold, but commented at his press conference: 'Actually I prefer to sing with a bit of a cold; it adds depth and resonance to my voice.'[5] Four days later, at the new airport in New Zealand's capital city, Wellington, a crowd of well-wishers sang 'For He's a Jolly Good Fellow'; Paul shook hands with everyone and patted a Māori boy on the head.[6]

The New Zealand concert tour

The friendly welcomes were a hint of what was to come—a successful concert tour alongside many opportunities to speak and meet with New Zealanders. The success of the concert in Brisbane, with its ensuing favourable reviews, would be repeated throughout the New Zealand tour: the concerts were largely sold out, loved by their audiences and well received by the music critics.

Paul sang a total of eight concerts—three in Auckland, two each in Wellington and Christchurch, and one in Dunedin. It seems that in addition to the two official programmes he added songs, possibly in the encores, that New Zealanders had specifically requested. From early in the tour, he learned that many New Zealanders wanted to hear him sing songs they knew from phonograph records and the radio, some of them decades old. They told him so in person and by mail.[7] In an interview with the *Evening Post* in Wellington conducted three days after he arrived in the country, Paul remarked that the people he was meeting in New Zealand were wanting to hear not so much new songs as those he had recorded twenty-five years earlier. As he had sometimes forgotten the words of these old songs, he was 'busy learning the songs again'. He would sing, he said, whatever people wanted.[8]

Throughout the tour the concerts were held either in a picture theatre owned by Robert Kerridge or, more often, in the local town hall, which had a larger capacity. The first concert, held in Auckland on Tuesday 18 October, took place at the Kerridge-owned St James Theatre, which is still standing, though it has been closed since 2007 and is scheduled for restoration. As Linden Saunders, the influential music critic for the *New Zealand Herald*, reported, the capacity audience gave Paul an ovation at both the beginning and the end of the concert. Paul delivered the programme in an informal manner; he 'patted his foot, swayed to the rhythm, gestured freely and by his running commentaries added humanity and interest to his singing'.[9] Saunders was not only music critic for the *New Zealand Herald* but also a leading figure in Auckland's musical world, being director of music at King's College, in which role he directed musical performances, including musical theatre.[10] In a similar vein, Desmond Mahoney reviewed the concert for the *Auckland Star*, commenting that as a singer of spirituals Paul Robeson was 'superb, nothing less', but it was in songs fitting his ideology that he 'came over as Robeson in the round'.[11]

The pattern was set of enthusiastic audiences and favourable reviews in major newspapers. Both concerts on 20 and 22 October in Wellington Town Hall, known for its excellent acoustics, attracted large, enthusiastic audiences. As Russell Bond commented in Wellington's *The Dominion*, the audience 'completely filled the hall, choir seats and all', and Paul showed a 'vivid personality that quickly had his listeners hanging on every word and note'.[12] Owen Jensen in the *Evening Post* expressed some excitement: 'Paul Robeson had arrived, stepping from the anonymity of records and the impersonality of films straight into the affections of the expectant audience.'[13] Jensen was also a leading figure in New Zealand music as a musician, tutor, composer, promoter and broadcaster. On stage, he reported, Paul talked quite a lot—about a song such as 'Jerusalem', about his grandchildren, or about the pentatonic scale. In everything, he showed that he was a 'really great artist'. Jensen loved his voice, the voice of an orator, which was appropriate since Robeson believed that 'singing is but oratory turned into melody and made more lyrical'. He also praised Larry Brown, commenting that between them 'they make music that is more than a concert, a unique performance, spontaneously joyous, almost homely, but alive with the spark of a creative personality'. Bond, too, absolutely loved Robeson's voice, so 'vastly resonant and deep'.

Though both reviews were warm and enthusiastic, they criticised Paul's use of a microphone. Bond thought Paul's voice was 'unfortunately a little larger than life last night because of his use of a public address system'. Jensen also criticised Paul's use of a microphone, commenting that when he stepped away from it 'the voice becomes more mellow, intimate, and no less rich'.[14] They were not the first to complain, several critics having done so after his Albert Hall concert in London in 1958. Musicologist Grant Olwage points out that in England the critics had seen the microphone as somehow getting between Robeson and his listeners, and in Auckland, Mahoney thought so, too.[15] Paul was undeterred, and in response to the English criticisms said that if hadn't used a microphone he would no longer be singing well in his sixties.[16] In his press conference at Heathrow Airport when he had first arrived back in the United Kingdom, he explained that he had used microphones in his concerts for two decades but whereas once he did this unbeknown to the audience, now he did it openly. He was, Olwage suggests, experimenting with new technologies and especially seeking to produce on the concert stage the kind of sound people could now hear on records.[17] In a number of interviews in New Zealand, as we shall soon see, he talked extensively about why he used microphones.

For Paul, music and politics were inextricably mixed and in New Zealand he frequently spoke about their connections, expressing his ideas about the universality of music and of humanity itself. It was not only Paul who mixed music and politics: many of those who went to his concerts did so for a mix of political and musical reasons. Ian Prior, for example, was a distinguished doctor widely credited with being the founder of epidemiology in New Zealand; later he was an active participant in the group International Physicians for the Prevention of Nuclear War. His daughter Bettina Bradbury tells me that her father, who attended the second Wellington concert, had developed an interest in 'progressive, anti-racist American singers' when he spent a year at the Peter Bent Brigham Hospital in Boston on a Fulbright scholarship. There, Prior 'was taught a lot about anti-communism, racism, etc., by the wonderful Dr Bernard Lown who later shared the Nobel Peace Prize with his Russian counterpart for their work in trying to minimise risks of nuclear war'. Prior brought with him back to New Zealand not only stories about how Lown as a suspected communist had been blacklisted in the profession for a while, but also records of singers such as Pete Seeger, the Weavers, Harry Belafonte and Paul Robeson. With him at the Wellington concert were his parents, his wife, Elespie, and his daughters. Elespie's diary for 22 October 1960 reads in part: 'Take them [the family] to hear Paul Robeson—a wonderful voice & such a personality.'[18]

The concerts in Christchurch, on Tuesday 25 and Thursday 27 October in the Kerridge-owned Majestic Theatre, sold out.[19] The audiences loved them. As the *Christchurch Star* reported, 'the large audience was vociferous in its approval of his chosen items, particularly those songs which Paul Robeson has made famous all over the world'.[20] Some audience members wrote to Paul afterwards. After the Thursday concert, Mary Donnell wrote to him to say his singing encouraged people like her to 'stop being armchair socialists and to get out as you are doing and make a heaven for our Family of Man right here on earth ... now that you have given us hope and courage we can no longer be quiet'.[21]

The music critics were also delighted. One of them, Charles Foster Browne, had two months earlier anticipated that Paul would be wonderful. As well as being the music critic for *The Press*, Browne was an organist, composer and teacher who had the previous year, as organist and master of choristers at Christchurch Cathedral, been awarded an OBE (Officer of the British Empire).[22] A few months earlier he had been in New York, and on his return in August had commented that the Cathedral of St John the Divine in New York included African American singers in its choir, something that was unusual in the United States. They made 'an artistic contribution to the music of the cathedral' and had been 'delightful people to work with'. He had expressed great pleasure then that Paul Robeson would visit soon and had predicted: 'As a concert artist he will sweep the country.'[23] Now, after the concert, he said he was delighted that 'the reality exceeded the expectations'. In listening to him, 'we seem to bathe in the beauty of the sounds he produces', the product of perfect technique and high artistry. 'He obviously feels deeply the message of his songs, and through his treatment of them they achieve a greatness.'[24]

After a busy few days in Christchurch, Paul and Eslanda returned on 28 October to Auckland for two more concerts, on 29 and 31 October. At Auckland Airport they met, quite by chance, Dizzy Gillespie and Sarah Vaughan, who were arriving in New Zealand for performances in Auckland and Wellington.[25] They had just finished performing at the Australian International Jazz Festival in Sydney, which had been organised by the unstoppable Lee Gordon.[26] Both were at the peak of their international careers, Vaughan as a jazz singer and Gillespie as a jazz musician and composer. Gillespie had in 1956 undertaken an international tour under the State Department's goodwill ambassador program, after which he had telegraphed President Eisenhower to say that the tour had 'proved conclusively that our interracial group was powerfully effective against Red propaganda. Jazz is our own American folk music that communicates with all peoples regardless of language or social barriers.'[27] If one might have expected Paul and Dizzy to be wary of one another given their divergent politics and experience with US officialdom, this seems not at all to have been the case. Commenting on Louis Armstrong's similarly sponsored tours a few years before, Paul had defended performing artists who went on such tours 'because they needed work and … were out to show the world, as they did, that the American Negro has talent and dignity deserving of respect everywhere'.[28] He would make similar comments in Christchurch.[29] The chance meeting showing smiles all round was captured by a news photographer and would later become one of the iconic images from the New Zealand tour.

The concerts on this second Auckland visit took place in the Auckland Town Hall; with its large auditorium, it is still very much in use as a performance venue. This time the *Auckland Star*'s reviewer was Paul Callan, a 21-year-old Englishman who would later make his name in Fleet Street. 'For those who have heard this remarkable performer only on record,' he wrote, 'seeing him is a truly exciting experience.' He also praised Robeson's personal performance style: 'It was as though he was singing and talking personally to each member of the capacity audience in the privacy of their own drawing rooms.' There was an 'overwhelming impression of sincerity, true culture and huge artistic stature'. Paul had, he said, done what few artists could, which was overcome the 'atmosphere of formality which the Town Hall seems to generate, and replaced it with a charming, spontaneous feeling of easiness'.[30]

Paul's final sold-out concert took place in the southern city of Dunedin on Wednesday 2 November in the large Dunedin Town Hall. With capacity for 3000 people, it was then, and remains today, New Zealand's largest auditorium.[31] In the city's *Otago Daily Times*, 'KG' was just as fulsome in their praise as their fellow critics. Paul, they wrote, had charmed a capacity audience in the Town Hall. Despite the political controversy surrounding him, KG thought that 'Paul Robeson still has the power to speak directly to the hearts of men everywhere'. The voice was still 'glorious ... incomparable in quality and resonance' and his diction exemplary in its clarity. He charmed his audience by interpolating between songs 'many engaging comments and anecdotes about the songs and people associated with them'. KG particularly admired Paul's singing of spirituals and songs for which he was especially well known, including 'Ma Curly Headed Baby', 'Scandalize My Name' and 'Water Boy'. The audience, KG thought, especially liked Paul's recitation of a few verses by William Blake.[32]

Musical talk

Throughout the New Zealand tour, Paul told reporters his ideas about music, in particular its universal character. He was articulating and explaining ideas he had outlined in *Here I Stand* a couple of years earlier—ideas that were drawn in part from his experience as a singer of spirituals, folk songs and classical pieces, and in part from his reading during the constricted 1950s, especially the work of composer and musicologist Ralph Vaughan Williams, a friend in the United Kingdom, who in *The Making of Music*, published in 1955, sought to explore and expand the connections between classical and folk music.[33] At a press conference in Auckland on Monday 17 October, the day after he arrived, Paul talked extensively about the importance of song. This press conference was nothing like the one in Sydney that had caused so much trouble. It was large and diverse; the *Weekly News* commented that it had been a while since so many Auckland journalists—'from the newspapers, the weeklies, the fashion magazines, even the teachers' college paper'—had gathered to interview just one person. He held their attention for an hour and a quarter, talking mainly about music and the book he was writing. The mention of the Teachers' College paper is interesting, the Māori group welcoming the Robesons at Auckland Airport having also been from that college, a point to which I will return in the next chapter.

At this media conference and in many interviews thereafter, Paul stressed his themes of music and humanity. The *Auckland Star* report, along with a photograph, quoted him as saying he aimed for the middlebrow and that what he valued most of all was 'songs that come from the hearts of the people'.[34] When asked by a reporter at Wellington Airport a few days later whether there was any theme to his tour, he replied that the theme was 'all men are brothers … that's the choral melody of Beethoven's 9th symphony'.[35] In Christchurch, where Paul and Eslanda arrived on Sunday 23 October,[36] he again talked to an interviewer about the importance of folk music and of singing for the people, and the universality of the pentatonic scale: 'Sitting at a piano in the drawing-room of a Christchurch hotel last evening, Paul Robeson ran a finger over five black keys and said, "Do you know that 95 per cent of the world's folk music can be played using these as a base?"'[37] Several journalists during the tour reported him saying he was writing a book about music.[38] He told *The Press* in Christchurch, 'I've been working on it for about two years. It should be ready for printing soon.'[39]

As indicated earlier, one of the themes in his New Zealand interviews was his use of microphones in concerts. He canvassed it during his first press conference in Auckland the day before his first concert, explaining that having been 'born into the radio age, the age of microphones and amplifiers', he had learned how to use these technologies. His use of microphones was the reason he could still sing at the age of sixty-two—he hadn't been 'screaming my head off like an opera singer'. He revealed that against the producers' wishes, and unknown to the audience, he had used a microphone in *Othello* in Stratford.[40] When he talked to James Homes of *The Press* in Christchurch, he returned to the subject and spoke at some length about how valuable microphones were in concert halls, just as they were when recording:

> With a microphone I can reach millions of people—on radio and records. Yet in a hall I have got to start yelling and shouting to reach the back of the hall. Makes no sense at all. So I use the hall just like a radio station. You only have to sing in somebody's ear; therefore I don't shout, I don't strain my voice like most opera singers. Because of this I am singing at 62 instead of being through at 50.

Using microphones when playing Othello, he explained, had enabled him to perform eight times a week without straining his voice:

> [P]laying Othello once a week is bad enough, but if you have to play it four times a week, or all week, that's a pretty rough road. I have mikes put in the theatre. I don't like mikes like some of those rock'n'rollers screaming into a microphone. I mean you put them in and nobody can tell they are there if you have the right engineers. I would say that what I have fought for is to make the stage like a bathroom—very resonant—then you have no tendency to force your voice. We did that in the theatre and I played Othello for 296 performances—eight times a week—with no strain.[41]

Despite Paul's spirited defence of his use of microphones, some critical commentary persisted. Almost four decades later, Eric Beardsley, a former journalist and subsequently information officer for the University of Canterbury at Christchurch, when recalling a

Christchurch concert noted regretfully that Paul had used a throat microphone 'to enhance the volume he could no longer produce'.[42]

In the interview in *The Press*, Paul also spoke at some length about folk music. He quoted approvingly from a book by Vaughan Williams, who sought to base an English national music on folk music and who placed folk music side by side with the classical songs of Schubert; in the same vein, Paul commented, 'I sing a lullaby by Schubert which was a folk song to begin with.' For him, 'the common man, the ordinary man, the divine average [Walt] Whitman had in mind, the common man [Franklin D] Roosevelt had in mind, is the salt of the earth and the guy who is the heart of any country in the world'.[43] The newspaper report virtually ends there, but the recorded interview is longer and goes on to explain how his concert programmes in Australia and New Zealand were designed around these ideas. He sang folk music alongside classical composers 'who built their music on folk music', such as Bach, Dvořák, Bartók and Schubert.[44]

The longest and most detailed interview with Paul about his music, and his politics, was that in the *New Zealand Listener*, a cultural and current affairs journal owned by the NZBC and described by Andrew Mason in the *Dictionary of New Zealand Biography* (*DNZB*) as 'a unique institution at the centre of New Zealand's cultural life'.[45] Here, again, Paul defended using a microphone: 'I've got now my own little gadget. I put this in my ear and it's like I'm standing in a very wonderful bathroom. Now all I have to do is be very quiet, and I hear my voice about five times as loud.' Olwage is intrigued by Paul's reference to his 'own little gadget', commenting that it is unclear whether this was an early in-ear performance monitor, a modified hearing aid, or some combination of the two. What we do know, he suggests, is that it was an example of Paul's desire to control his acoustic space and to aid his task of 'easy singing'.[46]

The *Listener* interview covers a lot of ground. When asked for his thoughts about Louis Armstrong, Paul replies that Armstrong is 'a very great artist'. While Paul himself sings 'the religious songs of my race', he thinks 'the blues are just as important, if not more important, as an expression of what our people suffered and went through. The blues are a very important part of our culture.' Armstrong represents 'one of the most important sides of what we have given to the world'. When asked what he thinks of the opera *Porgy and Bess*, Paul responds that he thinks it 'a fine musical, beautifully written music by Mr [George] Gershwin, and beautiful singing by all of the groups I have heard sing it'. Later, asked about his favourite film role, he says it is in *Proud Valley*, made in Wales, which has become home to him, and his second most favourite would be in *Show Boat*, with Jerome Kern's music and Oscar Hammerstein II's lyrics. And he can name no others that he likes, they could all 'easily be forgotten'.

Paul expands in this interview on why he thinks folk music is so important. It is, he says, 'by its very definition the product of the collective growth of centuries of people. Is that not so? It is in this sense that I would always want to remain a folk singer, and sing that music that comes from composers who had respect for the creations of the generations of their people.' When asked about the book he says he is writing, he describes it as having 'to do with the fact that many folk songs of the world are very close one to the other'. He explains, as he often did, that '95 per cent of all the folk music of the world can be played on the five black keys of the piano' and 'I am writing a book to suggest that there is in existence a universal language ... a musical one'. Even the great Johann Sebastian Bach, he adds, 'in many of his chorales, belongs in the folk stream of the world'. Béla Bartók, he continues, is a modern composer who builds his harmony on folk music. While most arrangers of folk songs impose what he calls 'West European harmony', he, Paul, has 'written a book to suggest that we have found another harmony, and the harmony is Bartók's and Mussorgsky's and Janáček's and Dr Vaughan Williams's and Mr Johann Sebastian Bach's'.

Paul's talks in New Zealand

Paul and Eslanda were thoroughly political people, wanting to spread their ideas about peace, socialism and racial equality. They were always available for an interview touching on political issues. Even at

Paul's first New Zealand press conference, where the focus was music, there was some politics, about his passport struggles and his belief in fair pay for everyone, 'whatever his colour'.[47] Paul explained to the assembled journalists that he was a true American: 'when you love your country, it is your duty to point out its faults'.[48] The United States had departed from its constitutional principles, he suggested, in supporting autocrats like [West German chancellor Konrad] Adenauer, Franco and Chiang Kai-shek. He expressed regret at the non-violent stance taken by African Americans at Little Rock, Arkansas, where in 1957 plans to integrate nine African American students into the Little Rock Central High School had met with angry demonstrators and opposition from the state governor, who deployed the Arkansas National Guard to exclude the students from the school. Only the intervention of President Eisenhower enabled the integration to proceed. Paul commented that if he had been involved, 'I would have asked thousands of Negroes from all over the United States to go there armed. I'm sure that nothing would have happened then … I would have walked my children to school, and if anybody had attempted to start anything—man, he would have been dead.' Paul may have been a man advocating peace as a necessary solution to the world's problems, but he was clearly no pacificist. He explained that he had refused to answer the HUAC some years earlier because the chair was a senator from Mississippi—to have been judged by him would have 'been like being judged by [South African prime minister] Dr [HF] Verwoerd'. Interestingly, the report in the *New Zealand Herald* based on this press conference was the first of the communications on the tour from the State Department to the FBI; the State Department seems to have been slow to catch up with him in Australia.[49]

While many interviews covered the same ground, and in Paul's case highlighted the same key points in his life story, some comments stand out.[50] At his press conference in Auckland, for example, he spoke about the importance to him of acting the role of Othello in Stratford in 1959. After the hard Cold War years, when he couldn't sing or act in the United States or travel outside it, that role had been 'the high point of his life'. He recalled how he felt at the end of the first performance: 'when I came off the stage that night, I knew the sheet was clean. I was starting again, a new life as good as ever.'[51] He felt like a new man.

Another memorable interview with Paul occurred in his hotel room in Auckland with Noel Holmes, a journalist who had a popular daily column in the *Auckland Star* called 'Just Looking, Thanks'. The DeBrett is a beautiful Art Deco hotel in central Auckland that still exists in its more or less original form today. I visited it in February 2023 and could easily imagine Paul feeling relaxed and expansive as he chatted with Holmes.

The two seem to have talked about *Sanders of the River*, which Paul now disavowed but which New Zealanders had loved, because Holmes begins by describing Paul singing two lines from the song but with a twist. Where the original song had praised Sanders, the British administrator, with the lines 'Sandy the strong/ Sandy the wise/ Righter of wrong/ Hater of lies', he altered the words to praise instead Chaka, the Zulu chief, and sang to Holmes: 'Chaka the strong/ Chaka the wise/ Righter of wrongs/ Hater of lies'. When he finished singing, Paul said, 'That's the way I'd sing it now if I were making *Sanders of the River* again.' Holmes commented on Paul's impromptu performance: 'The deep chocolate-coated voice rolled down the corridor of the DeBrett hotel in Auckland. You could almost see the notes surging along the body carpet and rebounding like big soft rubber balls off the Peter McIntyre pictures.' (Peter McIntyre was a well-known and sought-after New Zealand artist.) The interview, however, mostly concerned politics, to Holmes' surprise, an agent having warned him not to ask political questions. Paul again expressed his bitterness at his treatment in his own country, his disagreement with the policies of non-violence the civil rights movement was adopting, and his view that the African people in South Africa would eventually win their freedom. Holmes responded warmly to him and thought him a man 'who will fit in anywhere'.[52]

One of the most extensive political discussions occurred in the *New Zealand Listener* interview referred to earlier. The questions from the unidentified interviewer ranged far and wide, designed to elicit

Paul's views on a range of people and issues. When asked who he most admired, he first mentioned Dr WEB Du Bois, one of 'our great scholars' and 'one of the great authorities on Africa' as well as one of the founders of the NAACP. He also mentioned New Zealander Raymond Firth, who was now a professor of anthropology at LSE and whom he had met through Eslanda when she was an anthropology graduate student in London. Paul found Firth interesting for his extensive knowledge of 'this section of the world—Melanesian cultures, and Polynesian cultures as well'. Later in the interview, he describes himself as an optimist, as people of all colours and all societies will learn how to live together in peace, and also a great believer in the power of the collective to achieve change: 'I see history being written in terms of the people, not individuals, and I have great faith in masses of people.'

Towards the end of the interview, the *Listener* journalist asks Paul about his ancestry. He gives an extended reply, discussing his background in much more detail than in any other interview on the Australian and New Zealand tour. Martin Duberman in his biography comments that Paul identified much more with his father's side of the family, 'scarcely ever referring to his Bustill relatives'.[53] This interview in New Zealand, then, is one of the rare instances when he does refer to them. On his mother's side, he explains, he is descended from Samuel Bustill, an American of Scottish descent who was a member of Benjamin Franklin's scientific circle, and an unnamed 'Indian coloured woman' whose son, Cyrus Bustill, 'was the ancestor of my mother's family'. However, the 'American Indian felt himself superior to the Negro you know, he had not been a slave—he'd rather be wiped out. Okay. So I've never stressed that part of my heritage.' He goes on:

> I think it's interesting, this mixture, for I can be very patient and very kind—I guess that's the African in me—and then sometimes I can get very angry, and in my football games at various times I guess I used to go back to my Indian forebears. But I'm trying very much to get back to my African ancestors these days.

And there this rather remarkable interview ends.[54]

7

New Zealanders Meet the Robesons

PAUL AND ESLANDA met an extraordinary range of people in New Zealand, both Pakeha and Māori. Despite the fact there was no civic reception or formal welcome for them (to the pleasure of the Department of State and the FBI in the United States), they did in fact meet several senior politicians and officials, first in Wellington, the national capital, and later in Auckland.

On 19 October, the day they arrived in Wellington, they met Sir Arthur Harper, a senior civil servant, who was variously, one biographical entry records, patron, president, vice-president, chairman, trustee and member of forty national, local and community enterprises.[1] One wonders which of his many hats he was wearing when he met the Robesons. Two days later Paul and Eslanda met the Labour prime minister, 78-year-old Walter Nash, in his office at Parliament House. Paul had met Nash when they were both guests on the Voice of America radio program in 1942. Now, it was the last month of Nash's term in office as prime minister—on 26 November Labour would lose the election and be replaced by a conservative government. They also met Minister of Internal Affairs Bill Anderton, whose portfolio included arts and culture and who had that year formed an arts advisory council and substantially increased government funding for the arts.[2] When he met with Paul in his office, he invited him to return to New Zealand to do a series of professional appearances with state-supported theatre and opera groups.[3]

Most of the people the Robesons met in New Zealand, however, were far from the seat of power. They included journalists, musicians, trade unionists, writers, academics, theatre people and Unitarian churchgoers. That they met so many and so varied a group of people was due largely to the energetic role of some key individual peace activists, such as Flora Gould in Auckland and the married couple Rona and Chip Bailey in Wellington. In Christchurch, there was a welcome committee that included Frank Langley and Lincoln Efford.[4] Gould, the Baileys and Langley were all members of the CPNZ and of their local peace council, the bodies that Paul and Eslanda insisted arrange a limited number of political and social events, while Efford was an independent peace activist in Christchurch. One problem was that neither the party nor the peace councils were strong organisations. Though the CPNZ was delighted the Robesons were visiting New Zealand,[5] it was in a seriously diminished state, its membership now less than 300 in the whole country.[6] The communist-influenced peace councils had also shrunk and weakened, and the emerging Campaign for Nuclear Disarmament was challenging their leadership.[7]

The success of the extra-concert aspects of the tour was due in part to the remarkable organising capacities of these key individuals. Important for helping Eslanda meet New Zealanders was the United Nations Association in New Zealand, which would host her public lectures. In addition, through their tour manager, Dan O'Connor, the Robesons met a wide range of people in music and theatre. Paul took time, for example, between his two Wellington concerts to meet with a group of opera singers at the Opera Centre, home of the New Zealand Opera Company, which baritone Donald Munro had formed six years earlier. He spoke to the cast of the company's *Don Pasquale*, who were rehearsing in preparation for their first performance on 29 October 1960.[8] A photograph of Paul with the cast appeared in *The Dominion* the next day.[9]

Their hosts in Wellington for political and social activities were principally Rona and Chip Bailey. Chip was a member of the CPNZ and secretary of the Wellington Drivers' Union, which had had a chequered career since a crisis in New Zealand trade unionism in 1951 when the government had crushed a waterfront strike led by the Waterside Workers' Union. As organiser and secretary, Chip had been a leading figure in reorganising and rebuilding the union in the 1950s, especially in promoting internal democracy—including regular delegates' conferences, election of officials, and stop-work meetings—and in successfully advocating its reaffiliation to the overarching union body, the Federation of Labour. As Peter Franks writes in the *DNZB*, Chip's 'greatest legacy was the methods of organisation he pioneered in the Wellington Drivers' Union'.[10] He would help arrange one of the key events of the Robesons' tour, when Paul spoke and sang to waterside workers. He also gave Paul a Wellington Drivers' Union badge that Paul wore on his lapel when later interviewed in Christchurch.[11]

Rona Bailey was even more directly involved than Chip in organising the political side of the Robesons' visit to Wellington.[12] An ardent admirer of Paul's, she was an indefatigable organiser, a member of the CPNZ, and secretary of two organisations that were significant for the Robesons' visit. One was the Wellington branch of the NZ Peace Council, and the other was the Society for Closer Relations with Russia, of which she had been secretary since 1956, and which had encouraged an increasing number of visits between New Zealand and the Soviet Union in 1958–60.[13] She had also been involved earlier in the year in the campaign against the all-white rugby tour of South Africa. Her interest in the Robesons, especially Paul, was not only political but also cultural. As a teacher of physical education, she had studied in the United States in 1937–38; there, she had been deeply influenced by the radical modern dance movement, which was closely associated with theatre. Back in New Zealand she joined leftist theatre groups, and in Wellington became the treasurer for Unity Theatre, a radical group inspired by Unity Theatre in Britain. It was through Unity Theatre that she came into contact with and then joined the CPNZ.

As mentioned earlier, Rona had heard Paul sing at a concert in Colón in the Panama Canal Zone in 1947. She had not only heard him sing, but she and her friends had also met him briefly at the after-concert reception attended, she later recalled, 'by what I would call the Black elite of Panama', where she spoke to Robeson 'and we had a good laugh at how we New Zealanders had got there'.[14] In 1998, in a program aired on Radio New Zealand celebrating the centenary of Robeson's birth, Rona would describe attending this concert and meeting Paul as one of the defining moments of her life. His influence, she said, had helped her stay 'staunch and firm'.[15] Given her activist and cultural interests, she was an ideal person to introduce Paul and Eslanda to the kind of people they wanted to meet, such as trade unionists, peace and anti-apartheid activists, musicians and actors.

Singing to waterside and railway workers

Given his membership of the ILWU in the United States, it is not surprising that Paul readily agreed to speak and sing to waterside workers in Wellington, and indeed this engagement would be the first of four occasions—the other three in Australia—that he would do so. Also involved with the Baileys in organising Paul's meeting with striking waterside workers were Ken Douglas, president of the Wellington Drivers' Union, and Ted Thompson, delegate for the Waterside Workers' Union in Wellington. The two unions had been strongly associated ever since the Drivers' Union's support for the waterside workers' strike in 1951; indeed, the Drivers' Union included in its membership a number of former waterside workers who had been banned from waterside work since the failed 1951 strike.[16]

The Wellington meeting and concert for waterside workers took place on Friday 21 October. Rona later recalled that when Chip called at Paul's hotel to take him to the venue, Paul could barely fit into their small car, a Volkswagen Beetle: 'he managed with much laughter but only just'.[17] Paul addressed a waterside special stop-work meeting on the Wellington waterfront, sang to the workers, and accepted life-membership in their union. As well as the waterside workers, many representatives from other unions were present.[18] The *People's Voice* described the event, saying the 'air was electric' with anticipation as Paul took the microphone and gave a special hello to 'my Māori brothers and sisters'. In his speech he stressed the importance of class struggle, something he had learned from the Welsh miners, who had helped him realise that in the case of his own people, 'the struggle of the Negro people was a class struggle based on plain economic facts, that the bosses wanted their labour for nothing', and that 'the struggle of the Welsh miners was a class struggle'. He supported the men on strike: 'when men are on strike, I man the picket line with them'. He told his audience, 'To participate in the struggle you must fight for the unity of the working class of the world.'

It was clear that quite a number of the workers present had come to New Zealand from the United Kingdom, the *People's Voice* reporting: 'Speakers from the floor went to the microphone and expressed their thanks to Paul Robeson, and some recalled occasions when they had heard him sing in England.' The report continued:

> The most moving scene occurred when Robeson stepped down from the platform and waterside workers lined up to shake him by the hand and thank him personally. Soon he was surrounded and willingly signed men's union cards with the same friendly smile and gesture which had endeared him to the union for life.[19]

Rona later recalled Chip telling her: 'it was just so moving and you could feel how comfortable he was among the workers there. There were lots from other unions to[o] of course.'[20] Many years later, Thompson recalled how Paul had walked into a packed hall, immaculately dressed, a big strong man whose presence was electrifying.[21] Douglas remembered the visit with awe—'they were two exceptional days, one continual adrenaline rush'.[22] When Paul sang to the waterside workers, the performance was 'packed out', with well over 1000 people attending. They were 'so electrified, so stimulated by this person's presence and the words that he spoke in such a gentle but commanding way' that everyone there was 'convinced he was talking to him'.[23]

The next day, Paul and Eslanda met even more people. On the evening of Saturday 22 October they attended a major post-concert reception at the Wellington Town Hall, with unionists, representatives from the Soviet and China friendship societies, and a range of writers and artists all invited and present. As Rona later recalled, Paul and Eslanda insisted on the inclusion of trade unionists. On the Peace Council's request, Bruce and Diana Mason were hosts.[24] Bruce was an ideal host, well known in musical, dramatic and left-wing circles. An influential playwright, his popular play, often taught in high school, *The Pohutukawa Tree* (1955), explored the conflict between Māori and European values. He seems to have been something of a polymath, for he also directed plays at the Wellington Unity Theatre and was the radio critic for the *New Zealand Listener*, the drama critic for *The Dominion* newspaper, and editor of *Te Ao Hou*, a magazine about Māori issues produced by the Department of Māori Affairs.[25] He had visited the Soviet Union in 1958 and in that same year became president of the New Zealand China Friendship Society.[26] Diana was just as well known, as a leading obstetrician and medical superintendent of the Alexandra Maternity Hospital and Home for unmarried mothers in Wellington.

The next morning, enthusiastic supporters gave Paul and Eslanda a fond farewell at Wellington Airport.

Among those who welcomed them to Christchurch was Frank Langley, president of the Christchurch Peace Council. Now aged sixty, he had a long trade union career behind him, including as founder and first president of the nationwide New Zealand Carpenters' Union in 1942 and a period as national councillor in the Federation of Labour.[27] They also met Lincoln Efford. Coming from a family who had been social activists and trade union supporters since their initial immigration from Devon in the 1870s, Efford had been committed to a variety of peace and socialist causes from an early age. During World War II, he became probably New Zealand's most prominent pacifist. Immediately upon learning of the bombing of Hiroshima, he began organising anti-nuclear activity, including a large public meeting on 23 September 1945. In 1947, he had helped unite several different peace organisations to form the Peace Union and became its secretary, but he left it in 1953 disappointed by the lack of support. He remained, however, a keen supporter of peace. During the 1950s, he had been the full-time secretary of the Workers' Educational Association Canterbury District Council and the Canterbury Council for Civil Liberties, and had been involved in campaigns for prison reform.[28] He was later one of the founders of the Christchurch branch of the New Zealand Campaign for Nuclear Disarmament.[29]

On behalf of the city's welcoming committee, Efford organised a late-night reception for Paul after his first concert in Christchurch, on 25 October. The venue was the Workers' Educational Association Centre, which Efford himself had been instrumental in establishing the previous year. About 200 people attended from a wide variety of organisations, including the Canterbury Housewives' Union and the Christchurch branches of the Peace Council, the NZ China Society and the Campaign for Nuclear Disarmament. George Manning, the mayor of Christchurch, attended, as did Mr and Mrs JL Hay from the NZ Music Council; Jack Palmer, Labour Party election candidate, with his wife; welcoming-committee members Jack and Elsie Locke; and Frank Langley. In his welcome speech, Efford noted that those present came from a wide cross-section of political opinion but otherwise avoided talking about politics. In contrast, when Paul spoke he freely addressed both political and musical matters and was well received. As the event drew to a close, Paul and Eslanda both signed the back of an invitation card, inscribing it 'All the best and thanks, a wonderful evening'.[30]

Efford also helped organise what would become one of the best-remembered events of the New Zealand tour. This was Paul's singing and speaking to the workers at the Addington Railway Workshops during their lunch hour on Wednesday 26 October.[31] The workshops had been in existence since 1877 and were still important in the New Zealand railway system. Together with Efford in arranging this event was Jack Locke, a member of the CPNZ, whose wife, Elsie Locke, was an ex-communist and a well-known writer of children's books. Norris Collins, general secretary of the Amalgamated Society of Railway Servants, chaired the meeting, at which every seat was taken. This time someone recorded the impromptu concert, and radio producers have used parts of that recording ever since.[32]

Paul began by referring to his wonderful concert the previous evening, and then spoke of the importance for him of talking to the workers, the people who create the wealth. He talked, as he so often did, of singing in his father's church and then at school but not at college. He had begun to sing professionally after impromptu sessions when performing *The Emperor Jones*. He would, he said, sing a few songs, and noted that many songs come from working on the railroad. He sang 'Water Boy' to huge applause, then 'Joe Hill', at first loudly and then very softly, followed by 'Ol' Man River', again to much applause, and a Chinese children's song. He spoke about the pentatonic scale, which he explained as a sequence of notes that everyone has used at some point. Paul then talked about the unity of the world's peoples and the unifying effect of song, poetry and music. 'Poetry and music', he said, 'go together. In Negro life you never know where to start and where you leave off.' Negro spirituals, he added, showed just how close was the connection between speech and song, and he sang 'Swing Low, Sweet Chariot' to illustrate his point. He recited William Blake's 'Jerusalem', which was, he commented, about England but could be about New Zealand, or any country. He was keen to emphasise the importance of the working class worldwide. The Welsh miners, the Scottish miners and the London dockworkers, he continued, had taught him that we are all of one race, one family—the human family. The civil rights movement in the United States, he said, had arisen in a spirit not of vengeance, but of simply wanting to be treated as full human beings. He illustrated his points with a recital of Langston Hughes' 'Freedom Train', which he explained was about a Black soldier and a white soldier and how they had to fight together. The audience was spellbound and Collins later said that Paul's visit was 'one of the highlights of my life'.[33]

There was more to come. The initial visit to Auckland had been brief, and two days later, on Friday 28 October, Paul and Eslanda were back there for two more concerts and a round of political and social engagements. Their main contact with the political left in Auckland was Flora Gould, secretary of the New Zealand Peace Council. Flora had worked for the *People's Voice* and for many organisations of the far left, often as secretary, including the Society for Closer Relations with Russia, the Women's Union, and from 1956 the Peace Council.[34] Now, she became the link between the Robesons and a variety of people who wanted to meet them.

The pace was hectic. On Sunday 30 October they had morning tea with the mayor of Auckland, Sir Dove-Myer Robinson, and his wife Thelma at their home. Dove-Myer was an unusual politician, an independent, flamboyant man from a Jewish family; Thelma was his third wife and twenty-six years his junior. Paul sang 'Ma Curly Headed Baby' to the couple's newborn, leading to a photograph in the *New Zealand Herald*.[35] Next came lunch at the home of Dan and Shirley O'Connor, followed by dinner with Robert and Phyllis Kerridge at their home.[36] One can imagine them all celebrating the financial, musical and social success of the tour: all performances had been sold out and the reviews were uniformly warm and enthusiastic.

The following day, a Monday, the whirl of activities and meetings continued. Paul spoke and sang to a small audience at the Unitarian Church in Ponsonby Road, Auckland.[37] He had close connections with churches and their music; his father and brother, after all, had both been pastors. This particular church would have been of interest as its lay minister was an American, Maurice Wilsie, whose wife, Diana, was a member of the CPNZ. The church had attracted lovers of music ever since its acquisition of a stereophonic organ in 1904, and often invited high-profile speakers on social justice issues. With its radical tradition, musical history and excellent acoustics, it was thus an ideal venue for Paul to speak and sing at.[38] Afterwards, that evening, he sang his last Auckland concert, followed by a reception attended by a wide range of people, including some from Unity Theatre.

One guest that evening was Bill Airey, associate professor in history at Auckland University College, who would retire the following year. He was a contemporary of Paul's, having been born in Auckland in 1897, the year before Paul. Like Paul, he admired the Soviet Union and was interested in Marxism; he did not, however, join the Communist Party.[39] Airey was a highly respected historian who trained many people who would become New Zealand's leading historians in the 1960s and 1970s. A political and social activist, he had been involved earlier in the League of Nations Union of New Zealand, the New Zealand Spanish Medical Aid Committee, the Workers' Educational Association and the New Zealand China Friendship Society, and had been chairman of the New Zealand Peace Council from 1953 to 1956. In an essay in *Bulletin of the World Council of Peace* in 1959, he had reflected on what the peace movement needed to do in New Zealand. He had argued that 'Direct cultural contact is perhaps the greatest penetrator of the curtains of prejudice' and had given as examples the visit of the Chinese Classical Theatre and the exhibition of the *Hiroshima Panels* in New Zealand. He had welcomed the formation of new bodies 'wholly devoted to the question of nuclear weapons' and emphasised the importance of mobilising 'widening circles of the people' in support of peace and equality, concluding that the 'Cold War must be buried by the unity of the peoples'.[40] One can imagine that Bill and Paul may have got on rather well.

There is one couple that Paul and Eslanda may well have met while in Auckland, though I have been unable to find direct evidence that they did so. This is Bob and Augusta Ford, left-wing Americans who had lived in Auckland for ten years. Bob had been a member of the Abraham Lincoln Brigade and served in Spain from May 1937 to December 1938.[41] He had a background in Hollywood cinema, with his father an actor and film director and his uncle the famous director John Ford, who cast him in several small parts in films. He was also a Communist Party member. With this background, it is no surprise to learn he was a fan of Paul Robeson and long regretted that he hadn't managed to hear him sing in Spain. In one of his postcards to home, he had commented in March 1938 that although he had missed seeing or hearing Paul, 'I am glad that he came to Spain. I believe that he is a communist and if that is true, it is a good thing. We need men like him in the revolutionary movement as he is both popular and intelligent.'[42] Bob then served in World War II and married Augusta Bebel Ain, the daughter of Russian Jewish immigrants who had named her after the German socialist Auguste Bebel. She had written a thesis on US folk music while a student at University of California, Los Angeles (UCLA) in the late 1940s.

Weary of endless surveillance in the McCarthy era, Bob and Augusta left the United States for New Zealand in 1950, where Bob worked as a lathe operator and Augusta as a lecturer at Auckland Teachers' Training College. There, historian Mark Derby writes, 'she exerted a profound and lasting influence on many of her students and colleagues'. It may have been she who helped connect the visiting Robesons with the Auckland Teachers' College at the beginning of their New Zealand tour. Augusta also presented broadcasts on Radio NZ on American literature and music, especially noting, as Derby says, 'Black and feminist artists'.[43] Later, she would help introduce New Zealand women to American feminist Betty Friedan's *The Feminine Mystique*.[44] I hope the Fords and the Robesons did meet in Auckland—they had so much in common.

Meeting Māori

Māori perspectives and struggles had been at the forefront of public debate throughout the year the Robesons arrived. One issue, which would have been of particular interest to Paul as an outstanding and famous footballer in his youth who had personally experienced racism in sport, was a rugby tour of South Africa by New Zealand. The New Zealand Rugby Football Union (NZRFU) sent in May 1960 an all-white team to South Africa, explicitly excluding Māori players in obedience to South African requirements under the apartheid policy. Rugby was an extremely popular national sport in New Zealand and an important part of NZ national identity, and issues affecting the sport were liable to have much wider ramifications. The NZRFU had sent the racially selected team despite a strong protest movement, which had begun with church criticism in 1958 and strengthened through 1959 with Māori protests, including from the Māori Women's Welfare League and other organisations. Notably, a Māori member of parliament, Eruera Tirikatene, on 16 June 1959 issued a strongly worded press statement that indicated he was speaking 'as a chief and spokesman of the Māori race and not as a government official'.[45]

Labour prime minister Walter Nash refused to intervene and sought to stifle caucus and public discussion of the issue, banning the state-owned NZBC from reporting news of the public debate, a ban that was later lifted after public protest.[46] With the formation in mid-1959 of the Citizens' All Black Tour Association to coordinate the protest movement under the slogan 'No Māoris—No Tour', the protest gathered strength, with actions including large marches in Wellington and Auckland, circulation of a petition signed by almost 160,000 people, and a deputation in February 1960 to Prime Minister Nash and the acting leader of the Opposition that led to angry exchanges and Bishop Wiremu Panapa, the Anglican bishop of Aotearoa, leading the Māori delegates in a haka.[47] After news came of the Sharpeville massacre in South Africa in March 1960, protest further increased, with a march and rally of 7000–8000 people occurring in Auckland on 8 May, two days before the rugby team was due to depart. Nash remained firmly in support of the NZRFU, and on 10 May the all-white All Blacks departed for South Africa.

Though unsuccessful on this occasion, historians and others now regard the protests of 1958–60 as the beginning of the anti-apartheid movement in New Zealand. In addition, although the protests focused on the rugby tour, they broadened to the question of racial discrimination towards Māori. On 22 September, a little over three weeks before the Robesons arrived, Tirikatene presented a petition in parliament on behalf of Bishop Panapa and fifteen others. While the NZRFU had committed 'the most flagrant, single act of racial discrimination ever to have taken place in New Zealand', there was, it said, a wider context of discrimination against Māori, in 'hotels, boarding houses, cinemas and barber shops, and in certain spheres of employment'.[48] The petition sought a government statement on New Zealand race relations policy that would commit the government to act on domestic issues and on racial discrimination in sporting contact with South Africa.

There would be no response, either by the sitting Labour government—which would six weeks later call a national election—or by the incoming conservative government led by Keith Holyoake.[49] Yet change was on the way. As Richard Thompson, author of an early historical account of the movement, wrote in 1961, New Zealand was entering a period of 'intense preoccupation with the place of the Māoris in New Zealand society', with questions of 'Māori health, housing, leadership, vocational training, crime and urban drift' receiving sustained attention in the press.[50]

Paul addressed Māori concerns during the tour. At the Addington Workshops, he told the workers to 'look at your coloured brothers here and coloured sisters and see that they, not just in words, not just on paper, somewhere they've got to feel full parts of your life in New Zealand. Full citizens, full citizens. And I know that you will achieve it.'[51] Soon afterwards, he received a letter from twenty-three union officials in Auckland that indicated they were aware of his comments in Christchurch and perhaps elsewhere about standing up for Māori workers. The letter praised his struggle for civil rights and world peace:

> We in the New Zealand trade union movement are resolutely opposed to any and all forms of racial discrimination. We know the bitter consequences of any division in our ranks. In New Zealand you will witness Māori and Pakeha brothers working shoulder to shoulder and uniting to make common cause for common objectives. However, we cannot rest on past achievements, as the racial discrimination question is continually before us. Your tour of New Zealand will add to our determination to completely eliminate the remaining features of the racial question from the face of New Zealand.[52]

Paul was interested not only in Māori political struggles but also in Māori music. The tour had begun at Auckland Airport with a Māori welcome that included the performance of songs and a haka. As one newspaper reported,

> The tempo of the Māori music soon had its effect, and Mr Robeson was tapping a foot to its rhythm. He said later that the music was similar to other cultures, and particularly reminiscent of Hawaiian

music. It was his first experience of Māori singing and a Māori welcome, he said, although he had met many New Zealanders during the war.[53]

He retained this interest in Māori people and music throughout the New Zealand tour, and both Pakeha and Māori people he met shared with him their knowledge of Māori culture. In Auckland, an unidentified Māori person had given Paul a copy of a book by Māori anthropologist Peter Buck.[54] At Wellington Airport, Paul had said, 'Now I'm in New Zealand I'll be listening to Māori music. I want to take some with me, and sing it, and record it.'[55]

Paul had a chance to learn more about urban Māori musical culture when he and Eslanda, at 9 p.m. on Sunday 30 October, their second-last day in Auckland, attended a weekly talent night at the city's Māori Community Centre, a focal point for Auckland Māori. The prime minister had granted the building, originally a warehouse for the American Army stationed in Auckland, to Auckland's Māori community in 1947, leading it to become the city's only marae.[56] Through the 1950s, it had become, as NZ music writer Chris Bourke points out, a critical venue for a generation of Māori musicians; on Friday and Saturday nights it regularly attracted crowds from the Māori population of the area. It also frequently gave a Māori welcome to visiting performers, such as Trinidadian-British pianist Winifred Atwell, and now Paul.[57]

The talent quest that evening was much more packed than usual as word had got around that Paul would be dropping by. As the *People's Voice* reported, he spoke of the 'struggle for brotherhood' and sang 'Ol' Man River', which was 'thunderously applauded'. The report said that 'Mr Paikea, MP jocularly sang his own version and the talent quest got under way with a bigger zip than usual'.[58] 'Mr Paikea' was the forty-year-old member of parliament Tāpihana Paraire Paikea, who had held the Northern Māori seat for Labour since 1943 following the death of his father, its previous incumbent. Through his parliamentary career he pressed a range of Māori concerns in parliament, especially those affecting New Zealand's increasingly urban Māori population.

A large man, 193 centimetres in height, he would have been one of the few people Paul met on his tour who was taller than Paul was at 190 centimetres.[59]

The New Zealand tour draws to an end

Although Paul, Eslanda and Larry flew to Dunedin on 1 November and Paul sang one concert there the following day, their stay would last less than forty-eight hours and they appear not to have met people to the extent they had in Auckland, Wellington and Christchurch. Paul did, however, meet some press as usual; during the afternoon before the evening concert, he listened to the Melbourne Cup, Australia's most famous horse race, with an unnamed journalist, and they spoke about racing, rugby and music.[60]

There had been, in fact, even before Paul arrived in Dunedin a rare instance of controversy over his politics. Catholic authorities told children attending at least two of the city's Catholic schools, St Dominic's and Christian Brothers', that they should boycott the Robeson concert. In a letter to the *Otago Daily Times*, 'Shocked' expressed annoyance that this had happened. When the paper sought comment from the Right Reverend Monsignor GT Hussey, the director of education in the Dunedin diocese, he replied, 'So what?'[61] The responses the next day in the same paper were generally critical of Hussey, one saying he was supporting children at Catholic schools being 'brainwashed against the possible political influence of a great artist's singing', another commenting 'I believe that Paul Robeson has done more for his own people than anybody of his profession in the world today', and a third expressing sadness that 'McCarthyism still lives in the hearts of men'.[62] Paul and his promoters seem to have been unconcerned, for the concert was fully booked and would, in fact, turn out to be a huge success, marking the end of the New Zealand tour.

On 3 November, Paul and Eslanda flew via Christchurch to Sydney. During the several hours they spent at Christchurch Airport, Paul spoke at length to the communist newspaper *The People's Voice*. He spoke of the warmth of his reception in New Zealand, which he attributed in part to people who had heard him as children and had waited a long time to hear him sing in person. 'It has been obvious', he said, 'that many working people went outside their budgets to attend my concerts.' He was especially pleased to have been able to visit the Community Centre and reaffirmed that he wished to learn Māori songs and expressed a desire to learn more when he came to New Zealand again. He had been glad to have the opportunity to sing and talk to workers on the waterfront and in the Railway Workshops. He wanted to come again, not on a concert tour but as a peace activist, possibly when he came to Indonesia in the early part of 1961—a comment he would repeat frequently throughout his Australian visit.[63]

Yet his views about New Zealand were not quite as warm as expressed in this interview. A few months later, he expressed his concern to a reporter in the Federal Republic of Germany that he had witnessed racial discrimination in New Zealand, and even more in Australia.[64] Still, Paul and Eslanda had generally a positive impression of New Zealand, and the New Zealanders who met or heard them were thrilled to have done so. Rona Bailey was thoroughly delighted and for the rest of her life did her best to ensure New Zealanders remembered the Robesons, especially Paul. He was, she would say at a commemorative event on the occasion of his 100th birthday in 1998, a towering figure and for New Zealanders a 'giant kauri tree in the Waipoua Forest'.[65]

For their part, Paul and Eslanda now turned their thoughts to Sydney and what this second, much longer visit to Australia would bring.

8

'I'm a good union man'

Sydney and the Workers

PAUL AND ESLANDA'S second visit to Sydney was quite different from the first. Where the initial visit three weeks earlier had lasted barely two days, this one, from 3 to 15 November, would last for eleven full days and twelve nights, with one successful concert, meeting or interview after another. Not only would Paul sing four sold-out concerts in the Sydney Town Hall and speak and sing at several well-attended meetings of workers, peace activists and supporters, but Eslanda would also speak, once to a women's group and once alongside Paul at a major public meeting. In addition, both would be interviewed several times, in the press and on radio and television. The original press conference held when they first arrived was not forgotten, but it did seem on the whole to have been forgiven. As one newspaper commented after Paul had spoken and sung at the Sydney Journalists' Club, he had 'more than redeemed himself for that flag-waving, US-baiting performance when he arrived in Sydney from London'.[1]

While this second Sydney visit repeated many of the features evident in Brisbane and New Zealand, and indeed in visits worldwide—a mix of commercially successful concerts, speaking and singing to unionised workers, and public speaking on political matters—these elements played out in a distinctive way in this, the largest and most cosmopolitan city of the entire tour. We have for Sydney an unusually rich visual account of the Robesons' visit. Not only was there good film coverage of Paul singing to workers at the Opera House worksite, but we also have two ABC television programs involving him.[2] Furthermore, the Sydney visit was the subject of a half-hour documentary made for the ABC in 1979, three years after Paul's death. Entitled *Paul Robeson in Australia* and written and narrated by Wendy Charell, it made extensive use of photographs, recordings and ABC film footage as well as interviews with people who met Paul in Sydney. By contrast, newspaper coverage of the Sydney visit was decidedly patchy.

The Robesons arrived in Sydney on the evening of Thursday 3 November, where they were met by admirer and activist Faith Bandler—of whom more in following chapters—and quietly checked in again to the Hotel Australia.[3] The next day, they met Sydney's lord mayor, who would be the sole elected official to meet them on their Australian tour. Harry Jensen, who was four years into his (unusually long) nine-year tenure in the role, arranged for a press photographer and television coverage, ensuring a photo of the three of them in the *Daily Telegraph* the next day and perhaps an item on ABC-TV news.[4] Though Australia nationally was now in its eleventh year of conservative government, the Sydney City Council tended to be Labor-dominated, and Sydney had had a Labor mayor since 1949. Some years earlier, Jensen had been a co-founder of the ALP's New South Wales Industrial Group, created to fight the influence of communism within the trade union movement.[5]

Despite these clear political differences, Jensen welcomed Paul and Eslanda to Sydney at his office at the Sydney Town Hall the day after they arrived. When recalling for *Paul Robeson in Australia* the welcome he had given the Robesons, Jensen commented that when peace movement visitors came to the city, establishment figures were reluctant to acknowledge them, but in this case 'I had no such reluctance. I thought this man was a great man and I happened to agree with the point of view he was expressing, which made it easier for me.' He does not state which point of view he means here, but perhaps he was referring to Robeson's emphasis on peace.

Though now careful not to jeopardise the tour through angry proclamations of unpopular views, Paul's loyalty to the Soviet Union would be evident during his stay in Sydney. He spent the evening of Saturday 5 November celebrating the anniversary of the Russian Revolution at an event, probably organised by the Australia-Soviet Friendship Society, at the Waterside Workers' Federation Hall in Sussex Street, Sydney.[6] *Tribune* had called on its readers to join these 'celebrations of Nov 7 Achievements' at this event, where there would be 'Refreshments—Chinese Supper—Dancing'.[7] (The WWF Hall was, as labour historian Lisa Milner points out, used extensively for cultural events such as 'choir and orchestral performances, journalism, dance, theatre and art groups and classes, as well as film screenings', and Paul would visit it several more times during his Sydney stay.)[8] Two days later, during his first public concert, he would pay tribute to the Soviet Union as 'a new society whose anniversary is being celebrated tonight'.[9] The Soviet Embassy, which had been re-established in March 1959 after a five-year freeze on relations following the defection of Vladimir Petrov from it in 1954, returned the compliment, Ambassador Ivan Kurdyukov attending Paul and Eslanda's public meeting in Paddington Town Hall on 10 November and the reception afterwards.[10]

The Sydney concerts

Paul would sing four sold-out or nearly sold-out concerts at the Sydney Town Hall—three evening concerts, on Monday 7, Tuesday 8 and Monday 14 November, and one matinee performance, on Saturday 12 November. Many in the audience had waited a long time to hear him, and some had taken a lot of trouble to be there. The Newcastle branch of the CPA organised a busload of excited fans to make the five-hour journey to Sydney for one of the concerts.[11]

There was a large, appreciative audience at the first concert, after which *Tribune* wrote, 'The applause which echoed and re-echoed throughout the Sydney Town Hall was more than applause for a great musical artist, it was an expression of comradeship, of solidarity, with a man whose whole life has been devoted to the greatest cause on earth—the liberation of mankind.'[12] After the concert, Paul held a greeting session in the Town Hall basement. Ron Witton remembers attending the concert and the reception afterwards, saying this was 'I think, through the good offices of Faith (and Hans) Bandler who must, I think, have gone to the concert with my parents'. He remembers 'VERY clearly the way my (tiny) hand disappeared into his (gigantic) grasp when we shook hands'.[13] Another person who was there as a child was Chris Hamerton, who remembers that Paul 'was very kind to an eleven-year-old red-headed kid who asked for (and got) his autograph (and one for his schoolteacher)'.[14]

The first concert was reviewed in all the major dailies, plus weeklies such as *Tribune* and *The Bulletin*, while the *Sydney Morning Herald* also reviewed the matinee concert. The reviews were uniformly warm, admiring and enthusiastic, as they had been everywhere thus far on the tour. Many emphasised Paul's warm, enveloping presence as well as his performance as a singer. Roger Covell (signed 'RC') in the *Sydney Morning Herald* described the concert 'as much an exercise in the ethics of brotherliness as it was a collection of short songs of suffering, endurance and hope'. Covell, aged twenty-nine, had only that year become music critic for the *Herald*, a position he would hold, influentially for Sydney's and indeed Australia's musical life, for the next four decades.[15] In his review, he observed perceptively that the concert had clearly been designed to emphasise 'the universality of basic human wishes and needs'. In common with many other reviewers on the tour, he commented that while Robeson's voice was extremely well known to Australians from films and recordings, it was still a shock to hear in person his first spoken words and the first notes of his singing. His voice, Covell thought, was truly astonishing and magnificent.[16] The *Herald* reviewer of the matinee concert on 12 November, 'AW', was just as fulsome as Covell. AW described Robeson as 'a man who stands alone in his field of art'. His singing was marked by 'eloquent sincerity' and his recitations were superb. From the moment he walked onto the stage, 'the large audience was completely with him'.[17]

Several reviewers, including those who disliked Robeson's politics, were especially impressed by his speaking voice and verse recitations. In the Sydney afternoon newspaper *The Sun*, music critic Julian Russell described Paul's voice as rich and expressive, 'still grandly eloquent though brief in register', but thought the concert would have been even better 'had he left many of his protests unspoken'. Still, Russell concluded, not even Paul's 'naive political propaganda' could 'rob him entirely of nobility'.[18] Frank Harris in the *Daily Mirror*, another Sydney afternoon paper, saw Paul as a powerful, if tormented, personality who took off too much time from his singing for 'his political spruiking', though his verse speaking was a 'magnificent sidelight'.[19] In the *Daily Telegraph*, Martin Long, though reserved about the effect of the microphone on Paul's singing, was impressed by his speaking voice, his skill as an orator and his recitation of two Blake poems. He thought the transition from speaking to singing seemed 'astonishingly slight', making his rendition of folk songs 'vivid and immediate'.[20] In one of the longer reviews, 'SWK' in *The Bulletin* described Paul's singing voice as 'perfectly produced' and showing no sign of wear, while his speaking voice was 'equally musical'.[21]

SWK also mentioned a song that had been sung as an encore—'Zog Nit Keynmol', the song of the Warsaw Ghetto—which was 'deeply moving', 'a cry of defiance from the dead who fell under the German machine-guns in the ghettos of Warsaw'.[22] The music came from a Soviet song, the 'Terek Cossacks' March Song', popularised by the Soviet Army during World War II and with lyrics by Hirsh Glick, a young Jewish man imprisoned in the Vilna Ghetto in 1943.[23] Along with almost 40,000 other inmates in the ghetto, Glick subsequently died in the Holocaust. This was the song that Paul had sung in Moscow on 8 June 1949 to a stunned audience. He had sung it again, along with three Yiddish songs, in Moscow in February 1959 as part of a tribute to the recently deceased Jewish writer Sholem Aleichem.[24] It had a powerful effect in Australia, too, where there were many post-war refugees and other immigrants from Eastern Europe, and where memories of World War II were still strong.

Speaking and singing to the workers

Paul loved to speak and sing to workers, and on the tour thus far had memorably met waterside workers in Wellington and railway workers in Christchurch. In Sydney, he spoke and sang to at least three groups of workers: journalists, building workers and waterside workers.

Journalists' Club

The first occasion was a luncheon on 4 November at the Sydney Journalists' Club where Paul was guest speaker. Alan Knight writes of the club, which started in 1939 and by this time owned its own premises, as 'one of the world's wildest and woolliest journalists clubs'. Its building was a centre for strike and union meetings, presenting literary awards, and hosting 'a star-studded guest speaker series' in which Robeson was now the featured guest.[25] The *Canberra Times* reported that Paul gave a brilliant performance, singing songs in several languages, including Japanese, reading three or four poems, and reciting the final speech from *Othello*. He told the spellbound audience that 'he liked Australia so much he would come back again', a statement he made many times during the tour.[26]

In his history of the club, Don Angel adds a little more detail about Paul's visit:

> His magnificent voice reverberated throughout the club as he sang snatches of folk songs in English, Chinese and Swedish and then in the Scottish dialect and the dialect of the American Deep South. His vocal illustrations included several other languages. Paul Robeson was demonstrating his thesis that music and song in all countries seemed to have a common basis.[27]

The club made both Paul and Eslanda, who was herself a journalist, honorary members.

Opera House building site

A few days later came the best-remembered event on the tour. This was Paul singing on Wednesday 9 November to the workers who were building the city's new opera house. The event is remembered in Australia partly because for many years ABC-TV played a short five-minute segment depicting it and acknowledging Robeson as the first person to sing at the wonderful Jørn Utzon–designed Sydney Opera House. Also assisting public memory is Jeff Sparrow's book on Robeson, *No Way But This*, which starts with an account of Paul singing at the Opera House site.[28] Yet if Australians, especially Sydneysiders, remember the event well, with much media coverage of its fiftieth anniversary on 9 November 2010 and its sixtieth anniversary in 2020, it is less remembered elsewhere. Martin Duberman's biography mentions it only in a footnote, while the biographies by Gerald Horne and Paul Robeson Jnr do not mention it at all. There are signs this may be changing, with American historian Shana Redmond's warm evocation in her 2020 book *Everything Man*.[29]

The idea of inviting Paul to sing to the workers at the Opera House site came from the BWIU. While Paul was in New Zealand, Pat Clancy, secretary of the NSW branch, wrote to him on 27 October 1960. 'Building workers employed on the Sydney Opera House project', he informed Paul, had asked the union to invite him to sing at the site. 'Peace lovers in this country', he continued, 'would regard it as most fitting that your voice, which has been consistently heard in the cause of peace, should be the first to be heard on the site of our Opera House.' Clancy had clearly done his homework concerning the way such arrangements were made. He assured Paul that Bill Morrow was enthusiastic but also concerned not to place too much strain on Paul while he was in Sydney. Dan O'Connor, he added, is 'very enthusiastic indeed about the idea and has no objection to your singing there'.[30]

In the film *Paul Robeson in Australia*, Lord Mayor Harry Jensen says it was his suggestion that Paul sing at the Opera House, and while the BWIU had already floated the idea and sent the invitation, it may be that Jensen's support was important in securing permission for Paul to sing there. Jensen had his own motivations for wanting Paul to sing at the site. As he says in the documentary, the Opera House project was controversial at the time given its huge cost, and he wanted to increase public support for what had originally, in 1954, been a Labor state government initiative. He posed for a press photograph with both Robesons in front of a model of the proposed building;

although the *Sydney Morning Herald* did not publish the photo at the time, it was recovered many years later for a story in the paper's *Good Weekend* magazine.[31]

When Paul arrived from New Zealand on 3 November, the BWIU was delighted and relieved to learn that he had agreed to sing. It suited Paul to sing to large groups of workers whenever he could, and this was, of course, a site connected to his own professional life as a singer. At noon on 9 November Morrow took Paul to the huge site, with the building foundations evident and lots of scaffolding, located in a prominent position on Sydney Harbour with ferries, boats and tugs frequently passing by.[32] First, Paul toured the site with Morrow, Clancy and the site manager, Mr D Holland, who explained the project to him. Then it was time to sing. Waiting for Paul to perform were more than 250 workers, whom the *Daily Telegraph* described as sitting on 'tiles, pipes, timber and scaffolding', in their lunch hour. They gave him a 'rousing reception'.[33] As Paul remarked the next day, 'They wanted to get their lunch, I know, but they chatted about and talked, and I could see some of the workers said, "I could not go for all that you say", we had some differences here and there.'[34] He realised he needed to win them over and told them they were working on a project they would be proud of one day.[35] He sang, said the *Daily Telegraph*, 'from a rough concrete stage before a broken-down microphone'. One of those present, BWIU official Tom McDonald, later recalled that Nelson Mandela stood at the very same spot thirty years later.[36]

There are three filmed recordings of this event, made by ATN Channel 7, Cinesound Productions (who made *Cinesound Review*, a weekly newsreel shown in cinemas) and ABC Television. The surviving Channel 7 news clip, lasting just under a minute, shows Paul singing 'Ol' Man River' and enthusiastic clapping by the workers at the end.[37] An excerpt from the Cinesound news item, now available on the National Film and Sound Archive (NFSA) website, shows Paul singing 'Ol' Man River' interspersed with shots of a passing boat and the workers perched on the scaffolding, some eating lunch, and it concludes with narration by newsreader Brian Henderson: 'Paul Robeson, first celebrity to sing at the Sydney Opera House'.[38] In an interview almost fifty years later, Howard Rubie recalled making the Cinesound news film along with sound recordist Bill Dukes. He begins by talking about the camera used—'a Wall with a 1000-ft load in a magazine, a real bastard to lift and carry'—and continues:

> My lasting memory of using the Wall was with Bill Dukes as the sound recordist, photographing the great baritone Paul Robeson in the early foundations of the Sydney Opera House on a wet and drizzly Sydney afternoon. Robeson called the workers around him with the words 'Comrades gather round. Let me sing you a song.' He sang 'Ol' Man River' for those of us lucky enough to be there. I firmly believe that was the first performance at the Opera House, an emotional fifteen minutes I shall never forget, the feeling of his voice resonating around the concrete structure sending waves of sadness through the audience of mostly migrant construction workers.[39]

A longer (six-minute) clip filmed by the ABC and first screened on 13 November shows Paul praising Australia for its opera singers: 'You have to go a long distance to find greater opera singers than you turned up here in Australia. In fact, it must have something to do with the climate, I don't know, you've turned up so many of them.' Then he begins to sing. Wearing a large coat, though it was late spring, he cups his ear and sings solo without accompaniment to the building workers on site. He begins with 'Water Boy' and as he sings we see a ship going past, shots of the construction site and views of the harbour seen through scaffolding, and at the end of the song, workers standing around him clapping. Then he speaks: 'This is one about Joe Hill, one of our great heroes in the American working-class movement. They framed him on a murder charge, but his spirit still lives in the hearts of all the American working class.' He occasionally swats away a fly, and it seems a hotter day than he had bargained for, in his suit and long coat. As he sings 'Joe Hill', there are more shots of extensive scaffolding and of cargo boats, passenger ships and ferryboats going past. The clip ends with 'Ol' Man River' as the camera takes in the

Sydney Harbour Bridge and the workers, who respond again with loud, hearty clapping.[40]

There was a huge response when Paul finished singing. After extended applause, the workers 'mobbed Robeson for autographs', presented him with a hard hat and asked him to sign their working gloves, which he did.[41] As he put it the next day, 'they all came up afterwards and just wanted to shake my hand and they had me sign gloves. These were tough guys, and it was a very moving experience.'[42]

The next day saw news of John F Kennedy's election as US president dominate the newspaper headlines, though the *Canberra Times* did include a photograph of Paul singing to the workers on its front page.[43] The conservative tabloid *Daily Telegraph* somewhat ironically provided the only mainstream press story, accompanied by a photograph.[44] *Tribune*, a weekly paper, made a brief mention of the Opera House performance as part of a story on the Robesons' visit to Sydney.[45] The BWIU's own newspaper, *The Building Worker*, briefly listed it as a highlight, together with Paul's singing at WWF meetings, of the Robeson tour.[46] Much more extensive than the print media coverage was the filmed reporting for *Cinesound Review* and by all three television stations operating in Sydney at the time—the ABC, ATN7 and TCN9 (using an excerpt from the Cinesound film). Both the Cinesound and the ABC-TV news films, each of good visual and sound quality, would have a long afterlife, to which I return in the final chapter of this book.

Those present remembered Paul singing at the Opera House site long after, and their stories were often passed down to their family members. One striking example is a speech in the NSW Parliament in 1976 marking Paul's death. John Aquilina, a minister in the NSW Labor government, said his father had been a carpenter working on the Opera House site and had been there that day: 'Dad told us that all the workers—carpenters, concreters and labourers—sang along and that the huge, burly men on the working site were reduced to tears by his presence and his inspiration.'[47] Sometimes the story grows when passed along. When a man asked American folk singer John McCutcheon to sing 'Joe Hill' at a concert in Melbourne in 1988, the man explained: 'I'm an electrician by trade and the biggest job I ever did in my whole life was I helped build the Sydney Opera House.' When Robeson arrived, he continued,

> he called us all down and of course we all came, hundreds of us plumbers, masons, carpenters, electricians like me sitting around on scaffolding and sandbags and all around the ground and this guy sang for like two hours and it was fantastic. His voice filled the harbour. He sang this ['Joe Hill'] as his last song. We all knew it and, you know, without even being invited we started to join in and sing. And guys that I'd grown up with, I'd worked with all my life, were singing away like they were in church with big tears rolling down their cheeks. And it was just one of the greatest days of my life.[48]

Waterside workers at Sydney Town Hall

The next day, Friday, was another big day, with Paul again speaking and singing to the workers. This time it was at a stop-work meeting of about 3000 waterside workers in the Sydney Town Hall, called by the WWF to protest against proposed amendments to the *Crimes Act* that were then before parliament. The union had a tradition of taking an interest in political matters and protesting against various actions of Australia's conservative federal government. Its general secretary since 1937 had been Jim Healy, a towering figure in the Australian trade union world and a member of the CPA, who was especially noted for his pragmatic approach to union matters. The union, like the Communist Party, was extremely concerned by the government's proposal to amend the *Crimes Act* in a way that would restrict its ability to take industrial action on political issues. Attorney-General Sir Garfield Barwick had recently introduced into federal parliament a series of amendments to the Act that defined the crimes of treason, treachery and sabotage in extremely broad terms that would make any public discussion of foreign policy matters open to charges under the Act. The bill was so wide-reaching that Barwick biographer David Marr comments: 'Perhaps no Bill in the history of the Federation contained such complex dangers for the liberty of Australian citizens.'[49]

The proposed amendments were in part a response to the success of the 1959 Peace Congress, and both the peace movement and the trade unions had good reason to fear the government would use the proposed amendments against them.[50] Like many other unions, the WWF had expressed strong opposition to this 'fascist-like law' since early October, and in early November the ACTU had called for rallies against the proposed amendments.[51] The legal profession was generally strongly opposed, and the ALP wanted substantial amendments. Only two days before Paul spoke to the waterside workers, the new ALP leader, Gough Whitlam, had argued forcefully for major changes to the proposed amendments.[52] The campaign was gathering force and Paul's presence at a stop-work meeting would surely be an advantage.[53]

Paul seems to have had a particular affinity with waterside workers, though he was close to miners, too, especially in Wales. This was the second of four such meetings with waterside workers on his Australian and New Zealand tour. Each time, he drew attention to his close connections with longshoremen, the workers' equivalents in the United States. It is interesting, too, to reflect that several of his film roles were as a dockworker—think of *Show Boat*, *Song of Freedom* and *Big Fella*—and his most famous song, 'Ol' Man River', is sung by a dockworker. Three weeks before this meeting in Sydney, he had sung to waterside workers in Wellington, much to their delight.

We can now join him at the Sydney Town Hall, as he sits patiently while the stop-work meeting hears and endorses reports from the union's federal council, given by Healy and the Sydney secretary, Tom Nelson, which takes some considerable time.[54] He is introduced by the Sydney branch president, Jim Young, as a member of the ILWU of America and a personal friend of its Australian-born leader, Harry Bridges.

Once he has the stage, Paul speaks about his connections with the waterside workers on the West Coast of the United States, the importance of peace, and the letters of support he received from Australia while he was unable to travel. He sings 'Joe Hill' and 'Ol' Man River'.[55] At the end of his talk, Paul is presented with gifts and votes of thanks, the gifts including a painting by Aboriginal artist Albert Namatjira, recordings of a radical musical entitled *Reedy River* and of convict and folk songs, copies of Henry Lawson's works, drawings by the WWF Children's Art Group, and an unnamed presentation from the Sydney WWF Women's Committee.[56] Tom Supple of the Waterfront Peace Committee gives a vote of thanks, praising Robeson as one who 'fought in America similar attacks to those planned on the Australian people through the *Crimes Act*'. Later, Paul chats with the workers.

This meeting stayed long in WWF memory. Ralph Sawyer, a waterside worker and artist, later commented, 'I was overawed, he was a giant, he was a *massive* person ... But in his conversation downstairs with the boys, we were all talking to him about his football career and that. He seemed a very gentle person, extremely compassionate and very gentle.'[57] Sawyer's large (2.7 × 2 metres) painting of Paul, completed from photographs hung for many years in the WWF Hall, on one occasion served as a banner on top of the car leading the 1975 Labour Day parade in Sydney.[58]

That evening, when speaking at Paddington Town Hall, Paul gave his own account of how his meeting with the waterside workers had gone:

> This morning I had a chance to sing to, and say hello to, guys that I know very well, workers on the waterfront, workers who have played a magnificent part in the democratic struggles in your country. [Applause.] And I was able to sit in part of the meeting, while my friend Jim Healy was giving us a few ideas there [laughter from audience]. It was like being on the waterfront back in San Francisco or the east coast, because as a youngster who had to start working when he was very young, 14 or 15 to earn a living, whether it be in a brickyard or a hotel, or on the waterfront, wherever it might be, or on a farm ... through the years, in England and Britain, with the Welsh miners, with the dockers in Glasgow, I sort of feel I ... earned my membership in unions ... I feel I can say I'm a good union man. [Applause, cheers.][59]

For many, this was a wonderful event. In an article in the *Maritime Worker* on 1 December, WF Burns wrote: 'The thousands of Sydney wharfies to whom Paul Robeson sang at our last stop work meeting will all agree that they listened to a great man … He made it the best stop work meeting ever.' The author was William Fardon Burns, whom we met in Chapter 3: he had, like Robeson, suffered for expressing support for the Soviet Union at the time of the outbreak of the Korean War. Burns was scornful of the *Daily Telegraph* journalist who a few weeks earlier, just after Paul's first Sydney press conference, had written that he had met Robeson and gone away disappointed. In response, Burns now wrote: 'I met him and went away ready to fight the world.'[60]

9

Two Television Appearances and a Visit to the Theatre

One distinctive feature of the Sydney leg of the tour was that Paul recorded two television programs, both on the ABC. He appears to have given several brief TV interviews in other cities, but only in Sydney was he invited to contribute to longer, pre-recorded programs. Despite his enormous fame and popularity, he had not had extensive experience of television, though he had made an early appearance on British TV on 23 August 1939 singing at the Alexandra Palace, just before he returned to the United States.

The medium had been closed to him through the 1950s in the United States. He had, however, recorded a number of programs in Britain since his return there in mid-1958, including *Val Parnell's Sunday Night at the London Palladium* on ITV.[1] He also made three half-hour programs for ATV entitled *Paul Robeson Sings*, each devoted to a specific musical genre—folk, spirituals and popular songs.[2] There were further television appearances in 1959, twice on a BBC arts program called *Monitor*; for one of these, screened on 12 April, he was interviewed about his performance in *Othello*.[3] An ITV program featuring a conversation between him and violinist Yehudi Menuhin in November 1959 was a huge success.[4] Just before he left London for Australia, Paul hosted and headlined an ITV variety show entitled *Saturday Spectacular*.[5]

Yet he was still fairly new to the medium, and so, too, were Australian viewers, for TV had arrived only four years earlier after considerable hesitation by the socially conservative federal government. In those four years, Australians had taken to television with gusto, watching mainly imported American and British material along with an increasing range of locally made news, discussion and entertainment programs. Paul appeared in an ABC interview program, *Spotlight*, taped on 5 November and broadcast in Sydney and Melbourne at 9 p.m. on Sunday 13 November.[6] The ABC had originally sought a half-hour musical show, but in order to protect attendances at the concerts the promoters insisted Paul could do interview shows only.[7] He would, though, sing in another ABC-TV show, made possible by the fact it would not be shown until Christmas Eve, well after the concert tour was over. This was a children's session, part of a fortnightly music and entertainment program called *Hal Lashwood's Minstrels*, taped on 7 November.[8] These two programs are both of interest, but in quite different ways.

Spotlight

Spotlight typically consisted of a panel of three people with appropriate expertise, together with Alan Manning as chair, questioning and chatting with a featured guest for half an hour. The eighteen people interviewed before Robeson's appearance included academics (historian Asa Briggs, economist Ungku Aziz), poets (Roland Robinson), media figures (Rupert Murdoch), politicians (Robert Askin, Gough Whitlam) and performers (singer and comedian Anna Russell).[9] The panel interviewing Paul consisted of Ronald McKie, Eunice Gardiner and Cecil Robert Quentin, all well known in the arts. McKie was a journalist and author with a particular interest in South-East Asia; Gardiner was a concert pianist and music critic who had hosted both radio and television shows interviewing guests about their music. Quentin, an Englishman, had migrated to Australia five years earlier to assume the position of manager of the Australian Elizabethan Theatre Trust, which would establish many cultural institutions in opera, ballet and orchestra.

He was also professor of drama at the University of New South Wales and the year before this interview had become the founding director of the university's National Institute of Dramatic Art, from which many famous stage and screen actors would later emerge.[10]

The program producer was Englishwoman Joyce Belfrage, who most likely initiated Paul's appearance. On Sunday 13 November, just hours before *Spotlight* appeared on ABC-TV, Paul and Eslanda would have lunch with Joyce and her husband, Bruce, who was the younger brother of Cedric Belfrage, one of the organisers of the British 'Let Robeson Sing' campaign.[11] The couple had been living in Australia for two years. Like Paul, Bruce had been an actor on the London stage and in films in the 1930s. He later became a BBC newsreader and announcer and is remembered most of all for unflappably continuing to read the news while the BBC studio was being bombed around him on 15 October 1940.[12] Joyce had been a radio and television producer with the BBC in the 1950s and was now a TV producer for the ABC, making programs that explored topics such as homelessness, alcoholism and the difficulties facing migrants, including *Inquiry into Migration* in 1960.[13]

The result was an extraordinary program, surely one of the best TV interviews Robeson ever did. Though many of his comments repeat points he often made elsewhere, some arise directly from being in Australia or are prompted by the questions, which are respectful, sometimes knowledgeable, and genuinely curious. When asked how to explain his own achievements, he speaks of the influence of his father, who urged him to get an education, and comments that for peoples who have to fight their way up, 'education becomes life and death'. 'All coloured peoples', he continues, 'in Australia, in New Zealand, if given the opportunity, can be just as cultured.' As he had in Brisbane a few weeks earlier, he made a point of using the term 'Indigenous', saying he had been welcomed by 'the Indigenous peoples of Australia. I don't like to call them Aborigines—I call them the Indigenous people of this country.' There is also a long discussion of musical matters, especially of Paul's ideas about the universality of folk music and its importance for all kinds of music, including symphonic music. He talks at some length about the pentatonic scale, using the black piano keys, and says 90 per cent of folk music rests on those five notes. From time to time in the discussion he breaks into song, singing 'Sometimes I Feel Like a Motherless Child' and snippets from 'Didn't My Lord Deliver Daniel?' and 'Greensleeves'.

Paul comes across as relaxed, a mix of serious and light-hearted. Three minutes of the program are now freely available online, picking up a discussion that comes near the end of the interview when McKie asks how it is that the 'American Negro', treated as a second-class citizen, has contributed so much to American culture. Robeson replies that 'the Africans and the American Negroes have turned out to be an extraordinarily gifted people' and goes on to draw attention to the role of slavery in the development of the wealth of the United States: 'I am an American. Born there, my father slaved there. Upon the backs of my people was developed the primary wealth of America. The primary wealth. You have to have accumulated wealth to start, to build.' He takes the opportunity to highlight Australia's own history of creating wealth by taking from others, referring to taking the land itself: 'You did it another way here in Australia. You had to build your accumulated wealth, too. You just came and took it; you know what I mean? And that's what they did in most of the countries. That's what you Europeans did—you just took it.' Robeson is articulating here a sense of the connections between 'race' and capitalism that we would now describe as racial capitalism—that is, as a system that depends on racial categorisation of people to enhance profit-making and economic expansion.[14]

He returns to the relationship between his African ancestry and American identity:

> But just like a Scottish American is proud of being from Scotland, I'm proud for being African. In our schoolbooks they tried to tell me that all Africans were savages till I got to London and found most of the Africans that I knew were going to Oxford and Cambridge and doing very well and learned their culture … So I would say today that I'm an American who is infinitely proud to be of African descent, no question about it, no question about it.

In the full interview, held in the ABC Archives, there is much else of interest. When asked whether he looked forward to the development of a distinctive African American theatre, he commented: 'I went to see *Porgy and Bess* [the 1959 movie] in Christchurch, New Zealand, and I was deeply moved ... the singing of that chorus, the folk culture that was embedded in this, you know, was simply ... it shows what the theatre could be.'[15] It seems this had been his first chance to see the movie, which had started screening the previous year. In fact, Paul had his own history with *Porgy and Bess*, having acted and sung in the musical play in New York for six weeks in 1928 before leaving for the United Kingdom to perform in *Show Boat*, and he had recorded several songs from the play for HMV in 1938, two of which were released on a record that year.[16] Much later, in 1959, when the movie version appeared, HMV released in the United Kingdom a new record with four songs, possibly from this earlier recording, entitled *Paul Robeson: Highlights of Porgy and Bess*, and subsequently released it in 1960 in Australia, New Zealand and South Africa.[17]

One of the most striking moments comes when Quentin asks Paul what his suffering has taught him. Paul replies at length, saying 'it's a very interesting thing'. Anger at his treatment 'pops out once in a while', and he makes a point of distancing himself from his angry outburst at that first press conference in Sydney: 'It popped out when I first got off the plane here.' Looking at it more generally, he sees his own experience as different from that of most African American people, as he has travelled widely and seen many places. During his years of isolation, he was encouraged by the support he received from around the world, including the hundreds of letters he received from Australia and the enormous support in the United Kingdom with the 'Let Robeson Sing' committee. He knew he was loved in places Americans didn't like, such as the Soviet Union with its 200 million people and China with its 600 million: 'But it was tough, and I got angry ... then I got interested in my music ... I'm writing a book ... So, I sort of stayed with myself, investigating the pentatonic scale, [I'm] called by my friends "Oh, Mr Pentatonic".' The interview ends with Paul talking about the need for Black and white people to get along together—just as in music, where the black and white keys have to play together. His final comment is that he hopes people enjoy his concerts, and 'I've already decided that I'm coming back soon again'.

The *Spotlight* interview was well received. Nan Musgrove, one of the earliest journalists to write extensively about Australian television, observed the recording session and, in her column in the *Australian Women's Weekly*, described it as delightful. Robeson, she wrote, had taken over, making the panel hardly necessary, and talked and sang his way through the half-hour. Paul told Musgrove afterwards how much he had enjoyed the interview, and that he liked TV as a medium.[18] In her tour report, Eslanda commented that many people had praised the interview. His 'friendly and gay (not angry) manner' had done much to mend fences after the disaster of the initial Sydney press conference. Paul had been able to communicate directly with people 'without the interposition of a biased Press', and people came to understand and respect his views. 'It was shown in all the major cities and was said to be the best interview *Spotlight* has ever done. It had a very fine effect.'[19] The interview was so successful that the ABC planned a re-broadcast for 29 November, but later abruptly cancelled it, apparently for political reasons.[20]

Local commentators were enthusiastic. The Melbourne newspaper *The Age* said that Paul Robeson had been a trump card for Channel 2.[21] A column entitled 'Close-Up with Dolly Shot' in *TV Week* (hardly a left-wing journal) gave it a rave review, commenting, 'What a rare giant of a man is Paul Robeson' and, 'A rich deep voice, a *summa cum laude* mind, and a soul as compassionate as a mother's hand, filled this half hour with warmth, enthusiasm and understanding.' The column noted that Paul moved easily between speech and singing; he sang to illustrate a point, make his meaning clearer, or because 'that is what he was born to do'. Apparently uninhibited by the contractual restrictions that made it impossible for most overseas artists to sing during guest appearances on television, he 'studded his replies with jewelled chunks of song', such as 'Sometimes I Feel Like a Motherless Child', 'Going Home' and several others 'that made his material rich'.

The review ends: 'A great sad man has stepped into our lives and we shall not forget him.'[22]

Paul's *Spotlight* interview is of special interest now, as the three-minute segment from it on YouTube continues to attract attention. It also remains on the Australian ABC Education website as number 10 in a series of programs used for educational purposes headed 'Becoming Equal in the USA'.[23]

Hal Lashwood's Minstrels

Two days later, on Monday 7 November, Eslanda, having recovered from illness over the previous couple of days, accompanied Paul to his second television recording session. They met with Hal Lashwood, who wished to record with Paul a program for his regular show on ABC-TV.

Lashwood was an important figure in early Australian television, having been a vaudeville performer, dancer and radio and theatre entertainer before becoming a TV host soon after television began. He was also president of the Actors and Announcers Equity Association of Australia, a role he had taken up in 1951 and would hold for twenty-five years. Lashwood saw clearly and early the entertainment possibilities offered by TV, and even before it arrived in Australia he was a fierce advocate for ensuring it had significant Australian content. In September 1952 he had helped form the Australian Culture Defence Movement (ACDM), based in Melbourne, which argued to the Royal Commission on Television in 1953 the case for a solely national television system and for protection of Australian artists and cultural workers within that system. Other members of the ACDM included left-wing organisations—sometimes with some communist influence—such as the Fellowship of Australian Writers, the Children's National Theatre, the Australian Songwriters and Composers' Association and the Australian Journalists Association.[24] In 1954 Lashwood published an article in the literary journal *Meanjin* entitled 'Television and Australia', emphasising the entertainment possibilities of the medium and the responsibility to use it wisely; and in 1955 he stood unsuccessfully for parliament on this issue.[25] His close association with communist-led peace and cultural activities in the early 1950s had earned him the attention of ASIO, which in December 1959 noted that at a welcome organised by the Australia-Soviet Friendship Society for visiting Soviet artists, he had spoken on the importance of cultural exchange between Australia and the Soviet Union.[26]

The program on which Lashwood invited Paul Robeson to appear was the Christmas edition of *Hal Lashwood's Minstrels*, an ABC variety series that had started as *Alabama Jubilee* in March 1958 and been renamed *Hal Lashwood's Minstrels* in July 1960. It typically featured white performers in blackface make-up.[27] It is puzzling to modern audiences that someone with progressive politics would choose blackface minstrelsy when developing television light entertainment. Part of the explanation may come from the fact that Lashwood had grown up in a minstrelsy world. His father, an Englishman who migrated to Australia as a young man in the early twentieth century, was, as *ABC Weekly* records, 'a cornerman in many minstrel shows such as Fullers, Rickards and Clays, and was recognised as one of the greatest bones' players in the world'.[28] Bones players, who initially used animal bones to make a clacking sound but later used wooden or bone-shaped sticks, had been prominent in minstrelsy since the nineteenth century. In both Britain and Australia in the late 1950s, this older minstrelsy and blackface tradition was moving to television. In September 1957, the BBC broadcast a successful discrete one-hour program, *The 1957 Television Minstrels*, and on 14 June 1958, three months after Lashwood developed the *Alabama Jubilee* show for the ABC, the BBC began a twenty-year run of the hugely popular *Black and White Minstrel Show*. It involved, as historian Christine Grandy explains, a 'mix of highly choreographed dance pieces, regular solo performances by blacked-up minstrels Leslie Crowther and George Chisholm, and guest appearances by comedians, actors, and singers who did not don blackface'.[29] Though minstrelsy in blackface is now recognised as profoundly offensive, there appears to have been little recognition of its offensiveness in either Britain or Australia in 1960; this would change as the decade progressed.

So how did Paul Robeson come to appear as a guest on a minstrel show involving extensive blackface on Australian television in 1960? He certainly shared the African American opposition to blackface that had made the practice taboo in American culture by the 1960s.[30] In the ABC documentary *Paul Robeson in Australia*, made in 1978, Lashwood describes both the program and his invitation to Paul to be a part of it. He says that when he mentioned to Paul that he had his own TV show and it was a minstrel show, Paul was shocked, since minstrelsy denigrated and made fun of African Americans. Lashwood explains his own approach to minstrelsy, which involved white men blackening their skin but doing so to address the sufferings of Black people:

> I told him my minstrel show was different from the other types of minstrel shows in which they all had these large white mouths and white rings around the eyes and rolling eyes. I told him that we were blackened up completely and I wrote the introductions, and the introductions to the songs spoke of the sufferings of the Black Americans and that I used a lot of working songs and spirituals and gospel in the show.

Lashwood also explains that what he wanted Robeson to do was 'be seated on a stool and I'd like you to be speaking to six little children—two Aborigines, a boy and a girl; two Asians, a boy and a girl; and two white children'. He'd like Paul to 'talk about peace and the need for people to come together of all races and colours and creeds, and the need for peace and love amongst all people'. He continues: 'Well, without any further consideration he said I'll do it. We didn't even discuss whether there was a fee attached to it.'

Paul and Eslanda went to the ABC studios on Monday 7 November 1960 to record Paul's segment of *Hal Lashwood's Minstrels*. Among those observing the recording along with Eslanda was the indefatigable Nan Musgrove from the *Women's Weekly*; her subsequent story was accompanied by an excellent colour photo of Paul with the children and another of Eslanda watching the performance. Musgrove loved the show; 'Robeson', she wrote, 'was in wonderful form'.[31] Also present was a reporter from *The Biz*, a variety magazine that published a detailed summary of the performance shortly before the ABC screened it on Christmas Eve.[32]

On 7 November 2022, sixty-two years later, at the Sydney branch of the NFSA, I watched the thirty-minute episode of *Hal Lashwood's Minstrels* in which Paul appears.[33] The archivist warned me that I would see a lot of blackface, and indeed I did. The performers, all seemingly white men and women, were all in blackface and played stock minstrel characters. Lashwood is 'Mr Interlocutor', traditionally the host in minstrel shows and dressed a little more formally than the others with a high hat, though he shares the white gloves they nearly all wear. He introduces the other performers, who perform a jolly group rendition of 'Jingle Bells', followed by 'Miss Sunshine' (a character played by Peggy Mortimer, a popular singer, variety performer and pantomime actor) singing 'Santa Claus is Coming to Town'. Next, 'Mr Melody', wearing a huge striped bow, sings 'Little Donkey', a new Christmas song written the previous year by Eric Boswell, a British songwriter, evoking Mary's journey to Bethlehem. 'Mr Melody' was Neil Williams, a versatile performer who would two years later become best known for singing the jingle in the extremely popular 'Louie the Fly' advertisement for the pest control brand Mortein.

To this point in the program, the singers, though all in blackface, do not have the large white mouths typical of the genre, just as Lashwood had said. The next act, though, is 'Mr Dixie', who has a huge white mouth, much closer to the stereotypical image we associate with minstrelsy in blackface. Performed by Dave Wheeler, a seasoned vaudeville performer, 'Mr Dixie' sings 'Jingle Bell Rock', another recently composed Christmas song, this time from the United States. The interlocutor reminds the audience that Christmas is a time to celebrate and remember the importance of peace on earth and goodwill to all. Jesus Christ, he says, advocated peace, and so should we. The longest song comes next, and that is 'Mary's Boy Child', first recorded by Harry Belafonte in 1956, which had become hugely popular in the United Kingdom. On *Hal Lashwood's Minstrels*, Helen Lorain playing 'Miss Carolina' sings it wearing a headscarf, suggesting Mary as a peasant woman. In quite a different register,

Sydney Haylen appears as 'Uncle Bones', the second minstrel character to be represented with a huge white mouth; he is dressed in a loose checked jacket and trousers, suggesting a clown figure. Haylen had performed in vaudeville with Lashwood and would later become a very well-known actor on Australian television; his song, 'Little Red Riding Hood', was a nonsense song resting on spoonerisms such as 'Little Red Hooding Ride'. 'Miss Sunshine' and 'Mr Melody' then return with 'The Christmas Story', the last song before Robeson appears.

At last Lashwood as 'Mr Interlocutor' introduces Paul Robeson, expressing his delight in being able to welcome such a 'world-famous actor and singer', who is in his field 'the greatest the world has ever known'. He is not only a great man, says Lashwood, but a great scholar and, more importantly, humanitarian. This would be, he said, Robeson's 'only appearance on Australian television as an artist'. We then see Paul sitting on a chair and facing a row of Australian children. They were, we know from the report in *The Biz,* Anglo-Australians Cam Webber and Amanda Alcock, Chinese-Australian brother and sister Mark and Amanda Jong, and Aboriginal children Noel Murray and Fay Groves. (Fay was very likely related to Bert Groves, a leading figure in Aboriginal protest for several decades and a member of the Aboriginal-Australian Fellowship.)[34]

Paul's performance is remarkable for its warmth and focus on the children. He begins by speaking affectionately of his own grandchildren, Susan and David, saying, 'I miss them very much.' He sings a Mexican lullaby, first in English and then in Spanish, saying as it ends that 'by that time, little Susan should be fast asleep'. He then addresses the children, saying how wonderful it is to meet children from diverse groups of people, 'because, you know, in America where I come from people came from all parts of the earth to build it. You know my people came from a land called Africa, wonderful people, and we helped build America like your parents helped build Australia.' He mentions a little Chinese song that he helped write 'and I'm very proud of that', which may be a reference to the song that became the Chinese national anthem; and then speaks of his interest in Australian songs, especially those by 'a wonderful composer named Mr Hill'.

He seems to be referring here to Alfred Hill, an Australian-New Zealand composer who had died just the week before. Hill composed extensively and in many genres but is now best remembered for a short song, 'Waiata Poi', inspired by Māori music; it is possible that Paul had learned of him through obituaries published while he was performing in New Zealand. Having mentioned Hill, Paul says, 'I just came from New Zealand incidentally, where I saw some very interesting people too, some Māori people and had wonderful concerts over there.'[35]

As he sings the next song, the popular gospel 'Get On Board, Little Children', Paul encourages three of the children—Fay, Mark and Cam—to stand beside him. Then, after reciting a little *Macbeth*, he asks them to tell him some stories or what they want for Christmas, but they are too shy to speak. Still seeking to engage with the children, he talks about how much he loves looking at little lambs from train windows and then recites the last two lines of the first verse and the whole of the second verse of William Blake's 'The Lamb'—'Little Lamb who made thee?/ Dost thou know who made thee? … Little Lamb I'll tell thee/ He is called by thy name … Little Lamb God bless thee'.[36] Paul explains that in this poem 'we are talking about a very wonderful person who lived on this earth. He was like a little lamb, sweet and wouldn't hurt anybody.'[37] After singing 'Silent Night', with its famous line 'Sleep in heavenly peace', Paul asks, 'Wouldn't it be wonderful if—I think of my little grandchildren and you—if all the people on earth can just sleep and rest forever?' He says to the children:

> You go home and tell your parents, you know, I think we can live in a world where all the children like us are friendly. We can get along in peace and we must work for that because we don't want to live in a world that isn't here, we want to live in a nice world. You tell 'em I said that.

He ends with the words: 'I've had a wonderful time with you and when I come back to Australia I'll come and see you and we'll gather together again once more. Thank you very much, you've made me very, very happy. And say hello from me to all the folks in Australia. Bye.'[38]

The ABC screened the program on 24 December, long after the Robesons had returned home, and it is probable that they never saw it.[39] *Hal Lashwood's Minstrels* would not last much longer, the ABC discontinuing it in August 1961. Minstrelsy, however, retained a following for several more decades. In 1962, a stage version of the British *Black and White Minstrel Show*, with British principal artists and Australian singers and dancers, successfully toured Australia and New Zealand.[40] In Britain, complaints by Caribbean immigrants and others from the late 1960s led to extensive debates and finally, in 1978, cancellation of the TV show. Until the late 1980s, however, old episodes were screened on Australian television and the stage version toured the country with little public criticism; and as screenwriter and playwright Stephen Vagg points out, while blackface became rare in Australian-produced television drama after 1973, it continued to thrive in TV comedy until very recently.[41]

An evening at New Theatre

Paul's background in theatre would lead to another memorable cultural event towards the end of his visit to Sydney. On Sunday 13 November, Bill Morrow escorted him and Eslanda to the WWF Hall to see a performance of Arthur Miller's *All My Sons*.

New Theatre was a left-wing theatre similar to the Unity Theatre in Britain, with which Paul was familiar. Formed in 1935 by a group including Herbert Marshall, whom Paul had met in Moscow in 1934,[42] Unity had featured Paul in the leading role in its third play, *Plant in the Sun*, about Black and white workers conducting a sit-down strike.[43] In Australia, New Theatre was a thriving part of mid-twentieth-century left-wing cultural activism that was both locally attentive and interested in other cultures.[44] Formed in Sydney in 1932 (Melbourne followed in 1935, Brisbane and Perth in 1936 and Adelaide in 1937), it shared Unity's left-wing politics and emphasis on volunteer labour (Paul had performed for free). The Melbourne branch produced *Plant in the Sun* in 1939 as a curtain-raiser for a new anti-war Australian play by Catherine Duncan, *The Sword Sung*.[45] New Theatre also had strong trade union connections, having played in 1942 songs in praise of union leader Harry Bridges.[46] Its most successful enterprise was the musical *Reedy River* by Dick Diamond, based on events after the defeat of a major shearers' strike in 1891, first performed in Melbourne in March 1953 and attracting 450,000 paying customers in subsequent years.[47]

New Theatre had long admired Robeson, sometimes playing records of his before a performance—such as in 1941, when it preceded performances of Clifford Odets' play *Till the Day I Die* with a record of Robeson singing 'Arise, arise ye who refuse to be bond slaves', otherwise known as 'March of the Volunteers', the song that would in 1978 become the Chinese national anthem. The theatre followed his travails during the 1950s, and in April 1958, shortly before he regained his passport, the New Theatre national conference sent him greetings for his sixtieth birthday.[48] The theatre's energetic secretary was Miriam Hampson, who, like many of those involved in New Theatre, was a member of the CPA.[49] In August she had written without success to Harry Belafonte, then touring Australia, inviting him to see the performance.[50] She was absolutely delighted when, a couple of months later, the Robesons accepted. Hampson had been present when Paul sang at the Opera House site, and afterwards escorted him to a well-known seafood restaurant named Doyles at Watsons Bay (we see the restaurant in the documentary film). The reaction to his presence there, she recalled, was 'absolutely electric', with many people speaking to him in appreciation of his films and music.[51]

All My Sons was an appropriate play to present to the Robesons. Its criticism of America had brought Arthur Miller before the HUAC on 21 June 1956, nine days after Paul himself had appeared. It concerns two business partners who manufacture aircraft parts during World War II; when one batch is faulty, the senior partner, Joe Keller, nevertheless dispatches it, resulting in a substantial loss of life. His innocent junior partner is gaoled but Joe is wrongly exonerated and continues to live a very comfortable life, justifying his actions to himself that he owed it to his family to save the business. Finally, his adult son forces him to recognise that he is responsible not only to his family but to everyone else as well—that is, to all his sons. Miller's first theatrical success, the play had its opening performance in New York in 1947 and was performed frequently thereafter, as it is today.[52] This production of *All My Sons* was significant for New Theatre also because it saw the end of a mainstream press boycott on reviewing its plays. As a communist-influenced organisation, it had for thirteen years been unable to gain reviews. Now, its long campaign to end the boycott finally succeeded when the *Sydney Morning Herald* sent its main theatre reviewer, Lindsay Browne, to the opening night of *All My Sons*. Hampson was amazed; as she later wrote to a friend, 'I didn't believe it till I saw Lindsay Browne walk through the door.'[53]

When Paul and Eslanda came to New Theatre, they saw a packed-out performance. It was presented especially for them, as the play's run had ended a few weeks earlier. Hampson was an indefatigable organiser and had invited many in Sydney's theatre world to attend; acceptances included some well-known figures, including actor Ron Haddrick, theatre entrepreneur Hayes Gordon, and theatre publicist and arts administrator Noel Pelly. One member of the theatre's management committee had suggested they invite Margaret Fulton to prepare the supper.[54] This is an interesting detail, as Fulton played a role in Australia somewhat similar to that of Julia Child in the United States or Elizabeth David in the United Kingdom in helping to transform Australians' cooking skills and food knowledge and introducing them to a wide range of world cuisines. Eight years later, she would become the author of the bestselling *Margaret Fulton Cookbook*. At the time the Robesons visited, Fulton had recently married New Theatre actor and member of its management committee Denis Doonan. She had also recently become food writer for the popular magazine *Woman's Day*, a position she would hold for nineteen years. It is unclear whether Fulton did help with the supper; the report in the theatre's newsletter simply thanks 'the good ladies who prepared the supper' and she didn't mention doing so when years later she recalled meeting Paul at New Theatre.[55] 'On meeting Paul Robeson,' she wrote in her autobiography, 'I shook hands with him and remarked that I didn't think that I would ever see this day. "Nor did I", was his simple reply. For me it was an unforgettable moment.'[56]

The presence of Paul and Eslanda at *All My Sons* was a thrill for many.[57] At the post-performance ceremony, Paul spoke first to the audience about 'culture and its place in a socialist society' and then later to the actors about his stage experiences. He said he would write to Miller and tell him this performance had 'a clear ring of truth'.[58] In his report on the event in the theatre's newsletter, actor Mark McManus described Paul's comments as 'informal, pleasant, informative'. Paul, he said, spoke about the language of the people, and to 'demonstrate the power of simple language he quoted lines from Shakespeare'. These lines, Paul said, showed 'the simplicity and timeless force of that dialect, sprung direct from the people of Warwickshire'. Characteristically, he also drew a parallel between the yeomen of Shakespeare's England and the Russian peasant tongue of Pushkin's play *Boris Godunov*.[59] McManus concluded, 'It is a night the theatre will long remember.' He was not wrong. There is mention of the visit on the theatre's website today, almost seven decades later.[60]

10

'I wept and wept'

Sydney and Aboriginal Rights

AUSTRALIANS SHOWERED PAUL and Eslanda with Aboriginal gifts throughout their tour. Mainly given by non-Aboriginal people, they were a sign of support for Aboriginal people and their campaigns and included books, handicrafts in Australian wood, boomerangs, woomeras and other Aboriginal artefacts, necklaces, rugs, and much else.

A group of people from Randwick and Coogee (two adjacent eastern Sydney suburbs), autographed and gave Paul a copy of a well-known book by Daisy Bates entitled *The Passing of the Aborigines* (1957).[1] New Theatre gave Paul a 'real boomerang', possibly so described to differentiate it from the boomerangs produced specifically for the tourist trade, and in Adelaide the Waterside Workers' Federation would give Paul 'an authentic woomera throwing stick', which would 'remind him of his desire to learn more about the problems of the old Australians in our midst'.[2]

As *Tribune* commented:

> Everywhere gifts were showered on them—drawings from the wharfies' Children's Art Club—Australian handicrafts in Australian wood,—Australian books,—Australian music. The gifts came from the unions, women's committees, the Union of Australian Women, the Communist Party, the Eureka Youth League, the Junior Eureka League,

> Aborigines, the peace movement and from individuals who wanted to express their solidarity with Mr and Mrs Robeson in the struggle.[3]

The most frequently given gift of all, however, was a print of a painting by well-known Aboriginal artist Albert Namatjira. Lord Mayor Harry Jensen and Jim Young, president of the Sydney branch of the WWF, both gave them Namatjira painting prints, and there were many more as the tour progressed.

The Namatjira paintings told a complex story. On the one hand, they were evidence of Aboriginal artistic achievement and acceptance: Namatjira was an Arrernte man whose watercolour paintings of Central Australian landscapes had been extremely popular since the 1930s, leading to many a print on the walls of Australian homes. In the film documentary *Paul Robeson in Australia*, Jensen says he chose the Namatjira painting because he saw similarities between the two men as gifted representatives of their people. On the other hand, the paintings hinted at the tragic story of Namatjira himself. In the Northern Territory, where he lived, there were laws at that time that made most Aboriginal people wards of the state, with limited legal rights and thus subject to oppressive government regulation. The government could grant an exemption to individuals who could claim to be 'assimilated' to general community 'standards', allowing them the same legal rights as non-Aboriginal people. These newly achieved rights included the right to vote, to marry without needing government permission, and to obtain alcohol—all rights denied to wards of the state. Namatjira had been granted an exemption in 1957 but in 1958 was sentenced to three months gaol for supplying wine to a relative who was not exempt.[4]

During the trial and after Namatjira was sentenced, there was a widespread public outcry and some soul-searching about the racial inequality his case revealed. Protests came from left-wing unions such as the Seamen's Union and the BWIU, both of which subsequently welcomed the Robesons. Further protests came from a wide variety of organisations and concerned individuals. Noel Counihan, the Australian artist who had been present when Robeson spoke and sang at the Paris Peace Congress in 1949, coordinated a letter of protest against Namatjira's imprisonment from twelve eminent Australian artists, including John Perceval, John Brack, Charles Bush, Arthur Boyd and Clifton Pugh.[5] For health and humanitarian reasons, Namatjira was released after serving two months of his sentence; in August 1959, six months later, he died of heart failure, to the concern and distress of many. His case became a symbol of what was wrong with current discriminatory policies, leading many people to express support for Aboriginal rights through purchase and display of his paintings and, more often, of Namatjira prints.[6]

From the beginning of the tour, when Paul and Eslanda spent a few hours on a stopover at Darwin Airport, they expressed their desire to meet Aboriginal people and learn more about their struggles. Especially important for developing a connection between the Robesons and Aboriginal people and organisations was Faith Bandler, an Australian of Pacific Islander descent. In Sydney, Bill Morrow had the role of managing Paul's non-concert-related activities, but it was Bandler who ensured that Aboriginal matters came to the Robesons' attention. She grew up aware that her father had been an indentured labourer from Ambrym Island (now part of Vanuatu) who was brought to Australia to work in Queensland's emerging sugar industry in slave-like conditions. She and her brothers were keenly aware of the situation of Aboriginal people and the civil rights struggles of African Americans. A long-time admirer of Paul, Bandler had a good singing voice herself and later recalled that the first movie she ever saw was *Show Boat* and that she and her brothers 'used to save up to buy a record of Paul Robeson's and we would all sing with him, as well as singing the songs of his people'.[7]

Bandler was secretary of the Aboriginal-Australian Fellowship (AAF), an organisation she and Aboriginal woman Pearl Gibbs had co-founded in 1956.[8] It sought a range of changes to government policies and social practices in New South Wales: freedom of movement to and from the reserves; equal access to education, decent housing and medical services; and especially freedom from the petty police surveillance that governed their lives. Its members wanted the freedom to maintain family life, and to end the pernicious system where governments granted full citizenship rights only to those who had acquired an exemption certificate (Aboriginal people contemptuously nicknamed it the 'dog tag'), which in effect required the cutting of all family ties.[9] The AAF was active in the ultimately successful campaign for the 'Yes' vote in the referendum of 1967 to change the Australian Constitution to allow the federal government to legislate on Aboriginal matters and to include Aboriginal people in the census. When the Robesons arrived, the campaign, which had begun in 1957, was gathering momentum.[10]

A film viewing

Bandler and a company named Marngoo Films arranged for Paul and Eslanda a private viewing of two short films about Aboriginal conditions and struggles. They were screened in the function room of the Hotel Australia, where the Robesons were staying, on the afternoon of Thursday 10 November, just after Paul had spoken and sung to the waterside workers at Sydney Town Hall. Those present included Bandler; Helen Hambly, a non-Aboriginal member of the AAF and a shareholder in Marngoo Films; Alec Robertson, reporting for *Tribune*; documentary filmmaker Cecil Holmes with his wife, Sandra Le Brun Holmes; and the writer Frank Hardy.[11] These films would have a major effect on the Robesons and their tour.

Both films concerned Aboriginal groups in Western Australia. The first was *Manslaughter*, sometimes referred to as *Their Darkest Hour*, which Western Australian MP Bill Grayden had made three years earlier. It contained confronting images of Aboriginal poverty, starvation, injury and disease in the Warburton Ranges and Purli Yurliya (Rawlinson Ranges) in the Central Aborigines Reserve, now known as the Ngaanyatjarra lands. The film had been prompted by the Australian Government's authorisation of British nuclear testing on Australian soil, on land in the western part of South Australia called Maralinga. The tests would affect Aboriginal people in both South Australia and Western Australia. Grayden, an 'independent Liberal' member of the WA state parliament, became concerned with the plight and possible impact of the tests on the Wongi (Wangkatha) people of the Warburton Ranges, a mountain range north-west of Maralinga, on the WA side of the border. He said in parliament that it would prove difficult to warn the 800 Aboriginal people who lived and moved on the large area on both sides of the border of the dangers of radiation.[12] The way of life of the Wongi was threatened also by the building of a weather station on their land, and by mining projects authorised by the WA and SA governments.

The tests were held from 27 September to 22 October 1956. As they were ending, Grayden successfully pressed on 17 October for an inquiry by the WA Parliament into 'Native Welfare Conditions in the Laverton-Warburton Range Area'. The resulting inquiry report in December 1956 was extremely critical of the condition of Aboriginal people in that area. Its findings were publicised first by *Tribune* and then the mainstream press, shocking many with its description of starvation and extreme deprivation. It was, however, strongly criticised by two Rupert Murdoch–owned papers, the *Sunday Times* in Perth and *The News* in Adelaide, for giving a misleading and exaggerated account. In response to his critics, Grayden returned to the area in February 1957 with a movie camera, accompanied by other WA parliamentarians and, crucially, by Melbourne-based pastor Doug Nicholls, leader of the Aboriginal Church of Christ in Gore Street, Fitzroy and an outspoken activist for Aboriginal rights.[13] Nicholls later told journalists, 'I wish I had not gone to the Warburton Ranges. I wish I hadn't seen the pitiable squalor, the sights of my people starving—the most shocking sights I have ever seen. Never, never can I forget.'[14]

Nicholls was not the only one to find the filmed scenes shocking. With its depictions of Aboriginal dislocation and poverty in the wake of the Maralinga tests, the film had by late 1960, when Paul and Eslanda saw it, shocked and troubled audiences across Australia. Activists had been using it to alert other Australians to the injustices experienced by Aboriginal people and to press governments to take greater responsibility.[15] In Sydney, the AAF had screened it many times, including at a Sydney Town Hall meeting in April 1957 inaugurating the campaign for a referendum to change the Australian Constitution. Television stations in Sydney and Melbourne screened it in May 1957.[16] Screenings were usually to non-Aboriginal audiences, but in September 1957, AAF members had shown it to a meeting in the small NSW town of Walgett, which about forty Aboriginal people attended; half of those present signed the AAF petition requesting a change to the Constitution.[17]

Though *Manslaughter* did give impetus to the emergence of Aboriginal advancement leagues around the country, it is important to note that it did not present the views of the Yarnangu ('Yarnangu' being the Ngaanyatjarra term for Aboriginal people) about their own lives or about their being filmed in this way. Today, Yarnangu regard the film as a gross invasion of privacy. Anthropologists Pam McGrath and David Brooks point out that Yarnangu both then and since have sought to stress their own agency and choices rather than the film's portrayal of them as victims of government neglect.[18] On their request, the ABC no longer makes the footage available to the public.

The second film was *People of Pindan*, which Cecil Holmes had made earlier that year as a pilot for a larger film project provisionally entitled *The Flung Spear*. Holmes was a New Zealander who had migrated to Australia in 1949 and worked in the film industry as a director, writer and producer. As a left-wing filmmaker he often had trouble having his projects funded, but he had directed bushranger film *Captain Thunderbolt* (1953) and, with photographer Ross Wood, had made a three-part feature, *Three in One*, based on stories by Henry Lawson and Frank Hardy (1957).[19]

In an article in the Melbourne *Age* two days after the private screening for the Robesons, Holmes talked about the gestation of the pilot and his plans for the longer film. Influenced by novelist Gavin Casey and filmmaker Paul Rotha (a leading figure in the British documentary film movement who visited Australia in 1958), he had wanted to make a film on an Aboriginal subject 'truthful and non-partisan, yet passionate and angry'. Casey had alerted Holmes to the cooperative movement that was becoming popular among Aboriginal people in Western Australia, Queensland, South Australia and New South Wales, and especially to the mining cooperative at Port Hedland as evoked in Donald Stuart's novel *Yandy*.[20] That cooperative, known as the Pindan Cooperative, was formed in the aftermath of the Pilbara pastoral workers' strike of 1946–49 led by tribal elders Clancy McKenna and Dooley Bin Bin along with white man Don McLeod.[21] Holmes describes how in late 1959 and early 1960 he had visited the Pindan community, 'a thousand miles [1600 kilometres] north of Perth and a thousand below Darwin', where he 'stayed at the Aboriginal camps, sat all night listening to their songs, watched their corroborees by the streaming bonfires', made a short film, and 'took hundreds of stills and some hours of tape recordings'. When he returned to Sydney, he met with people and organisations concerned with Aboriginal rights and, after discussion, helped form Marngoo Films Limited in order to make an hour-long colour picture suitable for television. In this article Holmes is enthusiastic about the forthcoming film, which he hopes will 'penetrate the hearts and minds of the Australian people'.[22] As it turned out, the company could never raise sufficient funds and *The Flung Spear* was never made. The pilot that the Robesons saw was, however, later sold to the ABC.[23]

We have several descriptions of Paul's response to these films. They mainly concern reactions to *Manslaughter*. Sandra Holmes says in her autobiography that when Paul saw *Manslaughter* he was 'angry and upset'. 'He stood up and, throwing his cap on the ground, said, "You, all of you are to blame for letting this happen." Then he hastened to add that he was not referring to us and could see that we were trying to do something about it.'[24] *Tribune* reporter Robertson also reported Paul's reaction to the two films:

> When he saw two films—one showing the misery of tribal aborigines in a WA desert reserve, and the other showing confident and healthy tribal aborigines running their own mining cooperative at Pindan—Robeson was beside himself with anger, compassion and determination to arouse more international action to assist the emancipation struggle of those he calls 'the indigenous people of Australia'. 'Why are you Australians tolerating that?' Robeson

> demanded. 'This is unbelievable. There is nothing primitive about these people's ability. There are no backward people anywhere—only people held back or forced back, by "overlords".'[25]

Bandler recalled the event over thirty years later, giving a graphic description that has been much quoted since.[26] It refers only to *Manslaughter* and does not mention *People of Pindan*.

> I shall never forget his reaction to that film, never ... as he watched the film the tears came to his eyes and when the film finished he stood up and he pulled his cap off and he threw it in his rage on the floor and trod on it and he asked for a cigarette from someone. Well, a lot of people smoked in those days so there was no shortage of cigarettes and Eslanda said to me, 'Well it's many years since I've seen him do that.' He was so angry, and he said to me, 'I'll go away now, but when I come back, I'll give you a hand.' He was beautiful, but he died, and he didn't come back.[27]

While both Bandler and Robertson focused in their comments on Paul's reaction, Eslanda was shaken too, and the film would influence the Robesons' thinking and actions for the rest of the tour. Their anger would be clearly evident just a few hours later at Paddington Town Hall.

Speaking at Paddington Town Hall

The meeting at Paddington Town Hall on 10 November was organised jointly by the Peace Council and the AAF. It had been well planned and organised; 1500 people were reported present, including about thirty Aboriginal people whom the AAF had helped to attend.[28] The organisers had worked hard to publicise the event, and invitations headed 'Meet the Robesons' featured both Paul and Eslanda. Those wishing to attend had to apply and to pay in advance for the souvenir programme.[29] Though the organisers attempted to ban the press from attending, as this was technically a private rather than a public event, a *Sunday Mirror* reporter was there. He or she noted that while the function was 'communist-inspired', it was attended by 'many non-communist trade union officials and well-known people from various walks of life'.[30] An ASIO agent who was present listed by name thirty-six of those attending, including some we have already met, like Hal Lashwood, who was master of ceremonies, Alec Robertson, Bill Morrow and Faith Bandler.[31] Jack Tarlington, Sydney organiser of the BWIU, was also there, along with his wife, June.[32]

One of the Aboriginal people whom Paul met at this meeting was sixty-year-old Charles Leon.[33] A Worimi man from the NSW mid north coast, Leon had in his youth been a dancer and vaudevillian. Later he had moved to Sydney, where he became a builders' labourer and a political activist. He joined the CPA but, like many others, left it in the mid-1950s. In 1956 he joined the AAF, becoming in 1958 its president.[34] Almost the same age as Paul, one can imagine they would have had a lot to discuss.

Paul spoke and sang, and Eslanda also spoke. BWIU organiser Tom McDonald later recalled:

> The place was crowded, and he performed solo for a couple of hours without any musical instruments and it was one of the most remarkable performances by an individual I can recall. What he did was, you know, he talked about some of the struggles he'd been involved in. He'd then recite a bit of poetry. He'd then say a bit about his philosophies.[35]

Ernie Boatswain, the assistant national secretary of the BWIU who had helped bring Paul to the Opera House the day before, told journalist Bob Evans thirty-seven years later:

> The main hall was pretty well packed. We had everyone sitting at tables so we could all see and when the time came to sing, Paul just stood up at the table up the front. He was a pretty big guy and very serious. He was in his 60s by then but he still held deeply felt convictions. There was no doubt about that. He didn't talk about war and oppression on the basis of complex theories. He talked about how it was for people.[36]

The *Seamen's Journal* printed the full text of Paul's speech, and the organisers distributed a recording.[37] Paul says he was glad to learn that the struggle for 'the freedom of my people has meant that much to you so far away' and stresses the importance of making our voices heard 'in order to see that there will be peace in our time, that our children and grandchildren can live in prosperity and progress'. After singing 'Didn't My Lord Deliver Daniel?', 'Water Boy' and 'Joe Hill', he recites the Langston Hughes poem 'Freedom Train', introducing it by talking about Jim Crow. He then speaks about being born in America of a slave father in a white civilisation and since he was four or five feeling he had to prove something. When he was trapped in the United States, in Harlem, he saw what was happening at Little Rock on TV. He saw children leading the struggle: 'I knew what the children were carrying because I carried it at their age. And now the older ones, youngsters sitting down in Woolworths Stores [referring to the Greensboro lunch counter demonstrations earlier that year], are the youth carrying this burden.'

Paul then turns to the question of Aboriginal rights, first by critiquing the notion of 'backwardness'. 'They will tell you', he says, 'that Africans are savages', and goes on: 'As a boy I looked at my father [and thought] is someone going to tell me my father is a savage, that my father is not a human person?' He explains, as he so often did, why he was so much a supporter of the Soviet Union. In 1934 he had visited there, and 'lo and behold I did not feel myself a black man any longer, I just felt myself a man.' Paul then comes to a crucial point:

> You have a serious problem here, and I am going to have to come back and help join up. I looked at a couple of pictures [movies] today and read in your books about some 'backward people' who had been shunted off into the centre of Australia. And then [referring to *People of Pindan*], I saw a picture of the Cooperative and I looked at the man and he looked just as intelligent to me as any man I ever saw, and he was running the Cooperative and so forth.

He then referred to his meeting Samoyedic people in Soviet Asia:

> I read about the people called the Samoyeds, a very backward people in 1917 when there was a revolution. In 1934 I saw these people in the universities and know they had fisheries in the Arctic. And one

> thing I learnt in the Soviet Union is that there is no such thing as a backward People, but that it is only society which can force people to be backward.[38]

The critique of the notions of 'primitive' and 'backward' that Paul had first developed in the Soviet Union had been a continuing theme in his essays and speeches for years afterwards.[39] Now, in Sydney, he again finds it important to critique the notion of backwardness and to express his belief that Indigenous peoples can rapidly participate in modern industrial and agricultural societies. Turning to the Aboriginal struggle, he says:

> I am coming back I hope very soon, and I am going to join in the struggle for peace, in the struggle for friendship of all peoples and in the struggle in Australia to see that my brothers and sisters in the centre of this earth, in the centre of this country, can grow to human beings. I know you help them and thank you from the depth of my heart, but I assure you when I saw that picture today, I wept and wept.

As the *Sunday Mirror* reported, Paul said he would return to Australia within six months to campaign for greater help for Aboriginal people and people of colour:

> If necessary, I will stomp up and down the country to help them ... These people need someone to fight for them ... I hope and I feel certain that Australia will do the right thing by its colored people. I have nothing but admiration for Australia. I feel at home here, it is my kind of country and I am sure you are my kind of people.[40]

In her speech, Eslanda brought together the key themes of peace and race relations. She spoke intimately to her audience. 'People are people,' she says. 'We belong to the human race.' Before she came to Australia, she had thought it 'was in almost another world, far far away, and that the people would be different and the climate would be different, and everything would be different'. Now she is here, she says, 'I find that New York is far away, London is far away and you are people like me and we already are friends.' It is important to realise that 'regardless of colour, race, background, religious beliefs, political ideas, we are members of the human family ... This is very important because this is a matter of peace or war.' We think our beliefs are worth fighting for, she continues, and people 'in other places quite different from ours' also think their beliefs are worth fighting for, so we have to find a way to live together: 'It is a waste of time to fight, it is destructive and, anyway, as a very practical woman I summon women all over the earth to remind their men that, after all, after wars peace eventually has to be established, so why in the name of heaven don't we do the peace first and let the fighting go.'[41]

A few days later there was a burst of publicity concerning Paul's call for action to support Aboriginal people, starting with the *Sunday Mirror*'s detailed report, which was picked up by other Murdoch-owned papers.[42] It would reverberate through the rest of the tour.

Eslanda goes to La Perouse

On 11 November, while Paul was resting and preparing for his fourth and final concert the next day, Eslanda visited the Aboriginal community at La Perouse, in Sydney's south, with AAF member Helen Hambly as her guide. One part of the suburb was a government reserve for Aboriginal people, the closest one to central Sydney, that the NSW Government had gazetted in 1895. Adjacent to the reserve, many Aboriginal people lived in houses dating from the 1930s Depression, usually lacking basic amenities. People at La Perouse were connected through kinship to Aboriginal people on the coast south of Sydney, where many obtained seasonal work such as crop-picking or timber-getting.[43]

The community had long welcomed international visitors, such as African American soprano Dorothy Maynor, who had met Yankunytjatjara woman Nancy Brumbie there in 1952.[44] It was also a politically active community. A leading figure was Jack Simms, one of the vice-presidents of the AAF. The year before, he had addressed an audience of 2000 people in Martin Place, in the heart of Sydney, on the occasion of National Aborigines Day, appealing for 'full citizenship rights' for Aboriginal people.[45] In May 1960, Simms was one of the instigators of a petition to remove from the NSW *Aborigines Protection Act* the section concerning exemption certificates.[46]

In November 1960, when Eslanda visited the community, the residents on the reserve were refusing to pay rent. In doing so, they were part of a much larger pattern of Aboriginal resistance to the Aborigines Welfare Board. The board had introduced rent payment in 1949, partly to recoup costs, for it was perennially short of funds, and partly to 'train Aboriginal residents on its reserves to conform to white society's norms of financial behaviour', but it had quickly found a widespread refusal to pay.[47] Earlier that year, at the annual meeting of the Federal Council for the Advancement of Aborigines, Len Fox of the AAF reported that the reasons for not paying rent included a feeling of being 'stood over', the continued refusal of full citizenship rights, and the operation of an assimilation policy that openly set out to destroy their culture and identity.[48] Furthermore, Aboriginal communities across the state saw the reserve as having been given to their communities in perpetuity—that is, as their own land.[49] They did not see themselves as renters.

During the Robeson tour, complaints about housing and rent strikes had been occurring around the country, ASIO noting especially a rent strike in Acacia Ridge in Brisbane and another in the Purfleet reserve north of Taree in New South Wales. In both cases, ASIO suspected communist involvement. In the case of Purfleet, Barbara Curthoys, my mother (who was indeed a communist), supported the rent strike. She helped establish a subcommittee of the Newcastle Trades Hall Council that would raise money for the court case of the community's most outspoken resident and leader of the rent strike, Horrie Saunders. These events helped shape my own understanding of Aboriginal rights and struggles. Although Saunders eventually lost the court case, the campaign had indicated rising Aboriginal protest.[50]

While La Perouse residents of the reserve were challenging their housing conditions and rents, the community continued to attract many visitors. Being a pleasant place near a beach with a park nearby, and accessible at the end of the tram line from the city, La Perouse had become a tourist spot, where people could visit for a day and see some Aboriginal culture. Visitors to Sydney from all over the world would often make their way there, especially on weekends. The local community would meet them, selling weaponry, coolamon bowls, and boxes decorated with shells. There would often be a gum-leaf band, in which Aboriginal musicians would perform using eucalyptus leaves, sometimes accompanied by a didgeridoo, a bullroarer or chanting.[51] Both Black and white Americans had been going there at least since the great African American boxer Jack Johnson visited in 1907 and 1908, calling in so often that he finally left with an excellent collection of boomerangs and weaponry.[52] Men on the ships of the American Pacific fleet would, when it docked in Sydney in 1925, visit La Perouse, and a highlight for the Americans was usually a boomerang demonstration. When Harry Belafonte was in Sydney two months before the Robesons, he visited the Timbery family boomerang shop at La Perouse, where he watched Joe Timbery throw boomerangs for visitors and threw a boomerang with him.[53] Belafonte also visited Bill Onus's boomerang shop just outside Melbourne, where he was taught by famous Aboriginal country-and-western performer Harry Williams how to throw a boomerang.[54]

Though we have few details of Eslanda's visit, it is likely that she, like Belafonte, saw an exhibition of boomerang throwing at the Timbery shop and perhaps she, too, heard the didgeridoo. We do have one brief report on her response to what she saw and heard at La Perouse. In 1989, Hambly recalled:

> Everybody went there [La Perouse], even tourists went there to see them. I took Mrs Paul Robeson there and she was horrified. She said, 'If this is what you show the tourists, what the rest of it must be like?' And I said, well, it really is terrible, you know. And they were all humpies out there then, they weren't houses like they are now.[55]

A private recital

The Sydney visit was almost over. Just before his final Sydney concert on 14 November, Paul recorded a remarkable message for Kate Morrow, wife of his host Bill Morrow. She had been too ill to attend any of the events held in his honour, having suffered a stroke in 1955; she would die in 1963. Kate, whose maiden name was Katherine Scateni, had been born in 1886 in Gympie, Queensland, the daughter of an Italian miner, and had met Bill when both were members of the Workers' Political Organisation, the predecessor of the Labor Party in Queensland. They had married on 22 November 1910, almost fifty years before Paul made this recording.[56] In his goodwill message to Kate, he begins:

> We've had a wonderful trip here. I've been with Bill a good deal and met your daughter. Almost got out to see you and certainly hope to get back to see you very soon again. The audiences have just been wonderful, I've been able to get around to great sections of the community. I've had a wonderful tour in New Zealand and here. I certainly want to thank you for all that you've done for peace and a decent world and it's been just good for the soul to meet folks like Bill and those in the peace movement and what I would call the progressive section of Australia. I know there are many, many fine folks but it's nice to be with those who understand that deeply.

He then tells Kate that he will recite a poem for her: 'Bill tells me that you are very fond of the poem by Blake which is also one of my favourites. It's called "The Little Black Boy: The Song of Innocence". I've done it at the concerts, and it's had great success.' Before reading the poem, he promises her that he will be back, 'I think to Indonesia and India in the early spring. I hope to get to see you. So, I'll read this "Little Black Boy" for you. Take care of yourself and all the best from Essie, my wife, and from Mr Brown, Larry, and from me, Paul.' He explains to her that he is reading the full poem: 'As I always say when I do this poem, if Blake were alive today, he wouldn't worry about whether souls were black or white. So, I usually leave out the first verse, but I'll read it now.' Paul then recites:

> My mother bore me in the southern wild,
> And I am black, but O! my soul is white.
> White as an angel is the English child:
> But I am black as if bereav'd of light.

He comments: 'I'll intervene for just a moment and say that … of course I came up thinking that black was very beautiful, that night is a wonderful time, and that black skins are beautiful so that I could hardly agree with Blake there. So, I usually start with the next verse.' Paul then recites the poem in its entirety. The recording ends: 'All the best to you. Hope to see you when I get back again.'[57]

The next day, 15 November, after the last concert, Paul and Eslanda left Sydney laden with gifts. They still had three cities to go—Melbourne, Adelaide and Perth—and would receive many more gifts in each.

11

Eslanda's Tour

As they flew from Sydney to Melbourne, Paul and Eslanda could reflect that they were now more than halfway through the tour. They had covered six of the nine cities in their itinerary and Paul had given thirteen of his twenty concerts to full houses. He had spoken and sung to half-a-dozen mass meetings of workers and supporters, Eslanda had given four public lectures with three more to come, the press and radio had interviewed them both extensively, and Paul had appeared several times on television. They had met a large number of people they had never met before and gifts had been showered upon them wherever they went. In their sixties, with a history of health problems and having travelled long distances, they were surely tired, though they were likely also buoyed by the near-universal acclaim they had both received. They had three more cities to visit—Melbourne, Adelaide and Perth—and each would involve concerts, lectures, media interviews, and meetings large and small with sympathisers.

While they are in the air on their way to Melbourne, we can pause and look more closely at Eslanda's tour. She was a more significant force on the tour than anyone, including Eslanda herself, had expected. We have seen how, as Paul's manager, she was involved from the beginning in tour arrangements, including the social and political dimensions, and that during the tour itself, those seeking additional meetings with Paul dealt with her first.

Given her desire to protect Paul from becoming overcommitted and overworked, she could at times seem forbidding to those who wanted to meet him. Rona Bailey, for example, described many years later her trepidation when she called on Paul and Eslanda at their hotel, the St George, the morning after they arrived in Wellington: 'To say I was scared is putting it mildly. Robeson is not a man to be trifled with or beat around the bush—and I also had to contend with Eslanda, his wife, who was very worried for his health'.[1]

Rona would find Eslanda somewhat imposing a little later, when she took her to her home while Paul was rehearsing. Situated high on a hill above central Wellington, the home has a stunning panoramic view of the city and its surrounding hills and waterways, as my husband and I saw when we visited Rona's daughter, Meg Bailey, who lives there now, in February 2023. When Eslanda and Rona arrived at the house, Rona's black cat ran inside and Eslanda said 'there was no way [she] would go into a house with a black cat'. So, Rona recalled, 'I had to chase Gypsy out from under my bed and she wasn't easy to get hold of!' The two women, though, then settled into a friendly conversation where Eslanda talked about her worries regarding Paul's health.[2] Driven by such concerns, she often accompanied Paul to his engagements, including some media interviews. During his concerts, as she told one newspaper, she stayed in the wings backstage, having each piece of music ready when he needed it, and 'fresh clothing ready for him to change into during the interval because singing makes him very hot'.[3]

Yet her role in the tour was also as an independent writer, journalist, anthropologist and advocate of women's rights. She was able to draw on her experiences as a journalist and her travels in Africa and the Caribbean to great effect both in media interviews and in talks and lectures. Her public lectures were hosted in New Zealand mainly by the local branches of the United Nations Association, a worldwide organisation to which Eslanda belonged that sought to enhance public knowledge of and support for the principles and activities of the United Nations, especially in promoting peace and preventing war, safeguarding human rights, and promoting human welfare. One of its principal activities was to host international speakers.[4] In Australia, the Union of Australian Women, a communist-led organisation focusing on women's rights and issues such as kindergartens, rising prices and equal pay, organised events for her in each city.[5]

Recent scholarship on Eslanda has emphasised her role as a well-travelled international African American citizen fighting racism, sexism, colonialism and capitalism. Imaobong Umoren, in particular, has tracked in detail Eslanda's anti-colonial feminist politics.[6] We can see Eslanda in this light in Australia and New Zealand too, constantly raising questions for her audiences and listeners to consider concerning the need for peace, the struggle for independence in Africa, the participation of women in those and other struggles, the emerging civil rights movement in the United States, and the role of the United Nations in the modern world. Another theme she turned to from time to time was the responsibility of journalists to inform.

Eslanda in the press

Eslanda received substantial press coverage in both Australia and New Zealand despite the fact that she was far less well known than Paul. Journalists had access to a press release sent by the tour entrepreneurs, with the result that each newspaper reported the same aspects of her life and work—her training as a chemist, her study of anthropology, her trips to and study of Africa, her books *Paul Robeson, Negro* (1930), *African Journey* (1945) and, with Pearl Buck, *American Argument* (1949), and her work as a freelance correspondent at the United Nations.

Some newspapers supplemented this information with her comments made in interviews, as happened in her first published interview, conducted by the *Sydney Morning Herald* on her arrival at Sydney Airport on 12 October. She revealed that in her youth she had been 'offered a singing scholarship at the Ziegfeld School of Music in Chicago, but I wasn't interested'. Of her role at the United Nations, she said she only covered subjects that interested her, 'particularly the activities of the Fourth Committee, which deals with the problems of the non-self-governing territories of Africa and Asia'.[7] Two days later, in Brisbane, the *Courier-Mail* interviewed her, giving the usual list of her achievements, including that she had written 'two and a half books'. That half, she commented, 'was highly controversial'. Buck, she explained, 'wrote the half defending the American way of life and I wrote the second half, attacking it', and the book had since been taken off the American market.[8] She also said that she had met 'most of the present African leaders when I visited their countries in 1936 and later when the younger ones were still students'. She had foreseen then that independence was coming, 'and the only thing that amazes me is that the movement for independence has been so slow'.[9] In response to questions from the *Otago Daily Times* and later from the Melbourne *Sun*, she commented on discrimination and racial segregation in the United States.[10] *The Sun* quoted her on how far African Americans had to go before achieving equality. In the southern states, many had never been able to vote, owing to threats of physical violence, 'even murder'. They were, however, becoming increasingly militant, 'the women even more than the men', she said, pointing out that it was a 'middle aged Negro housewife [presumably Rosa Parks] who set off the bus boycott in Montgomery, Alabama—where they now have integrated buses'.[11]

In an early interview in Brisbane, Eslanda showed the *Courier-Mail* reporter photos of her two grandchildren, David Paul, aged nine, and Susan, aged seven—something she would do regularly throughout the tour. As she said to the reporter, 'I show people pictures of my two grandchildren at the drop of a hat.'[12] This was true, and perhaps Eslanda was not only talking about a subject close to her heart but also presenting a relatable view of both her and Paul. In Auckland, the *New Zealand Herald* mentioned her photo of her two grandchildren, indicating her great pride in being a grandmother.[13] The *Evening Post* also noted her grandmotherly pride, commenting, 'On her dressing table in her Auckland hotel were two large portraits of the children, who are dark-eyed and dimpled.'[14] Though a proud grandmother, Eslanda did comment to *The Press* in Christchurch that her grandchildren were not showing 'any particular talent for the music that made their grandfather famous'.[15] In Melbourne, the grandchildren provided the title of a story in *The Age*, 'Singer's near "flop"—no cowboy song', in which Eslanda recounts her grandchildren's disappointment that Paul knew no cowboy songs, though he had saved the situation by learning several songs such as 'Home on the Range', 'and he was really tops then'.[16]

Several published interviews commented on Eslanda's personality and appearance in similar terms, apparently drawing on the promoter's press release. The first published interview report in New Zealand, entitled 'Mrs Robeson is notable too', described her as 'a warm person who is deeply interested in other people, their cultures and ways of life'. The *Evening Post* thought her a person 'of great charm and intelligence', while the *Otago Daily Times* in Dunedin headed its story 'Paul Robeson's wife charming, intelligent'.[17] In Melbourne, a journalist said Eslanda had a 'dynamic personality, with an easy, friendly manner', and in Perth another journalist used almost the same words, saying she had a 'charming, friendly manner, a dynamic personality and can speak with authority on many subjects'.[18] Some stories emphasised Eslanda's appearance, especially that she was short. The most effusive and detailed was the story in *The Age* in Melbourne that said that in contrast to her 'husband's towering six feet three inches, Mrs Robeson is small. She wears her grey hair neatly parted in the centre and swept back into plaited coils. Alert brown eyes sparkle from behind attractive glasses.'[19]

Eslanda speaks

Eslanda impressed many people during the tour, both in personal interactions and more formal public lectures. The first event held in her honour was a garden party in Brisbane hosted by the Enoggera branch of the UAW. Connie Healy, one of those attending, reflected later that Eslanda was 'a lovely woman', 'very friendly, made people feel at home'.[20]

This ability to charm and impress carried over into her public lectures, for she was an eloquent and well-informed speaker. Each speech was distinct, sometimes referring to very recent events, and adapted for her audience—for example, in paying more attention to the United Nations when hosted by the United Nations Association in New Zealand and to women's rights and roles in Australia when hosted by the UAW.

The most detailed account we have of her New Zealand lectures is that in *The Press*, which reported on her lecture in Christchurch called 'The United Nations and Africa'.[21] This talk, like most of her public lectures, drew on her extensive knowledge of Africa. She had been there three times, first in 1936 to conduct fieldwork for her doctoral studies at LSE. Then, in 1946 from May to November, she had visited the Congo and Chad, where she spent part of her time investigating the life story and retracing the steps of Felix Eboué, an African man born in French Guiana in 1884 who had become a successful colonial official. Eboué had served two years as the governor of Guadaloupe in the mid-1930s, making him the first Black governor of a French colony; he also notably supported de Gaulle and the Free French during World War II. Eslanda's interest in Eboué indicated her liking for biographical studies of individuals, evident also in her first book, *Paul Robeson, Negro*, and in much of her journalism during the 1950s. At the same time, during that tour in Africa she interviewed and spoke with many women activists, attended a conference of missionaries, and, as she had done in 1936 in Uganda and South Africa, spoke extensively with both white officials and ordinary Black Africans. On her return to the United States in November 1946 she had toured the country, speaking of the backward social conditions arising from colonisation and the possibility of revolution in Africa. Based on her travel diaries, she wrote several essays for the *Amsterdam News* and an unpublished movie script.[22]

In December 1958, when able to travel again, Eslanda had returned to Africa. This time she went to Accra, in Ghana, which had gained its independence the previous year. There, she attended the All-African Peoples' Conference from 5 to 13 December 1958, where the major themes were anti-colonialism, pan-Africanism and non-alignment. Conference delegates came from twenty-eight African countries, and there were observers from Europe, India, Indonesia, Canada and Australia.[23] Several African Americans attended, including Shirley Graham Du Bois on behalf of her famous husband, WEB Du Bois,

Foyer display in the State Theatre, Sydney, for the British adventure film *King Solomon's Mines*, 1937, starring Paul. *Courtesy Sam Hood/Home and Away 8229/ State Library of New South Wales.*

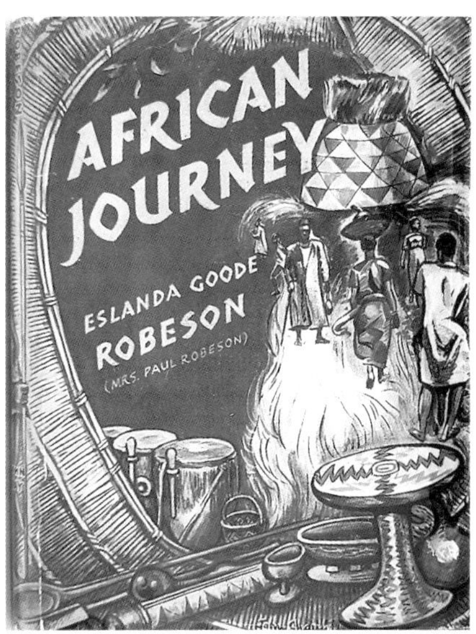

Eslanda's second book, *African Journey*, published in 1945. Note that she is described as 'Eslanda Goode Robeson (Mrs Paul Robeson)'.

Irene Gale meeting Paul and Ahmed Kheir, secretary for Africa and Asia, at the International Institute for Peace and Friendship in Vienna in 1959. Irene and her husband Jim worked at the Institute. *Jim Gale, courtesy Irene Gale.*

PAUL ROBESON

The Epic Hero is not very fashionable at the moment. The trend is towards uniformity and conformity, lines of little toy soldiers standing neatly to attention. A certain current sickness of the human spirit tends to make most of us uncomfortable at the mere thought of moral greatness, so we shuffle uncomfortably and feel unaccountably ashamed in some obscure way. And most exasperating of all, we cannot wholly explain any kind of greatness, not with all our scientific sorcery, our statistics and our psychology. That is why the figure of Paul Robeson, as it towers over us, enigmatic and strangely moving, baffles so many of us.

His career is more astonishing than that of any other popular entertainer or artist of the twentieth century; more astonishing perhaps even than Chaplin's or Marie Lloyd's or Louis Armstrong's. For it has not been just a professional career, but an expression of something

4

Signed Paul Robeson concert program.

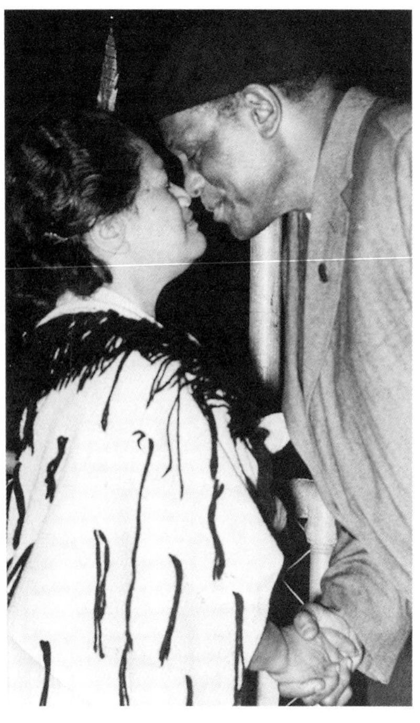

Mrs KG Bidois gives Paul a traditional Māori welcome at Whenuapai airport, Auckland, on 16 October. *Courtesy New Zealand Herald.*

Eslanda arrives in Melbourne holding the *rakau*, a challenge stick, given to her by Māori students at the Auckland Teachers' College. *Courtesy The Sun/Newspix.*

Paul at a desk in his Wellington hotel. *Courtesy Spencer Digby Studios/Museum of New Zealand/Te Papa Tongarewa.*

Paul bumps into jazz musician Dizzy Gillespie and jazz singer Sarah Vaughan at Auckland airport on 28 October. *Courtesy Auckland Star/Hannah Middleton Collection/Sydney Trades Hall Archives.*

Paul with waterside workers Bill Napier, Bill Sandlands, Chip Bailey and Tom Wells at the Wellington Waterside Workers Office on 21 October. *Bailey, Rona, 1914–2005: Photographs. Ref: 1/2-179679-F. Alexander Turnbull Library, Wellington, New Zealand.*

Paul and Eslanda with children of their hosts and supporters at Wellington airport on 23 October. *1998. Papers relating to centennial of the birth of Paul Robeson. Ref: 2006-041-091. Alexander Turnbull Library, Wellington, New Zealand.*

Paul speaks and sings to the workers during their lunch hour at the Addington Railway Workshops in Christchurch on 26 October. *Locke, Elsie Violet, 1912–2001: Photographs of Paul Robeson's visit to Christchurch, 1960. Ref: PAColl-5405-1 and Ref: PAColl-5405-3. Alexander Turnbull Library, Wellington, New Zealand.*

Lord Mayor Harry Jensen with Paul and Eslanda inspecting a model of the Sydney Opera House, then under construction, on 8 November. *Courtesy Fairfax Syndication.*

Paul speaks and sings to the workers at the Sydney Opera House construction site on 9 November. *Courtesy SEARCH Foundation/CPA Collection/Mitchell Library, State Library of New South Wales.*

Paul on ABC TV show *Hal Lashwood's Minstrels* on 7 November. The children are Anglo-Australians Cam Webber and Amanda Alcock, Chinese-Australian brother and sister Mark and Amanda Jong, and Aboriginal-Australian Noel Murray and Fay Groves. *Courtesy Collection of the National Archives of Australia.*

Paul receives an Albert Namatjira print from Mayor Jensen on 8 November. *Courtesy Fairfax Syndication.*

Flyer featuring Paul and Eslanda at an event sponsored by the Aboriginal-Australian Fellowship and the NSW Peace Committee. They attracted 1500 people. *Courtesy Hannah Middleton Collection/Sydney Trades Hall Archives.*

Miriam Hampson and Eddie Allison, of New Theatre, present Paul with gifts at a performance of Arthur Miller's *All My Sons* in Sydney on 13 November. *Courtesy The New Theatre/Mitchell Library, State Library of New South Wales.*

An excited crowd meets Paul and Eslanda at Melbourne airport on 14 November. *Courtesy The Herald/ News Ltd/Newspix/ University of Melbourne Archives.*

Reverend Alfred Dickie and Sam Goldbloom welcome Paul and Eslanda at a reception hosted by the Victorian Peace Council at the Palais de Danse in St Kilda on 20 November. *Courtesy Search Foundation/CPA Collection/ University of Melbourne Archives.*

Paul in conversation with renowned sports coach Percy Cerutty at the Palais de Danse, St Kilda on 20 November. *Courtesy Search Foundation/CPA Collection/University of Melbourne Archives.*

Eslanda speaks at a Union of Australian Women event at Willard Hall, Adelaide, on 25 November. With her are secretary Beryl Jury, president Val Howe and treasurer Irene Bell. *Courtesy State Library of South Australia.*

Young girls present Eslanda with gifts at Willard Hall. *Courtesy State Library of South Australia.*

Paul greeted by fans and supporters at Perth airport on 30 November. *Courtesy West Australian/7West.*

Paul at the Palace Hotel reception hosted by the WA Peace Council on 2 December. *Courtesy Sharon Connolly.*

Five women (unidentified) celebrate Paul's sixty-fourth birthday at an event organised by the Victorian Peace Council in April 1962. *Courtesy Search Foundation/CPA Collection/University of Melbourne Archives.*

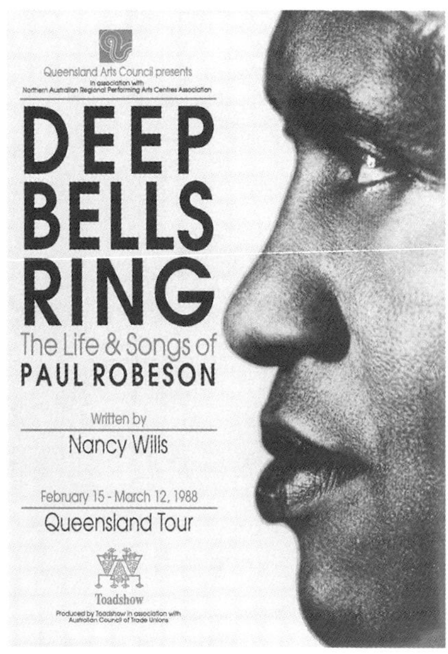

Deep Bells Ring, a play performed in Brisbane, Sydney, Canberra and Melbourne in 1987 and in rural Queensland in 1988.

Program for concert on 27 November 2004 commemorating Paul Robeson's visit to the Midland Railway Workshops in Perth.

Rachel Bate sings in front of the Sydney Opera House on 9 November 2020. The fiftieth anniversary commemoration was sponsored by the Construction, Forestry, Maritime, Mining and Energy Union. *Courtesy Fairfax Syndication.*

who was ill.[24] Though there was much agreement on the key themes, there was also strong disagreement on whether violence against colonialism was justified, with Frantz Fanon, representing Algeria, controversially arguing that violence would be necessary to defeat it.[25] On this trip, Eslanda greatly enhanced and updated her knowledge of African affairs and met several future leaders—Tom Mboya from Kenya, Patrice Lumumba from Congo, and Hastings Banda of Nyasaland (Malawi). She spent time with the other women at the conference; the two she most enjoyed meeting were Saiza Nabarawi, a leading Egyptian feminist, and Geeta Mukherjee, an Indian communist and future member of the Indian Parliament.[26] In her speeches in New Zealand and Australia, she would especially draw on this 1958 visit.

For Eslanda's lecture on 'The United Nations and Africa' in Christchurch, the hall was filled to capacity. She gave her address sitting down, explaining that she would soon be sixty-four and spoke best when she was comfortable. She emphasised the importance of learning about an issue and then fighting for what you think is right, 'but don't kill anyone—let everyone else have their opinions'. She described the United Nations as 'the most important organisation in the world' and spoke of the desire of Africans for self-government: 'they looked after themselves before anyone exploited their labour'. It was absurd to think that Africans needed Europeans to teach them self-government, she said. One reason for the Western fear of the emergence of the new independent African nations, she suggested, was that they 'would change the colour of the UN politically' and render the Soviet countries less isolated. 'The African nations will not be reckless', she suggested—they will 'step carefully so long as no-one calls them names'; she went on: 'People that mean no harm to Africans and Asians need have no fear of them.'[27]

The question of Africa was prominent in her talk at a women's meeting the following day organised by the Christchurch welcoming committee for her and Paul. Mary Woodward, an activist in the Campaign for Nuclear Disarmament, chaired the meeting.[28] Eslanda began her talk on the question of peace and the need to get along with other people 'no matter what their colour, religion, ideology or nationality'. Doing so starts in the home, she said, with relatives, and then extends out to 'neighbourhood, community and national levels'. New Zealand could preserve its European culture, but 'you must respect other people's cultures and backgrounds'. Turning to Africa, she talked about the 'countries she had visited—the Congo, South Africa, Kenya, Tanganyika and the Central African Federation' and predicted that 'Africa is going to move more and more swiftly'.[29]

Another key theme in Eslanda's public lectures throughout the tour was China, in which she had long had a special interest. Most notably, in December 1949, she and her travelling companion Ada Jackson had been the first African American women to visit China after the proclamation of the new People's Republic of China on 1 October that year. Jackson was a Brooklyn-based activist who was a member of the Congress of American Women, the US affiliate of the Soviet-aligned Women's International Democratic Federation.[30] After attending the WIDF Conference in Moscow, Eslanda and Ada participated in an Asian Women's Federation meeting in Beijing (then known as Peking), at which speakers for the new government outlined its policies and plans. In Shanghai, she met Soong Ching-ling, the widow of Dr Sun Yat-Sen who was often known as Madame Sun Yat-Sen, who was president of the All-China Women's Federation as well as vice-chairman of the republic. Over dinner, the two discussed the recent granting of new rights to Chinese women.[31] After her return to the United States in early 1950, Eslanda conducted a speaking tour to describe what was happening in China. She spoke of the emancipation of the peasants from feudalism and argued that the United States would eventually have to recognise the new regime. She addressed varied audiences in St Louis, Detroit, Oakland, Minneapolis and other towns and cities and urged her audiences to become involved in world affairs.[32]

Eslanda's knowledge of and attachment to China led her through the 1950s to become a fierce opponent of China's continual exclusion from the United Nations. In her talk to the UN Association in Christchurch, she argued that the United Nations could not function effectively without China: 'The West is insulting China by keeping it out.' She predicted, wrongly as it turned out, that China would be in the United Nations by the following year—it was not admitted until 1971. When asked in question time about her view of Indian prime minister Jawaharlal Nehru, she revealed her remarkable cosmopolitanism by replying that he was a good friend, she had known him for thirty years, and she hoped he would 'follow the Chinese experiment'.[33]

These themes of Africa and China's exclusion from the United Nations would reappear in her lectures in Australia, where she gave four major public talks as well as speaking alongside Paul at several other events. She gave the first of these speeches in Sydney on 9 November at the same time as Paul was making history singing to the workers at the Opera House building site. About 300 women attended a luncheon at which she was the guest speaker, an event organised jointly by several left-wing women's organisations—the UAW, the WWF Women's Committee, the Seamen's Women's Committee and the Miners' Women's Auxiliaries.[34] The text of her speech was reproduced in a special supplement to the *Seamen's Journal*.[35] It is the only verbatim account of Eslanda's speeches during the tour, and she herself was so delighted to see it when she received a copy back in London that she asked the union to send her ten copies since she didn't have any speaker's notes.[36] I was curious at first why the journal of such a male-dominated union had so much coverage of Eslanda's role in the tour, but soon learned that since 1955 the editor had been Della Elliott, a UAW member and wife of the union's leader, Eliot V Elliott. As historian Diane Kirkby points out, the journal under Della's editorship reflected 'Cold War antagonisms, the Soviet-aligned leadership of the SUA, the hostility to US imperialism in south-east Asia, support for decolonisation and anti-Fascism', but also, she continues, 'Della's unique style', and it often included material concerning women's rights and equality. The journal devoted eight pages to the Robesons' visit and Della made sure it covered Eslanda as well as Paul.[37]

The special supplement's coverage of the visit began with: 'In October–November two outstanding peace fighters, Paul and Eslanda Robeson, were in Australia. These two people personify for all lovers of humanity their aims—peace and the brotherhood of man.' The journal introduced Eslanda to its readers as an anthropologist, writer and activist against racial discrimination and for peace and friendship: 'Mrs Robeson's charming personality and informal manner sets one at ease immediately; when she speaks it is with sound knowledge of her subject and in the language of the people.'[38]

Eslanda began her speech by listing the three subjects she wished to talk about: 'Africa, the United Nations and race relations'. Starting with Africa, she spoke of being interested, as an 'American Negro', in the problems of 'American Negroes' since her student days, and her realisation when she went to live in London that the 'Negro problem was not just the 13 million Negroes in America, but also the 200 million Negroes in Africa'. She began to learn about Africa from Africans themselves and from studying anthropology at LSE. Whereas most of her fellow students were 'Administrators, District Commissioners and others who were learning how to go out to Africa and take over the African people and govern them', she was there 'trying to learn how to help the Africans' liberate themselves from government by others. She explained that though she had also studied at LSE with professors Bronisław Malinowski and Raymond Firth, both 'authorities on the peoples of the Pacific', her main focus was Africa. She had eventually done her African fieldwork in Tanganyika, Kenya and Uganda in 1936, 'when things were just beginning to cook in Africa; leaders were springing up and the African people were very much interested in considering the possibility of getting out from under colonial government'. She spoke of her return to Africa in 1946, to French and Belgian Congo, where, also, 'things were beginning to come to a boil and the now leaders were then students and very active and very vocal, very articulate'. She explained that she had maintained her connections with Africa for five years from 1953 to 1958 as an accredited correspondent to the United Nations.[39] She also described her third visit, in 1958, this time for the All-African Peoples' Conference in Accra, where she met the present leaders of African countries—Banda of Nyasaland, Mboya of Kenya, Madame Andrée Sékou Touré of Guinea, Lumumba of Congo, and many others.

In pointing to her work as a correspondent in the 1950s, Eslanda thus arrived at her second topic, the United Nations. Her 'original time at the United Nations', she said, was during its inauguration in San Francisco in 1945. There she met Vijaya Lakshmi 'Nan' Pandit, sister of Nehru, now prime minister of India. They teamed up, both working for their causes—Pandit for Indian independence and Eslanda for 'Negro rights' in America and independence in Africa. Pandit later became the only woman president of the United Nations and was now India's ambassador in London. Eslanda took time to point out that the United Nations did many wonderful things, such as UNICEF and the WHO, but said that when she had to leave her UN work as she and Paul were moving to London, she was not as regretful as she thought she would be. She was furious that China was not in the United Nations, as its absence had major implications for the organisation of the United Nations itself. The exclusion of China was the work of her own country and, with a gentle nod to Australia, of its 'sometimes reluctant allies'. When Khrushchev said the United Nations had to include China and expand the secretary-generalship, his demands offended many people, particularly because of 'the manner in which he made them'. But 'manner or no manner, he did express a very great question which was in the minds of many of the member nations who were afraid or unwilling to express these questions themselves'.[40]

On her third topic, race relations, Eslanda had run out of time, so she concluded by making a few general remarks about the importance of people from diverse backgrounds getting along together.[41] As would be the case for her talks on the tour generally, there would be many questions from the audience. When someone asked what role women were playing in the 'Negro struggle' in the United States, she replied that they were playing an important part. 'I am not a feminist,' she said, 'but I believe very strongly that since women are half the population on earth that they should exert at least half the power.' As noted earlier, many women associated with the socialist and communist left at the time made similar remarks, seeing feminism as a bourgeois phenomenon attractive to well-off women with little or no class awareness or class-consciousness. Her hosts at the UAW would have thought similarly, distancing themselves from feminism but nevertheless fighting hard for women's rights and women's equality. Women, she said, should have influence in the kitchen, the living room, the nursery, the parliaments, and the United Nations: 'they should make their contribution at every level'. She concluded her answer by saying that women were playing a significant role in China, the Soviet Union and Africa.[42]

On a different topic, in question time at one event in Sydney (probably this one), an audience member asked Eslanda 'whether it was possible for some international body to insist journalists publish the facts without colouring reports and giving them a bias'. Eslanda responded by saying that publishers who 'are fighting the Cold War' owned the newspapers. Even when journalists presented factual reports, publishers could override them and 'reports can be altered and re-arranged'. The situation was serious: 'many honest reporters have lost their jobs, many editors also have lost their jobs, many radio and television commentators have lost their jobs because they have dared to present honest news'.[43]

Eslanda returned to many of these themes during a radio interview with Tom Jacobs on Sydney's popular commercial radio station 2UE, recorded and broadcast on 10 November. The State Library of New South Wales has a recording of this interview, and it makes for remarkable listening.[44] Jacobs had conducted interviews on commercial radio for many years, first for 2SM from 1946, and since 1957 at 2UE. One can hear the effect of the voice lessons he received early in his career from the ABC's chief announcer, Bryson Taylor—a cultivated, perhaps faintly British version of an Australian accent.[45] There is also something about his interviewing style that his biographer describes by saying, 'Jacobs had a cheekiness about him but also a sincerity enabling him to ask direct and penetrating questions', which seems to me to apply quite well to his interview with Eslanda.[46]

At first Eslanda talks of her interest in Africa, her visits there, her sympathy as an African American with the African people, and the importance of the right to self-government. The interview becomes tense when Jacobs asks her if Paul is a communist, which she says is a very rude question and robustly refuses to answer, saying that membership of the Communist Party is illegal in the United States and that in any case it has nothing to do with the purpose of the interview. Though Jacobs' tone is patronising and aggressive, interviewer and interviewee do settle into a lively exchange. Eslanda speaks of her admiration for the Soviet Union and for China, both 'powerful nations with an enormous future', and contrasts the Soviet lack of racial prejudice, as she sees it, with her experience of racial prejudice in the United States. And she speaks strongly of her view that women should be able to play an equal role in the world with men. 'I think a woman who stays in the kitchen is stupid,' she says, 'and I think a woman who never goes into the kitchen is stupid.' Women should contribute wherever they can, in the kitchen, the nursery, in government or in international affairs. That morning, the Sydney newspapers had carried the news that John F Kennedy had won the US presidential election, and when Jacobs asks Eslanda her view on this, she replies cautiously that it is a healthy sign that the American people want a change, and she hopes it is a change for the better. Americans cannot contribute to the freedom of the world, she also says, until there is freedom at home, especially for what she calls the 'Negro American'. At the end, undeterred by her earlier comment that such questions are very rude, Jacobs asks her if *she* is a communist, and she replies robustly that she will not tell him, but she *will* say she likes the Soviet Union, which is 'another matter altogether'. There are two especially interesting features of her comments here: first, they betray no inkling of the emerging Sino-Soviet split, and second, her sharp distinction between being a communist and being an admirer of the Soviet Union.

Eslanda was out in public again the next day, 11 November, firstly for another radio interview. Though 2UE had received telephone complaints about Jacobs interviewing her the day before, since she was, supposedly, a communist, Jacobs was undeterred and interviewed her again for another program, *My World*, which he hosted jointly with the well-known and outspoken Dorothy Jenner, known to all as Andrea.[47] He interviewed Eslanda for over half an hour, the discussion interspersed—disconcertingly to modern ears—with advertisements read out by Jacobs himself. This second interview covered new ground. Jacobs' questions led Eslanda to explain her racial background as both African American and, through her Cardoza ancestors, Sephardic Jewish; her Spanish given name; her childhood; the family emphasis on the importance of education; and Paul's childhood, where she extolled his father as a marvellous man, a 'brilliant Negro leader'. She talked about her experience of the 'unnecessary humiliations in daily life' as an African American in America, and when asked whether she believed in God replied that she had been raised an Episcopalian but really preferred African beliefs that saw the individual as a drop in the river of life, commenting: 'I'm a drop in the river of life.' When pressed on her views on Christianity, she replied that she would have more faith in Christianity if Christians would actually practise Christian ideals.

The conversation turned to the White Australia policy when Jacobs asked her what she thought of the comments made in London by Lord Slim, a former governor-general of Australia, which local papers had published that morning. Slim had supported the White Australia policy on the grounds that 'coloured' immigrants would be labourers who 'would depress the general standard of living' and commented: 'If you dilute the populations too much Australia can no longer be a bastion of Western civilisation in the southern hemisphere.' Slim said he liked his Asian friends and comrades, who were cleverer and better educated than he was, but would rather they stayed in their own countries than become 'a third-class community' in Australia.[48] Eslanda commented that it would have been far better for Slim to speak of policy concerning the introduction of technically trained or skilled people rather than of 'white' or 'non-white' people. The conversation then shifted to Paul's movies, Jacobs commenting that no-one could forget that popular movie *Sanders of the River* and playing a record of Paul singing 'Canoe Song'.[49] The interview ended amicably.

The Sydney visit was a full one for Eslanda, but in fact her public lecture in Melbourne was the best attended—though not the best reported—of the whole tour. On Monday 21 November, she spoke to almost 400 women at a luncheon hosted by the UAW, the Victorian branch of which was strong and closely connected with the Victorian peace movement through its president, Alison Dickie, the wife of 'peace parson' the Reverend Alfred Dickie.[50] Held in St Kilda, the event was chaired by Dr Elwyn Morey, a lecturer in psychology at the University of Melbourne who would soon become a leading figure in child psychology in Australia.[51] According to the Melbourne *Guardian*, Eslanda spoke with 'decisiveness and humour' on Africa, race relations and the United Nations, emphasising the role of women in movements for freedom—for example, in the campaigns for integrated schools in Little Rock, Arkansas, and for desegregation of buses in the American South.[52] She particularly stressed the absurdity of China's exclusion from the United Nations and called the US position on this 'stubborn and mulish'. Referring to the UN recognition of Taiwan rather than the People's Republic of China, she pointed out that no other government-in-exile was allowed such a role in the United Nations.[53] Though her comments in this lecture were similar to those made in Sydney, she added the striking point that Australians who called themselves white were living in the middle of a coloured area, among the people of Asia: 'You may be sitting in the Pacific, but you're really in the midst of Asians. You call yourselves Europeans, but you're a very long way from Europe.'[54] It was a theme she would return to with effect in subsequent speeches.

In raising the question of Australia's relationship with Asia, Eslanda was strengthening local voices making similar points. During the 1950s, there had been new interest as governments and business wanted to trade with Asia as never before and Australian travellers went to Asian countries in increasing numbers. History syllabuses in schools and universities placed more emphasis on Asia and its future relations with Australia. Lloyd Evans' high school history text *Australia and the Modern World* (1957), to take just one example, stressed that Australians had once thought of Asia as 'a distant region with which Australians have little in common'. Asian government officials, it pointed out, come to study forms of government, and students come to gain qualifications: 'We, in return have much to learn from Asia, and in years to come civilisation in Australia will undoubtedly reflect Eastern influences.'[55]

Almost 100 women heard Eslanda speak in Adelaide on Friday 25 November at a reception hosted by the UAW at Willard Hall in Wakefield Street.[56] Named after Frances Willard, the founder of the international Woman's Christian Temperance Union, the local WCTU had owned the hall since 1907, meaning it had been host to women's activism for many years. It had also been the site of the first meeting three years earlier of the Federal Council for Aboriginal Advancement, a national body bringing together the various Aboriginal support organisations across the country. (From 1964, it would be known as FCAATSI, to indicate that Torres Strait Islanders were included.) Just a few months before Eslanda spoke there, the hall had hosted the world premiere of Alan Seymour's *The One Day of the Year*. Though it would become one of Australia's best-known plays, at the time it was controversial, posing challenging questions about the meaning of Anzac Day, which was (and is) observed in both Australia and New Zealand each year on 25 April as an almost sacred day of remembrance of those who served in wars, conflicts and peacekeeping operations. When the organisers of the inaugural Adelaide Festival of Arts refused the play a spot, the Adelaide Theatre Group staged its very first performance on 20 July 1960 at Willard Hall.[57]

There is a photograph of Eslanda in Willard Hall standing behind a table, flanked on her right by Beryl Jury (UAW secretary) and on her left by Val Howe (president) and Irene Bell (treasurer), all four women laughing heartily.[58] Eslanda is clearly enjoying herself. Her speech, which lasted for forty-five minutes, was similar to that given in previous cities. One ASIO agent present, after listing about fifty people by name and estimating attendance as 'about 86', reported that when asked by an audience member how capitalism compared with communism, Eslanda replied, after some hesitation, 'Communism is here to stay whether it is liked or not. Capitalism is sheer waste. It is only a matter of time before Capitalism is extinct. Communism and socialism will then take [their] rightful place in the world.'[59] Howe, the chair, wrote a detailed and enthusiastic report for the local *UAW*

News Sheet. She was particularly impressed by the way Eslanda was able to communicate anthropological knowledge in an accessible way: 'she translates anthropology into terms of human relationships, from race relationships down to family relationships, and stressed the need for the peoples of the world to live in friendship'. Eslanda also gave 'a fascinating account of Africa today, the changing character of [the] UN, the racial problem in America and the courage of the young people who dared to stand on their constitutional rights and attend school with white children in the face of mob violence'. Major worldwide changes were coming, Eslanda had said: '"don't look now" but the peoples of the world who were still under colonial domination were not going to stay there'.

Now that Eslanda had been in Australia for three weeks and met and spoken to many people, she began to articulate more freely some criticisms of the country. As Howe reported, 'She also rather wryly told us to look to the situation in our own country where maybe everything wasn't quite as it should be, from the treatment of our aborigines to the encroachment on our civil rights', the latter referring to the recently passed *Crimes Act*.

The audience was enthusiastic and at the end the UAW presented Eslanda with 'a beautiful sheaf of flowers together with a scarf and handkerchief printed with Australian wildflowers. Individual members also gave flowers and gifts, the Port Group provided 'a lovely corsage'[60] and, as ASIO reported, Eslanda was given (yet another) Namatjira reproduction.[61] Although they had not previously known Eslanda, Howe wrote, 'now we have met her we realise that she, no less than her husband, is a fearless fighter, and a distinguished and accomplished woman in her own right', who 'charmed her audience with her informality, her rich sense of humour and by the wealth of knowledge she passed on to us'. The report ended: 'Thank you, Eslanda Robeson, for a wonderful afternoon. We hope that in the future there will be further opportunities to meet you, and we wish you safe journeying. With you go our warmest wishes.'[62]

In Perth, the last city of the tour, Eslanda spoke twice, first alongside Paul at an event at the Palace Hotel organised by the local

Peace Council, and then by herself at the final UAW event. The Peace Council speech is short but striking and is the only audio recording we have of her speeches on this tour. She begins by telling of her day so far, which was spent meeting students at the University of Western Australia, but unfortunately she gives no details of that meeting and I have been unable to find out more about it. Then she says something quite remarkable. She has been thinking about the implications of Australia's geographical location for its politics and foreign policies. In Sydney she had said that before coming to Australia, she had thought Australia was far away but now she was here it was New York and London that were far away. She develops this thought further. 'I've been thinking about you', she says

> When I was in England preparing for the trip … I thought of coming to Australia as coming to the other end of the world and when I got here in two days flying, I found I wasn't at all at the other end of the world … I feel very much in the centre of the world here and I think it's extraordinary that I should have made such a mistake because I should know better … I went out and bought a map, it's a great big map but it has Australia in the centre, and I particularly wanted this kind of map so I could see where I was in relation to all the other places. I find that I really am in the centre in a way and I think that it is in thinking of Australia as an outpost as I've often heard it called, I think either I'm wrong or somebody else is wrong, because it looks to me like a bridge, not an outpost at all, but a bridge connecting Asia, India, Africa, China's just up there, Indonesia, Oceania's right here.

Australia, she says, is in the *middle* of things:

> One extremely important contribution you could make to peace in a very confused and upset … world is to regard yourself as a bridge. You Australians may be European, but Europe is way, way over there and … here you are sitting out in the middle of Oceania and right next door to Asia and very near to Africa and I think if you were to regard yourselves as a bridge you could make a very great contribution to peace.

She goes on to comment that:

> in a young and vigorous and powerful country as you are, with a vigorous and developing and growing people, I don't see why you shouldn't grow in a big direction … and have world connections and make *your* policy. I don't see any sense in taking over or copying anybody else's policy which may not be a good one.[63]

Here, she was clearly being critical of Australia's abject conformity with US policy, especially on excluding China from the United Nations. She thanks everyone for the warm welcome, and the immense pleasure she and Paul have had in finding themselves not strangers in a new part of the world.

Eslanda's last public appearance in Australia was at a UAW reception at the Builders' Exchange in West Perth the following day, Saturday 3 December. This, too, was a success.[64] The WA branch of the UAW, formed in 1951, worked closely with allied organisations such as the Native Welfare Council, the Combined Equal Pay Committee, and the women's committees of the Seamen's Union and the WWF. During the 1950s and early 1960s, the UAW in Perth provided a monthly forum for interstate and overseas speakers and maintained some excellent international connections. Mary Lester, UAW secretary since 1954, was also secretary of the Perth-based International Women's Day committee, and in that capacity had invited German, French and Indonesian women activists to speak.[65]

Eslanda's talk and afternoon tea were exceptionally well attended, having been publicised not only by the UAW itself but also that morning by *Women's Session* on ABC Radio Perth, a popular program that had been hosted by Catherine King since the 1940s and often featured interstate and international speakers.[66] In her book on trailblazing Australian women broadcasters, Kylie Andrews says of King's daily radio shows that they often involved interviews with an expert to discuss their work, and in general they 'interrogated contemporary issues and covered a wide spectrum of cultural, political, and social discourse'.[67] Eslanda would likely have appealed to King's audience. Lester wrote gratefully to King the following Monday, thanking her for the publicity and informing her excitedly, 'The hall was crowded, in fact there were more standing than sitting', and estimating the audience as about 200.[68] As one ASIO agent present reported, some members of the audience were Aboriginal women, but as in the ASIO report on the Palace Hotel reception, they were not named.[69]

I don't have the full text of this talk, but it was clearly similar to the ones given at UAW events in previous cities. Activist Annette Aarons later recalled that Eslanda spoke of her 'association with women in the USA, with negro women and children, and the many things of concern in this sphere'.[70] One ASIO report said she spoke in some detail about Khrushchev's behaviour at the United Nations, commenting that he 'shouts in a loud voice and does a lot of table thumping but actually what he is doing is the correct thing' (referring to Khrushchev's advocating the admission of China to the United Nations).[71] Another reported that that she spoke about 'the Negro problem around the world; Peace; Africa and the Congo; the United Nations; Equal rights and power to vote for American Negroes; and the rights of the Australian Aboriginal'.[72] A third report outlined her admiration for aspects of African culture, such as marriage laws, and quoted her as saying 'they are happy with their way of life and do not want the white man nor his ways because all he does is take away their land and give nothing in return'. It also said that when a man in the audience asked whether Africans accepting aid from Russia would mean they would still have no freedom, she characteristically replied that the African people would not be concerned about being tied to Russia, which was at least 'offering ways and means to make their lot better than the others had ever done'.[73]

In her letter of thanks to King, Lester said she hoped the Robesons would return as they had suggested they would, given Paul's 'fearless humanitarianism', and referred to Eslanda as 'so well-informed, friendly and charming'. *News for Everywoman*, the newsletter of the local branch of the UAW, expressed delight with Eslanda's talk:

> What an exhilarating afternoon it was. What a pleasure and honour to be able to meet Eslanda Robeson and speak with her. This was

> one of the most successful functions we have held, and although we were sorry to see so many having to stand, it gave us all a thrill nevertheless to see such a crowd.

The newsletter also reported: 'we gave Paul a mounted, enlarged photo of Albert Namatjira, and Eslanda a wall plaque of mounted West Australian flora, together with a large bouquet'.[74] The plaque and bouquet for Eslanda were very local gifts that would have meant a lot to those who gave them, for WA wildflowers are exceptionally beautiful and plentiful and Western Australians are, and have long been, extremely proud of them.

12

'I shook his hand'

Melbourne Welcomes the Robesons

Let us now return to Eslanda and Paul in their plane on its way from Sydney to Melbourne. It is time to backtrack a little and follow them as they touch down on Tuesday 15 November in the city that had first invited Paul to Australia ten years earlier.

While for Paul and Eslanda each new city meant yet another concert, talk or interview, for the people in those cities their presence was, of course, something fresh and new. Those on the left were meeting someone whose politics they respected and admired, while a wide range of people who loved Robeson's voice and remembered his movies now had the chance to see and hear him in person. Melbourne had waited ten years for Paul's arrival. This was, after all, the city in which the peace activists of 1949–50 had twice invited him to be a keynote conference speaker only to find that he was unable to come owing to other pressing commitments and to his loss of passport. Now that he was at last in Australia, Melbourne's peace activists were delighted, and so too were a range of journalists, unionists and music critics.

The general buzz about Paul and Eslanda's forthcoming visit began with a page-two story in the city's morning broadsheet newspaper, *The Age*, on 1 November 1960, a fortnight before they arrived. The 'News of the Day' reporter said that Dan O'Connor had first tried to get Paul for the Australasian circuit as far back as 1928 and had tried many times since. His concerts would feature both singing and speaking, including recitations from *Othello*, of which American drama critic Alexander Woollcott had once said that 'listening to Robeson in *Othello* was like listening to Beethoven's great symphonic passages'. Furthermore, Eslanda was 'a remarkable woman in her own right', a distinguished anthropologist, chemist and author.[1]

Clearly excited by the Robesons' imminent visit, *The Age* published two further articles just three days before they were due to arrive, one on Paul and the other on Eslanda.[2] Geoffrey Hutton—theatre critic, literary reviewer and the chief leader-writer on *The Age*—wrote of Paul's 'magnificent voice', which rolls out 'in Negro spirituals, popular songs, in oratorio or opera' and his many talents, in all of which he was a 'self-dedicated champion of his people'.[3] Melburnians were also alerted to Robeson's presence in Australia by the screening on ABC-TV in prime time on Sunday 13 November of his *Spotlight* interview.[4] They may also have seen clips of him singing at the Opera House site either on television or in cinemas that screened *Cinesound Review* from 17 November.[5]

When Paul and Eslanda arrived at Melbourne Airport in Essendon in the early afternoon of Tuesday 15 November, they were given what *The Sun*, a local morning tabloid newspaper, described as a 'rowdy, flower-strewn welcome' by trade unionists and peace movement officials.[6] Channel 7 filmed their arrival, showing a welcoming crowd and a woman presenting Paul with a bouquet.[7] The broadsheet *Herald* had a photograph of a rather tired-looking Paul being welcomed, with the comment 'World famous Negro singer Paul Robeson towers over well-wishers'.[8]

Had they arrived in 1950, when Paul was first invited, the Robesons would have found quite a different city from the one they were now visiting. Melbourne had been a grand Victorian city in the nineteenth century, based on wealth springing from the gold rushes and associated economic development and expansion. Indeed, their hotel, the Menzies, was a product of this era in Melbourne's history, having been built in 1867 just in time for the visit of Prince Alfred, son of Queen Victoria. It had long been regarded as Melbourne's finest, with celebrity visitors including Mark Twain, Anthony Trollope and HG Wells. By the time the Robesons arrived, however, it seems to have become a little dated, and more modern establishments were beginning to displace it.

After the goldrush period, Melbourne's growth and cosmopolitanism had stalled during two world wars and the severe economic depression of the 1930s. It recovered during the 1950s with the influx of both capital and labour, a baby boom, high immigration and economic prosperity, including the development of heavy industry and car manufacturing. The large numbers of Italian, Greek and other migrants in the 1950s were beginning to transform the city, with Italian cafes appearing in Bourke Street. It still had a long way to go, though, and when it won the bid to host the 1956 Olympic Games, many wondered how it could ever feed the competitors, their staff, the international media and visiting spectators. As journalist Nick Richardson writes, the problem was solved by the importation of hundreds of European chefs and a smaller number of Asian chefs from shipping liners, many of whom stayed on after the Olympics.[9]

As a former elite athlete himself, Paul may have appreciated the fact that Melbourne was a sports-loving city, as it is now. Despite early concerns, the Olympic Games had been a success, with extensive volunteer involvement and high levels of attendance at the major venues. Each year Australian Rules football attracted huge crowds throughout the football season, and on 1 November, just two weeks before the Robesons arrived in the city, the Melbourne Cup, the famous horse race that attracted national attention every year, had run its 100th race at Flemington.[10] Paul had listened to it on radio in Dunedin.[11] When he and Eslanda arrived on 15 November, Melbourne was buzzing with excitement over the visiting West Indies cricket team, which had dominated other cricketing nations in recent years.

One distinctive feature of Melbourne that was important for the Robesons was its significant Jewish population, higher than that of any other Australian city. There had been several waves of Jewish migration from Europe to Melbourne, especially in the wake of World War II.

In the 1961 census Melbourne's Jewish population was approximately 30,000, about half of Australia's total Jewish population. Many were Holocaust survivors; a survey in 1961 revealed that in Melbourne only 12 per cent of Jews over the age of twenty-one had been born in Australia. Many of Melbourne's Jewish community were of Eastern European origin, and a majority of Jewish adults in Melbourne were from a Yiddish-speaking background.[12] The Robesons would meet some of the leading left-wing Jewish activists in Melbourne, notably peace movement leader Sam Goldbloom, who had been secretary of the very successful peace congress in Melbourne in 1959 and was now secretary of the ensuing peace organisation, the Campaign for International Co-operation and Disarmament.[13] He was a member of the ALP, and also, as his daughter Sandra Goldbloom Zurbo reveals in her memoir and as ASIO thought, a secret member of the CPA.[14] Goldbloom was also very much a Robeson fan, Zurbo recalling in a letter to me that 'In our house, to our family, he was a hero of the people … My sisters and I were raised on his music, his songs, his films and the knowledge of his political activism.' Zurbo remembers Paul and Eslanda coming to the Goldbloom house on one occasion, commenting, 'When he and Eslanda came to dinner, I was completely in awe.'[15]

During their first afternoon in the city, both Paul and Eslanda conducted interviews at the hotel with press, radio and television reporters. Paul's interview with a group of reporters from *The Age*, *The Sun* and *The Herald*, which included some singing as well as talking, lasted over an hour.[16] In its third item on Paul that month, *The Age* featured his arrival with a smiling photograph on the front page and the caption that of his many expressions during an interview, his 'big, warm smile' had appeared most often.[17] He spoke of having been deprived of his passport and of access to stage and theatre, and said that, as *The Age* put it, he had 'just been coming awake again in these past two years'. Paul spoke of both politics and music. Describing himself as a socialist, he said the socialist world wanted peace whereas those in control in the United States, his own country, did not, since capitalism needed war to survive. He also spoke about his love of folk tunes, sang for the journalists both 'Ode to Joy' from Beethoven and 'Deep River', that popular spiritual expressing a longing for a place of peace that he had sung at his very first solo concert in 1925.

While both Robesons gained favourable coverage from the Melbourne media, there were occasional signs of hostility to their views on the Soviet Union. JS Lennie, a former army intelligence officer and interpreter and a frequent letter writer to newspapers, asked in a letter to the editor of *The Age* on 19 November, probably in response to the story on Paul three days earlier, what Robeson thought of 'the Russian colonial policy which has enslaved Hungary, Czechoslovakia and Poland', whether he condoned 'the brutal treatment meted out to the Hungarians who tried to gain their freedom', and what he thought would happen 'if he went to Russia and adversely criticised the socialist rule there'.[18] Yet comments of this kind, which seem pertinent to us now, were fairly rare. Most of those who opposed Robeson's support for the Soviet Union—and they were the majority—did not do so publicly.

The Melbourne concerts

With so much positive and informative media coverage, the stage was set for successful concerts in Melbourne. The first three took place on Wednesday 16, Friday 18 and Monday 21 November in the Melbourne Town Hall, a commanding nineteenth-century building with a huge auditorium that had hosted many concerts, theatrical plays, exhibitions and civic events since its completion in 1870. Every concert was filled to capacity; Vaughan Greenberg remembered in 2008 being 'with friends in an enormous queue at the Melbourne Town Hall, waiting for ages to get in and gradually creeping along the pavement'.[19] After the tour manager received hundreds of requests for an additional concert, he scheduled a fourth at the Palais de Danse in St Kilda on Tuesday 29 November. Paul and Eslanda would visit Adelaide, as planned, between the third and fourth concerts.

Audiences loved the performances. The agent reporting to the FBI on the first concert emphasised the enthusiastic response from the capacity audience, of which, they noted, a large percentage was from 'older age groups'. The audience, said the agent, loved the mix of Beethoven, Schubert, Negro spirituals, poetry, the speech from *Othello*, and spoken references to 'peace', 'injustices' and 'brothers under the skin'—and it seems the agent agreed, commenting that the audience applause was 'applause for a great and superb artist.'[20] Well-known Australian singer Margret Roadknight later recalled that she had as a schoolgirl attended a Robeson concert that was so packed she and her sister 'had to sit behind him on the stage'; and that despite her politically conservative upbringing, she was 'mightily impressed'.[21] In an interview in 2008, Jane Mullett remembered attending a Robeson concert in Melbourne and hearing him sing and speak: 'I remember him speaking, I remember that incredible deep baritone.'[22] Bronwyn Silver remembered going to a Paul Robeson concert in Melbourne when she was eight years old. Her parents, Charles and Olga Silver, were communists. 'I was in about the fourth row from the front and during an interval between songs, Paul looked at me and said I was just like his granddaughter. I had very curly hair. I have always found it amusing to think back on this.'[23]

Les Rosenblatt also remembered attending a Robeson concert at the Melbourne Town Hall. A writer who would later be active in the Australian Jewish Democratic Society (a left-wing Jewish organisation critical of Israeli actions towards Palestinians), he remembered in 2008 that 'I was fourteen and had never heard such a deep rich bass voice'; he was struck also by Paul's 'seriously intense dignity'. He recalled Paul singing 'Water Boy' and 'Ol' Man River', and especially 'Sometimes I Feel Like a Motherless Child'. While he later became interested in many other singers, including Nina Simone, Rosenblatt thought 'Robeson was on his own really and the concert left a mysteriously enduring impression of importance that my subsequent interest in jazz and classical music never quite overtook'.[24] Ila Marks, who was sixteen when Robeson visited Melbourne, wrote to me: 'My memories of Paul Robeson's visit and concerts, the Palais and the Melbourne Town Hall, are of joy, coming together of people and the beginning of the end of the Cold War period. Which was symbolically very important.'[25] Juliet Flesch recalled that there had been trouble with the sound system reverberating and that once it had been solved, he 'filled every corner of the Hall with sound'. When the audience applauded 'a particularly political comment', he said 'for that, he was prepared to sing "Ol' Man River"'. Her memories, she wrote to me, almost sixty-five years after the event, were 'still vivid'.[26]

On a lighter note, Jim Falk remembers the last, additional concert at the Palais de Danse in St Kilda:

> It had these huge urns—one on each side of the stage, and really all I can remember is that Paul was incredibly charismatic and at one stage walked over to one of the urns, slapped it hard and said, 'Wake up'. Then he laughed and said, 'I have been wanting to do that ever since I saw them.' He really had everyone eating out of his hand.[27]

Robeson appears to have met admirers and supporters at receptions after some or perhaps all of the concerts. Mullett remembered meeting him after one concert:

> my memory is of being with my parents, being the smallest person, being surrounded by all these really big adults and must have been backstage, must have been after the concert, and Paul Robeson just being this imposing, jet black, sort of fabulous presence and this hand coming down … shaking my hand, and just being in the presence of a celebrity … there was quite a lot of fuss made of me, because you know, I had shaken Paul Robeson's hand.

Greenberg remembered: 'After the concert I recall queuing once again to get his autograph, just to shake his hand. I don't think I would have washed it for weeks … But he was a wonderful human being.' Leo Sanderson recalls: 'I remember shaking Paul Robeson's hand. My hand is not small, but I remember how large Paul's hand was.' Paul must have shaken many hands in Melbourne, for it is one of the key themes in the oral histories Sari Braithwaite and I collected in 2008.

As always, local newspapers reviewed the concerts favourably.[28] Felix Werder, the music critic for *The Age*, was one of the German Jewish refugees whom Britain had expelled as supposed enemy aliens and transported to Australia on the *Dunera* in 1940. Most of the more than 2500 detainees were in fact anti-Nazi Jewish civilians, and many later made, as Werder did, major contributions to Australian cultural and economic life. He was a composer, critic and music educator who helped establish musical modernism in Melbourne; he had only recently become the paper's music critic.[29] His review of the first concert described Paul as a 'singing legend, who possesses a glorious resonance which he uses with superb artistry, both technically and musically'.[30] His review of the second concert commented on the 'fathomless depth of his voice, with its organ-like sonorities' and described his rendition of Negro spirituals as 'overwhelming in its impact and will surely never be bettered'.[31]

Equally impressed was Linda Phillips in the *Sun News-Pictorial*. A noted composer, pianist and music critic, also Jewish, who had represented women composers in Victoria at the International Conference of Women held in Venice in 1956, she began by describing the concert as 'great entertainment by a great man', noting Paul's 'glorious voice' and the 'depth of his sincerity and his humanity'. She mentioned him singing Mussorgsky's 'The Orphan', 'Song of the Warsaw Ghetto', and spirituals including 'Swing Low, Sweet Chariot'.[32] In her review of the second concert, she noted that 'every seat was taken' and that this concert 'proved as entertaining as the first'. His performance of a speech from *Othello*, she thought, gave the audience a glimpse of 'what he would be like performing in Mussorgsky's *Boris Godunov*'.[33] Particularly moving for Phillips, who had studied Jewish and Middle Eastern melodies, was his singing of '"Yisgadal Shema Rabboh", a Rabbinic Chassidic air (a Jewish song or prayer), scolding, imploring, and then extolling the Omnipotent on behalf of oppressed people'. The song, she continued, 'was sung partly in Hebrew and partly in English with great fervour and dramatic expression'.[34] Phillips was especially interested in this song, for she had composed *Exaltation: Chassidic Air and Dance*, a work for oboe, violin, cello and piano.[35]

The *Jewish Herald*, based in Melbourne, commented that Paul had sung Jewish melodies at both concerts, at the first the partisan 'Song of the Warsaw Ghetto' and at the second the air 'Yisgadal Shema Rabboh', which he had sung with 'great fervour and depth of expression'.[36] Paul's version was what he called 'Hassidic Chant'. Jonathan Karp has written at length about Robeson's singing of this Hassidic chant at Carnegie Hall two years earlier. It was, he informs us, a version of the Kaddish (Memorial Prayer) attributed to an eighteenth-century master, Levi Yitzhak of Berditchev.[37] The song is both a protest to God at the sufferings of the Jewish people and an affirmation of faith.[38] The song as Robeson sang it strikingly begins:

> A good day to Thee, Lord God Almighty
> I, Levi Isaac, son of Sarah, from Berditchev,
> Here am I before thee
> with a grave and earnest plea for this my people
> What has thou done to this thy people?
> Why has thou so oppressed this thy people?

It ends with the title words of the song, first in Hebrew and then in English: 'Magnified and sanctified is only Thy Name'. It is a truly striking song. As Karp explains, the version of the chant that Robeson sang was arranged by Joel Engel, a Russian Jewish folklorist, in 1923.[39] When Paul sang it at Carnegie Hall and elsewhere, he gave a long spoken introduction, tracing the song's genealogy from Levi Yitzvak through Czech and African chants to African American church music and finally to his father's speech-song as a preacher.[40] This musical tradition, expressed also in speech, led Robeson to feel an affinity for the Hebrew language and, Karp suggests, for Jewish people, who, he felt, had stuck by him even when his own Black leaders had disowned him.[41] Karp says that it was often in remarks preceding singing 'Hassidic Chant' that he articulated his theory both of the universality of music and the close relationship between speech and song, and it seems very likely that he did so here.[42] It was clear in Melbourne, more than anywhere else on the tour, that Paul had strong affinities with Jewish people and musical culture, as did Eslanda, who valued her Jewish ancestry.

Paul sings to Melbourne waterside workers

If Paul's Melbourne concerts were an outstanding success, equally memorable for those who were there was his speaking and singing to about 4000 waterside workers on Friday 18 November, two days after his first concert.[43] The venue was what waterside worker Jim Beggs recalled was 'the old boxing stadium', and some workers had family members with them; author Kerry Greenwood has a strong memory of sitting on her father's shoulders while Robeson sang on the waterfront.[44] The workers had been on strike for a week. Whereas the Sydney Town Hall meeting of striking waterside workers had been about the Crimes Bill (the bill had by this time passed through federal parliament and become law), this Melbourne strike was over working arrangements and conditions. It would end, on the union leadership's urging, three days later.[45] As Beggs later recalled, Paul spoke about the condition of Aboriginal people in the outback and 'the plight of the Indigenous people of every country'. He urged trade unionists to do more to support Aboriginal people and commented: 'Democracy needs a good shepherd and you in the trade union movement must be that good shepherd for all the oppressed. You cannot live on an island of wealth in a sea of poverty. You men are the hope of the world.'[46]

As in Sydney, Paul received a tumultuous reception. After singing 'Joe Hill', 'Water Boy' and 'Ol' Man River', he led the 4000 people present in singing 'John Brown's Body', explaining that John Brown had died that his (Paul's) father, a slave, should be free.[47] John Brown was a radical opponent of slavery whom the state of Virginia executed on 2 December 1859 for conducting a raid on a federal armoury at Harpers Ferry, intending to seize munitions for use in slave rebellions. Union troops in the early months of the American Civil War began singing 'John Brown's Body', a marching song, and news of its instant popularity reached Australian newspapers. One story in November 1861 told of soldiers in New York singing it on their way to the battle zone, joined as they marched by thousands of private citizens singing the chorus, 'John Brown's Body lies a-mouldering in the grave' (sung three times), followed by the last line, 'His soul's marching on' (in later versions 'But his soul goes marching on').[48] It soon became well known and was sung by the Fisk Jubilee Singers during their Australian tour in the 1880s and others after that.[49] Given that many people knew the chorus, it was ideal for mass singing. When Paul sang it, the waterside workers were delighted to join in.

The Melbourne branch of the union made him a life member and when he left the stadium there were unprecedented scenes. The *Maritime Worker* described it: 'Members climbing over seats to grasp his hand and the whole gathering was on its feet, stamping, shouting, and clapping. It had to be seen to be believed.'[50] Beggs, then a rank-and-file delegate, walked with Paul to his car and the two men talked about an African American singer named Muriel Smith whom Jim had met at a Moral Re-Armament conference in the United States two years before; Paul responded that he knew Muriel to be a courageous woman. Begg's account of these events concludes: 'As we shook hands I felt I was in the presence of a very special human being, a man misjudged by his country at that time, simply because he had the courage to speak out for equality and justice for his people.'[51] In his memoir, Beggs reflects that Paul and Harry Bridges, the Australian-born leader of the ILWU, whom Beggs looked after whenever Bridges visited his original home town of Melbourne, had a lot in common: 'both were men who loved their country, but because they fought against injustice, McCarthyism put them in the "communist box" in the USA'.[52]

The Melbourne peace movement meets the Robesons

Had he been in Melbourne a little longer, Paul Robeson would very likely have spoken and sung at the CICD's first-anniversary conference, held from 25 November to 2 December.[53] However, he had concert commitments in Adelaide and in lieu of attending he recorded a message, as he had done the previous year, to be played when the conference officially opened on 26 November.

The journal *Peace Action* printed an account of his speech, which had two main themes: the importance of peace, and the struggles of

African American and colonised peoples for freedom. He began with his usual comments concerning 'our great joy to be here with you in Australia. The last weeks have been deeply moving and inspiring ones. We have met so many of you who are actively engaged in making Peace on This Earth a reality. We certainly feel ourselves a part of you on this historical occasion.' Paul referred to what he believed the people in the socialist bloc wanted: 'As I have said on many recent occasions, I deeply and firmly believe, and know, that the people of the lands of Socialism want peace dearly, need peace. They remember at very close hand what the terrible ravages of war mean.' He concluded on a positive note, saying there was a strong peace movement in the world: 'They march in thousands; they march to and from Aldermaston; they march for peace in New York; they cry out for a decent America in San Francisco.'[54] His answer to the question of whether peace and disarmament were possible was 'A thousand times, YES'. During the talk he indicated he would soon sing 'some of the songs of other days of struggle for the defence of our sacred constitutional liberties, for an America of Peace and Plenty', such as 'Which Side Are You On?', 'Gonna Lay Down My Sword and Shield' and 'Walk Together Children'. Perhaps he ended the recording by singing these songs.[55]

The CICD organised a reception for Paul and Eslanda in Melbourne on Sunday 20 November that would prove to be an outstanding event. The venue was the Palais de Danse in St Kilda, a seaside suburb where Sam Goldbloom lived and where he had formerly been a member of the local council. It was a sign both of Robeson's popularity with Melburnians and the strength of the city's peace movement that thousands attended, ASIO estimating 3000.[56] Along one wall was a banner flown down from Sydney with the slogan 'Greetings to Eslanda and Paul/ Long may you sing speak and write for Peace'. Goldbloom chaired the meeting and the Reverend Alf Dickie gave a fulsome speech of welcome. Eslanda spoke next, bringing a strong feminist perspective to the event. She was pleased, she said, to see the women at this event 'playing a proper role', and emphasised the importance of women's involvement in the movement for peace. Since women were half the population, they should have 'half the say about how the earth should be run'.[57] Paul then spoke at some length; as one ASIO agent who was present commented, not unfairly, 'Robeson is a dramatic, forceful, impressive speaker who introduces subtle humour at the right moment, yet the speech itself is disjointed. He intersperses his delivery with singing but overall it appealed to the crowd which clapped his every statement.'[58] The somewhat wandering nature of this speech is an indication, perhaps, of Paul's growing exhaustion.

We have an audio recording of this event, from chairman's welcome to conclusion, made by Norm O'Connor. A founding member of the Victorian Folklore Society, O'Connor had for many years been recording local songs and stories of colonial origin.[59] On the St Kilda recording, now held in the National Library of Australia, we hear Paul begin by singing 'Water Boy', 'Ode to Joy' and 'Down by the Riverside' (inviting people to join in the chorus, 'I ain't gonna study war no more'). He then talks, as he often did, about his father having been born a slave, but with more detail this time, emphasising his father's huge influence on him as his mother died when he was only six years old, and how as the youngest in the family, his older siblings gradually left home so that for a long time it was just Paul and his father. His father's favourite sermon, he recalled, was from Isaiah, that you lay down your sword and you turn it into a ploughshare. When his father lost his position as pastor (at Witherspoon Church in Princeton, New Jersey), 'I came up in complete poverty, complete poverty, lucky to have a pair of shoes', so that when he met the wharfies, as he had earlier that day, he knew immediately 'that's where I belong'.

As he had done in Sydney, Paul refers to events in Little Rock, and now adds New Orleans, 'the toast of our country' and his pride in seeing the courage of children combating racism and segregation. Paul was here referring to events occurring during the desegregating of two elementary schools in New Orleans in mid-November 1960, which *The Age* had reported.[60] Each day, as four six-year-old African American girls went to their newly desegregated schools, white parents and others taunted them with racial slurs and subjected them to death threats. The treatment of six-year-old Ruby Bridges in particular, who was confronted with a screaming, abusive crowd when escorted to her first day at a previously all-white elementary school, attracted international attention.[61] A little later, Paul expresses concern for what is happening to the (Aboriginal) people in 'the middle part of your country', for 'they're my brothers and sisters too'. He also criticises Australia for following American policy too closely: while here in Australia, he says, 'I don't know where I am sometimes, I look around and I don't know if I'm in Australia or New York, I don't know sometimes.' He concludes by reciting Blake's 'Jerusalem', followed by extended applause.[62]

After the speeches, Paul introduced the ten girls nominated in a 'Princesses of Peace' competition; there is a photograph of him meeting the 'princesses' in the local communist newspaper *The Guardian* on 1 December.[63] This was a fundraising competition, and it sounds similar to the 'Queen' competition I participated in as a seven-year-old in the Australian mining town of Broken Hill in 1952, which was organised by my mother and her friends to raise funds to establish the town's first kindergarten. I also remember my princess dress on a May Day float in Newcastle a couple of years later. Communist women seem to have had a liking for queen and princess competitions to raise money.

Either before or after the speeches, Paul spent time shaking hands with some of those present. Alan Anderson wrote to me in 2008 saying he remembered attending a large gathering in St Kilda 'where many people of the Peace movement the Left and politicians like Jim Cairns were in attendance ... I shook his hand and was bowled over.'[64] Lorraine Paul also remembers lining up to shake his hand: 'What a beautiful hand it was! Strong and warm, much like the man himself I would say.'[65] Mullett recalled, 'I was about eleven ... Paul shook my hand, I was in awe.'[66] Author Barry Hill wrote many years later, in 2018, about attending this event in an essay in letter form to his father:

> 'Stand here', you told me once, when we were in a crowd at the Palais Theatre [*sic*] in St Kilda, and I did. I joined the queue that slowly approached the huge black man at the edge of the stage. 'You'll remember this', you said, and I knew I would as my fingers slipped

> into the big, warm, dark brown and pink hand of Paul Robeson. And in case I forgot, you bought the record of that wonderful event, when Robeson spoke of being with Welsh miners and workers in Russia (a nation that had welcomed his son into an unsegregated school) and then he sang 'Water Boy', and 'Old Man River', and of course 'Joe Hill', the name I would one day choose for my son.[67]

Another recent recollection is more troubled. In his memoir *No Country for Idealists*, social theorist and cultural critic Boris Frankel writes of attending both a concert and this meeting at the Palais when he was about fourteen years old. Having grown up in Melbourne in a left-wing family (his father, born in Russia, was a communist and both parents were members of the Australia-Soviet Friendship Society), he had listened to Robeson recordings for years, and at the concert, he remembers, Paul's 'magnificent voice thrilled me'. He was less impressed by Paul's speech, with its 'cringing apologetics for the Soviet Union'. In Frankel's view, Robeson was a courageous fighter of racism but a coward in relation to the Soviet Union. Apparently referring to the case of Feffer and Mikhoels discussed in Chapter 2, Paul 'closed his eyes to the terror and the repression of people he knew personally'.[68] Frankel's distance from the 'uncritical supporters of the Soviet Union' he saw around him at this meeting came from his own experience as a teenager. Unlike most of the audience in Melbourne, he and his family had experienced the Soviet Union firsthand, from their arrival there in 1956 expecting a successful socialist society until their return to Melbourne in 1960, thoroughly disillusioned by what they had seen and experienced.

That evening, the Reverend Archibald Crichton Barr, minister at the Scots Church since 1947, said in his sermon that while he did not like Paul Robeson's politics, he wanted to 'salute a great man who makes us like himself, if only for an hour'.[69] Though Barr may seem at first glance an unlikely Robeson supporter, in fact he was very well informed. His wife, Anne, who had died only seven months earlier, had in her youth been an opera singer, had sung in the church choir, and had been instrumental in popularising the spiritual in Scotland in the 1930s.[70] 'The great thing', Barr said, 'about Paul Robeson was his heart, which felt strong, clean emotions, and his power to make one feel them.' The visit was, he thought, 'an event of real significance'. Paul 'reminds us that there are bigger and more enduring things than race, class or political affiliations'. Barr also said, 'Paul Robeson reminds us that every race has its contribution to make to truth and beauty and the understanding of life.'[71]

Aboriginal Melbourne

As I researched this book, I wondered if Paul or Eslanda had met Aboriginal people in Melbourne as they had done in Brisbane and Sydney and would do in Perth. There is good reason to think they might have, as Melbourne was the Australian city in which the Aboriginal advancement organisations of the era were most prominent. The Council for Aboriginal Rights had formed in March 1951 and was actively campaigning for equal opportunity, full citizenship rights, the repeal of discriminatory legislation, the development of greater economic opportunity, and equal pay. It had many similarities with the Aboriginal-Australian Fellowship based in Sydney, but the personal relationship between one of the council's leading members, Shirley Andrews, and Faith Bandler was strained, perhaps inhibiting communication between the two organisations.[72] The Victorian Aborigines Advancement League (VAAL), which is still operating as the Aboriginal Advancement League, was formed in early 1957 by Pastor Doug Nicholls and non-Indigenous supporters Gordon Bryant (Labor Party MHR), Doris Blackburn (feminist peace activist) and Stan Davey (Church of Christ pastor). As historian Richard Broome points out, the organisation was based on Nicholls' philosophy 'that, like the keys of a piano, black and white needed to work together to create racial harmony'.[73]

If the Robesons were to make Aboriginal connections, it would most likely be through the VAAL. Previous African American entertainers and musicians visiting Melbourne, including Harry Belafonte two months earlier, had often met Aboriginal people at Nicholls'

Aboriginal Church of Christ in Gore Street, Fitzroy.[74] Yet I have found no record of a similar visit by Paul or Eslanda, or of a meeting with Harold Blair, the Aboriginal tenor whom newspapers had in 1947 hailed as 'an Australian Paul Robeson'. Blair lived in Melbourne and often sang at the Gore Street church, but as a frequent traveller he may not have been in Melbourne in November 1960.[75] Nor have I found any mentions of the Robesons meeting with representatives of the VAAL or similar organisations.[76] One reason may be that the league was going through a difficult period in 1960, financial difficulties forcing it to retrench staff and move to a different office.[77] Another may be that in Melbourne the Robesons' connections were firmly with the peace organisations, whose links with Aboriginal communities and organisations seem to have been relatively slight. Whatever the reason, the paucity of contact in Melbourne with Aboriginal people and their music would have been a disappointment for Paul and Eslanda.

In other respects, however, the Melbourne visit was remarkable for them both. The concerts were sold out, receiving rave reviews, and they both enjoyed positive media coverage. The attendance at the concerts, public lectures and meetings came to over 10,000 people. Melburnians would not forget them, as many subsequent Paul Robeson evenings, birthday celebrations and, later, memorial services for Paul would indicate. As we shall see in the concluding chapter, one young member of Paul's concert audiences in Melbourne, Margret Roadknight, would decades later have a special role to play in keeping his memory alive in Australia.

13

'A family party'

Five Days in Adelaide

After six weeks in the major cities in New Zealand and on Australia's east coast, the Robeson group—Paul, Eslanda and Larry Brown—turned west, flying along the southern edge of the continent to Adelaide, the capital city of South Australia. Adelaide in 1960 was, and remains, a much smaller city than Sydney and Melbourne, its 1960 population of 572,000 being less than a third that of Melbourne. It had a distinctive history, as South Australia had in the nineteenth century been a free rather than a convict colony. The city had developed a reputation in the nineteenth century for its liberalism, being early to introduce democratic reforms such as secret ballot (1856) and women's suffrage (1894). Yet the colony, later the state, also developed a substantial pastoral industry that entailed the dispossession and exploitation of Aboriginal people on a large scale.

The twentieth century saw the state lose some of its liberal reputation to such an extent that, when Paul and Eslanda arrived, the conservative politician Thomas Playford, leader of the Liberal and Country League, was in the twenty-second of his twenty-seven years as premier. Under his leadership the state saw a rapid expansion of its manufacturing capacity, which transformed the city and brought waves of British and other European immigrants. Its port, known as Port Adelaide, was only 14 kilometres north-west of the central business district but, with its resilient working-class culture, highly unionised workforce and sense of being separate and distinct, seemed a lot further.

Adelaide had strong cultural institutions. Eight months before the Robesons arrived it had hosted its first ever Festival of Arts, a major national cultural event that has been held ever since—biannually from 1960 to 2012 and annually since then, even during the pandemic. As the festival's public relations officer, author George Farwell, commented in the first festival program, 'Like another Festival City, Edinburgh, Adelaide is a compact city. You can walk without much trouble from one end of the inner city to the other ... Theatres, halls, galleries and exhibition buildings are all within easy reach of one another.' Farwell also pointed out that the state's pastoral wealth made Adelaide a 'comparatively well-endowed city', with wealthy people willing to make huge donations and bequests to support large cultural and educational institutions—the Elder Conservatorium of Music, the Barr Smith Library and the 'magnificent Bonython Hall'. The musical component of that first Festival of Arts was eclectic, including Dave Brubeck's jazz quartet, the Sydney Symphony Orchestra and the Victorian Symphony Orchestra.

Sometimes Adelaide was included in the itinerary of the string of African American performers brought out by Lee Gordon and others from the mid-1950s. Audiences had been able to hear classical singer Mattiwilda Dobbs in 1955 and 1959, Louis Armstrong in 1956, and Nat King Cole in 1957. Armstrong's visit was a sensation in Adelaide, as Johanna McMahon of the NFSA reports. As an aside, she notes that 'Satchmo jammed and dined at the home of jazz musician and 5DN radio broadcaster Mal Badenoch', where he ate his first-ever meat pie ('Meat pies, man? I heard of eating apple pies, mulberry pies, raspberry pies, but never meat pies. I'm heading out the back to eat meat pies').[1] Such visits, however, were uncommon—Harry Belafonte, for example, had not come to Adelaide—adding to the sense of excitement as people anticipated Paul's arrival. The Adelaide *Advertiser*, the city's morning broadsheet paper, published a customary preparatory article two weeks beforehand that, while distancing itself from Paul's politics, was pleased that Adelaide would have the chance to hear and see 'one of the most remarkable men of this century'. 'Almost everybody', it said, 'has come to regard this tall, calm, dignified man as the living symbol of the sorrows and hopes of the Negro race.' It was clear from his performances in England since regaining his passport, where he sang at the Albert Hall in six languages and performed Othello, that 'his voice was unimpaired by time'. The paper hoped that the people of Adelaide would receive Robeson warmly.[2]

Two key figures in hosting the extra-concert aspects of the Robesons' Adelaide visit were married couple George and Edna Hutchesson, both musically inclined activists in the peace movement, who helped promote with other activists the sale of concert tickets.[3] George was a violinist and Edna a pianist, and as their daughter, Margaret Kartomi, records, they met when Edna accompanied George on stage, and 'they kept on playing together all their lives'. They were Quakers, members of the Religious Society of Friends and, as Margaret explains, many Quakers 'display a special love for music in daily life'. The family attended each Sunday the Friends Meeting House in North Adelaide, a notable wooden construction built originally from prefabricated material transported from England in 1840.[4] As Quakers, they had something in common with Paul given his background as the son of a pastor. In fact, his mother, Maria Louisa Bustill, who had died when he was very young, came from a family with a mix of African, Delaware Indian and English Quaker ancestry, and had taught at Roberts Vaux High School, named after a Quaker abolitionist.[5] George and Edna were both members of the Quakers Peace Committee and the South Australian branch of the worldwide Peace Pledge Union, and Edna was also a member of the active local branch of the Women's International League for Peace and Freedom.[6] Like Melbourne's three 'peace parsons'—the reverends Alfred Dickie, Frank Hartley and Victor James—the Hutchessons represented the Christian part of the peace movement. Although not communist themselves, they were prepared to work with communists on questions of peace. They had, for example, attended two international peace conferences in 1955, each of which had close links with the communist strand of the world peace movement; on their return to Australia, their involvement in the peace movement had continued.[7]

The Hutchessons were present at the airport welcome on Wednesday 23 November organised by the small South Australian Peace Committee, along with about fifty others, including peace activists, members of the UAW and the Australia-Soviet Friendship Society, whose representative, Carrie Keith, presented them with flowers on behalf of the society.[8] Most of those ASIO listed as being present were members of the CPA, some of them leading figures, such as John Sendy, Alan Finger and Jim Moss. Also present was the secretary of the Peace Committee, Syd Lovibond, a party member and senior lecturer in psychology at the University of Adelaide who was becoming a distinguished academic and whose obituaries would later describe him as the 'father of Australian psychology'.[9] ASIO also noticed the presence of Stavros Pappas, who had arrived in Australia from Greece in 1927 and joined the CPA during the Depression, at one time chairing its Adelaide branch.

Paul's interviews in Adelaide

Once settled in at the South Australian Hotel, Paul and Eslanda conducted, as they had in every city, several press and radio interviews. The result was a range of appreciative newspaper stories and radio programs.[10] One story appearing the next day in the afternoon tabloid, *The News*, was especially warm, with the interviewer, 'JM', describing Paul as 'a big wide man, warm, human, polite and intelligent' and his voice as 'a sound never to be forgotten'. The interview ranged widely, including Paul's comment that he withdrew from Hollywood because its film directors 'insisted on portraying the negro as a clown or a plantation hallelujah shouter'.[11] When Paul said he was a strong union man, JM reflected: 'He is a strong man in many ways, this giant who has weathered years of storms around his majestic head.'

Another interview conducted that day was by rising ABC star Bob Moore.[12] It was the best radio interview with Paul of the entire tour.

Moore was an unusually educated and knowledgeable interviewer, having studied at the University of Adelaide and Oxford University and having worked at the BBC from 1958 to 1960 as a current affairs producer for radio. Now twenty-seven years old, he had recently returned to Australia and was working as a talks assistant for ABC Radio; he would later become well known as a leading interviewer, presenter and producer on ABC-TV. His questions make it clear that he knew Paul Robeson's career well, assisted perhaps by the fact that both men had lived and worked in London for the previous two-and-a-half years.[13]

The interview focuses on music, song, and acting on stage and film, and has many interesting moments. When asked about his musical and acting training, Paul says that 'from the age of five my father taught me how to use my speaking voice', commenting that for his father, 'oratory was the great art'. His singing came naturally from speaking: 'as Dr Vaughan Williams points out in his book *The National Music*, perhaps folk song is only an extension of speech'. Paul recounts how he went to a teacher to study opera once, but after three weeks felt that opera was not for him and he was naturally far closer to folk music. He is a singer, he says, of folk songs, and of 'that opera which is close to the folk tradition', such as Mussorgsky and Debussy, and refers again to Vaughan Williams, much of whose music, he says, was based on the folk music of Britain.

Paul talks about his time in London in the 1930s, a time he will never forget for the opportunity to act with leading British actors in *Othello*. He emphasises how he has become part of British life and got to know English, Welsh and Scottish working-class people, to whom he still feels 'very close today'. They discuss musicals, Moore asking about the recent tendency to make the songs a part of the story and Paul commenting on *West Side Story* as a great advance in musical theatre and film. On his film acting career, Paul says he was in those movies mainly to sing, with little attention to his acting; when he looks back at them, he thinks 'the acting is not so hot'. When Moore asks him how his concerts differ from drama, Paul responds that he turns his concerts into a drama, talking directly to the audience, creating the feeling of a welcoming, enjoyable evening: 'I come on talking to my audience, conversing with them, explaining, talking about some of the songs, and making it rather a family party in which … they come into a theatre perhaps, and I even read poetry you know, I read some Shakespeare.'

When Moore asks about the biggest audiences he has ever had, Paul refers to singing in Paris (just two months earlier) for *L'Humanité*, a newspaper there, 'and there were about 200,000 people floating about, about 100,000 or more in the place and 100,000 more outside where they could hear through loudspeakers'.[14] When asked about the most *satisfying* concert he has ever performed, Paul mentions his comeback concert in Oakland, California, in February 1958, remembering that the place was packed 'and I was frightened to death', but the concert went well and 'I was back in business'. He also alludes to concerts in London after his return there, and one in Moscow in August 1958 where he received a 'wonderful reception'. He is quick to add that the current tour of Australia and New Zealand, where so many people have said they have been waiting to hear him for thirty years, is 'one of the most moving experiences of my whole professional life'. When Moore asks Paul what kind of auditorium Adelaide should have for music festivals in future, the recent Festival of Arts having been such a tremendous success, Paul suggests an outdoor setting. The interview continues with a discussion of African American achievements in music, leading Paul to refer warmly to Billie Holliday as 'one of the greatest who ever lived' and to reflect sadly on the 'conditions under which she had to live'. In pondering the successes and struggles of African American singers, Paul comments, 'I'm not one for the great suffering of the artist all the time, got to be joyful too, and it isn't easy to be happy under pressure.' Throughout the interview he seems relaxed, responding to questions seriously and with good humour.

Towards the end of the visit, Paul had a rather different interview with sportswriter Ray Polkinghorne of *The Advertiser*. It was about football. Headed 'Singer keen to see "Rules"' (referring to the local football code, Australian Rules), the story was one of the few on the tour to focus on Paul's earlier career as a star footballer. It was accompanied by two photographs, one of him as a footballer and the other as he looked at the time of the interview. Paul expressed interest in Australian Rules and asked many questions about the rules and principles of the game. He also reflected on the influence of his time as a star footballer on his singing and acting career. 'I have had no formal training in singing or the theatre,' he said, 'but sport taught me how to breathe deeply, and playing football to crowds of up to 100,000 gave me stage confidence.'[15]

The Adelaide concerts and Kamahl

The first Adelaide concert, on Thursday 24 November, was a full house at the Odeon Theatre. A palatial and extravagant cinema building in the inner suburb of Unley, just south of the city centre, it had opened in 1928 under another name, the New Star Theatre, at the height of the cinema building boom before the Great Depression.[16] Nadra Penhalurick, a pianist, music teacher and musical arranger for live performances who reviewed the concert for *The News*, was bowled over.[17] 'The magic of Paul Robeson,' she wrote, 'touching on every last one of our emotions, held us all spellbound last night just as we had always known it would.' Along with the audience, she loved the well-remembered favourites such as 'Shortnin' Bread', 'Ol' Man River', 'Ma Curly Headed Baby', 'Water Boy' and 'Swing Low, Sweet Chariot', and his 'brilliantly humorous comments'. With Othello's speech, she noted, 'the crowded house roared, cheered, and stamped'. Doug Eason, in his column 'Odd Spot' in *The News*, reported on attending the concert and noted approvingly the remark of an elderly woman afterwards that 'It is not simply the voice of a person, it is the voice of a people'.[18]

Both concerts were reviewed for *The Advertiser* by its longstanding music critic John Horner, an organist born and educated in Scotland and since 1928 a teacher at the Elder Conservatorium of Music at the University of Adelaide. Horner was delighted with the tremendous success of the first concert, which he called a 'fine celebrity concert';

for him, what made it truly memorable was Robeson's role as 'a kind of one-man band (or league) of nations' who sang songs first in English and then in their original language (German, Welsh, Russian, Yiddish), hammering home the theme of universal brotherhood.[19] Horner noted of the second concert, on 26 November, that it was, like the first, fully booked, making 4500 concert attendees in all.[20] He said that this time Paul 'added Norwegian and Czech to his list of languages', including a 'Norwegian version of Luther's "A Stronghold Sure" as sung in Trondjheim Cathedral during the occupation' in defiance of a Nazi ban. Revealing his own musical priorities, Horner commented that the 'greatest moment occurred at the end of Mussorgsky's Death of Boris', which 'lifted us right out of the Negro spiritual class … into the wider realms of art—and of criticism'.[21]

In the audience at one of these concerts was 26-year-old Kandiah Kamalesvaran, better known as Kamahl. He had arrived in Adelaide as an eighteen-year-old student in 1953 and turned to singing through hearing Nat King Cole on the radio. So great was his admiration that when Cole was on his third Australian tour in 1957, Kamahl went to his hotel in Adelaide and, amazingly, sang one of Cole's own songs, 'Nature Boy', to him.[22] He had just begun his own singing career, originally choosing the first part of his surname, Kamal, as his name but soon changing the spelling to Kamahl to stop people pronouncing his name as 'camel'. Eight months before the Robesons arrived, he had appeared in the role of a calypso singer in *Moon on a Rainbow Shawl*, a play staged at the Adelaide Festival of Arts. Written by Errol John, a Trinidadian who had migrated to England in 1950, it depicted life in a poor black community in Port of Spain, Trinidad, and had been first performed at the Royal Court in London in 1958.[23]

Kamahl went on to have an immensely successful singing career and has recalled in several interviews over the years what an enormous impact hearing Paul sing at the Odeon Theatre had on him. 'I remember feeling', he recalled in 2009, 'the vibrations through the floorboards on the stage, hearing him. He was a very big man, with a great mind.' At the time, young Kamahl was still beset by feelings of inadequacy: 'The inferiority complex is a feeling that, as a Black, you think, regardless of your achievements, you'd never be considered equal. That whatever you do, you're secondary, because you're Black.' He saw Robeson as Black and proud, noting that in Australia Paul had taken up the cause of Indigenous people, declaring 'there's no such thing as a *backward* human being, only a society which says they are backward'. Kamahl reflected, 'It was Robeson who really paved the way for the likes of Martin Luther King to do what he did'—he helped desegregate America. 'Unfortunately, in spite of his intellect, he was naive enough to believe that the Russians were angels; he couldn't see that the Russians were doing worse things than the Americans. He was myopic in some respects, he had the blinkers on.'[24]

In a later interview, with Brian Nankervis on ABC Radio in 2021, Kamahl talks of Paul's attempted suicide, which he believes to be the result of Paul's realising the Soviet Union was not what he had always thought. He also talks about meeting Paul at the reception after the Unley concert. Though Eslanda, he says, prevented him from speaking to Paul directly, he did shake his hand. Paul, he recalled, dwarfed him: 'He was a huge man in every sense of the word, his intellect, and his sporting ability, he was a Shakespearean actor … He could do everything.' Of hearing him sing, he said, 'it was like a mountain murmuring. It's an experience I've never had since. I mean, he was an amazing man.' He also recalls that the audience 'all loved him'. The interview ends with Kamahl describing Paul as 'perhaps one of the greatest Americans ever' and as having a 'voice like the earth would have if the earth could sing'.[25]

Singing at the port

As in Sydney and Melbourne, Paul sang to waterside workers and their families, this time to a crowd of about 1100 in Port Adelaide on Friday 25 November. This was not a stop-work meeting, as in Sydney, or a strike meeting, as in Melbourne, but simply a lunchtime concert for a working-class community. Many of the workers in Port Adelaide were British immigrants—English, Welsh, Scottish and Cornish—who had been assisted by government immigration programs to provide the labour needed for the state's growing industrial sector. As such, they would have known of Paul from his twelve years in Britain and his return there to live and perform in 1958. The venue was the Waterside Workers Hall in Nile Street, Port Adelaide, which had been used extensively from its foundation in 1926 through to the 1960s for workers' entertainment and community activities, such as providing food for striking workers and their families. Arthur Shertock, a union organiser, later recalled that the hall, with its concerts and community support role, helped maintain a sense of solidarity and unity in the community.[26] It is still standing today, and is still used for radical theatrical and other entertainments.

When Paul entered the hall, the workers gave him a standing ovation. As always, he both spoke and sang. A reporter from *The News* was there, and quoted Paul as saying, 'My people have struggled and suffered for a long time, and we want to inherit a decent world.'[27] He spoke about Aboriginal issues, saying that he would 'return early in the new year to help working people in their fight for peace and to learn more of the plight and problems of the Australian Aborigines', a statement that brought 'special applause'.[28] The 25-minute concert consisted of recitations of 'Freedom Train' and the speech from *Othello* together with about twelve songs. As one news report put it, 'The songs and poetry were not given as a recital, but as part of a talk on the trials of the coloured races, the importance of unionism and the urgency of obtaining lasting peace.'[29] There is a film recording in the NFSA of part of this event, where we see Paul emphasising his solidarity with unions, reading William Blake's 'Jerusalem', singing 'Water Boy' and 'Ol' Man River', and, finally, leading the audience in singing 'John Brown's Body'.[30] As *The News* reported:

> eleven hundred watersiders and their families broke into spontaneous song with American negro singer Paul Robeson at an informal concert at Port Adelaide today. They sang 'John Brown's Body Lies a-Mouldering in the Grave'. Then the crowd went wild—shouting, applauding, whistling and calling for more.[31]

At the end, Robeson said, 'I am a people's artist. Wherever I go people want me to belong to them, and for me—nothing could be finer!' The audience was thrilled, Jim Mitchell reporting in the *Maritime Worker*, 'The final three cheers at the end of the concert lifted the roof.'[32]

Shertock, a member of the Communist Party and a job delegate for the WWF in Adelaide, had helped sell tickets to Paul's concerts.[33] He wrote to me in 2008 about Paul's informal concert at the WWF Hall:

> On that day it was jam packed with not only wharfies and seamen but also with shop workers and people from offices and banks … The lunch hour was long gone; I guess it was after three o'clock when finally he concluded his magnificent performance, with no musical accompanists. [As] far as I could see no one had left the hall.[34]

Also present was Rex Munn, a waterside worker and staunch unionist who loved to sing. When interviewed in 2012 by oral historian Allison Murchie, he, too, remembered the concert well:

> When Paul Robeson came to the Wharfies Hall in Port Adelaide it was absolutely packed … Shop assistants walked off, took time off their job … There wasn't any standing room. It was packed. Everybody standing up and down the aisles. And Paul Robeson came in and he sang to us and recited 'Freedom Train' … as Paul Robeson left he put his hand out and he shook, and I was lucky enough to shake hands with him. Yeah, it was great.[35]

After the concert, the union officials took Paul to a nearby pub, the British Hotel, for a drink and relaxation. There he 'downed a couple with the lads' and then, in response to requests, sang two songs 'to the great delight of the many regulars'.[36] He also met an African American seafarer from one of the ships then in port, who, as Paul later commented, 'looked if anything a little bigger than me' and who had come 'from the very part of North Carolina where my father was born and where I was reared as a child'.[37] When the seafarer, whom Paul named as Mr Byers, came up to him, Paul was delighted.

That evening, 25 November, both Paul and Eslanda attended a social event jointly organised by the Eureka Youth League (EYL), a youth organisation sponsored by the CPA, and the Australia-Soviet Friendship Society to welcome a Soviet youth delegation to Adelaide.[38] The delegation, consisting of Yuri Yelchenko (aged 31), Anatoly Shutov (27) and Victor Kuzmin (29), had just missed connecting with Paul and Eslanda in Sydney and Melbourne, but now, in Adelaide, they met.[39] Shertock recalls that when he and Carrie Keith took Paul and Eslanda to the venue, 'I couldn't believe it—we ran out of petrol. A taxi out of petrol … Paul is making jokes about the situation and Carrie and I are feeling so embarrassed … Finally we get to the reception and it was absolutely jam packed full of people.'[40] About 600 attended the reception for the Soviet delegation in the Caledonian Hall in King William Street, in the centre of Adelaide, making it standing room only.[41] ASIO reported that Paul was 'the centre of much attention and applause, but insisted that the Soviet Youth Delegation be given the first place, as the Reception was in their honour'.[42] Paul spoke, using a microphone, from the side of the hall, saying he was thrilled to be in Australia at the same time as the Soviet youth visitors.[43]

Someone recorded his speech and thirty-eight years later the tape recording was forwarded to the organisers of a Sydney event celebrating Robeson's 100th birthday. On it, we hear Paul begin by mentioning how wonderful it had been to meet Mr Byers, who was present, at the WWF Hall earlier in the day. He then mentioned, as he had done in Melbourne, the children suffering angry racist demonstrations when first attending a desegregated school in New Orleans: 'we are very proud standing here to see our children, yes children, yes teenagers, even at the age of four and six and eight, going into those schools in New Orleans'.[44] Given that this was a pro-Soviet event, Paul spoke more expansively about the Soviet Union than in his other talks and speeches. He spoke of having visited in 1934, where for the first time in his life he felt himself a full human being. Most of his speech, though, was about the importance of peace. Noting that he was a member of the World Council for Peace, he said 'we must have peace with all folks on this earth'. As Khrushchev had recently said at the United Nations in New York, there were two particularly important struggles: the end of colonialism, and the achievement of disarmament and peace. Paul went on: 'I have just come from many of the socialist lands. I know they want peace, know it from the depths of my soul. With my own eyes I saw it. They want peace in the world. So let's have it!' He continued, 'The socialists are going to stay, they're going to build their way of life, and they are going to have an influence on ours', and as a result, we have to learn to live together: 'There is only one earth and no matter what colour we may be, no matter what our opinions, whether we are black, brown, white or yellow, whatever our political opinions, in the end we are one human family …'

Paul thanked people in Australia for their courageous struggles for peace and for giving him such a warm welcome. It had been wonderful to see both 'the older ones who say "Paul, we've been waiting 35 or 30 years to see you, 20 years", and then to see the young who say, "we've only been waiting 20 months but we're glad to see you"'. He concluded by expressing a warm welcome to the Soviet youth delegation, asking them to 'take back to your people our love and friendship'. He then sang several songs: 'Water Boy', 'Ode to Joy' ('Build the road of peace before us/ Build it wide and deep and long/ Speed the slow and check the eager/ Help the weak and curb the strong/ … All for one and one for all'), and a song in Russian. Speeches done, Paul and Eslanda spent the rest of the evening signing autographs and answering questions.[45]

A musical evening

As happened in every city during the Australian part of the tour, Paul and Eslanda attended a 'private function' organised by the local Peace Committee, but in this case, on the evening of Sunday 27 November, it was a meeting with a difference. Where in other cities these Peace Council (or Committee) events had tended to be political rather than musical, in Adelaide the Peace Committee organised a buffet supper and a classical musical programme.[46] It seems likely that George and Edna Hutchesson, with their musical and peace connections, were deeply involved.

Though a smaller meeting than its equivalent in Sydney and Melbourne, this one attracted 150 people to the community hall in Belair, a middle-class suburb in the south-eastern foothills of the Adelaide Hills.[47] It began with Paul and Eslanda giving speeches similar to those given in Melbourne, followed by Paul singing several songs, illustrating, according to ASIO, 'the link between African songs and modern jazz'.[48] Next on the program was a Czech violinist, described by ASIO as 'possibly Ladislav Jasek', who played three pieces accompanied by Larry Brown. Jásek, an esteemed violinist in Czechoslovakia, had in 1959 begun a three-year term as professor of violin at the Elder Conservatorium; he was also leader of the conservatorium's string quartet. In coming to Adelaide, he would be part of a strong Czech immigrant influence on Australian classical music in the late 1950s. His connection with the Robesons may have been through Janette McStay, with whom he had played two chamber music concerts in New Zealand in May 1960.[49] Jásek was followed by the Hutchessons' daughter, Margaret, who played a piano solo, which as she later recalled was 'one of Bach's preludes, because of Robeson's liking for Bach's music'.[50] Her father, George, she says, also loved Bach, along with Handel and Mozart.[51] As musical as her parents, Margaret would later become an eminent ethnomusicologist with a specialisation in Indonesian music, an interest sparked by a family trip to Indonesia in 1959.[52]

At the end of the reception in Belair, the organisers gave Paul a boomerang and an 'aboriginal shield'.[53] Earlier, the Port Adelaide branch of the WWF had given him 'an authentic woomera throwing stick' with the explanation that 'the name of this peaceful aboriginal hunting equipment had been grossly misappropriated in this age', referring to the fact that the name of the area where British atomic testing had been conducted in 1946–47 was the Woomera Rocket Range.[54] While these gifts signified sincere support for Aboriginal rights, it seems that, as in Melbourne, neither Paul nor Eslanda was able to meet with Aboriginal people in Adelaide. While Paul had on his arrival told *The News* he was 'deeply concerned in the problems of the people who were here before you, the indigenous people of

Australia', he had little opportunity to express this support directly to Aboriginal people.[55] Where Faith Bandler had been able in Sydney to bring the peace and Aboriginal movements together and thus connect the Robesons to Aboriginal people, there seems to have been no-one playing this role in Adelaide.

The reception at Belair was the last organised event in Adelaide, and on Monday 28 November Paul and Eslanda flew back to Melbourne for the newly scheduled and sold-out concert in St Kilda on Tuesday 29 November. For those who met and heard them in Adelaide, the visit was a tremendous success. The American consul in Adelaide, John C Ausland, in a patronising and somewhat spiky report to the US State Department, judged the Adelaide visit to have been a 'complete propaganda success ... He was accepted by South Australians with the naive, uncritical welcome they extend to almost all entertainers from "overseas", regardless of merit.' Ausland continued:

> Australians are by no means pro-Communist; the great majority are strongly anti-Communist. However, they are eager for novelty and, for the most part, completely indifferent to international politics. The few who are politically aware are proud of their political tolerance and would not miss a chance to show how much more broad-minded they can be than the Americans. For this reason, the years of controversy caused by refusing Robeson a passport undoubtedly increased the impact of his propaganda.[56]

The Adelaide leg of the tour showed more starkly than anywhere else Paul's ability to communicate with people across class barriers. He turned his concerts into a 'family party', chatted freely with his largely white, middle-class audiences, talked learnedly and enthusiastically to a well-prepared and well-educated interviewer like Bob Moore, and was equally—or probably more—at home singing and talking to waterside and other workers in Port Adelaide. Eslanda, too, though not a famous musical performer, had some of this same relaxed cosmopolitan quality. As Val Howe put it excitedly in her report to the UAW, the Robesons had 'been and gone, but they left with us something of their feeling for humanity. They came, we saw, and they conquered us completely.'[57]

14

'A kind of farewell'

Four Days in Perth

On the evening of Wednesday 30 November 1960, Eslanda and Paul Robeson touched down in Australia for the last time. Perth audiences would hear Paul's last-ever performance on a concert tour, for a health crisis forced him to retire soon afterwards. This last stop would prove to be a huge success, with capacity appreciative audiences, delighted rave reviews, over 2000 people attending an additional impromptu concert at the Midland Railway Workshops, and a chance to hear memorable speeches, in person and on radio, by both Robesons. Precisely because it was the last stop, it led Paul and Eslanda to reflect on their experiences and the tour as a whole.

A memorable welcome

Paul and Eslanda arrived from Melbourne in the early evening. Hazel Butorac, who was then twenty-three and pregnant with her third child, remembers the airport arrival clearly. It was, she told me in 2019, at the old TAA (Trans Australia Airlines) terminal, where there was a pathway from the plane to the airport building, with doors opening into the arrival area. For the waiting crowd of about 200 people, suddenly, there he was.[1] Katharine Susannah Prichard, a well-known communist and a member of the Western Australian Peace Council, gave the welcome speech. Prichard was a writer with an international reputation; she was especially known as the author of *Coonardoo* (1929), one of the first novels to depict Aboriginal characters sympathetically.[2] She was also a fan of Robeson's, having hosted a local celebration of his birthday in April 1959.[3]

This welcome seems to have been a moving event. While there had been few Aboriginal people involved in the welcomes in Melbourne and Adelaide, they were well represented in Perth, the WA Peace Council having ensured they were aware and invited to attend.[4] *Tribune* reported Paul as saying to the Aboriginal people in the welcoming crowd, 'I hope that soon they will treat you as well as they treat me.'[5] Lloyd Davies later recalled that Paul instantly walked up to the Aboriginal members of the crowd and hugged some of them.[6] A lawyer who had frequently advocated for workers during numerous industrial disputes in the 1950s, Davies had helped form the Committee for the Defence of Native Rights, who supported Aboriginal strikers in the Pilbara in 1946.[7] Sam Aarons, a former member of the International Brigade in Spain in the 1930s and now a leading member of the Communist Party in Western Australia, was there, too. With him were his wife, Annette, their eleven-year-old son, and his young Noongar friend and neighbour, Robert. Annette later recalled:

> we stood at the very back, and I lifted young Robert up so he could see. Paul and Eslanda came through, waving and looking very alertly around. Robert, who was somewhat used to discrimination against him, said in amazement: 'he looked at me! He looked and smiled and waved straight at me!'[8]

Butorac remembers that she and her father, a leading communist trade unionist named Paddy Troy, were standing near the back, next to a tall white man holding his adopted two-year-old daughter, whom she described as 'a beautiful little Aboriginal girl with curly hair'. Paul immediately espied the little girl and came straight across the room and started to sing to the child 'Ma Curly Headed Baby'. The crowd went quiet, and when he stopped singing, she looked up to him with a smile and said, 'Daddy.' Margaret Lindley remembers being at the airport welcome as a child with her family, too. She told me, 'I remember vividly the sound of Paul's voice as he sang "Oh my baby, my curly-headed baby" to a young Aboriginal girl at the airport. My father hoisted me onto his shoulders, and I wished that I could be that girl.'[9] It was an emotional moment for everyone there.[10] Though most listeners would not have been aware of it, 'Ma Curly Headed Baby' was Paul's especially apt choice of song, for it was composed in 1897 by a 31-year-old Australian, George H Clutsam, who at the age of twenty-one migrated to the United Kingdom.[11]

When the airport welcome was over, Paul conducted a press conference that started at 9 p.m. and lasted over an hour. In the city's major broadsheet newspaper, the *West Australian*, the next day, journalist Frank Harvey reported that Paul spoke animatedly about Aboriginal rights, challenging those who spoke of 'backward races' and drawing connections with racial questions in 'Fiji, Honolulu, Ghana, Nigeria, the Arctic Circle, the Congo, and Russia'.[12] Harvey commented, a little sardonically, that:

> by 9.35 we had visited France, Spain, and the Fascist West generally. By 9.40 we had raced through North Carolina and Kentucky and we were having a short stopover in the United States … By 9.45 we had passed through Britain ('I have the warmest relations with the British people and have my roots in the British working class') and had arrived in Australia where, the singer said, 'he had received the warmest welcome—particularly from the wharfies'.

At 9.48 p.m., Harvey reported, Paul turned to the topic of singing, saying his voice was in good shape and he liked singing folk songs. He said, 'One reason my voice has lasted is because I sing like I speak. I hope I will be able to talk as long as I live.'

The presence of Aboriginal people at the airport welcome indicates the connections between the local Peace Council and Aboriginal people living in Perth, especially Noongar, the large language group of Australia's south-western corner. John Clements, president of the WA Peace Council, coordinated the political aspect of the Perth visit, which, with his extensive connections, he was well placed to do. Born in 1908 in Greenhouse near Cambridge, England, he had migrated to Australia in 1929, served as an ABC radio announcer during World War II, and was a member of the CPA, New Theatre and the Fellowship of Australian Writers.[13] His wife Margaret Clements worked as both kindergarten director and clinic nurse at Allawah Grove, an Aboriginal settlement near Perth; she would later be described by Noongar leader Robert Bropho as 'the black people's Florence Nightingale'.[14] Other key members of the Peace Council included not only Prichard but also the Reverend Peter Hodge, who had been a leading non-Aboriginal supporter of the Pilbara strike in 1946, and the writer Bert Vickers, who had been chair of the Council during the 1950s and whose novel *The Mirage* (1955) dealt with the situation facing Aboriginal people in the north-west and had been translated into several European languages.[15]

Making connections in Perth

The connections did not stop at the airport. A local newspaper reported that Paul bought one of the forty-five paintings displayed in an exhibition of Aboriginal artists that had opened in the Perth city centre two days before they arrived; a representative may have purchased it on his behalf.[16] The artists were all prisoners at Fremantle Gaol who had been sponsored and encouraged by Doreen Trainor in her role as prison visitor for the Department of Native Affairs.[17] Trainor, a social anthropologist, was an important non-communist figure in Aboriginal support organisations, having been president of the Original Australians Progress Association until it was dissolved just a few months before the Robesons arrived; she was now vice-president of its replacement, the WA Association for the Advancement of Coloured People.[18]

Had Paul and Eslanda arrived a year or so earlier, they would have been able to visit the Coolbaroo Club as a number of African American visiting performers had done before them, exchanging culture and having fun.[19] This was an Aboriginal club that had thrived through the 1940s and 1950s in a situation where, as historian Anna Haebich puts it, 'department officers and police controlled where Aboriginal people could live, walk, work, their associations, their children and entertainment'.[20] Its political wing, the Coolbaroo League, published a newspaper, the *Westralian Aborigine*, between 1953 and 1957. Dances, held on Friday nights, had been a major feature of the Coolbaroo Club's activities, and through the 1950s they expressed a variety of musical and dancing styles. The club had been influenced by its African American connections. In 1955 African American drummer Michael Silva and members of the Norma Miller Dancers, starring in a show called *Coloured Rhapsody* at His Majesty's Theatre, introduced club members to modern dances like the jitterbug, the jive, the hokey pokey and the conga.[21] In January 1956, African American jazz singer and pianist Nat King Cole performed at the Ambassadors Theatre in Perth and invited members of the club to his hotel, where activist and elder Bill Bodney presented him with a boomerang on behalf of the club.[22] In 1959, the Harlem Blackbirds performed at Perth's Capitol Theatre and on Friday nights, after their show, they, too, attended the Coolbaroo Club dances.[23] However, unfortunately for the Robesons, the energetic and visionary club and its political wing, the Coolbaroo League, had both ended in 1960, before they arrived. Clements, Davies and the Peace Council would be their main point of contact with Aboriginal people.

Paul and Eslanda spent Thursday 1 December at the prominent Palace Hotel in the inner city, which had, like the Menzies Hotel in Melbourne, been built during a gold rush, though this time it was the Western Australian gold rush, which occurred in the 1890s. With a reporter from the *Daily News* present, Paul heard John Joseph Jones, a London-born schoolteacher at Perth's Christ Church Grammar School, sing what the paper described as, but did not identify specifically, an 'Australian folk song'. Jones had responded to a call from Clements to supply for Paul information on Australian folk music, and this well-reported meeting was a result.[24] Jones gave Paul the manuscripts of seven songs he had composed, writing the lyrics of three himself and for others using poems written by Patsy Durack, Jack Sorenson and

Victorian lyric poet John Shaw Neilson.[25] Paul also met with a group of ten members of the EYL, which was a thriving organisation across Australia in 1960, as I can attest from my own teenage membership of it in Newcastle from 1958 to 1963, attending summer camps. In Perth, as Hugh Webb reported in the EYL magazine, *Target*, the group of ten went up cautiously to the Robesons' hotel room where they were greeted by 'a booming "Come in". From that moment on formality was forgotten.' Webb continued, 'Talking with Paul is like talking to the whole mass of genuine, friendly, progressive people of the world who stand for a policy of honesty, peace and above all—progress.' For the group, Paul became 'a symbol of all that is good on this earth … we all knew that this was one of the finest hours of our young lives.'[26]

That evening, Thursday 1 December, Paul gave his first Perth concert at the Capitol Theatre. According to the *West Australian*, it drew 'one of the largest audiences the theatre has seen for a musical affair in many moons'.[27] Butorac remembers it was a full house with a 'rapturous crowd', while Lindley recalls, 'We went to one of the concerts at the Capitol, and I remember how Paul would cup one hand to his ear and the astonishing sound of that voice.'[28] In his review of the concert, 'Fidelio' described it as unorthodox, informal and lively, and Paul's voice as noble, deep and sonorous, though perhaps with not quite the 'splendid power' of thirty years before. Fidelio was the pseudonym of 67-year-old Albert Kornweibel, a journalist who had been the *West Australian*'s music critic since, astonishingly, 1916 and who had played a significant role in the development of music in Western Australia.[29] Himself bilingual in German and English, and a lover of Beethoven, from whose work he took his pen-name, he noted approvingly that Paul sang the 'Ode to Joy' from Beethoven's Ninth Symphony, one verse in German and two in English, which he thought Beethoven, that 'apostle of human brotherhood, would not have minded'.

The Midlands Railway Workshops concert

The best-remembered parts of the Robesons' tour of Australia and New Zealand are those to do with the informal concerts to workers, such as at the Addington Railway Workshops in Christchurch and the Opera House building site in Sydney. The same is true in Perth, where he again sang to workers at a railway workshop. His doing so came about at the initiative of Colin Hollett, a union official, ALP member and Robeson fan. He owned and loved many Robeson records and had seen a television documentary about Paul meeting the Welsh miners. As he told an interviewer in 2002, 'I loved Paul Robeson as a person and his politics.'[30] Hollett worked at the Midlands Railway Workshops, the largest industrial workshops in the state, employing thousands of workers, where he was secretary of the Joint Railway Unions Committee.[31] He knew that Paul liked to sing at worksite concerts and for a couple of weeks had been unsuccessfully seeking management approval for such a concert at the Midlands Workshops.[32] On 1 December he decided to take a more direct approach and went to the Palace Hotel to ask Eslanda if Paul would come to the workshops and sing. He hoped that the chief mechanical engineer, Bill Britter, would grant permission once Robeson agreed to perform.[33] Eslanda told Hollett he would have to wait till after Paul's concert that evening to hear Paul's answer. When she rang Hollett after the concert at 2 a.m. to say yes, Paul would sing at the workshops that day, Hollett was delighted and immediately began organising.[34] He rang everyone to let them know and then, at 9 a.m., when Britter firmly maintained the ban, started another ring-around 'to tell them we were having it outside and to let the general public know'.

Tony Thomas, who at the time was a twenty-year-old CPA member and a cadet at the *West Australian*, was present at the workshops that day and provided a detailed account of the event.[35] Hollett and the others 'lined up a truck, public address system and facilities for the massive turnout, and the Mayor of Midland, Wal Doney, agreed to join Robeson on the truck and take him to a civic reception afterwards, a rare example on the tour of official endorsement'. Somehow, a piano was found and Larry Brown joined in despite the contract forbidding accompaniment outside the formal concerts. With only one more formal concert to go, the contract didn't matter.

The midday concert was a tremendous success. Over 2000 people from the Midland area came, children climbing trees to get a better view.[36] The audience from the workshops would have included many European immigrants and perhaps some Noongar workers, especially as apprenticeships for Noongar people were being encouraged at the time.[37] As the *West Australian* reported the next day, Robeson sang many of the songs he had sung the previous evening at the Capitol Theatre—'Water Boy', 'Joe Hill', 'Ol' Man River', other American folk songs, classical themes, Chinese tunes—and performed Shakespearean extracts. Hollett later remembered him singing 'Swanee River' and 'Jordan' as well as doing the recitation from *Othello*. Alongside his singing, Robeson spoke about the ways in which folk music was international, as tunes from one part of the world would appear in another. 'What is Dvořák's *New World Symphony* but my people's folk music?' he asked at one point.[38] *Tribune* described the audience joining in on one particular song as they had in Melbourne and Adelaide: 'As the great bass voice rolled out, the applause grew until finally the whole audience joined in "John Brown's Body"—"a song that honors a white American who gave his life so that my people should not be slaves", as Robeson put it.' At the end of the concert, the audience carried by acclamation a message of solidarity to the trade unions and to the 'Negro' people of the United States of America.[39] Afterwards, the mayor hosted a reception at the council chambers in Paul's honour, where Paul and Hollett talked. Hollett recalls: 'I had one of my first driver's licences and he signed it for me … He was just a wonderful, wonderful person.'[40]

Reception at the Palace Hotel

That same afternoon, Friday 2 December, the Peace Council hosted a well-attended reception for Paul and Eslanda in the dining room at the Palace Hotel.[41] Originally there had been no plans for any such event in Perth, Eslanda having rejected an earlier proposal, saying, 'This tour is so strenuous and the distances so great that Mr Robeson will have neither time nor energy for such an affair.'[42] Evidently, time had been found after all. For this reception we have recordings of the speeches, together with an ASIO report, from which we learn there were between 200 and 250 people present, so that the dining room was full and some people were standing.[43] ASIO described the audience as 'a very mixed gathering, with a representative group from practically all walks of life, professional, artistic, and working class. There did not appear to be a great number of New Australians [recent immigrants from a non-Anglophone background] present.' Those listed as attending included Paddy Troy, Bert Vickers, Katharine Susannah Prichard, and 'two women by the name of Durack, who were writers and/or artists' (one most likely was Mary Durack).[44]

At one point, Paul joined the table of Prichard, Troy and Sam Aarons. Troy fitted Paul's political leanings perfectly. He was a maritime union leader and the state's most well-known communist, and was noted for his actions in support of peace and Aboriginal rights.[45] Aarons had been a member of the International Brigade in Spain at the same time as Robeson visited in January 1938, though the two men had not met.[46] As Amirah Inglis explained in her book *Australians in the Spanish Civil War,* over sixty Australians joined the International Brigade, but as they arrived separately and were insufficient in number to form their own brigade, they were distributed among the other brigades.[47] Aarons and another Australian volunteer, Lloyd Edmonds, were both assigned as transport drivers with the Americans in the 1st Transport Regiment of the International Brigade, and Aarons was involved in the fighting fronts in Aragon, Madrid, Teruel and the Ebro.[48] Later, Annette Aarons would pass around at the Leederville branch of the CPA photographs of the event featuring Paul, Sam and several others.[49]

Fortunately, there is a tape recording of this event that includes the speeches given by both Paul and Eslanda (Eslanda's speech is discussed in Chapter 11). As secretary of the Peace Council, John Clements fulsomely introduced Paul. We can hear him on the recording saying in his cultured English voice that for those present, having Paul Robeson, a 'fellow member in the World Council of Peace' here to speak was 'a great and glorious occasion'. Clements hit a serious note when he said, 'We welcome Paul as an artist—an artist who has come down on the side of the people, and who by the sheer weight of creative and interpretative skill has destroyed those who sought to relegate him to artistic oblivion and thus destroy his work. We pay tribute to Paul the man.' He turned to a biblical allusion, saying:

> A long time ago, there was another man called Paul, who saw the light on the road to Damascus and when later on he was writing to his friends the Ephesians he gave them some advice, saying, 'Question all things and hold fast to that which is true.' Paul's life has been an elaboration and development of that theme, and nothing could have been better.

Clements went on:

> We acknowledge Paul as a leader of millions of people, including the Sacco and Vanzettis, the Rosenbergs, Linus Pauling and, oh, millions of others who have not and will not bend the knee or bow the head to the McCarthyist tyrants of our time … So you can see why we gain such inspiration from a visit from Paul Robeson and his great little standard-bearer, Eslanda, and might I say his protector too.[50]

Paul's half-hour resumes the themes he had used many times in speeches all over the world, but it also has a special quality to it as he reflects on the tour coming to an end. He began by saying:

> this is a very moving occasion for me. I'm about to say certainly not goodbye … but sort of see you again soon … I certainly hope to be able to get back very soon again … But I am saying just a kind of farewell tomorrow to a country which certainly has treated us so warmly and with such deep understanding … It is one of the great tours of my whole life … I am happy that it could come at this time in my own life, which has been a sort of gathering together of many strands after years of difficulties … It has been a chance for the first time to visit another continent on this earth and to feel that I could give, and we've been able to give, with a richness that wouldn't have been possible before and to have had it received in the way that it has been received.

His theme throughout the speech was the one he had been emphasising the whole tour: that we are one human family. He picked up on Clements' mention of the biblical Paul, saying his own father, a pastor, had often told him about Paul the Apostle. His father's favourite sermon, he said, was from Isaiah: 'When I lay down my sword and shield and turn them into ploughshares'. Then he broke into song: 'I'm going to lay down my sword and shield/ Down by the riverside/ ... I ain't gonna study war no more ...' He followed this with the first verse of 'There Is a Balm in Gilead': 'There is a balm in Gilead/ To make the wounded whole/ There is a balm in Gilead/ To heal the sin-sick soul'. Later in the speech he expressed concern at the role Australia was beginning to play in supporting US foreign policy aims and military objectives, commenting that 'somewhere the masters sitting in the Pentagon have mapped out a strange role for you here in Australia if you're not careful. [They want you] to play a main role here in Australia against peace, yes, because a lot of guys over there don't want peace, in my own land.' He thanked the peace movement in Australia for 'the struggle that you are making, it's a very magnificent one', noting that it was 'a source of great pride that I can be met in every city by peace groups. You couldn't do that in America today, couldn't quite do it.'

Yet again, Paul took up his critique of the idea of backwardness: 'It's running out now, the idea that people are so backward you can't educate them. That is running out now, fast, even in your country.' He reflected that he has been told Aboriginal people are good stock workers: 'they know how to handle a horse and the sheep, they ain't too dumb for that, not too dumb to labour for nothing. Well, they won't be too dumb to be full citizens and to function like anybody else.' He expressed his sense of kinship with Aboriginal people and said, 'as I told my brothers and sisters when I saw them at the airport, I hope they begin to treat you like they treat me'.[51]

He also talked about music, saying he loved to sing folk songs made by people of generations gone. He remarked on his amazement at the way Australians knew him and particular songs through his records, and commented that 'to walk out to face an audience that just wants to hear this song or just wants to *see* you somehow, it's been an amazing experience'. He went on:

> And so I have talked to the audience—I wouldn't dare talk this much, as much as I talked to you audiences here on platforms in Australia. They [managers] say wait a minute Paul, hold that, get onto another song. But you've been so patient and so understanding. A lot of things I've wanted to do, the concert's too short … but I want to … talk about so many things and haven't had the time and I won't have it this time.

Paul concluded his speech by saying, 'I hope to get back very soon. I hope they won't stop me coming in—they did that once in Canada—and I hope to get back to my own land to see my people … I wish you all success in your struggles.'[52] He then sang Beethoven's 'Ode to Joy'.

Clements supplied local radio station 6PR with a copy of the recording of this event that, when broadcast, aroused considerable interest. As he later reported to Peace Council members, the 'switchboard was jammed for two hours and the staff gleefully announced that [the program] would be repeated'. However, as *Tribune* reported, there was no repeat as the station executives, who had not previously heard the original recording, now objected. In its place was an interview on non-controversial issues, and some recorded songs.[53] When the repeat didn't happen, probably for political reasons, the Peace Council found there was great demand for copies of the tape of Paul Robeson's 'banned broadcast'.[54] Also available from the Perth leg of the Robeson tour was a 33 rpm record called *Big Paul*, featuring his recitation of 'Freedom Train' and singing of 'Ode to Joy'.[55]

The last concert and saying farewell

That evening, Friday 2 December, Paul gave his final concert of the tour at the Capitol Theatre. James Penberthy, the *Sunday Times* music critic, was fulsome in his praise, describing the concert as 'one of unmistakable greatness' and Robeson as 'a master of himself and of the warm, rich singing which has made his the world's best-loved voice'.

Penberthy was not only the paper's music critic but also a well-known composer, lecturer in composition, and musical director of the West Australian Ballet; earlier in the year he had composed the music for the ballet *Kooree and the Mists*, which would feature Mary Joyce Miller who had been accepted into the company the previous year and was possibly the first Aboriginal ballet dancer in a professional company.[56] Now, he wrote of Paul: 'He is a proud, fearless, majestic figure, but his easy informal friendliness reaches out through songs and spoken word to embrace all the members of his audiences.' He is beyond criticism: 'He is what he is—there are no rivals, no comparisons.'[57] There could be no greater praise.

There was one more day to go. A document written subsequently by ASIO summarising its surveillance of the Robesons' Australian visit suggests that on Sunday 4 December Paul and Eslanda met with members of the CPA in Perth and that Paul promised to help in any campaign on Aboriginal issues.[58] One agent reported him saying 'this was to be his last professional tour and that he will be returning to Australia in March 1961 as a "Peace" delegate'. Paul emphasised, the agent reported, his interest in Aboriginal people's struggles, telling the CPA that if it could 'supply the necessary information concerning his "Black Brothers" he would endeavour to assist their cause where possible'.[59] Paul and Eslanda had had a similar meeting in Adelaide, as ASIO reported, meeting with Dr Alan Henry Finger, state president of the CPA.[60] They had clearly developed quite close ties with the CPA during the tour.

It was time to leave, and as usual a group of well-wishers accompanied the Robesons to the airport. One of them was Brian Fleay, who reported later at a Peace Council meeting that he had had a good chat with Paul, who said he would be returning, but not on a concert tour. Fleay also quoted Paul as saying, 'the Peace Movement in Australia has made more progress than in any other place in the Western world that he had visited'.[61] Prichard was among those who went, writing a letter full of praise later that day to her son, diplomat and author Ric Throssell: 'No man I've ever met has so impressed me with his personal greatness. He's so simple and unaffected in his manner, so dignified, yet straight forward & uncompromising in what he says.' 'While his voice is deeply moving,' she continued, 'it's the man himself, I think, who demonstrates the greatness of the human spirit.'[62]

Finally, at midnight on Sunday, Paul and Eslanda boarded a Qantas plane to Jakarta, the first leg of their long journey home to London. It would take well over forty hours, with nine stops along the way, before finally reaching London on Tuesday morning. They had plenty of time to reflect on the fact that the visit had been both a financial and a political success.

15

'A symbol of hope for many'

Aftermath, Tributes and Reanimations

When it comes to memory in Australia and New Zealand of the Robesons and their tour, Paul's and Eslanda's stories differ markedly. Paul has been quite well remembered and acknowledged, though he is not well known to younger generations. Eslanda, on the other hand, is now little known in either country and, indeed, I hope *The Last Tour* goes some way to restoring knowledge and appreciation of her life and achievements. While it is not surprising that people remember Paul better than they do Eslanda—his fame was much greater and we can still hear his extraordinary voice—it is also true that women have a way of dropping out of collective memory. The project of women's history, which took off in the early 1970s, has gone a long way to remedy this relative historical invisibility, but we still have a way to go.

Aftermath

Once they were back home, Paul and Eslanda gave conflicting accounts of the tour. On the one hand, as Paul wrote to a friend, Clara Rockmore, soon after their return to London, he had experienced 'a really wonderful—moving tour'. Audiences had loved him. Yet, unsurprisingly in the context of the distances travelled, their packed itinerary, and his age and state of health, he was exhausted. He told Rockmore that this was definitely his last tour.[1]

When he went to Moscow in late March 1961, he was, as usual, warmly received and gave several press interviews. One was with V Drannikov for a trade union newspaper, to whom he commented that in the year since his last visit to Moscow, the biggest thing that had happened was his visit to Australia and New Zealand. People had treated him like an old friend though they had never seen or met him before; they knew of him and his songs through his recordings. The visit, he said, had been full of meetings and 'concerts attended by ordinary people, by workers, farmers, and longshoremen. We all sang together, and when we got tired of singing I'd read verses by Shakespeare, [Robert] Burns and [Vladimir] Mayakovsky. After that, we'd return to singing.'[2] He gave a different account of Australia when interviewed by Henrik Gurkow, Moscow correspondent for the German Democratic Republic newspaper *Neue Zeit* (New Times):

> One thing has embittered me. On the fifth continent I encountered a phenomenon which I have experienced in Africa and America: racial discrimination in the most loathsome form. If we compare the situation of the Maoris [*sic*]—of the aborigines in New Zealand—with the situation of American Negroes from northern states, we can call the situation simply terrible in which they and the Australian aborigines [exist].[3]

Eslanda made similar comments in her report on behalf of both of them to TASS, the Soviet news agency. Though in general complimentary about New Zealand, her report was critical of the discrimination against Māori in housing, jobs and social life, and she strongly condemned Australia's treatment of Aboriginal people, whom she described as a 'desperately abused people'.[4]

In Australia, meanwhile, many looked forward to Paul's return. He had promised numerous times on the tour to come back to assist Aboriginal people's struggles, and had mentioned specifically to Kate Morrow his plans to visit Indonesia and India 'in early spring', possibly thinking of the World Council of Peace conference in New Delhi in

February 1961 and the Afro-Asian Peoples Solidarity Council meeting in Bandung in April 1961, two meetings Bill Morrow and other Australian peace activists would in fact attend.[5] Paul had said in Perth that he might come back to Australia after those two meetings, leading CPA members of the Victoria Park branch in Perth to comment, when they met in January 1961, that perhaps they ought to be doing more to involve Aboriginal people in the party, 'particularly in view of Paul Robeson's proposed visit here in May 1961'.[6]

Yet it was not only the prospect of Paul's return that galvanised people into action: it was also his and Eslanda's words of critique and encouragement. As the UAW's *News for Everywoman* put it, their visit had been 'an inspiration to all of us. We feel much stronger for our contact with them.'[7] In Perth, John Clements reported to the Peace Council on 22 December 1960: 'We have had an active and important year. The Robesons performed their miracle here too and did more good for the Peace Movement in three days than has been done in as many years.'[8] To maintain the impetus given by the visit, the NSW Peace Committee made and distributed widely a sound recording called *Paul Robeson for Peace*, which had his Paddington Town Hall speech on one side and him singing and reciting Langston Hughes' 'Freedom Train' on the other.[9] A New Zealand recording made at the time had Paul's message and reading of Blake's 'Little Black Boy' to Kate Morrow on one side, and songs by Unity Artists of New Zealand on the other.[10]

The Robesons certainly helped the peace movement, but their most important legacy was an enhanced determination by left-wing activists to support the struggle for Indigenous rights. As Lloyd Davies said at a meeting of the Fremantle branch of the CPA on 12 December, just a week after the Robesons had left the country, they should take up again the 'native question' in the north 'so that they would be able to help Robeson if and when he revisited the state'. (Paul had said expressly to Davies that on his return he proposed to tour the north-west of Western Australia.)[11] At a meeting of the party's Central Committee in February 1961, Sam Aarons spoke strongly on the subject, saying that in his view, 'A party worthy of the working class must oppose and fight against white chauvinism and racism in all its forms. The Communist Party … opposes all discriminatory legislation and actions on grounds of colour or race.' He stressed the importance of actions initiated and carried through by Aboriginal people themselves.[12]

During 1961 there was an increase in coverage of Aboriginal matters in the party's newspaper, *Tribune*, and several state conferences that year passed resolutions on Aboriginal affairs.[13] A special meeting on the issue by concerned party members was held in Brisbane on 13 April, with key figures present including Wally Stubbings, Ted Bacon and the poet Kath Walker, later known as Oodgeroo. Walker stressed the importance of Aboriginal leadership ('coloured people must be led by coloured people') and Aboriginal membership of the CPA if the party were to progress on Aboriginal issues.[14] Although Aboriginal membership of the party remained low, one important recruit during this period was Bob Anderson, who had met Robeson in Brisbane. A little later, Anderson became a leading figure in both the Queensland Council for Aboriginal and Torres Strait Islanders and a union organiser for the BWIU.[15] He became a leader in Queensland Aboriginal politics and eventually a revered and influential elder.[16]

Both Robesons influenced the Union of Australian Women. When its national committee met in Sydney on 19 February 1961, Barbara Curthoys, my mother, gave a report on Aboriginal policy.[17] She mentioned Khrushchev's comment to the UN General Assembly on 12 October 1960 in which, in the context of supporting colonial independence, he had said it was 'common knowledge how the native population was exterminated in Australia … Here open extermination is effected.' Curthoys also referred to the fact that the Warburton Ranges film had deeply affected the Robesons, and that Paul had said that nowhere else were people treated so badly. Aboriginal people, she continued, were being used as slave labour and there was a need for equal pay and equal education. She mentioned the cooperative movement then gaining popularity in northern New South Wales, and the remaining discriminatory legislation concerning Aboriginal people purchasing liquor. She outlined the work of the Newcastle Trades Hall Council subcommittee on Aboriginal affairs, which she had helped form, and described the struggle then occurring at the Purfleet mission north of Newcastle concerning payment of rent. Referring to a statement Eslanda Robeson had made concerning coloured world leaders (unspecified, but possibly at her talk to the UAW in Sydney on 9 November 1960 where she emphasised the role of women worldwide in independence and freedom struggles), Curthoys said Mrs Maher (Marjorie Maher, vice-president of the Aboriginal Advancement Committee at Purfleet mission) was an example, showing 'dignity in demanding rights for her people'. After Esther Aarons spoke in further detail about the Newcastle Trades Hall Council subcommittee, Ursula Southwell, from Victoria, commented that the Robeson visit had been 'very effective publicity' for the movement to support Aboriginal people.[18] A month later, on 22 March, the Sydney branch of the UAW listened to a recording of one or both of Eslanda's radio interviews with Tom Jacobs.[19]

Jessie Street, an Australian feminist activist for Aboriginal rights, wrote to Eslanda in April 1961 saying, 'They are still talking about the visit of you and Paul out here.' On several occasions, she wrote, she had heard people playing Paul's record, possibly the one of his speech and recitation of 'Freedom Train' at the Paddington Town Hall event.[20] Street and Eslanda had become friends, for the two women had a lot in common—both were pro-Soviet, feminist (though Eslanda did not describe herself that way) and active in the peace movement, and both had had UN accreditation as journalists and close connections with Pandit Nehru. They were both friends, too, of Peggy Middleton, who had been co-organiser of the *Let Robeson Sing* campaign in the 1950s. Street's letter summarised some of what had been happening in Australia concerning Aboriginal people as well as the growing opposition to apartheid in South Africa since Eslanda's visit. Street sent copies of this letter to several people, including Faith Bandler in Sydney and Shirley Andrews in Melbourne, attaching copies of her own *Report on Aborigines in Australia* (1957), which the Anti-Slavery Society in London had circulated widely.[21]

The expectation in Australia and New Zealand that Paul would soon return would never be realised, for in late March he faced a major health crisis. In a Moscow hotel room on 27 March 1961, Paul slashed his wrists.[22] There had been little warning. Only shortly before, he had told Drannikov he intended to be in Ghana and Guinea in the summer and would return to Moscow in the autumn for a concert tour that would also include London, Prague, Bulgaria, Hungary and Romania.[23] And he had said to Gurkow:

> I intend to return to Australia. I shall make films and give concerts. The proceeds shall benefit the aboriginal population languishing in poverty … For the rest of my life, I want to use my energies completely for the struggle for Africa's freedom, for the freedom of the American Negroes and of the Australian Aboriginal population—for the freedom of all who suffer from oppression.[24]

Yet, suffering from depression and exhaustion, he had attempted suicide. His promised visits to Australia, Africa, Indonesia and India, and the planned European concert tour, would never happen. The book on music and humanity of which he had spoken so frequently in Australia and New Zealand would never be written.

That Paul's suicide attempt happened so soon after his Australian and New Zealand tour raises the question of whether there is a link between the two. Was the tour responsible for his severe depression? It had not been unpleasant or unrewarding. While he did have moments of anger during the tour, prompted either by hostile questioning at his first airport media conference or by what he learned of the subjugation of Aboriginal people, in public Paul had remained generally cheerful. He welcomed the extended love and affectionate attention bestowed on him at his concerts and his encounters with people individually, in small groups, and en masse. He had, after all, told Clara Rockmore that he had 'a really wonderful—moving tour'.[25]

Yet it is undoubtedly true that the tour had been extremely tiring, leading both Robesons to a feeling of exhaustion for a month or two. Reflecting on events months later, Eslanda told a friend that Paul had been 'much too tired to make the Australian tour'.[26] And the tour itself was undoubtedly exhausting for someone of his age and disposition. To modern Australian travellers, who have the benefit of jet flight, their schedule looks utterly daunting. Both Robesons gave interviews at airports after long flights or series of flights that would make most people just want to get to their hotel and sleep. They seem to have had no rest days. When Paul had no scheduled concerts they were always meeting new people or giving radio and press interviews, and in Eslanda's case perhaps giving a public lecture and in Paul's the odd television interview or an informal concert to large groups of workers. Most people would be utterly exhausted after such a tour.

In addition to exhaustion, Paul had a history of depression. It had reached a crisis point in 1956 soon after a failed attempt to regain his passport. Given his experience of being an outcast at the height of the Cold War, so abruptly after his enormous fame and success in the 1930s and 1940s, some depression at his change in circumstances is unsurprising. Martin Duberman, however, suggests a little more than this, referring to the 1956 episode as an initial 'bout of what would later be called "bipolar disorder"',[27] and that one factor in Paul's suicide attempt may have been 'a bipolar depressive disorder'.[28]

Whatever the cause, Paul was clearly now suffering from severe depression. For almost three years he would receive treatment, including extensive shock therapy, in Moscow and the United Kingdom, and he was no longer able to perform or engage in public speaking. His friends and admirers everywhere were concerned and wanted to help. Shirley O'Connor, the wife of promoter Dan O'Connor, sent the Robesons a Christmas card in December 1961, to which Eslanda replied warmly in January 1962. Paul was, she wrote, 'suffering from acute and prolonged exhaustion, and your husband will remember signs of it when we were in Australia and New Zealand, when he was so terribly impatient with the press. He has always been forthright, but not so truculent.' She was still hopeful that Paul would recover and visit Australia and New Zealand again: 'I still feel that he would like to come again, when he is in fine voice, and sing properly to the Australian and New Zealand people. They would be surprised. Fortunately, his voice remains gorgeous ...'[29] Her suggestion that Paul had not been in 'fine voice' is, perhaps, a little odd, for most music critics had thought his voice was in excellent condition.

While Paul was undergoing treatment through 1962 and 1963, his birthday on 9 April continued to be an occasion for appreciation and celebration internationally, just as it had been during his years of confinement to the United States. One such celebration was organised by the Victorian Peace Council in 1962. Held in the Unitarian Church hall in East Melbourne, people could hear him speak and sing on record and listen to local CPA member Rex Mortimer talk about Robeson's life and the struggles of his people.[30]

As Paul's birthday loomed in 1963, Australians and New Zealanders became more aware that he was extremely ill. One meeting, in Sydney on 23 February, occurred at the home of Freda and Paul Katzmann in Clovelly, in order to 'enjoy recordings of the outstanding singer, peace worker and humanitarian Paul Robeson'.[31] Many organisations and individuals wrote to Paul that year, taking the opportunity to wish him well for his sixty-fifth birthday and to send good wishes for his recovery. The BWIU, which had retained its special sense of connection to Robeson since the Opera House visit, was one organisation that wrote to him, expressing the hope that he would one day visit Australia again. The union's newspaper, *Building Worker*, referred to 'the many cards sent to the great artist of song and fighter for freedom and Peace, Paul Robeson'. It urged 'his host of friends' and those 'who met him on jobs he visited and addressed' to send cards and messages and helpfully included his full London address so that readers could write to him directly. The paper urged children especially to send get-well cards.[32]

Individual admirers also wrote, expressing how much he meant to them. As Grant Olwage points out, letter writers often addressed him informally and expressed their sense that he was a friend for life; Olwage cites several Australians and New Zealanders among his examples. New Zealander John Dickens wrote around this time that 'you have been a friend to me, my parents and grandparents for almost as long as we can remember, although we have never met you in person'.[33] Dickens went on to say that Robeson's views had encouraged him to try to make friends 'with all races, so now in New Zealand my best friends are Maoris [*sic*], Samoans, and Fijian Indians'.[34]

From Australia, Elizabeth Perkins wrote that on the death of her father she listened to one of Paul's records and felt as if 'you sang to me alone'.[35] Mona Frame, in Sydney, wrote in March 1963 that playing Paul's records was like having him 'visit us in our own home'. She regarded him, she wrote, as a friend of her, her family, and 'of all the people you met (and many you could not) while you were in Australia'.[36]

After almost three years of treatment, on 22 December 1963 Paul and Eslanda returned to live in the United States.[37] Neither ever travelled overseas again. Though Paul lived quietly for the rest of his life, Eslanda remained an active journalist until her death in 1965. She published articles on a range of topics, including the United Nations, the emerging civil rights movement in America, and worldwide political events such as the Cuban alliance with the Soviet Union, the anti-apartheid movement, and turmoil in Congo and Kenya.[38] She also wrote about her delight at the upsurge in militant protest in the civil rights movement in 1963 and 1964, even as her cancer returned and was clearly terminal.[39]

On 13 December 1965, two days before her seventieth birthday, Eslanda died. A friend, journalist and activist Ruth Gage-Colby, wrote to her just before she died saying she had a 'bunch of rave clippings from Australia during your tour with Paul when you got rave notices too'.[40] There was, sadly, little notice of her death in the Australian and New Zealand press. *Tribune* carried a brief notice the following February, describing her as having acted as Paul's 'private secretary' during the 1960 tour and noting her 'important and dangerous work as liaison between the United Nations and independence movements in the Congo and other African colonies'.[41]

Both Robesons would have been relieved, and probably surprised, to see how rapidly the Aboriginal protest movement gathered speed after they left. Key events included the Yirrkala bark petitions for land rights in 1963, the Commonwealth Conciliation and Arbitration

Commission pastoral workers' equal pay decision in 1966, and the successful referendum campaign to amend the Constitution in 1967 so that the federal government had the power to legislate on Aboriginal matters.

Perhaps the best-known example of the acceleration of the Aboriginal protest movement in the years after the Robeson visit was the Freedom Ride of 1965 led by Charles Perkins and in which I was involved. As mentioned in this book's Introduction, the Freedom Ride was a two-week tour conducted by a busload of students from the University of Sydney protesting against racial discrimination in NSW country towns. It was in many ways inspired by the African American civil rights struggle. Martin Luther King, in particular, directly influenced its guiding principles, notably its strategy of non-violent protest and its approach of refusing to wait—to act now.[42] A group of African American singers farewelled us as we set out on our journey. Late in 1964, a production of *Black Nativity*, a song-play depicting the birth of Christ, came to Australia. Written in 1961 by Langston Hughes, whose 'Freedom Train' Paul had so often performed on his antipodean tour, it had opened on Broadway in 1961 and been adapted for television.[43] With an African American cast, the play opened in Melbourne in November 1964 and moved to Sydney in the new year. Five days before our bus left for the Freedom Ride, the ABC screened an American program on the history of gospel music called *Go Tell It on the Mountain* featuring singing by members of the local *Black Nativity* company.[44] A group from the company, now dubbed the Go Tell It on the Mountain Singers, then memorably sang 'We Shall Overcome' to farewell us as we left the University of Sydney on 12 February 1965.[45]

The Australian Freedom Ride was stimulated by many things, not least the conjunction of the growth of student radicalism and the Aboriginal protest movement, but one element in growing student awareness in the early 1960s on racial matters was Paul and Eslanda's public stance on the issue. Indeed, I first thought that I might write *The Last Tour* when I realised, while writing my 2002 book *Freedom Ride: A Freedom Rider Remembers*, that several of the freedom riders had heard Robeson sing in Sydney or knew about him from his records.

Tributes

When Paul Robeson died on 23 January 1976, mainstream newspapers paid attention. In New Zealand, the *Evening Post* reprinted the *Chicago Daily News* obituary, which portrayed his life as a tragedy: 'Paul Robeson, once one of the two or three most famous black men in the world, then vilified and cast into a historic limbo, died last Friday after suffering a stroke … his story had taken on the dimensions of a classical Greek tragedy.'[46] The *Courier-Mail* in Brisbane carried a US report saying that 'Paul Robeson, the Left-wing black singer-actor, who was persecuted in America more for the colour of his politics than that of his skin has died'. He was 'one of the century's great singers' and 'America's first fully-fledged black star'.[47]

The next day the paper printed another obituary, which noted that Robeson had visited Australia in 1960 and had sung at the Festival Hall in Brisbane to a packed audience.[48] Other major dailies also reported his life and passing. *Tribune* published a heartfelt obituary. For the middle aged and elderly, AK wrote, 'his passing reminds us of a man who was, for his time, the supreme representative of the struggle of oppressed peoples everywhere for emancipation and equality'. After outlining some key features of his life, the article commented that 'Australians came to know him personally when he and Eslanda, his exceptional wife, visited us in 1960'. The *Tribune* obituary ended, as so many commentaries on Robeson did, with a quote from author Alexander Woollcott concerning Paul's 'greatness as a person'.[49] To mark Paul's passing, the CPA produced for sale a cassette tape entitled *The Life of a Coloured Man*, which included an interview and songs recorded on Paul's visit and was described in an advertisement as a 'collector's item which includes Eslanda Robeson'.[50]

The Melbourne peace movement observed Paul's passing in several ways. The CICD magazine published in April 1976 a two-page tribute outlining his musical career and political activism.[51] On Dorothy Gibson's suggestion, it also organised an evening tribute at South Yarra Library on 9 April 1976. Hosted by Ted Laurie QC, a barrister and former communist who had played a leading role in successfully challenging the constitutionality of the 1950 legislation banning the CPA, the tribute was described as a 'program of music and commentary, to pay tribute to Paul Robeson on the occasion of the anniversary of his birth'.[52] As Ralph Gibson recalled later, a 'large hall filled to hear the recording of Robeson's voice in song and speech while the story of his life was told by Ted Laurie'.[53]

Reanimations

In Shana Redmond's view, Robeson has since his death been gradually 'reanimated', his reincarnation taking a variety of forms; her book sets out to trace some of these reanimations in detail.[54] They include holograms, theatrical commemorations, exhibitions, and places named after him. In Australia and New Zealand, reanimations—to adopt Redmond's term—have included musical evenings, audio recordings, plays, paintings, exhibitions, radio programs and re-enactments. In the years immediately after his death, his life was commemorated on radio, television and film. The ABC broadcast both a radio program (produced by Mark Aarons and Robyn Ravlich) and in 1979 the half-hour documentary *Paul Robeson in Australia*. On Channel 7, Peter Luck's popular television series *This Fabulous Century* in 1979 included in one episode, entitled 'Great Works', a clip of Robeson singing at the Opera House.[55] In the United States, a thirty-minute film made in 1979, *Paul Robeson: Tribute to an Artist*, narrated by Sidney Poitier, also includes footage of Paul singing at the Opera House. That film won an Academy Award in 1979 for Best Documentary Short Subject.[56]

For many years, knowledge of Paul Robeson's visit to Australia was spread by the playing as a filler on ABC-TV a shorter version of the original ABC film of Paul at the Opera House.[57] You can now see it on the NFSA website. This excellent clip did a great deal through the 1980s to inform Australians about Robeson and his visit, and helped ensure that Australian memories of the Robeson tour would be deeply connected to his singing at the Opera House site. When I mentioned my topic while researching this book, people would often respond, 'Oh, you mean the guy who sang first at the Opera House.'

An important event in keeping a broader knowledge of Paul Robeson alive in Australia was the performance in 1987 and 1988 of *Deep Bells Ring*, a musical play about his life. Through the 1950s, Nance Macmillan, now living in Brisbane and professionally and personally known as Nancy Wills, had helped keep Paul's struggle to regain his passport known to the Australian left and had urged the readers of *Tribune* to support the campaign for its return. By the mid-1980s, she had become concerned that the silencing of Robeson had succeeded and that young people no longer knew who he was. In 1986, the UN International Year of Peace, she had an idea: she would write a play about his life and achievements and would gather financial support for it from the BWIU, sponsor of the Opera House visit, and from the Brisbane Community Arts Centre.[58] She was inspired in part, she told an interviewer in September 1987, by seeing musician and actor Jeannie Lewis in her show *Piaf*, which told Edith Piaf's stories and in which Lewis sang Piaf's songs. Wills thought, 'I'd like to do it for Robeson. That's when I got the idea.'[59] At the time, the Australia Council, during the period of the Labor government led by Bob Hawke, was sponsoring an 'Art and Working Life Program' that enabled the council's Theatre Board to award the BWIU $26,000 to produce *Deep Bells Ring*.[60] Financial support came also from a group of Brisbane construction firms each granting $6000.[61]

Wills wrote the play with the extensive assistance of Errol O'Neill, who had been an actor, writer and director with the Popular Theatre Troupe in Brisbane in the late 1970s and early 1980s. Foundational to the project was Margret Roadknight as musical director, who had as a teenager heard Paul sing in Melbourne Town Hall and who worked with Wills in selecting the songs.[62] According to O'Neill, Wills' and Roadknight's 'knowledge of and respect for Robeson's songs, his life, and his beliefs, is the foundation stone upon which the show has been constructed'.[63]

In the play the narrator, Kate Daring, starts with her own experience of seeing and hearing Paul in *Sanders of the River* in the 1930s, and continues with a focus on some key episodes in his life. Interwoven with her narration throughout the play are Robeson's songs, performed by Australian singers on stage.[64] The play was extensively performed for over twelve months, both in full in theatres and in shorter versions as workplace lunchtime concerts.[65] Both the worksite performances (usually lasting twenty minutes) and the longer theatre performances attracted large audiences and were well received.[66] Local reviewers were keen to support a local production: even before the play opened, the Brisbane press gave it warm publicity, and warm praise followed its early performances.[67]

After its original successful run in April 1987, a revived version with a slightly different cast toured to several cities in September.[68] One of the best known singers for the revival was Jeannie Lewis, who had performed protest songs in the 1960s through to rock, blues and jazz thereafter, and her show *Piaf: The Songs and the Story*, which had sparked in Wills the idea for the Robeson play, had recently been successfully revived.

While the Brisbane press was enthusiastic, reviewers elsewhere had more mixed responses, both of the original production and its revival. Writing of the original production, Sue Gough in *The Australian* was rather critical of the script, though she did like the scene of Paul singing at the Sydney Opera House.[69] Barry Oakley reviewed the revival for the *Times on Sunday*, commenting: 'Though *Deep Bells Ring* is passionately felt and often moving, in dramatizing one evil (racism) it unforgivably ignores the fact that the Russia that practised the socialism Robeson gave his heart and mind to was worse.' Oakley continued: 'Robeson's victimisation in America is one tragedy. That it led him into political myopia is another.'[70] When the revived version reached Canberra, Ann Nugent, reviewer for the *Canberra Times*, was not impressed, describing the production as flat and observing that 'the tendency towards hagiography meant that the emotional force of his story and its relevance for today was largely uncommunicated'. Nugent also had problems with 'white singers presenting the songs of Robeson's inimitable voice'.[71] In Sydney one reviewer, Angela Bennie, thought similarly, commenting that while the 'commitment and dedication of the cast' were the play's strengths, its one-dimensional treatment of Robeson was its weakness. The result was that 'Robeson the man remains as elusive as ever, lost somewhere behind the heroic myth-making'.[72] Despite these reservations, the play was so successful on tour that a third production, with a somewhat altered cast, toured in 1988 to nine Queensland towns in February and March and concluded its run in Melbourne in April.[73]

There were plays remembering Robeson in New Zealand, too. One was *Song of Freedom*, written by British actor Andy Rashleigh, which had been performed in 1988 at the Young Vic in London.[74] Directed by Justine Simei-Barton, a New Zealand–born Samoan who had formed the Pacific Theatre company in 1987 with the aim of presenting plays written by Black writers from around the world, it opened in Auckland in September 1990.[75] Simei-Barton dedicated the play to her father, who had been a union delegate in a freezing works, loved Robeson's singing, and 'was keenly aware of the power of song as a means of cementing group solidarity and as a source of comfort and inspiration'. In her director's statement, she said she valued Robeson as someone who studied and practised and based his music on 'a careful academic analysis of music from around the world'. Bass-baritone Eddie Muliaumaseali'i, also a New Zealand–born Samoan and at the time a student at the University of Auckland's School of Music, played the role of Robeson.[76] Muliaumaseali'i went on to an illustrious international singing career.

Centenary celebrations

As the century came towards its end, the centenary of Paul's birth on 9 April 1998 prompted a further reclaiming and revival of his memory. With the Cold War formally over, though not necessarily the political conflicts informing it, the time seemed ripe for friends, colleagues and scholars to inform new generations about him and his music, acting, ideas and actions. Around the world supporters and admirers formed Paul Robeson centennial committees, with the Paul Robeson Centennial Project and the Center for Black Music Research, both located at Columbia College Chicago, acting as focal points. Meetings, concerts, exhibitions and other forms of celebration were organised in the United States, United Kingdom, Canada, Japan, Russia, and other European countries. Hollywood stars like Whoopi Goldberg and Paul Newman figured in a major celebration at Carnegie Hall.[77] Organisers and those wishing to pay tribute had access to a scholarly, detailed and invaluable biography of Paul, namely Martin Duberman's excellent *Paul Robeson*, which had appeared ten years earlier.

In Australia and New Zealand as the centenary date approached, radio stations began to play musical tributes. In October 1997, six months before the celebrations proper, there were affectionate tributes to Paul Robeson on Sydney FM radio station 2MBS and on ABC Classic.[78] Local organising committees began to form in Wellington, Sydney and Melbourne to arrange musical events, exhibitions and meetings in tribute to Paul. Through the initiative and organisational skills of two energetic women, the Australian and New Zealand organising committees were closely in touch with one another, sharing information and photographs. Those women were 83-year-old Rona Bailey in Wellington and 46-year-old Hannah Middleton in Sydney. Rona had been a driving force when the Robesons visited Wellington in 1960, while Hannah was the daughter of Peggy Middleton, one of the organisers in Britain of the *Let Robeson Sing* campaign.

Hannah had been in high school when that campaign was under way and as a university student had met the Robeson family when they lived in London in the late 1950s. She had looked after a young Susan Robeson in Hyde Park and would often help Paul remove his cufflinks so that he could change into a dry shirt at concert intermissions.[79] She had subsequently joined the Communist Party of Great Britain and graduated in African Studies from the University of London. In 1972, at the age of thirty, she completed her PhD in anthropology, concerning Australian Indigenous activism. Entitled *The Land Rights and Civil Rights Campaign of the Gurindji at Wattie Creek*, she had undertaken it in East Berlin, with fieldwork with the Gurindji at Daguragu (Wattie Creek) in northern Australia, under the supervision of British anthropologist Fred Rose, professor at Humboldt University. She migrated to Australia in 1974, where she has lived ever since.[80]

New Zealand celebrates

Rona Bailey began preparing for the centenary in April 1997, or perhaps earlier, leading the Trade Union History Project in organising the New Zealand commemoration.[81] The national executive of the NZ Council of Trade Unions on 10 February 1998 welcomed her initiative and asked its affiliated trade unions to support the Paul Robeson centennial celebrations.[82] At the same time, National Radio New Zealand began to broadcast programs featuring Robeson's music. To Bailey's delight, on 15 March 1998 it broadcast the 'legendary' 1949 Moscow concert, which had recently been released on CD. 'It is wonderful,' she wrote to Hannah Middleton, 'his singing in Russian, Chinese, Yiddish, and English quite superb.' It was more than the singing, she thought—some of its power came from the audience: 'The excitement and applause so intense and exciting he sang "Joe Hill" and "Old [*sic*] Man River" twice.'[83]

Commemorative activities stepped up in April 1998. On 6 April, the New Zealand Seafarers' Union at its monthly stop-work meeting noted that 9 April would mark the 100th birthday of Paul Robeson, 'great actor, athlete, scholar and fighter for the civil rights of people throughout the world'. The resolution went on to mourn that young people in the United States knew little about him, and to endorse efforts to celebrate the centennial and gain public recognition for his life, career and legacy.[84] The next day saw the main event: a meeting of around 100 people held in the Public Service Association building in Wellington that featured speeches, songs, recordings, an exhibition viewing, and reminiscences and commentary from the floor. Bailey gave a major speech outlining Paul's life and its significance and describing her experience of hearing him sing in Panama in 1947. Of that concert she said, 'that really was the event of my life—that concert and what happened there … Paul at his singing best was just magic.' She emphasised his linguistic skills, his extensive knowledge of music, his role in the labour unions and in African Americans' civil rights struggles, his book *Here I Stand*, and much else. Of the Australian and New Zealand tour, she said, 'How lucky we were to be able to hear him speak and sing in New Zealand and Australia in 1960. Indications of his later illness were there at times with Eslanda desperately trying, unsuccessfully, to protect him from doing too much. I know, I was there.'[85]

The audience then listened to recordings of Paul singing 'Deep River', 'Joe Hill' and 'Ol' Man River' and his speeches to the Melbourne waterside workers and Christchurch railway workers.[86] After a break to view the exhibition, people spoke from the floor, about the huge impact Robeson's visit to New Zealand in 1960 had on their lives. As Peter Franks reported,

> Ikar Lissienko said he had never experienced anything like the impression Robeson made on the audience when he read Blake's 'Jerusalem 'just before the interval in the Wellington concert. Ted Thompson talked about Robeson's meeting on the Wellington waterfront, organised with the assistance of the Drivers Union, and the watersiders' decision to make Robeson a life member of their union. Ted said, 'Paul Robeson was a symbol of hope for many.'

The meeting concluded with a resolution, passed unanimously:

> We congratulate those around the world who are organising celebrations of Paul Robeson's Centennial. We are proud to be part of the Celebrations for this giant of a Freedom Fighter, Political Activist, Singer and Actor. In particular we support the efforts of the Center for Black Music Research, Columbia College, University of Chicago, in working to restore Paul Robeson to his rightful place in American history.[87]

There were several stories in the print media, but it was probably on radio that most people encountered celebrations of Robeson's life and work.[88] Radio New Zealand had several broadcasts honouring him: on 8 April a one-hour program on Concert FM entitled *This Century: Paul Robeson, Nina Simone, and Winton Marsalis*; on 9 April, a half-hour radio documentary by popular New Zealand presenter Wayne Mowat; and on 12 April *Paul Robeson Speaks* on Jim Sullivan's long-running *Sounds Historical* evening program.[89] Most importantly for coverage of Robeson's New Zealand visit, Marie Russell, who worked with Bailey in organising the celebration, produced a documentary entitled 'Remembering Paul Robeson' for the *Spectrum* program on Radio New Zealand, which was broadcast on 12, 14 and 17 April. This program, whose oral histories have been so valuable for this book, has been re-broadcast several times since and is now available online.[90]

Australia commemorates

There were similar events in Australia, with the addition of a live concert featuring Robeson's songs. In Sydney, on Hannah Middleton's initiative, the Paul Robeson 100th Birthday Committee first met on 1 September 1997.[91] Middleton contacted many well-known local identities to act as patrons to be listed on the committee's letterhead. One was Peter Tighe, national secretary of the Communications, Electrical and Plumbing Union; others were performer Robyn Archer, Indigenous magistrate Pat O'Shane, ACTU president Jennie George, broadcaster Phillip Adams, and Greens Party founder and federal MP Bob Brown.[92] The committee's letterhead also listed singer Jeannie Lewis, playwright Nancy Wills, Aboriginal educator and activist Kevin Cook, national president of the Maritime Union of Australia (MUA) Jim Donovan, union leader and environmentalist Jack Mundey, and ALP politician Tom Uren.

Middleton began organising an exhibition and a concert to commemorate Paul's life and work. She placed an advertisement in the *Sydney Morning Herald* seeking 'programs, newspaper cuttings, photographs, and memorabilia' from his 1960 visit for the forthcoming centenary celebrations, eliciting many valuable responses.[93] It was her strong wish to draw in Aboriginal people as well as to support Aboriginal claims more broadly. A lot had happened in the arena of Indigenous rights and claims since the Robesons' visit: in addition to the developments in the 1960s there had been land rights legislation in the Commonwealth and the states in the 1970s and 1980s and, since 1990, a decade of reconciliation, meant to further the wider community's recognition of Indigenous people's rights and concerns.

A Labor government had developed the reconciliation project, but with a change to conservative government under John Howard in 1996, it had reduced government support. It nevertheless continued to have considerable grassroots impact, climaxing in the famous Walk for Reconciliation across the Sydney Harbour Bridge in 2000, in which 250,000 people participated. In her talks and letters concerning the Robeson centenary celebrations, Middleton often emphasised the commemoration's value for reconciliation.

A major challenge was fundraising. Middleton sought a 'substantial donation' from the MUA, pointing out that while in Australia in 1960 Paul had visited the old WWF Hall and had sung to the wharfies.[94] While the Opera House did not respond to her attempts to involve it in the celebrations, the City of Sydney Council made the Sydney Town Hall available for the exhibition free of charge and the Miners' Federation of Australia provided financial support for its production.[95] Strong union support was evident also for the proposed concert, the Australian Manufacturing Workers Union making its Tom Mann Theatre available at the nominal rent of $1.[96] Middleton succeeded in gaining some financial support from the NSW state government, the only Labor government in the country at the time, when Bob Carr, the premier of New South Wales and Minister for the Arts, approved government funding of the fee for Roadknight to sing at the planned Robeson concert.[97]

Bob Brown, best known in Australia for his environmental activism and role in founding the Greens party, spoke in parliament on Monday 6 April about the forthcoming centenary. This Thursday 9 April, he said, is the 100th anniversary of the birth of 'an outstanding, talented and courageous American, Paul Robeson', who fought 'against discrimination, racism and intolerance' and for 'peace, freedom, friendship, dignity and civil rights'. Experiencing 'full human dignity' in the Soviet Union prior to World War II had a profound impact on him, and later he became a victim of the 'blind hatred and anti-communist hysteria of the McCarthyist era'. Brown congratulated Middleton and her committee for ensuring recognition of the anniversary and told parliament of the forthcoming exhibition in the Sydney Town Hall and then the

Percy Grainger Museum in Melbourne, and the concert tributes in Sydney and Melbourne featuring Roadknight.[98]

Another parliamentary mention of Robeson came in the Queensland state parliament on 21 April 1998, when Naomi Wilson, National Party member and minister for families, youth and community care, spoke at length on the life and achievements of Mick Miller, a leading Aboriginal activist prominent in FCAATSI: 'Such was Mick's conviction to our people he epitomised through his actions the words of great Black rights activist Paul Robeson, "There is no such thing as a backward human being, there is only society that says they are backward."'[99]

As the date of Paul's 100th birthday approached, a revival of *Show Boat*, which had made him famous for his singing of 'Ol' Man River', coincidentally opened in Sydney on 7 April.[100] Then, on 8 April, the centenary exhibition opened at the Sydney Town Hall for a week, attracting approximately 1000 visitors.[101] It consisted of nine large boards displaying photographs, record covers and textual quotations illustrating aspects of Robeson's life and work and in particular his tour of Australia and New Zealand, and was accompanied by recordings of his music, speeches and interviews.[102] Middleton's call for mementos and memorabilia for the exhibition had brought to light several cherished audio recordings, such as the aforementioned one made by the NSW Peace Committee with Paul's Paddington Town Hall speech on one side and him singing and reciting 'Freedom Train' on the other.[103] Many people had kept their recordings for years.[104]

The concert, entitled 'Robeson Keeps Rolling Along', and devised by Roadknight, took place in Sydney on 9 April.[105] Middleton told me: 'The night of the concert we were in despair because there was a torrential downpour and we thought no one would come—but they poured into the Tom Mann Theatre, very damp but enormously cheerful.'[106] She noted in her report to the funding bodies that the committee had wanted the centenary celebrations to contribute to 'Reconciliation and justice for the Aboriginal community' as well as 'mutual respect, appreciation and harmony between the different components of our multi-cultural society'. In keeping with these aims, the concert programme began with a half-hour of 'Songs of Aboriginal Australia', sung by Aboriginal actor and writer Leah Purcell backed by her band.[107] Then followed a one-hour performance by Roadknight with Sue Porter on piano, consisting of anecdotes, history and songs. Over 200 people attended, and in Middleton's view the concert 'successfully portrayed Robeson's lifelong commitment to the fight against racism and for democracy, equality and social justice—values and ideals which are central to our own society'.[108] Bob Brown loved the show and admired the exhibition at the Sydney Town Hall.[109] Roadknight and Porter repeated their Sydney performance in both Melbourne and Adelaide.[110] A small segment of the exhibition is now presented permanently in a display case in Sydney Trades Hall.

Middleton took the Robeson exhibition to Broken Hill, a mining town in the far west of New South Wales.[111] One of those who saw the exhibition there was George Thompson, a Sydney Labor member of the NSW Legislative Assembly who was attending a ceremony to hand back the nearby Mutawintji National Park to its traditional Aboriginal owners. Viewing it prompted him to refer to Robeson in the NSW Parliament on 20 October 1998. He spoke of Paul at some length, and his learning about him through family friends who had many of his records. On the visit to Australia in 1960, he said, 'he sang to workers on the Opera House construction site. The film of that occasion is truly moving. He became aware of the plight of Australia[n] Aborigines and pledged to return to give them support.' The next speaker, John Aquilina, a minister in the NSW Labor government whose father, a carpenter, had been there that day, endorsed Thompson's speech, saying Robeson was 'truly not only a great singer but also a great symbol of the underprivileged'.[112]

21st-century commemorations

More anniversary celebrations were to come. In Perth in 2004, the Midland Redevelopment Authority organised a concert at the site of the former Midland Railways Workshops to celebrate the forty-fourth anniversary of Paul's singing there on 2 December 1960, as part of the centennial celebrations of the establishment of the workshops. They had closed in 1994, but the site remained as it was and in 2000 the WA Government had started its redevelopment. The authority hoped that the re-creation of Paul's singing at the workshop entrance on the back of a truck would remind people of the significant role the workshops had played in WA life. Rob Banks in the *West Australian* previewed the concert with a detailed account of the original event, and informed readers that the concert would feature Perth baritone Andrew Foote, who would sing many of the songs that Robeson had sung at the workshops forty years before.[113] On 27 November the authority held a 'free picnic concert' on the railway forecourt at the site. After the Kalamunda Youth Swing Band performed music from the era, Alannah MacTiernan, the minister for planning and infrastructure in the state Labor government, and Kieran Kinsella, CEO of the Midland Redevelopment Authority, gave official welcomes. Next came the Working Voices Choir and the Greg Schultz Band, before the main event of Foote singing a series of twelve Robeson songs, mostly his best-known spirituals.[114]

More than 5000 kilometres to the east, the Auckland Festival in March 2005 featured Kevin Maynor's series of three plays, one of which was *The Repertoire of Paul Robeson*, performed at the Holy Trinity Cathedral on 11 March. Maynor was a famous African American bass opera singer, and the programme lists seventeen songs, starting with 'Hammer Song', 'I Still Suits Me' and 'Ol' Man River' and ending with 'Lullaby', together with a monologue from *Boris Godunov*. Maynor's praise for Robeson in the programme was fulsome:

> Here we explore the wonderful programming of Paul Robeson and how he used music to say what was most urgent to him. His way of choosing music and placing it in an order unfamiliar to most listeners of the standard vocal recital is now famous to any music artist concerned with the needs of the people around her or him … Probably the most complete man to ever live, short of Jesus … He was a friend to humankind … the greatest of great Americans. He was art.[115]

Internationally, one of the most famous and long-running tribute shows is *Call Mr Robeson: A Life in Songs*, written and performed by Tayo Aluko, an Englishman of Nigerian descent. Since first presenting it at the Edinburgh Festival in 2007, Aluko has performed the show around the world ever since, including nineteen performances in Australia and New Zealand in early 2015.[116] Shana Redmond is critical of *Call Mr Robeson* for its insufficient attention to the music and song that meant so much to Paul throughout his life. 'Though described as "a life with songs",' she writes, '*Call Mr Robeson* errs in its singular attention to monologue as the exemplary means of narrative meaning making.'[117] Though I enjoyed the show when I saw it at the Marlborough Pub and Theatre in Brighton, England, in May 2016, it is true that I remember its politics rather than its music. In contrast, several tributes held in Christian churches have focused on Paul's music, especially his singing of spirituals.[118]

While the Sydney Opera House management's interest in Robeson's foundational performance has waxed and waned over the years, the building itself has become a focus for memorialising him. When it opened in 1973, the *Building Worker*, the journal of the BWIU, featured Paul's historic visit to the worksite in 1960.[119] In September 1987, the *Deep Bells Ring* actors performed there the half-hour version of the play, attracting media attention. Channel 7 ran a news item showing both the *Deep Bells Ring* performance and footage of Paul singing at the Opera House in 1960, along with commentary by union leader Ernie Boatswain.[120] In 2010, there was considerable media interest in the fiftieth anniversary of Paul's performance at the construction site. In the usually conservative paper *The Australian*, Mahir Ali wrote a substantial article and quoted Alfred Rankin, who had been there on the day, recalling this 'giant of a man enthralling the workers with his *a cappella* renditions of two of his signature songs, "Ol' Man River" and "Joe Hill"'.[121] A concert sponsored by the Construction, Forestry, Maritime, Mining and Energy Union (the successor to the BWIU), took place on the Opera House steps on 9 November 2020. Though Australia and New Zealand were both in the grip of the worldwide COVID-19 pandemic and 2020 was a year of many strict lockdowns, it so happened that in early November there was no lockdown in Sydney, though Australia was still closed to the world. The union invited Rachel Bate, 'acclaimed opera singer and daughter of an Illawarra coal miner', to sing two of the songs Robeson had sung at the site in 1960, 'Ol' Man River' and 'Joe Hill'. On the steps listening were construction workers involved in an ongoing major refurbishment of the Opera House Concert Hall, and sitting with them was 89-year-old John Clough, a long-time union member who had migrated from England as a nineteen-year-old in 1950. Clough had been at the site in 1960, and he commented, 'His Sydney performance was out of this world, he was an icon for me, I loved him all my life. Hearing those songs now, it's like the words in the song "Joe Hill", he never died.'[122]

For the union movement, and indeed many others, Paul Robeson and his songs live on.

Endings

Paul also touched people as their lives came to an end. As his admirers grew old, their love of his songs often came to the fore. In Sam Goldbloom's case, his daughter Sandra sang Robeson and Pete Seeger songs to him for three hours as he died.[123] From the 1960s onwards, it became extremely common for one or more of Paul's recorded songs to be played at funerals of communists and other left-wing people. In my husband's aunt's case, one item in the order of service was 'Beethoven/Schiller: Ode to Joy (vocalist Paul Robeson)'. Sometimes the song chosen was Paul's revised version of 'Ol' Man River', with its lines 'I must keep fightin'/ Until I'm dying'. Very often the chosen song was 'Joe Hill', as in the case of my father-in-law. Mary Okello, who had as a child helped farewell Paul and Eslanda in Brisbane, included excerpts from Robeson's records in her father's funeral service—a Russian song, and then 'Joe Hill'. Berenice Nyland, in Melbourne, told Sari Braithwaite in an interview that when her father was dying in 2007, he asked that 'Joe Hill' be played at his funeral.[124] With its idea of the radical activist who 'never died', 'Joe Hill' expresses for the dying person who has led a politically active life, and for the mourners of that person, a sense of continuity between the life now ending and a promising future that person will not live to see.

It will not do, though, to end on a note of sadness and death. Both Robesons are figures of the future. Interest in and scholarship on them continues to surge. Their shared anti-colonialism, anti-racism and critiques of capitalism, along with Paul's allegiance to working people and Eslanda's feminism, are just as relevant in our time as they were in theirs. So, too, are the connections Paul drew between music and political protest, even though the forms each takes continually change. People of their time in so many ways—musically, politically, filmically, personally—they speak, despite their Cold War context, to new generations facing huge challenges.

Acknowledgements

For this project, more than any other, I have been overwhelmed by the number of people ready to assist, donating old programmes, photographs, pamphlets, records, cassette tapes, invitations and other documents, emailing me with suggestions, alerting me to new publications or radio programs, setting aside time for extended interviews, and responding to queries. I hereby acknowledge and thank all who have assisted me.

I began researching the visit in 2007 with the help of my superb research assistant, Sari Braithwaite, and in 2010 published an essay entitled 'Paul Robeson's visit to Australia and Aboriginal activism' that narrated and discussed some of the results of our research thus far. Nine years passed while I worked on other projects. In 2019, just before the pandemic turned our lives around, I was free to return to this project, which had grown in scope and had now become a book that would deal with Eslanda Robeson as well as Paul, and with New Zealand as well as Australia.

The first person I need to thank is Sari Braithwaite, who not only worked as my research assistant in 2007 and 2008 but who has since sent me tips and suggestions over the years. What a wonderful research assistant she has been. The documentary research and the oral histories she conducted in 2008 have been essential. This book would never have happened without her.

Jordan Goodman, based in London, generously passed on to me copies of material he had gathered during research for his own important and excellent book, *Paul Robeson: A Watched Man*, published in 2014. The copied material has proved invaluable, especially during the pandemic when libraries and archives were so hard to access. This kind of generosity is unusual and extremely valuable, and I am deeply grateful.

Since 2007, three Australian universities—the Australian National University, the University of Western Australia and the University of Sydney—have offered me a hospitable home for my work as a historian and a scholar, and I have benefited from their institutional support and from excellent colleagues in each one.

I thank Joellen Albashir, archivist at the Moorland-Spingarn Research Center at Howard University until 2020, and her team for the excellent online finding aid they produced in 2015 for the Paul and Eslanda Robeson papers held at the Centre. I have, however, been unable to gain access to the papers themselves. My request on 22 April 2022 was referred to the Robeson family estate, who replied that they were unable to grant me access owing to 'various contractual commitments on the part of the estate'; they would let me know when the material again became publicly available. The Centre also holds the collection of letters sent from Australia to Martin Duberman in 1983 when he was researching *Paul Robeson: A Biography*. When I requested access, however, I was informed the collection had not been processed and was therefore not available.

While my lack of access to the Paul and Eslanda Robeson papers held at the Moorland-Spingarn Research Center was a setback, I hope I have made up for it by archival work in Australia and New Zealand. I am especially grateful to the librarians at the National Library of Australia; the state libraries of New South Wales, Western Australia, South Australia and Victoria; the National Library of New Zealand, especially its Turnbull Library; and the Auckland City Library. I am similarly indebted to staff at the University of Melbourne Archives, University of Queensland Fryer Library, the Noel Butlin Archives Centre at the Australian National University, the National Film and

Sound Archive of Australia, the National Archives of Australia, and the Sydney Trades Hall Archives.

Many groups and individuals offered valuable suggestions after hearing me deliver one of my work-in-progress papers. These papers began in the History Department at ANU in 2007 and concluded with the musicology series at the Conservatorium of Music in Sydney in 2023. Two of the papers between these two dates were conference keynote addresses—one to the National Labour History Conference in Perth in 2008, and the other to the Australian Women's History Network conference in Perth in 2019. Larissa Behrendt's probing questions during her extended interview with me on her ABC Radio program *Speaking Out* in February 2024 helped me articulate my ideas for a wider audience as I was in the last stages of writing the book.

Chapter drafts were discussed by two writing groups, one at the University of Western Australia and the other in Sydney. I thank the members of both groups for their astute suggestions. At UWA I thank Ethan Blue, Shino Konishi, Andrea Gaynor, Tony Hughes d'Aeth, Jeremy Martens, Catie Gressier, Cameron Muir, Daniel Juckes, Dylan Lino and Tanya Dalziell. In Sydney I thank Penny Russell, Kirsten McKenzie, Frances Clarke, Alecia Simmons, Zora Simic, Ruth Balint and Judith Keene.

I thank Diane Kirkby and Lee-Ann Monk for helping me with some Melbourne-based research. A special thankyou to Dale Jacobsen and others in the Queensland Society for the Study of Labour History, who in 2008 circulated my call for emails concerning memories of the visit. Sari interviewed many of them, and others wrote directly to me. I thank also Carmel Shute, who included a similar call in her email circular, *Shute the Messenger*, in 2023.

I thank all those in Brisbane and Melbourne whom Sari interviewed, including Uncle Bob Anderson, Wally Stubbings, Connie Healy, Jane Mullett, Vaughan Greenberg, Hilary Langford, Mary Okello, Jean Leary and Andrew Vickers. I also thank Hazel Butorac, whom I interviewed in Perth. I thank the many other people—too many to list individually—who wrote telling me of their memories of meeting, seeing or hearing Paul and Eslanda Robeson.

Others who assisted, some of them many times, include Brian Aarons, Martha Ansara, Meg Bailey, Norma Chalmers, Sarah Collins, Sharon Connolly, Stephanie Cronin, Joy Damousi, Desley Deacon, Philip Deery, Mark Derby, Heather Goodall, Pat Healy, Marilyn Lake, Margaret Lindley, Martie Lowenstein, Jane Lydon, Stuart Macintyre, Jill Matthews, Hannah Middleton, Doug Munro, Colin Penter, Jon Piccini, Graham Shirley and Flora Smith.

For the New Zealand part of the project, I especially thank Charlotte Macdonald for her advice and assistance.

John Docker, as always, has been a firm supporter, encourager and first and final reader of my drafts, from which I have benefited immensely and for which I am deeply grateful. Ned Curthoys has been a brilliant reader of several chapters, and I thank him for his valuable advice.

This book has benefited enormously from the hard-working team at Melbourne University Publishing. I especially thank Louise Stirling for her guidance—working with you has been a pleasure. I also thank Katie Purvis for her sharp-eyed copy editing.

This book has prompted me to think about many aspects of my childhood and teenage years, and the ideas, experiences and actions of my parents, Barbara and Geoffrey Curthoys, both now deceased. While my own political ideas have varied from theirs, especially concerning their attachment to the Soviet Union, I am aware of having grown up in a stimulating and happy household. I am especially indebted to my mother's activism and thinking about women's rights and Aboriginal rights, which have profoundly influenced my life and my scholarly concerns. She was, like so many communists of her era, a Paul Robeson fan, and this book is in part for her.

Notes

Abbreviations used in this section:

ADB	Australian Dictionary of Biography
ANU	Australian National University
CH7AR	Channel 7 archives via Archive Road
DNZB	Dictionary of New Zealand Biography
MSRC	Moorland-Spingarn Research Center (Howard University)
NAA	National Archives of Australia
NBAC	Noel Butlin Archives Centre (ANU)
NLA	National Library of Australia
NLNZ	National Library of New Zealand
RNZ	Radio New Zealand
SLNSW	State Library of New South Wales
SLSA	State Library of South Australia
SLWA	State Library of Western Australia
SMH	*Sydney Morning Herald*
STHA	Sydney Trades Hall Archives
UMA	University of Melbourne Archives and Special Collections
UNSW	University of New South Wales
UWA	University of Western Australia

Introduction

1 This was the version Paul had sung since he changed the words in 1937. The original 1927 version followed 'Tote that barge and lift that bail!' with 'Get a little drunk and you lands in jail'.

2 Shana Redmond, *Everything Man: The Form and Function of Paul Robeson* (Duke University Press, 2020): 5–6.

3 Ann Curthoys and Joy Damousi (eds), *What Did You Do in the Cold War, Daddy? Personal Stories from a Troubled Time* (NewSouth Books, 2014); Ann Curthoys, 'Writing Australia's Cold War through history and memoir', in Judith Keene and Elizabeth Rechniewski (eds), *The Cold War: Seeking Meaning, Seeking Justice in a Post-Cold War World* (Brill, 2018): 25–42.

4 Martin Duberman, *Paul Robeson: A Biography* (New Press, 1989): 487–91, endnotes at 738–40.

5 Ann Curthoys, 'Paul Robeson's visit to Australia and Aboriginal activism, 1960', in Ann Curthoys, John Docker and Frances Peters-Little (eds), *Passionate Histories: Myth, Memory and Indigenous Australia* (Aboriginal History Inc. and ANU E Press, 2010): 163–84.

6 Barbara Ransby, *Eslanda: The Large and Unconventional Life of Mrs Paul Robeson* (Yale University Press, 2013): 251–2.

7 Duberman, *Paul Robeson*: 34–9; Paul Robeson Jnr, *The Undiscovered Paul Robeson: An Artist's Journey, 1898–1939* (John Wiley & Sons, 2001); Paul Robeson Jnr, *The Undiscovered Paul Robeson: Quest for Freedom, 1939–1976* (John Wiley & Sons, 2010): 306–7; Jordan Goodman, *Paul Robeson: A Watched Man* (Verso, 2013); Gerald Horne, *Paul Robeson: The Artist as Revolutionary* (Pluto Press, 2016): 184; Jeff Sparrow, *No Way But This: In Search of Paul Robeson* (Scribe, 2017): 1–3, 8; Grant Olwage, *Paul Robeson's Voices* (Oxford University Press, 2023).

8 Ransby, *Eslanda*; Imaobong D Umoren, *Race Women Internationalists: Activist Intellectuals and Global Freedom Struggles* (University of California Press, 2018); Robert Shaffer, 'Out of the shadows: The political writings of Eslanda Goode Robeson', *Pennsylvania History*, 66:1 (Winter 1999): 47–64.

9 Duberman, *Paul Robeson*: 34–9.

10 Eslanda Goode Robeson, *Paul Robeson, Negro* (Harper and Brothers, 1930).

11 Duberman, *Paul Robeson*: 190.

12 Ibid.: 214.

13 Eslanda Goode Robeson, *African Journey* (John Day Company, 1945).

14 Pearl Buck with Eslanda Robeson, *American Argument* (John Day Company, 1949).

15 See, for example, Paul Buhle and Lawrence Ware, *Ballad of an American: A Graphic Biography of Paul Robeson* (Rutgers University Press, 2020): 116.

16 Horne, *Paul Robeson*: 184.

17 Kit Macfarlane, 'Paul Robeson: A resonant voice that will never be fully silenced', *Pop Matters*, 9 November 2010.

18 For an excellent example of this kind of tour history, see Katie A Callamet et al., 'Marian Anderson's 1953 concert tour of Japan: A transnational history', *American Music*, Fall 2019: 267–329.

19 Marie Russell (presenter), 'Remembering Paul Robeson' (12 April 1998) [radio program], *Spectrum*, RNZ, Wellington (replayed on 27 February 2015).

20 Penny Von Eschen, *Race Against Empire: Black Americans and Anti-Colonialism, 1937–1957* (Cornell University Press, 1997). See especially 126–8.
21 These appear to have been organised after she arrived in the country. During the welcome at Sydney Airport on 12 October, for example, Lurline Simpson of the UAW invited Eslanda to speak to a UAW luncheon when she returned to Sydney in November, and she agreed.

Chapter 1: Australia and New Zealand Love Paul Robeson, 1925–1939

1 Martin Duberman, *Paul Robeson: A Biography* (New Press, 1989): 62–6, 89–91.
2 'London's Week: Great Negro actor in new play', *Daily Telegraph*, 20 October 1925: 4. The same story appeared as 'Old Country Gossip: Great Negro actor in new play', *Poverty Bay Herald*, 7 November 1925: 8.
3 'Eugene O'Neill', *SMH*, 23 December 1925: 17. Other newspaper reports on Robeson in *The Emperor Jones* include 'Rose to fame: Negro slave's son', *Queensland Times* (Ipswich), 21 November 1925: 14; 'Negro star on London stage', *Bathurst Times*, 19 October 1925: 1; 'From London Town', *The Telegraph* (Brisbane), 12 November 1925: 7; 'Music and the Stage', *The Star* (Christchurch), 5 December 1925 (Supplement): 22.
4 Duberman, *Paul Robeson*: 77.
5 Lynn Abbott and Doug Seroff, *Out of Sight: The Rise of African American Popular Music, 1889–1895* (University Press of Mississippi, 2002): 3–27; Bill Egan, *African American Entertainers in Australia and New Zealand: A History, 1788–1941* (McFarland & Company, 2020): 32, 38.
6 One of the Fisk Singers, Robertson Bradford Williams, married a Melbourne woman named Katherine Burke and settled in Wellington, New Zealand. Chris Bourke, 'RB Williams: He came, he sang, he stayed', *Music in New Zealand*, 12 (Autumn 1991): 50–1, online.
7 Egan, *African American Entertainers in Australia and New Zealand*: 40.
8 Nicole Anae, '"They seemed to recognise us as brethren from a far distant tribe": The influence of the Fisk Jubilee Singers among Australian and New Zealand Indigenous communities, 1886–1936', *The Historian*, 80:2 (2018): 241–92.
9 WEB Du Bois, *The Souls of Black Folk* (Myers Education Press, 2018 [originally published in 1903]): 191. See also Hazel Carby, *Race Men: The WEB du Bois Lectures* (Harvard University Press, 1998): 87–9.
10 For a valuable history of spirituals, see Lawrence W Levine, *Black Culture and Black Consciousness: African American Folk Thought from Slavery to Freedom* (Oxford University Press, 1977): 30–55.
11 Grant Olwage, 'Listening B(l)ack: Paul Robeson after Roland Hayes,' *Journal of Musicology*, 32:4 (2015): 528.
12 Ibid.: 527.
13 Ibid.: 537, drawing on the work of Carby in *Race Men*: 93–4.

14 Ibid.: 529, 533–4; Doris Evans McGinty and Wayne Shirley, 'Paul Robeson, musician', in Jeffrey C Stewart (ed.), *Paul Robeson: Artist and Citizen* (Rutgers University Press, 1998): 109.
15 Alain Locke, 'Enter the New Negro', *Survey Graphic*, March 1925, available in 'The Making of African American Identity: Vol. III: 1917–1968' section on *National Humanities Center Toolbox Library* website (quotations on p. 6).
16 'Harlem in New York', *The Chronicle* (Adelaide), 30 May 1925: 58.
17 Quoted in Shane Vogel, 'Locke and the value of the Harlem Renaissance', in Rachel Farebrother and Miriam Thaggert (eds), *A History of the Harlem Renaissance* (Cambridge University Press, 2021): 368.
18 Ibid.: 369.
19 'American Negroes: Literary renaissance', *Daily Mail* (Brisbane), 1 November 1925: 8; 'Conflict of color: The Negro's race-consciousness', *The Sun* (Sydney), 6 December 1925: 3.
20 Egan, *African American Entertainers in Australia and New Zealand*: 154–5.
21 McGinty and Shirley, 'Paul Robeson, musician': 108.
22 'Edna Thomas: Interpreter of Negro songs', *SMH*, 27 October 1924: 8; 'Society News: Miss Edna Thomas', *The Mail* (Adelaide), 19 September 1925: 12; 'Edna Thomas and negro spirituals', *Waikato Times*, 13 June 1925: 15.
23 'Negro singer', *Queensland Times*, 1 May 1925: 4; 'Music and Musicians: Negro spirituals', *The Herald* (Melbourne), 27 July 1925: 16; *New Zealand Herald*, 27 September 1924: 20; 'Edna Thomas: Negro spirituel [sic] and Creole melodies', *The Star* (Christchurch), 14 April 1925: 6; 'Way down south: The lady from Louisiana', *New Zealand Times*, 15 April 1925: 6. Re her records, see *SMH*, 2 January 1926: 1. Her popularity was noted in 'Negro spirituals', *The Australasian*, 31 July 1926: 64. Letters written to her by Australian fans are now held in the Emory University Archives in Atlanta, Georgia.
24 See 'Plays, Players, Pictures', *Evening Post* (Wellington), 3 November 1928: 25; 'Coming age of Negro literature/ Story of a great colored singer: How he starved for art/ Paul Robeson in a talkie', *Daily Standard* (Brisbane), 5 January 1929: 4.
25 Gerald Marr Thompson, 'London Season', *SMH*, 20 October 1928: 13; John Carmody, 'Gerald Marr Thompson (1856–1938)', *ADB* website, 2006 (originally published in 1990).
26 *Auckland Star*, 8 December 1928: 18; 'Most popular song', *The Mercury* (Hobart), 15 January 1929: 3.
27 'Music in London', *The Age* (Melbourne), 26 October 1928: 13.
28 *Auckland Star*, 16 August 1928: 14.
29 Ibid.; 'Music Notes: Music in England: Negro spirituels [*sic*]', *Poverty Bay Herald*, 16 November 1928: 9.
30 'Tragedy of race', *The Advertiser* (Adelaide), 28 June 1930: 7; 'London Letter: A Negro Othello', *The Mercury* (Hobart), 28 June 1930: 6; CR Bradish, 'Robeson explains Othello', *The Herald* (Melbourne), 5 July 1930: 20.

31 Stephen Henry Roberts, 'America: An insistent Negro steps from the "melting pot"', *Sydney Mail*, 8 August 1934: 8.
32 See Lois Potter, *Shakespeare in Performance: Othello* (Manchester University Press, 2002); Lindsey R Swindall, *The Politics of Paul Robeson's Othello* (University Press of Mississippi, 2011).
33 Henry Reese, 'Protecting the national soundscape: The gramophone industry and the nation in the 1920s', *Australian Historical Studies*, 52:2 (2021): 269, 273.
34 'Music: Notes and Records', *Otago Daily Times*, 15 January 1926: 5; 'Mimes [column name]: Music: Records', *Evening Post* (Wellington), 23 January 1926: 21; 'Music Notes', *Catholic Advocate*, 4 February 1926: 23; 'Music in Britain', *The Sun* (Sydney), 1 August 1926: 36.
35 Advertisement, *Tweed Daily* (Murwillumbah), 7 January 1927: 1; 'Gramophone records and music', *The Sun* (Sydney), 13 February 1927: 36; 'Negro spirituals on gramophone records: Good batch just sold out', *Daily Standard* (Brisbane), 22 September 1928: 8.
36 AHT, 'The Gramophone: Remarkable Negro singer', *The Telegraph* (Brisbane), 11 January 1929: 16. See also 'The gramophone in the home', *The Examiner* (Launceston), 30 January 1929: 7; 'Latest recordings', *The Sun* (Auckland), 31 January 1929: 14: 'New records', *West Australian*, 16 February 1929: 5; AHT, 'The Gramophone', *The Telegraph* (Brisbane), 26 April 1929: 16. The average locally produced manufactured record cost between 2 and 4 shillings, according to Reese, 'Protecting the national soundscape': 274.
37 'Gramophone Music: Paul Robeson', *The Advocate* (Burnie, Tasmania), 18 May 1929: 12. See advertisement for another Paul Robeson record from the Gramophone Company, 'Sonny Boy' / 'De Lil' Piccaninny's Gone to Sleep', *The Sun* (Sydney), 26 June 1929: 1.
38 Advertisements, *Evening Star*, 15 June 1929: 3; classified advertising, *The Argus*, 20 July 1929: 32; Advertisements, *Evening Post* (Auckland), 2 July 1929: p. 4.
39 Grant Olwage, '"Warbling wood-notes wile": Nature, art, and race in Paul Robeson's "early singing"', *Musical Quarterly*, 98, 3 (2015): 271.
40 'Music of the Discs: Records reviewed', *Brisbane Courier*, 1 January 1930: 15.
41 'Royal Southern Singers', *The Register* (Adelaide), 15 June 1923, 12; 'Southern Singers: Their music and themselves', *West Australian*, 2 July 1923: 10; Egan, *African American Entertainers in Australia and New Zealand*: 150–1. By 1926, there were around 1600 jazz bands playing in Australia; see Bruce Johnson, *The Inaudible Music* (Currency Press, 2000): 10.
42 Alwyn Williams, 'Jazz and the New Negro: Harlem's intellectuals wrestle with the art of the age', *Australasian Journal of American Studies*, 21: 1 (July 2002): 1.
43 'Theatre Royal', *The Age* (Melbourne), 15 September 1924: 13.
44 Andrew Bisset, *Black Roots, White Flowers: A History of Jazz in Australia* (Golden Press, 1979): 45.

45 Deirdre O'Connell, *Harlem Nights: The Secret History of Australia's Jazz Age* (Melbourne University Press, 2021): 64.
46 Ibid., passim; Egan, *African American Entertainers in Australia and New Zealand*: 169–76.
47 Bisset, *Black Roots, White Flowers*: 36; See Deirdre O'Connell, 'Contesting White Australia: Black jazz musicians in a white man's country', *Australian Historical Studies*, 47:2 (2006): 241–58, especially 249; Egan, ibid.: 169–77.
48 Egan, ibid.: 187–93, 203–4.
49 Bisset, *Black Roots, White Flowers*: 45.
50 They could also hear spirituals sung on radio from around 1925. See 'Wireless Broadcasting', *Daily News* (Perth), 13 January 1926: 5.
51 3DB scheduled one such program on 22 June 1929, see 'Broadcasting Programmes', *The Herald* (Melbourne), 22 June 1929: 31, and another on 17 December 1929, see 'The Week's Broadcasting Programmes', *Weekly Times* (Melbourne), 14 December 1929: 12. So did 2BL in Sydney, see 'To-day's Broadcasting', *Truth* (Sydney), 26 January 1930: 15.
52 'Tonight's Radio: Masterton program,' *Wairarapa Daily Times*, 29 May 1929: 5.
53 Eslanda Robeson, *Paul Robeson, Negro* (Harper and Brothers, 1930); Robert Shaffer, 'Out of the shadows: The political writings of Eslanda Goode Robeson', in Joseph Dorinson and William Pencak (eds), *Paul Robeson: Essays on His Life and Legacy* (McFarland, 2002): 100; Fionnghuala Sweeney, 'Modernist biography and the question of manhood: Eslanda Goode Robeson's *Paul Robeson, Negro*', in Farebrother and Thaggert (eds), *A History of the Harlem Renaissance*: 144–58.
54 'Colored culture', *The Sun* (Sydney), 17 August 1930: 25.
55 Shaffer, 'Out of the shadows': 99.
56 Paul Robeson Jnr, *The Undiscovered Paul Robeson: An Artist's Journey* (John Wiley & Sons, 2001): 173.
57 Woollcott's oft-quoted comment that he thought Robeson someone who had been 'touched by destiny' appears in Alexander Woollcott, *While Rome Burns* (Simon & Schuster, 1934): 135; 'Woollcott Calling', *Daily Mercury* (Mackay, Queensland), 22 June 1946: 2.
58 Woollcott, *While Rome Burns*: 129–30.
59 SEN, 'Review: *While Rome Burns*', *Sydney Mail*, 30 January 1935: 10; Panache (pseud.), 'Meet Mr Woollcott', *Evening Star*, 6 June 1936: 2; John Random, 'The two million', *Daily Telegraph* (Sydney), 15 April 1937: 6; Mary Olivier, 'Mrs Robeson does exist', *The Queenslander*, 12 January 1938: 10; John Dempster, 'Musical Notes', *The Mail* (Adelaide), 25 June 1938: 5.
60 'Robeson "touched by destiny"', *Adelaide Advertiser*, 12 November 1960: n.p.; JM, 'His voice a gift—and a burden', *The News* (Adelaide), 24 November 1960: n.p.
61 Anae, '"They seemed to recognise us as brethren from a far distant tribe"'.

62 Amanda Harris, *Representing Australian Aboriginal Music and Dance 1930—1970* (Bloomsbury, 2020): 12, 49; see in the same volume Shannon Foster, 'Mungari Buldyan: Song for my grandfather': 16–20.
63 Harris, ibid.: 48.
64 Egan, *African American Entertainers in Australia and New Zealand*: 38; Frances Peters-Little, *Jimmy Little: A Yorta Yorta Man* (Hardie Grant, 2023): 9–14.
65 Harris, *Representing Australian Aboriginal Music and Dance*: 136.
66 '"One fella good Christmas" at Darwin', *The Argus*, 27 December 1937: 1.
67 'May be Paul Robeson of Australia', *Newcastle Morning Herald and Miners' Advocate*, 6 September 1947: 3.
68 'Entertainments', *New Zealand Herald*, 10 August 1935: 18; 'Adventure in the wilds', *Labor Daily*, 21 October 1935: 8; 'Current Entertainments', *Evening Post*, 2 September 1935: 5.
69 'Aborigines joined chant with film', *Daily News* (Perth), 25 January 1937: 2, also cited by Nicole Anae in '"They will all be my color": Nina Mae McKinney and Black internationalism in 1930s Australia', in Keisha N Blain and Tiffany M Gill (eds), *To Turn the Whole World Over: Black Women and Internationalism* (University of Illinois Press, 2019): 138.
70 Alec Robertson, 'Paul Robeson's advice: Stand with the people', *The Tribune*, 23 November 1960: 6.
71 JM, 'His voice a gift—and a burden'.
72 Jill Matthews, *Dance Hall and Picture Palace: Sydney's Romance with Modernity* (Currency Press, 2005): 126.
73 See 'Paul Robeson sings six songs: National film broadcast', *Wireless Weekly*, 17 September 1937: 5.
74 Olivier, 'Mrs Robeson does exist'.
75 The songs included 'Lazin'', 'I Got a Robe', 'Roll up, Sailorman', 'Ma Curly Headed Baby', 'River Steals Ma Folks from Me' and 'You Didn't Oughta Do Such Things'. See Barbara Ransby, *Eslanda* (Yale University Press, 2013): 124–5.
76 See Scott Allen Nollen, *Paul Robeson: Film Pioneer* (McFarland & Company, 2010): 106–17.
77 Mark A Reid, 'Race, working-class consciousness, and dreaming in Africa', in Stewart, *Paul Robeson*: 172. See 'Appealing drama: Robeson at his best', *Evening Post*, 11 December 1937: 7.
78 Stuart Cunningham, *Featuring Australia: The Cinema of Charles Chauvel* (Allen & Unwin, 1991): 110–16.
79 'Film Reviews: *Uncivilised*', *SMH*, 28 September 1936: 4.
80 See, for example, 'Songs to inspire: Robeson in Spain', *The Argus*, 29 January 1938: 7.
81 James Smethurst, 'London, New York, and the Black Bolshevik renaissance: Radical Black internationalism during the New Negro Renaissance', in Farebrother and Thaggert, *A History of the Harlem Renaissance*: 207.

82 Sparrow, *No Way But This: In Search of Paul Robeson* (Scribe, 2017): 128.
83 Marie Seton, *Eisenstein* (Bodley Head, 1952): 316.
84 Ransby, *Eslanda*: 94; Lisa Merrill and Theresa Saxon, 'Black Americans in Russia: Ira Aldridge and Paul Robeson', in David Featherston, Christian Høgsbjerg and Alan Rice (eds), *Revolutionary Lives of the Red and Black Atlantic since 1917* (Manchester University Press, 2022): 203.
85 Duberman, *Robeson*: 156.
86 Marie Seton, *Paul Robeson* (Dennis Dobson, 1958): 86.
87 Seton, *Eisenstein*: 327.
88 Seton, *Paul Robeson*: 86.
89 Merrill and Saxon, 'Black Americans in Russia': 203.
90 Jennifer Wilson, 'When the Harlem Renaissance went to Communist Moscow', *New York Times* online, 21 August 2017.
91 See Julia Dorn, '"I breathe freely": An interview in Moscow with Paul Robeson', *New Theatre*, 2:7 ('Negro Number', July 1935): 5.
92 Horne, *Paul Robeson: The Artist as Revolutionary* (Pluto Press, 2016): 61–2.
93 Ransby, *Eslanda*: 95.
94 Sharon Vriend-Robinette, 'Marian Anderson as Cold Warrior: African Americans, the US Information Agency, and the marketing of democratic capitalism', *American Studies*, 57:4 (2019): 46, n. 8.
95 Seton, *Eisenstein*: 352.
96 Dorn, '"I breathe freely"'.
97 For a detailed discussion of African Americans' attraction to the Soviet Union in the 1930s and in some cases after, see Kate Baldwin, *Beyond the Color Line and the Iron Curtain: Reading Encounters Between Black and Red, 1922–1963* (Duke University Press, 2002).
98 Stephen Bourne, *Deep Are the Roots: Trailblazers who Changed Black British Theatre* (History Press, 2021): 88.
99 Duberman, *Paul Robeson*: 196–7.
100 'Interviews: CLR James', *Black Scholar*, 42:2 (2012): 22–30.
101 See also CLR James, 'The most influential man of the 20th century: Paul Robeson Part 1' [speech], *Pacifica Radio Archives* website, 1989.
102 Duberman, *Paul Robeson*: 208; Seton, *Paul Robeson*: 109–10.
103 Paul Robeson, 'To you beloved comrade', *New World Review*, April 1953: 11–13, reprinted in Philip S Foner (ed.), *Paul Robeson Speaks* (Citadel Press, 2002 [originally published in 1978]): 347.
104 Seton, *Paul Robeson*: 109–10. The quote, slightly amended, also appears in Paul Robeson, 'The voice of freedom', in Edwin R Embree (ed.), *Thirteen Against the Odds* (Viking Press, 1944): 259–60.
105 'Paul Robeson may visit Australia: Views on race and colour', *The Argus*, 29 April 1937: 11. See, in particular, 'The boomerang and its vagaries', *Dublin University Magazine*, 40:62 (February 1838): 168–71; Stan Florek, 'Why a boomerang flies', *Australian Museum* website, 13 June 2023.

106 O'Connell, *Harlem Nights*: 87.
107 Duberman, *Paul Robeson*: 208.
108 Ibid.
109 Robeson Jnr, *The Undiscovered Paul Robeson: An Artist's Journey*: 289–90.
110 Ibid.: 306.
111 Smethurst, 'London, New York, and the Black Bolshevik renaissance': 200.
112 Horne, *Paul Robeson*: 72–3.
113 Ransby, *Eslanda*: 105–21.
114 Duberman, *Paul Robeson*: 212.
115 As cited by Duberman, ibid.
116 Horne, *Paul Robeson*: 74.
117 Seton, *Paul Robeson*: 112.
118 Duberman, *Paul Robeson*: 219.
119 McGinty and Shirley, 'Paul Robeson, musician': 116; Grant Olwage, '"The world is his song": Paul Robeson's 1958 Carnegie Hall concerts and the cosmopolitan imagination', *Journal of the Society for American Music*, 7:2 (2013): 191.
120 'Afterword', in Nikolay Gorbunov, *Feodor Chaliapin in Australia and New Zealand* (Kruk, 2015).
121 McGinty and Shirley, 'Paul Robeson, musician': 117.
122 'Paul Robeson may come here', *The Argus*, 29 September 1936: 8.
123 Anae, '"They will all be my color"': 139.
124 'Paul Robeson may visit Australia: Views on race and colour'.
125 'The march of events: The colour bar', *Sunday Mail*, 2 May 1937: 4; 'Robeson's hooey: About White Australia', *Sunday Times* (Perth), 2 May 1937: 2.
126 See, for example, 'Great Negro for Sydney', *Labor Daily*, 1 August 1938: 4; 'That mystery of black skin', *The Worker* (Brisbane), 23 August 1938: 3.
127 'Robeson, Gigli may be here next year', *The Argus*, 15 March: 1.
128 Duberman, *Paul Robeson*: 231.
129 'Robeson, Gigli may be here next year'. Duberman suggests the planned tour was called off because of the uncertain political situation in Europe, *Paul Robeson*: 228.
130 Duberman, ibid.
131 Ibid.: 232. See also Wilson, 'When the Harlem Renaissance went to Communist Moscow'.

Chapter 2: 'He simply electrifies you'

1 'Prominent guests inaugurate "Answering New Zealand" programs—David Jenkins, Mrs Franklin Delano Roosevelt, Paul Robeson, Mr Deems Taylor, Hon. Walter Nash and Mr George Palmer', Archives New Zealand, 3102/0034, Box 2596, 1942.
2 Martin Duberman, *Paul Robeson* (New Press, 1989): 259–61; Scott Allen Nollen, *Paul Robeson: Film Pioneer* (McFarland & Company, 2010): 145–51.

Although this production attracted widespread praise in the United States, it received little notice in Australian and New Zealand newspapers. For occasional mentions, see Pat Thompson, 'Drama: The new Othello', *Workers' Star* (Perth), 14 January 1944: 5; 'A prison resolve', *Auckland Star*, 29 November 1943: 4.

3 Barbara Ransby, *Eslanda* (Yale University Press, 2013): 152–3.

4 Mary G Mason, 'Travel as metaphor and reality in Afro-American women's autobiography, 1850–1972', *Black American Literature Forum*, 24:2 (Summer 1990): 337–56, especially 350.

5 Eslanda Goode Robeson, *African Journey* (John Day Company, 1945): 109.

6 Mason, 'Travel as metaphor and reality': 430.

7 Ernestine Evans, review of Eslanda Goode Robeson, *African Journey*, in 'Book Reviews', *New York Herald Tribune Weekly*, 12 August 1945: 2.

8 'The dark continent through a Negro's eyes', *The Age*, 20 July 1946: 25; 'A Negro looks at Africa', *The Telegraph* (Brisbane), 11 September 1946: 2.

9 'Native life in the African continent', *The Advertiser* (Adelaide), 19 October 1946: 6.

10 FB, 'A visit to Africa', *The Argus*, 7 December 1946: 16.

11 Russell Braddock, 'American Negro in Africa', *Daily Telegraph* (Sydney), 21 September 1946: 16. For a rare negative review, see SH O'L, 'Problem in black and white', *SMH*, 21 December 1946: 13.

12 For example, 'South African Customs ban Negress' book', *Evening Advocate* (Innisfail), 22 October 1946: 3.

13 Clare Corbould, 'Black internationalism's shifting alliances: African American newspapers, the White Australia policy, and Indigenous Australians, 1919–1948', *History Compass*, 15:5 (2017): e12377.

14 Sean Brawley and Chris Dixon, 'Jim Crow downunder? African American encounters with White Australia, 1942–1945', *Pacific Historical Review*, 71:4 (2002): 607–32.

15 See 'Paul Robeson visit sought', *The Herald* (Melbourne), 9 May 1946: 9; 'Paul Robeson's "dearest wish"', *The Herald*, 6 July 1946: 3; 'Robeson wants to sing here', *News* (Adelaide), 6 July 1946: 33.

16 Geoffrey Hutton, 'Why overseas stars are staying home', *The Argus*, 12 October 1946: 18.

17 Among many newspaper references to Duncan's performance in this movie, see 'Syncopation concludes at Johnson's', *Barrier Daily Truth*, 29 January 1943: 3; 'The new films', *Daily Telegraph* (Sydney), 24 January 1943: 23.

18 Jim MacDougall, 'Contact', *The Sun* (Sydney), 31 July 1946: 1.

19 'Negro baritone greets "great American"', *The Argus*, 13 June 1946: 7.

20 Lon Jones, 'Anti-Negro feeling rises in the US', *The Argus*, 26 October 1946: 2.

21 Kenneth Harrison, *Dark Man, White World: A Portrait of the Tenor Harold Blair* (Novalit, 1975): 77.

22 'May be Paul Robeson of Australia', *Newcastle Morning Herald and Miners' Advocate*, 6 September 1947: 3.
23 'This blackbird knows his song', *Courier-Mail*, 10 April 1948: 2; Harrison, *Dark Man, White World*: 148.
24 Alan T Duncan, 'Harold Blair (1924–1976)', *ADB* website, 2006 (originally published in 1993). See John G Mason, 'Youthful singer Harold Blair', *The Age*, 23 May 1947 (Junior Age Supplement): 2 for mention of Duncan's encouragement of Blair.
25 Duberman, *Paul Robeson*: 317.
26 Ibid.: 302, 316ff.
27 Gerald Horne, *Paul Robeson* (Pluto Press, 2016): 10, 73; Jordan Goodman, *Paul Robeson: A Watched Man* (Verso, 2013): 81.
28 Gus Hall, *Paul Robeson: An American Communist* (CPUSA, 1998), 11-page pamphlet. In Britain, the Metropolitan Police told MI5 that he had joined the Communist Party in 1937. See David Caute, *Red List: MI5 and British Intellectuals in the Twentieth Century* (Verso, 2022): 137.
29 Duberman, *Paul Robeson*: 317.
30 Katherine Zien, 'Race and politics in concert: Paul Robeson and William Warfield in Panama, 1947–1953', *Global South*, 6:2 (2013): 114.
31 NLNZ: Bailey, Rona, 1914–2005: Papers and recordings, Series 8: Race relations and Project Waitangi, Papers relating to centennial of birth of Paul Robeson, 2006-041-090 (hereafter NLNZ: Rona Bailey Papers), Folder 4, Bailey, 'Paul Robeson saga 1947 and 1960'.
32 Duberman, *Paul Robeson*: 327.
33 Ibid.: 675, n. 34.
34 'ILWU honorary member Paul Robeson memorialized at Rutgers University', *The Dispatcher* (ILWU newspaper online), 24 June 2019. Accompanied by a photograph from the *Dispatcher* archives of Harry Bridges presenting a certificate to Paul Robeson.
35 Duberman, *Paul Robeson*: 310–11, 676, n. 34.
36 'Faith in royal family: Menzies', *The Argus*, 10 January 1949: 2.
37 Duberman, *Paul Robeson:* 340; Nico Slate, *The Prism of Race: WEB Du Bois, Langston Hughes, Paul Robeson, and the Colored World of Cedric Dover* (Palgrave Macmillan, 2014): 96.
38 Duberman, *Paul Robeson:* 340.
39 See John Munro, *The Anticolonial Front: The African American Freedom Struggle and Global Decolonisation, 1945–1960* (Cambridge University Press, 2017).
40 Nancy Wills, *Shades of Red: Personal and Political Recollections of a Communist to Mark the Occasion of Our Sixtieth Anniversary, 1920–1980* (Communist Arts Group, 1980): 87; Nancy Wills, *Robeson* (Gem Publications, 1987): 45.
41 Wills, *Shades of Red*: 87. See also NLA: Wills, Nancy, 1920–2005 and Stevens, Adrian, *Nancy Wills Interviewed by Adrian Stevens* [sound recording], 1997,

transcript (TRC 2348) (hereafter NLA: Nancy Wills Oral History Transcript), cassette 1, side 1: 7–12; 'To be a housewife is not enough', *Weekly Times* (Melbourne), 23 April 1947: 37.

42 Duberman, *Paul Robeson*: 223; See also Jennifer Wilson, 'When the Harlem Renaissance went to Communist Moscow', *New York Times* online, 21 August 2017.

43 Wills, *Shades of Red*: 89; Charles L Blockson, 'Paul Robeson: A bibliophile in spite of himself', in Jeffrey C Stewart, *Paul Robeson* (Rutgers University Press, 1998): 240.

44 *Tribune* published this interview well after the 1949 Paris peace conference and its tumultuous events. 'Paul Robeson may visit Australia at end of this year', *Tribune*, 4 May 1949: 5.

45 Goodman, *A Watched Man*: 30, 34.

46 Philip Deery, 'The dove flies east: Whitehall, Warsaw and the 1950 World Peace Congress', *Australian Journal of Politics and History*, 48:4 (2002): 450.

47 Given Paul had left for the United Kingdom in February, it seems that either this dinner occurred before he decided to go to the Paris Congress, or that it occurred later, after he had decided to go; and that Eslanda was the host and Paul was not present.

48 Harry Belafonte, *My Song: A Memoir of Art, Race, and Defiance* (Vintage Books, 2012): 82.

49 Bernard Smith, *Noel Counihan: Artist and Revolutionary* (Oxford University Press, 1993): 230; Geoffrey Roberts, 'Averting Armageddon: The Communist peace movement, 1948–1956', in Stephen A Smith (ed.), *The Oxford Handbook of the History of Communism* (Oxford University Press, 2014): 325.

50 HCE, 'World Congress for Peace', *Salient: An Organ of Student Opinion at Victoria College, Wellington*, 12:7 (13 July 1949): 5; 'Eight NZ students in France', *Bay of Plenty Times*, 9 November 1948: 6.

51 Simon Pierse, *Australian Art and Artists in London 1950–1965: An Antipodean Summer* (Routledge, 2016): 29.

52 Smith, *Noel Counihan*: 230.

53 For the list of Australians at Paris in 1949, see Rowan Cahill, *Rupert Lockwood (1908–1997): Journalist, Communist, Intellectual* (PhD thesis, University of Wollongong, 2013): 260. See also Smith, *Noel Counihan*: 552, for a mention of Bruce Hamilton and his wife.

54 NLA: Papers of Noel Counihan, 1931–1994, MS 9107 (hereafter NLA: Counihan Papers), Box 1, Folder 2, Noel Counihan to his wife, Paddy Counihan, 9 April 1960. See also Box 13, Folder 3 for a typed statement of greetings to the Congress by about twenty Australian writers, painters, sculptors (Fredda Brilliant), scientists and other cultural workers.

55 NLA: Counihan Papers, Box 1, Folder 2, Noel Counihan to Paddy Counihan, 22 April 1949.

56 Ibid., 24 April 1949.

57 NLA: Counihan Papers, Box 13, Folder 3, 'Report on the World Congress of the Defenders of Peace held in Paris from April 20 to 25'.
58 Smith, *Noel Counihan*: 230.
59 KS Inglis, 'Stephen Murray-Smith (1922–1988)', *ADB* website, 2012; NLA: Counihan Papers, 'Report on the World Congress'.
60 'Lockwood at Paris peace talks for 3 Aust. unions', *Tribune*, 20 April 1949: 8.
61 Bernard Smith, *A Pavane for Another Time* (Macmillan Art Publishing, 2002): 286.
62 Rupert Lockwood, 'World's leading intellectuals appeal to Australians: "Unite for peace"', *The Guardian* online (Melbourne), 20 May 1949; Joan Mansfield, 'The Christian Social Order Movement, 1943–1951', *Journal of Religious History*, 15:1 (June 1988): 109–28. Later that year Chidzey would be married in Canterbury Cathedral by Hewlett Johnson, the 'Red Dean'; see Juliet Flesch, 'Merz, Blanche Isobel (1920–2007)', *Australian Women's Register* website, 2017.
63 NLA: Counihan Papers, Noel Counihan to Paddy Counihan, 22 April 1949.
64 'More vigorous peace action to follow Congress', *Tribune*, 30 April 1949: 2; Cahill, *Rupert Lockwood*: 231. See also several reports in *The Guardian* (Melbourne), 6 May 1949: 1, 2, 3.
65 Wills, *Shades of Red*: 98.
66 Lian Luo, 'International avant-garde and the Chinese national anthem: Tian Han, Joris Ivens and Paul Robeson', *Ivens Magazine*, 16 (October 2010): 16.
67 Ibid.: 7.
68 Goodman, *A Watched Man*: 44.
69 NLA: Counihan Papers, Box 1, Folder 2, Counihan to his mother and family, 12 May 1949.
70 Ibid.
71 Nance Macmillan, 'Robeson still with the people', *The Argus*, 30 June 1950: 2.
72 Duberman, *Paul Robeson*: 341–2; Barbara Beeching, 'Paul Robeson and the Black press: The 1950 passport controversy', *Journal of African American History*, 87 (Summer 2002): 339–54, esp. 341.
73 Duberman, *Paul Robeson*: 342.
74 Ibid.: 350.
75 Ibid.: 342.
76 Ibid.: 325.
77 Ibid.: 344.
78 '"US Negro will not fight Reds": Robeson', *Barrier Miner*, 21 April 1949: 1; 'Negroes in conflict: Attitude to Soviet', *SMH*, 22 April 1949: 3; 'Paul Robeson in plea against war', *The Age*, 22 April 1949: 1.
79 Duberman, *Paul Robeson*: 343.
80 'Negro spirituals', *The Argus*, 30 July 1949: 12; see also 'US singers "poles apart in politics"', *The Age*, 25 July 1949: 1.
81 Duberman, *Paul Robeson*: 352.

82 Lisa Merrill and Theresa Saxon, 'Black Americans in Russia', in David Featherstone, Christian Høgsbjerg and Alan Rice (eds), *Revolutionary Lives of the Red and Black Atlantic since 1917* (Manchester University Press, 2022): 198.
83 Daniel Soyer, 'Executed Bundists, Soviet delegates and the wartime Jewish popular front in New York', *American Communist History*, 15:3 (2016): 316–21; John Docker, *Growing Up Communist and Jewish in Bondi* (Kerr Publishing, 2020): vol. 2, 579–80.
84 Duberman, *Paul Robeson*: 353.
85 Tim Tzouliadis, *The Forsaken: From the Great Depression to the Gulags: Hope and Betrayal in Stalin's Russia* (Abacus, 2008): 361.
86 Duberman, *Paul Robeson*: 353.
87 Paul Robeson Jnr, *The Undiscovered Paul Robeson: Quest for Freedom* (John Wiley & Sons, 2010): 154–5.
88 Duberman, *Paul Robeson*: 352–3; Tzouliadis, *The Forsaken*: 269.
89 Maxim Matusevich, 'Paul Robeson's tragic love of Russia', *Past in Present: Blog of Seton Hall University History Department*, 8 November 2015.
90 Kate Baldwin, *Beyond the Color Line and the Iron Curtain* (Duke University Press, 2002): 246.
91 Paul Robeson, 'For freedom and peace', 19 June 1949, in Philip S Foner (ed.), *Paul Robeson Speaks* (Citadel Press, 2002): 201; Duberman, *Paul Robeson*: 357.
92 Paul Robeson, *Paul Robeson Calls on the American People to Fight for Freedom and Peace* (Current Book Distributors, 1949).
93 Foner, *Paul Robeson Speaks*: 203–4, 211; Duberman, *Paul Robeson*: 358.
94 Foner, ibid.: 205.
95 'Paul Robeson's wife explains how she found her loyalty', *Tribune*, 21 September 1949: 4.
96 Pearl Buck with Eslanda Goode Robeson, *American Argument* (John Day Company, 1949): 133.
97 Ibid.: 126.
98 Ibid.: 127.
99 'Controversial', *West Australian*, 19 August 1950: 22; 'Debate on wide range of topics', *The Advertiser* (Adelaide), 24 June 1950: 6.
100 Deery, 'The dove flies east': 450.
101 Malcolm Saunders and Ralph Summy, *The Australian Peace Movement: A Short History* (Peace Research Centre, ANU, 1986): 28.
102 Ibid.: 32.
103 Robin Gollan, *Revolutionaries and Reformists: Communism and the Australian Labour Movement 1920–1955* (ANU Press, 1975): 261.
104 Ralph Summy, 'The Australian Peace Council and the anticommunist milieu, 1949–1965', in Charles Chatfield and Peter van den Dungen (eds), *Peace Movements and Political Cultures* (University of Tennessee Press, 1988): 240.
105 Audrey Johnson, 'Morrow, William, 1888–1980', *Biographical Dictionary of the Australian Senate* website, n.d. [originally published in 2004].

106 Goodman, *A Watched Man*, Chapter 8: 115–37.
107 American Civil Liberties Union, *Violence in Peekskill* (ACLU, 1949).
108 This was probably *The Peekskill Story*, released in October 1949, Folk Archive de.
109 Audrey Johnson, *Fly a Rebel Flag: Bill Morrow 1888–1980* (Penguin, 1986): 193–4.
110 'Paul Robeson invited to Australia', *The Advertiser* (Adelaide), 4 February 1950: 3; 'Australian Peace Congress in April; Dean, Robeson invited', *Tribune*, 15 February 1950: 1. See mention of an invitation from the APC for its conference in April 1950 in *The Argus*, 22 June 1950: 2, copy held in NAA: Department of Immigration, Paul Robeson and Madam Sun Yat Sen—Proposed visit, 1950, A433, 1950/2/2697.
111 'Paul Robeson invited here', *The Age*, 16 February 1950: 3.
112 Craig McLean, *Fear of Peace? Australian Government Responses to the Peace Movement 1949–1959* (PhD thesis, Victoria University, 2001): 39.
113 The organisers wrote back to Robeson and asked him to name his own time for a visit to Australia; 'The story of a mighty challenge against war', *Journal of the Australian Peace Council*, 1:2 (1950): 7. 'Dean of Canterbury to attend Peace Congress', *Northern Standard* (Darwin, NT), 24 March 1950: 2; '"Peace only aim of Peace Council", delegates declare', *Illawarra Mercury*, 1 May 1950: 2.
114 Gollan, *Revolutionaries and Reformists*: 262.
115 Ralph Gibson, *My Years in the Communist Party* (International Bookshop, 1966): 164; '10,000 hear "Red Dean"', *The Age*, 17 April 1950: 1.
116 Australian Peace Congress Programme, 1950, available at *Reason in Revolt: Source Documents of Australian Radicalism* website.
117 Gibson, *My Years in the Communist Party*: 161.
118 Democratic Rights Council, *A Charter of Freedom: Report of a Conference for Democratic Rights Held in Melbourne Lower Town Hall, Sat. April 22, 1950* (DRC, 1950): 1.
119 Gibson, *My Years in the Communist Party*: 162.
120 Democratic Rights Council, *A Charter of Freedom*: 5.
121 Jordan Goodman, *A Watched Man* (Verso, 2013), Chapter 9.
122 Duberman, *Paul Robeson*: 386; Goodman, *A Watched Man*: 153–4.
123 Jill Roe, *Miles Franklin: A Biography* (HarperCollins, 2010).
124 Marilla North, *Yarn Spinners* (Brandl & Schlesinger, 2016): 308.
125 'Robeson may visit here', *The Argus*, 12 June 1950: 5. See *Liberty* (journal of the Democratic Rights Council), 1 (July 1950); 2 (September 1950): 9 (December 1950). Available in UMA: Consolidated Papers of Frank Hartley, 1980.0163, unit 16.
126 Hugh Buggy and Ron Stephens, 'News Diary', *The Argus*, 19 June 1950: 6.
127 Frank Doherty, 'Was his "no" due to "colour" politics?', *The Argus*, 22 June 1950: 2; Nance Macmillan, 'Robeson still "with the people"', *The Argus*, 30 June 1950: 2.

128 Fryer Library: Collection UQFL191—Constance Healy Collection, Box 14, Paul Robeson to Nance Macmillan, Australian Peace Conference, 330 Little Flinders Street, Melbourne, 27 June 1950. The letter is on Council on African Affairs, Inc. letterhead. It was subsequently printed in *The Guardian*: Paul Robeson, '"More power to you, Australian defenders of Peace"', *The Guardian* (Melbourne), 14 July 1950: 7.
129 The Scottsboro Boys were a group of nine African American teenagers from Scottsboro, Alabama, who were accused of raping two white women in 1931. Their case was taken up by both the CPUSA and the NAACP. Their trials and, in five cases, ultimate convictions have since been widely considered as exposing racial injustice within the Alabama legal system. Haywood Patterson, to whom Robeson refers, had been convicted and gaoled in 1936; he escaped in 1949 and was picked up in 1950 in Michigan.
130 Robeson to Macmillan, 27 June 1950.
131 Duberman, *Paul Robeson*: 388.
132 Goodman, *A Watched Man*: 154.
133 Duberman, *Paul Robeson*: 388.
134 Goodman, *A Watched Man*: 155; Duberman, *Paul Robeson*: 388; Ransby, *Eslanda*: 231; 'Robeson not coming: "Some other time"', *SMH*, 10 August 1950: 3. Confusingly, on 9 August *Tribune* incorrectly reported his acceptance: *Tribune*, 9 August 1950: 1.

Chapter 3: 'Let Robeson Sing'

1 Martin Duberman, *Paul Robeson* (New Press, 1989): 391.
2 Two months later, on 5 March 1953, Stalin died.
3 Duberman, *Paul Robeson*: 398.
4 Ibid.: 414.
5 Denouncing him would become a loyalty test for African Americans brought before the House Committee on Un-American Activities and other government committees investigating American communism; Victor S Navasky, *Naming Names* (Penguin, 2003): 187; Daniel A Holder, '"I got a home in that rock"': Paul Robeson's *Here I Stand* and Cold War resistance to McCarthyism', *Auto/Biography Studies* 27:1 (2012): 69.
6 Duberman, *Paul Robeson*: 391.
7 Stuart Macintyre, *The Party: The Communist Party of Australia from Heyday to Reckoning* (Allen & Unwin, 2022): 261; Roger Douglas, 'The ambiguity of sedition: The trials of William Fardon Burns', *Australian Journal of Legal History*, 9 (2004): 227–48.
8 WF Burns, 'Paul Robeson never was a "Bosambo"', *Maritime Worker*, 1 December 1960: 4.
9 Stuart Macintyre, 'Lance Sharkey (1898–1967)', *ADB* website, 2006 (originally published in 2002).
10 See *Liberty* (journal of the Democratic Rights Council), 2 (October 1950): 1, 2.

11 Angus McIntyre, 'The training of Australian communist cadres in China, 1951–1961', *Studies in Comparative Communism*, 11:4 (Winter 1978): 410–23.
12 Robin Gollan, *Revolutionaries and Reformists* (ANU Press, 1975): 260; 'Korean War, 1950–53', *Australian War Memorial* website, 2023.
13 The situation was similar in communist parties around the world. See Geoffrey Roberts, 'Averting Armageddon: The communist peace movement, 1948–1956', in Stephen A Smith (ed.), *The Oxford Handbook of the History of Communism* (Oxford University Press, 2014): 322–7, esp. 323.
14 Gollan, *Revolutionaries and Reformists*: 263; 'Political points', *The Bulletin*, 17 May 1950: 8.
15 Macintyre, *The Party*, Chapter 9.
16 'Robeson, Chaplin invited' and 'News from the States', *Australian Peace Review*, 1:2 (July 1956): 3.
17 Barbara Beeching, 'Paul Robeson and the Black press', *Journal of African American History*, 87 (2002): 353; Jordan Goodman, *A Watched Man* (Verso, 2014): 163.
18 Duberman, *Paul Robeson*: 392–3.
19 Jacqueline Castledine, 'In a solid bond of unity: Anticolonial feminism in the Cold War era', *Journal of Women's History*, 20:4 (Winter 2008): 57–81; Erik McDuffie, 'A "new freedom movement of Negro women": Sojourning for truth, justice, and human rights during the early Cold War', *Radical History Review*, 101 (Spring 2008): 81–106, quote on 82.
20 Gerald Horne, *Communist Front? The Civil Rights Congress, 1946–1956* (International Publishers, 1988): 13–21, 48, 69.
21 William L Patterson, *The Man Who Cried Genocide: An Autobiography* (New York International Publishers, 1971): 184; Gerald Horne, *Black and Red: WEB Du Bois and the Afro-American Response to the Cold War 1944–1963* (State University of New York Press, 1986): 181.
22 *We Charge Genocide: The Historic Petition to the United Nations for Relief from a Crime of the United States Government Against the Negro People* (Civil Rights Congress, 1951): 8; Ann Curthoys and John Docker, 'Defining genocide', in Dan Stone (ed.), *The Historiography of Genocide* (Palgrave, 2008): 15–20.
23 Castledine, 'In a solid bond of unity': 69.
24 John D'Emilio, *Lost Prophet: The Life and Times of Bayard Rustin* (Simon & Schuster, 2003): 178–9; Beeching, 'Paul Robeson and the Black press': 353; Duberman, *Paul Robeson*: 393, 414, 437.
25 Imaobong Umoren, '"We Americans are not just American citizens any longer": Eslanda Robeson, world citizenship, and the *New World Review* in the 1950s', *Journal of Women's History*, 30:4 (Winter 2018): 134–58.
26 Barbara Ransby, *Eslanda* (Yale University Press, 2013): 206.
27 Ibid.: 212.
28 Ibid.: 224; Duberman, *Paul Robeson*: 412.

29 'Majestic—Devonport—To-night' (advertisement), *The Advocate* (Burnie, Tasmania), 16 July 1951: 10; 'Radio and Television', *SMH*, 16 December 1956: 68; TV programme, *SMH*, 7 July 1958: 10.

30 The Sydney Cinema Group showed it in 1958; see advertisement in *SMH*, 27 September 1958: 20.

31 Morgan's Book Shop and Record Lounge advertisement, *SMH*, 28 April 1956: 11.

32 Paul Robeson, *Here I Stand* (Beacon Press, 1988 [1958]): 55.

33 Goodman, *A Watched Man*: 195–7.

34 'Lorraine reads the lesson', *The Advocate* (Burnie, Tasmania), 3 August 1954: 16; Ron Verzuh, 'Mine-Mill's Peace Arch concerts: How a "Red" union and a famous singer-activist fought for peace and social justice during the Cold War', *BC Studies*, 74 (Summer 2012): 87; Grant Olwage, '"The world is his song"', *Journal of the Society for American Music*, 7:2 (2013): 169.

35 Approximately 2000 copies of the record were made, of which 1700 had been sold by the time of the fourth and last Peace Arch concert in 1955; Laurel Sefton MacDowell, 'Paul Robeson in Canada: A border story', *Labour/Le Travail*, 51 (Spring 2003): 177–221. The second concert was also recorded, and much later the two recordings were combined in a single CD, *Paul Robeson: The Peace Arch Concerts* (Folk Era Records FE 1442CD).

36 MacDowell, 'Paul Robeson in Canada': 184.

37 'To Robeson lovers', *Tribune*, 9 October 1957: 10.

38 Mary Okello interviewed by Sari Braithwaite, 25 July 2008.

39 Charles Musser, 'Utopian visions in Cold War documentary: Joris Ivens, Paul Robeson and *The Song of the Rivers* (1954)', *Cinémas: Journal of Film Studies*, 12:3 (Spring 2002): 109–53, this information on 112.

40 Horne, *Paul Robeson*: 145. There is a German-language version on YouTube.

41 Scott Allen Nollen, *Paul Robeson: Film Pioneer* (McFarland & Company, 2010): 169.

42 Robeson, *Here I Stand*: 61.

43 Horne, *Paul Robeson*: 145; Robeson, *Here I Stand*: 60–2.

44 John Hughes, '*Indonesia Calling*: Joris Ivens in Australia', *Senses of Cinema*, 51 (July 2009); see also Gerald Peel, *Hands off Indonesia* (Current Book Distributors, 1945).

45 Norman Jeffery, 'WFTU film shows world struggles', *Maritime Worker*, 12 October 1954: 6.

46 '*Song of the Rivers*', *Tribune*, 23 November 1955: 6.

47 'Greetings to WFTU on anniversary', *Tribune*, 7 December 1955: 9; Musser, 'Utopian visions': 114.

48 Mary Dudziak, *Cold War Civil Rights: Race and the Image of American Democracy* (Princeton University Press, 2011): 61–2, 66; Penny Von Eschen, *Satchmo Blows Up the World: Jazz Ambassadors Play the Cold War* (Harvard University Press, 2006).

49 Katie A Callam et al., 'Marian Anderson's 1953 concert tour of Japan', *American Music*, 37:3 (Fall 2019): 267–329.
50 Sharon Vriend-Robinette, 'Marian Anderson as Cold Warrior', *American Studies*, 57:4 (2019): 46, n. 8.
51 *Sunday Herald*, 24 August 1952: 15 (2).
52 Robert Alan (pseud.), 'Paul Robeson: The lost shepherd', *The Crisis*, 58:11 (1951): 569–73; see Penny Von Eschen, *Race Against Empire* (Cornell University Press, 1997): 127.
53 'Your move—for Paul Robeson!', *Tribune*, 15 April 1953: 8; Goodman, *A Watched Man*: 203.
54 T Bell and others, Democratic Discussion Group to President Eisenhower, copy to Paul Robeson, 18 May 1953, photocopy in STHA: Hannah Middleton Papers, Misc. 5.
55 WJ Brown, 'Portrait of a people's artist: Paul Robeson', copy in Rona Bailey papers. The Australasian Book Society had been formed in 1952.
56 'Demand for Robeson passport', *Tribune*, 13 May 1953: 10; 'Crowds at Robeson night', *Tribune*, 3 June 1953: 3.
57 Duberman, *Paul Robeson*: 424; Goodman, *A Watched Man*: 273; Horne, *Paul Robeson*: 132.
58 'A cultural salute to Paul Robeson …', *Tribune*, 26 May 1954: 8; 'Seamen back Robeson', *Tribune*, 2 June 1954: 2.
59 STHA: Hannah Middleton Papers, Misc. 5, Australian Tramway and Motor Omnibus Employees' Association, Victorian branch, to Mrs I Deboissiere, 18 June 1954.
60 'Seamen back Robeson'.
61 'Robeson asks for passport', *The Argus*, 12 July 1954: 1.
62 'Help Robeson win back his passport', *Maritime Worker*, 13 July 1954: 7.
63 'Paul Robeson film, music evening', *Tribune*, 4 August 1954: 5. The Peekskill recording was probably *The Peekskill Story*, released in October 1949. *Tribune* says the speech celebrated the thirty-fifth anniversary of the *Daily Worker*, but that paper was founded in 1930.
64 'Grant passport', *Tribune*, 11 August 1954: 2.
65 '"I'll get over there soon"', *Tribune*, 6 October 1954: 7.
66 'Americans win ground on liberty front', *Tribune*, 6 July 1955: 5.
67 Duberman, *Paul Robeson*: 432, 444.
68 Goodman, *A Watched Man*: 275.
69 Ibid.: 277, 278.
70 'Americans win ground on liberty front'; 'Iron-Curtained', *Tribune*, 24 August 1955: 6; 'Let Robeson sing', *Tribune*, 12 December 1956: 7.
71 Gollan, *Revolutionaries and Reformists*: 279; Macintyre, *The Party*, Chapter 9.
72 Goodman, *A Watched Man*: 239.
73 Isaac Deutscher, 'The Russian Revolution and the Jewish problem', in his *The Non-Jewish Jew and Other Essays* (Merlin Press, 1981): 82–3; 'Khrushchev's

secret speech: Soviet history', and 'Doctors' Plot: Alleged conspiracy, Soviet Union [1953]', both on *Britannica* website, n.d.

74 Paul Robeson, 'To you beloved comrade', *New World Review*, April 1953: 11–13, reprinted in Philip S Foner (ed.), *Paul Robeson Speaks* (Citadel Press, 2002): 347.

75 Duberman, *Paul Robeson*: 417.

76 Ibid.: 443; Goodman, *A Watched Man*: 240.

77 RH Brookes, 'The CPNZ and the Sino-Soviet split', *Political Science* 17:2 (1965): 21.

78 Len Fox, *Broad Left, Narrow Left* (Len Fox, 1982): 145.

79 Ibid.: 147, 149. See a detailed account in Macintyre, *The Party*, Chapter 7.

80 Duberman, *Paul Robeson*: 449.

81 Goodman, *A Watched Man*: 279.

82 Ibid.: 252.

83 Ibid.: 280.

84 Robeson, *Here I Stand*: 56.

85 'Robeson recording', *Tribune*, 2 October 1957: 10.

86 'Robeson is heard again', *SMH*, 22 September 1957: 75.

87 Nancy Short, 'Letterbox: Robeson', *ABC Weekly*, 20:18 (30 April 1958): 2.

88 'Paul Robeson sings again', *Tribune*, 16 October 1957: 6.

89 Beeching, 'Paul Robeson and the Black press': 353; D'Emilio, *Lost Prophet*: 178–9; Duberman, *Paul Robeson*: 448.

90 Ransby, *Eslanda*: 235.

91 Nollen, *Paul Robeson*: 172.

92 Lloyd Brown, 'Preface' (1971), in Robeson, *Here I Stand*: xxvii–xxviii.

93 'I take my stand', *Tribune*, 22 April 1958: 7; KW, 'Great man, great artist', 24 March 1959: 6; 'Oustanding new books and reprints', 25 February 1959: 7.

94 Martin Long, 'A dedicated Negro', *SMH*, 8 November 1958: 12.

95 Duberman, *Paul Robeson*: 461–2.

96 Nico Slate, *The Prism of Race: WEB Du Bois, Langston Hughes, Paul Robeson, and the Colored World of Cedric Dover* (Palgrave Macmillan, 2014): 94.

97 Ibid.: 92.

98 Eslanda Robeson, 'How the world greeted Paul Robeson', *The Worker*, 27 April 1958: 6, as quoted in Kenneth O'Reilly, *Black Americans: The FBI Files* (Carroll & Graf, 1994): 374. A Paul Robeson evening had been held the previous year at the home of Win and Dick Surplus in Brisbane on 4 May 1957; see 'General', *Tribune*, 1 May 1957: 11.

99 Duberman, *Paul Robeson*: 460; Nollen, *Paul Robeson*: 173.

100 NAA: C100, 1201734, 'Interview singer Paul Robeson and Mrs Robeson, by Bob Moore', broadcast on Adelaide ABC radio station 5CL on 25 November 1960.

101 'Despite all attacks, he "just keeps rollin' along"', *Tribune*, 12 October 1960: 7.

102 'Downbeat', *SMH*, 21 August 1960: 110. The article refers to a 12-inch record issued by Top Rank (TRL-8530).
103 Jonathon Karp, 'Performing Black-Jewish symbiosis: The "Hassidic Chant" of Paul Robeson', *American Jewish History*, 91:1 (2003): 70–1.
104 Ibid.: 71.
105 Olwage, '"The world is his song"': 165–95.
106 'Passport for Robeson', *SMH*, 27 June 1958: 3.
107 Ron Tarrant, 'Robeson on the way back', *SMH*, 6 July 1958: 75.

Chapter 4: 'The world is his song'

1 Martin Duberman, *Paul Robeson* (New Press, 1989): 465; Lindsey R Swindall, *The Politics of Paul Robeson's Othello* (University Press of Mississippi, 2011): 172.
2 Quoted in Nico Slate, *The Prism of Race: WEB Du Bois, Langston Hughes, Paul Robeson, and the Colored World of Cedric Dover* (Palgrave Macmillan, 2014): 86.
3 Ibid.: 94.
4 Duberman, *Paul Robeson*: 466.
5 Barbara Ransby, *Eslanda* (Yale University Press, 2013): 240.
6 Paul Robeson interview with Therese Denny of Australia in London, August 1958, as described and quoted by Scott Allen Nollen, *Paul Robeson: Film Pioneer* (McFarland & Company, 2010): 175, 199.
7 Grant Olwage, '"The world is his song"', *Journal of the Society for American Music*, 7:2 (2013): 165.
8 Duberman, *Paul Robeson*: 467.
9 See listing for the Paul Robeson album *In Live Performance, London, Royal Albert Hall, August 10, 1958*, *MusicStack* website.
10 Duberman, *Paul Robeson*: 468–9.
11 'Hero's welcome for Robeson', *SMH*, 17 August 1958: 19.
12 STHA: Hannah Middleton Papers, cassette tape labelled 'Robeson: Moscow concert, 1 side only'.
13 Many thanks to Yoland Wadsworth, who posted me information (received on 7 May 2021) about these two records, which were part of Margaret Mortimer's estate.
14 Nollen, *Paul Robeson:* 176; Duberman, *Paul Robeson:* 471.
15 Swindall, *Robeson's Othello*: 173.
16 Geoffrey Hutton, 'The many-sided career of Paul Robeson', *The Age*, 12 November 1960: 19.
17 Duberman, *Paul Robeson*: 479; Sarah Mayo, 'Paul Robeson and the Cwmbach Male Choir', *Cynon Valley Museum* website, 2021.
18 Ransby, *Eslanda:* 236.
19 'Princess opens parlt. of new federation', *SMH*, 23 April 1958: 3.
20 Ransby, *Eslanda*: 237.

21 EG Robeson, 'The Accra Conference', *New World Review*, 27 (February 1959): 13–14, reprinted in 'Remembrances of Eslanda', *Freedomways*, 6:4 (1966): 349.
22 Ransby, *Eslanda*: 249.
23 Ibid.: 248.
24 Duberman, *Paul Robeson*: 473–4.
25 Ransby, *Eslanda*: 251.
26 Audrey Johnson, 'Morrow, William, 1888–1980', *Biographical Dictionary of the Australian Senate* website, n.d. [originally published in 2004].
27 Audrey Johnson, *Fly a Rebel Flag* (Penguin, 1986): 275.
28 'Broadcasting Programmes', *The Press* (Christchurch), 8 June 1960: 12.
29 Swindall, *Robeson's Othello*: 185.
30 Email from Gavin Edwards to author, 1 May 2023.
31 Jessica Mitford to Robert Treuhaft and Constancia Romilly, 4 May 1959, in Peter Y Sussman (ed.), *Decca: The Letters of Jessica Mitford* (Weidenfeld & Nicolson, 2006): 208.
32 Anthea Goddard, 'New triumph for Paul Robeson', *SMH*, 12 April 1959: 88.
33 'Paul Robeson's comeback as Othello', *Australian Women's Weekly*, 15 July 1959: 51.
34 Rob Baker, '100 years of protesting at Trafalgar Square (Part 2)', *Flashbak* website, 1 September 2014.
35 NLNZ: Adrienne Marie Simpson Papers: Dan O'Connor Material; Paul Robeson (hereafter NLNZ: O'Connor Material), MS-Papers-10782-117, correspondence between O'Connor and Harold Davison (theatre agency in London) concerning possible tour, July 1959.
36 Duberman, *Paul Robeson*: 479.
37 They would later attend one of his concerts in New Zealand.
38 Email from Irene Gale to author, 29 March 2023.
39 Barbara Ransby says there was now 'a brief window of simultaneous good health'. Ransby, *Eslanda*: 251.
40 Michael Sturma, 'Lee Lazer Gordon (1923–1963)', *ADB* website, 2006 (originally published in 1996); Michael de Looper (comp.), *Australian Concert Tours, 1950–1979* (Big Three Publications, 2014).
41 Jo Darbyshire, *The Coolbaroo Club, 1947–1960*, catalogue of exhibition *The Coolbaroo Club and the Coffee Pot: Two Extraordinary Places in 1950s Perth*, held at Perth Town Hall, 20 October – 5 November 2010 (City of Perth, 2010): 7.
42 Bill Egan, *African American Entertainers in Australia and New Zealand* (McFarland & Company, 2020): 225.
43 Penny Von Eschen, *Satchmo Blows Up the World* (Harvard University Press, 2006).
44 de Looper, *Australian Concert Tours*; 'Stage and Music: Harry Belafonte', *The Bulletin*, 24 August 1960: 23–4. Other stories related to his tour include Larry Foley, 'His songs are his protests', *Australian Women's Weekly*, 13 July

1960: 15; 'His folk songs sell millions', *Australian Women's Weekly*, 17 August 1960: 7; *Woman's Day*, 15 August 1960, cover photo. For an account of his Brisbane concert on 24 August 1960, see *Courier-Mail*, 25 August 1960: 3.

45 'Belafonte speaks out for peace', *Peace Action*, 1:4 (September 1960): 4.

46 Foley, 'His songs are his protests'.

47 CH7AR: Harry Belafonte interview, 10 August 1960, HSVXF-310-002.

48 Belafonte died on 26 April 2023.

49 Duberman, *Paul Robeson*: 738, n. 56.

50 See Tatlock Miller, Alec Murray and Loudon Sainthill, *Ballet Rambert: The Tour of Australia and New Zealand, 1947–1948* (Craftsman Bookshop, 1947). See also NLNZ: O'Connor Material.

51 Duberman, *Paul Robeson*: 487, 738, n. 56.

52 Arrangements were made through Harold Davison, an agent based in London, who sent Kerridge copies of a concert programme for a UK concert tour conducted by Harold Holt Ltd. See Auckland Central City Library, Program, 'Paul Robeson, with Lawrence Brown', presented by Harold Holt Ltd, performed in England, 1960.

53 NLNZ: O'Connor Material, copy of draft contract between Kerridge Theatre Ltd and Paul Robeson of 5/45 Connaught Square, London, 29 June 1960.

54 There is an early draft, listing more venues, in Dan O'Connor to Harold Davison, 12 July 1959, in NLNZ: O'Connor Material.

55 NAA: ASIO, Northern Territory Centenary Celebrations—Proposed visit of Paul Robeson to Northern Territory, F1, 1960/1747: 3, telegram from Mayell, President of District Association, Tennant Creek to Director, Centenary Celebration, 12 September 1960.

56 The song was collected by John Stokoe and included in his *Songs and Ballads of Northern England* (Walter Scott Ltd, 1893). Shirley Collins first recorded it in 1958 and included it on her 1960 record *False True Lovers*. See 'I Will Set/Put My Ship in Order / I Drew My Ship Into the Harbour', *Mainly Norfolk: English Folk and Other Good Music* website, 2023.

57 Marjory Kennedy-Fraser had collected it from the island of Eriskay in the Outer Hebrides in 1909 and written its English lyrics. See 'An Eriskay Love Lilt', *SecondHandSongs* website, n.d.

58 Swindall, *Robeson's Othello*: 128, 160. Kerridge liked the draft programmes sent to him in September but added that he would have expected an Othello recital included. Copy in NLNZ: O'Connor Material, letter from RJ Kerridge to Harold Davison, Harold Davison Ltd, Eros House, 29/31 Regent Street, London, 9 September 1960.

59 Marie Seton, *Eisenstein* (Bodley Head, 1952): 328. These songs had been made famous by Chaliapin, the celebrated Russian bass opera singer for whom Godunov was his signature role. Two years after Paul's visit to Moscow, Chaliapin would tour both Australia and New Zealand, to much acclaim.

60 Marie Seton, *Paul Robeson* (Dennis Dobson, 1958): 93.

61 See radio/TV supplement, *The Age*, 13 October 1960: 28; 'Downbeat', *SMH*, 21 August 1960: 110.
62 'Paul Robeson here next month', *Evening Post*, 17 September 1960, cutting in NLNZ: Rona Bailey Papers, Folder 4.
63 *Sunday Mail* (Brisbane), 2 October 1960: n.p.; 'Robeson the 3-way star', *The Telegraph* (Brisbane), 5 October 1960: n.p.
64 'Robeson … Now for a new future' and 'Margaret plans to meet Paul', *Truth* (Queensland), 9 October 1960: 24.
65 LR Swainson, 'A spiritual took Robeson to fame', *Sun-Herald*, 9 October 1960: 106.
66 *Daily Telegraph*, 9 October 1960: 10.
67 Ralph Summy, 'The Australian Peace Council and the anti-communist milieu', in Charles Chatfield and Peter van den Dungen (eds), *Peace Movements and Political Cultures* (University of Tennessee Press, 1988): 243–6.
68 Ibid.: 247–8.
69 UMA: Consolidated Records of Congress for International Co-operation and Disarmament, 79/152; 87/92; 87/93; 88/107; 88/121, Finding Aid: 56.
70 UMA: Consolidated Papers of Frank Hartley, 1980.0163, 80/163; 83/108, Box 16, Folder 4, report by Dorothy Gibson to executive of Victorian Peace Council, 22 February 1960.
71 Nita Murray-Smith, 'Dorothy Gibson (1899–1978)', *ADB* website, 2006 (originally published in 1996).
72 Ralph Summy, 'Militancy and the Australian peace movement, 1960–1967', *Australian Journal of Political Science*, 2 (1970): 148–62, quote on 150; Elsie Locke, *Peace People: A History of Peace Activities in New Zealand* (Hazard Press, 1992): 164; Malcolm Saunders and Ralph Summy, *The Australian Peace Movement* (Peace Research Centre, ANU, 1986): 35.
73 Aroha Harris and Mary Jane Logan McCallum, '"Assaulting the ears of government": The Indian Homemakers' clubs and the Maori Women's Welfare League in their formative years', in Carol Williams (ed.), *Indigenous Women and Work: From Labor to Activism* (University of Illinois Press, 2012): 226.
74 Sue Taffe, *Black and White Together: FCAATSI: The Federal Council for the Advancement of Aborigines and Torres Strait Islanders 1958–1973* (University of Queensland Press, 2005).
75 Both *Tribune* and *The Guardian* (Melbourne) told readers about his history and the forthcoming concerts: 'Despite all attacks, he "just keeps rollin' along"', *Tribune*, 12 October 1960: 7; 'Robeson arrives this week', *The Guardian*, 13 October 1960: 2.
76 NAA: ASIO, Robeson, Paul Volume 3, 1961–72, A6119, 5035 (hereafter NAA: ASIO, Robeson vol. 3), Bill Morrow to John Clements, 30 September 1960. It was also agreed that the Peace Council would receive a percentage from any concert tickets it sold.

77 SLNSW: Papers of People for Nuclear Disarmament (NSW Records), 1930–85, MLMSS 5522, Box 29 (74), Item 11, Eslanda Robeson and Lili Williams to Bill Morrow, 45 Connaught Square, London, W2, 4 October 1960. Williams is not mentioned in the Ransby biography. See also NAA: ASIO, Robeson, Paul Volume 2, 1961, A6119, 5031 (hereafter NAA: ASIO, Robeson vol. 2): 15, item headed 'Paul Robeson'.

78 Duberman, *Paul Robeson*: 483.

79 '"Old Man River" in Berlin', *The Press* (Christchurch), 28 June 1960: 18.

80 Duberman, *Paul Robeson*: 486–7.

81 'Paul Robeson on way to Australia', *The Age*, 12 October 1960: 1.

Chapter 5: Meeting the Robesons

1 Mickey Dewar and Kim Lockwood, 'Douglas Wright Lockwood (1918–1980)', *ADB* website, 2006 (originally published in 2000).

2 Douglas Lockwood, 'Paul Robeson lashes at "childish" US', *The Herald* (Melbourne), 12 October 1960: n.p. This story was published in slightly different versions in several newspapers owned by the Herald & Weekly Times group, for whom Lockwood worked—see 'Paul Robeson criticises PM', *Northern Star*, 13 October 1960: 1; 'Robeson still a bitter man', *News* (Perth), 12 October 1960: n.p., 'Robeson here—and still sour', *The Sun* (Sydney), 12 October 1960: n.p. Press clippings in NAA: ASIO, Robeson, Paul Volume 1, 1960–61, A6119, 5033 (hereafter NAA: ASIO, Robeson vol. 1): 72.

3 See Simon Hall, *Ten Days in Harlem: Fidel Castro and the Making of the 1960s* (Faber, 2020) for a detailed account of the Fifteenth Session of the General Assembly.

4 'Plan for leaders' meeting dropped', *Canberra Times*, 7 October 1960: 1.

5 NAA: ASIO, Robeson vol. 1: 88, 'Paul Robeson', 19 October 1960, lists the people to whom Paul spoke.

6 'Paul Robeson may sing here', *Northern Territory News*, 14 October 1960: 1.

7 JKB, 'Met Robeson', *Tribune*, 26 October 1960: 2.

8 'Paul Robeson may sing here'; *Northern Territory News*, 21 October 1960: 5, 25 October 1960: 1, 28 October 1960: 4. Email from Brian Manning to author, 6 March 2008.

9 'Robeson bitterly critical of US', *SMH*, 13 October 1960: 4; 'Met by Reds', *Northern Star* (Lismore), 14 October 1960: 1; 'Enthusiastic welcome for Paul Robeson', *The Age*, 13 October 1960: 5.

10 'Paul Robeson's feelings for Welsh miners', *Common Cause*, 1174 (1960). The Aboriginal-Australian Fellowship's monthly bulletin, *Fellowship*, 1:8 (November 1960): 1, also mentioned the presence of Aboriginal people at the airport welcome.

11 Ray Castle, 'I wish he was still Bosambo', *Daily Telegraph*, 13 October 1960: 4. 'Ray Castle' was the pseudonym for a number of journalists, being a play on the name of the street on which the *Daily Telegraph* was produced, Castlereagh.

12 'He would side with the Soviet', *Courier-Mail* (Brisbane), 13 October 1960: 5; Alec Robertson, '"I'm in the working guy's corner" says Robeson', *Tribune*, 19 October 1960: 2.
13 Robertson, ibid.
14 NLNZ: O'Connor Material, letter from Davison to O'Connor, 7 October 1960.
15 'Robeson hits straight from the shoulder in press interview', *The Guardian*, 20 October 1960: 8; NFSA: '[Robeson, Paul: Interviewed by Frank Proust]' (804482) [sound recording]; Malcolm Brown, 'Francis Evans (Frank) Proust (1917–2009), *Obituaries Australia* website, n.d. (originally published in 2009); CH7AR: 'Circa Oct/Nov Paul Robeson Australian visit', ARCH02-021.
16 Robert Johnston, 'He just keeps rollin' along', *The Sun* (Melbourne), 13 October 1960: 6.
17 'Robeson hits straight from the shoulder in press interview'.
18 Martin Duberman, *Paul Robeson* (New Press, 1989): 441.
19 'Robeson hits straight from the shoulder in press interview'.
20 'Robeson's wife is a writer', *SMH*, 13 October 1960: 40.
21 'Hotel Australia', *Dictionary of Sydney* website, 2008.
22 Gerald Horne, *Paul Robeson* (Pluto Press, 2016): 234, n. 93 citing Eslanda Robeson to Betty Bateman, 7 November 1961, in MSRC Robeson Collection.
23 'Robeson's wife is a writer'.
24 'World-famous Negro singer arrives for tour of Australia and New Zealand', *Canberra Times*, 13 October 1960: 1.
25 'Enthusiastic welcome for Paul Robeson'.
26 Robertson, '"I'm in the working guy's corner"'. See a similar report by Alec Robertson, 'Paul Robeson comes "as a fighter for peace"', *The Guardian* (Melbourne), 20 October 1960: 1.
27 Johnson, 'He just keeps rollin' along'.
28 'Robeson bitterly critical of US'.
29 Column 8, *SMH*, 13 October 1960: 1.
30 'Onlooker', 'Voice from the past', *SMH*, 16 October 1960: 46.
31 Castle, 'I wish he was still Bosambo'.
32 'He would side with the Soviet', *Courier-Mail* (Brisbane), 13 October 1960: 5; 'Robeson here: I'd back Russia in a war', *The Sun* (Melbourne), 13 October 1960: n.p.; 'Left-wing unionists clap and cheer Paul Robeson', *The Advocate* (Burnie, Tasmania), 13 October 1960: 5; 'Robeson lashes out at America, backs Soviet', *The Mercury* (Hobart), 13 October 1960: n.p. News clippings in NAA: ASIO, Robeson vol. 1: 70, 93, 97.
33 Castle, 'I wish he was still Bosambo'.
34 LP Fox, 'Artists and politics', *Daily Telegraph*, 15 October 1960: 2.
35 CW Steadman, 'Aborigines', *Daily Telegraph*, 15 October 1960: 2.
36 NLNZ: O'Connor Material, Kerridge to Davison, 16 September 1960.
37 Duberman, *Paul Robeson*: 488, 738, n. 59.

38 NLNZ: O'Connor Material, copy of unsigned letter (apparently from O'Connor) to Eslanda, 24 October 1960; Duberman, *Paul Robeson*: 488, 738, n. 59.
39 'Robeson lashes out at America, backs Soviet'.
40 Kenneth Brooks, *An Affirming Flame: Adventures in Continuing Education*, William Legrand Publishing, 1987: 25–6, 33, 56–7.
41 NLNZ: O'Connor Material, copy of letters from KG Brooks, Director of Adult Education, to DD O'Connor Productions Ltd, 17 October 1960.
42 George Sokolsky, 'America doing nothing about singer Robeson', *Bluefield Daily Telegraph*, 6 December 1960. Sokolsky had a history of extremely negative comments about Paul Robeson—see Duberman, *Paul Robeson*: 320, 406.
43 'Paul says no', *Courier-Mail*, 15 October 1960: 6.
44 Frank O'Neill, 'A song to remember', *Sunday Mirror* (Sydney), 16 October 1960: 17.
45 'Big crowd claps, cheers for Paul Robeson: Old Man River … in person', *Courier-Mail*, 14 October, 1960: 9.
46 Jean Leary interviewed by Sari Braithwaite, 25 July 2008; copy of photo in Fryer Library collection.
47 Ralph Summy, *Australian Peace Movement 1960–1967: A Study in Dissent*, MA thesis, University of Sydney, 1971: 113–14.
48 NLA: Hayes, Janet, 1948–2011 (interviewee), *Janet Hayes Interviewed by Rob Willis in the Voices of the Bush Oral History Project* [sound recording], 3 March 2004 (TRC 6125/15). At 78 minutes, Hayes talks about meeting Robeson in Brisbane and having a photo taken that was later enlarged for her birthday.
49 'Big crowd claps, cheers for Paul Robeson'.
50 'Chemist, student and writer, too', *Courier-Mail*, 15 October 1960: 13; Marjorie Stapleton, 'Robeson: Happy giant who loves children', *Australian Women's Weekly*, 2 November 1960: 71.
51 NAA: ASIO, Robeson vol. 1: 85, Staff Reporter, 'Robeson talks politics', press clipping from unidentified newspaper, date probably 15 October 1960.
52 'CPA interest in Paul Robeson', 15 November 1960, in NAA: ASIO, Robeson vol. 2: 97–8.
53 NLA: Nancy Wills Oral History Transcript. It is puzzling that she does not mention his Australian visit in her memoir, *Shades of Red* (Communist Arts Group, 1980).
54 'Margaret plans to meet Paul', *Truth* (Queensland), 9 October 1960: 24.
55 'Inspiration', *Courier-Mail*, 15 October 1960: 1.
56 Letter from Margaret Valadian to author, 9 August 2008.
57 Connie Healy, who was present at the cocktail afterparty, thought at least one Aboriginal woman was there, probably Sylvia Cairns. Healy interviewed by Sari Braithwaite, 25 July 2008.
58 'Airport meeting', *Courier-Mail*, 25 August 1960: 3. The photo was reproduced, captioned 'Sylvia Cairns meets Harry Belafonte', in Pam Young, *Daring to Take a Stand: The Story of the Union of Australian Women in Queensland* (Pam Young,

1998): 133. For an account of Belafonte's Brisbane concert on 24 August 1960, see *Courier-Mail*, 25 August 1960: 3.

59 NAA: ASIO, Union of Australian Women, Volume 6, 1956–61, A6122, 1450: minutes of the Second National Conference: 92.

60 NAA: ASIO, Union of Australian Women, Volume 6, 1956–61, A6122, 1450: 37, 'Second National Conference: Union of Australia Women', 2 June 1960.

61 NAA: ASIO, ibid.: 33. For surveillance of Sylvia Cairns, see NAA: ASIO, ibid.: 22, 'Sylvia Rosalind Cairns', 18 October 1960.

62 Ann Curthoys and Audrey McDonald, *More Than a Hat and Glove Brigade: The Story of the Union of Australian Women* (Union of Australian Women, 1996): 62–3.

63 Sylvia Cairns, *Uncle Willie Mackenzie's Legends of the Goundirs* (Jacaranda Press, 1967).

64 'Police guard for Robeson', *Truth* (Queensland), 16 October 1960: 1.

65 'Paul is "great"', *Truth* (Queensland), 16 October 1960: 2.

66 'An unexpectedly vivid life: Janetta McStay in conversation with David Guerin', *Music in New Zealand*, 40 (Summer 2001–02).

67 NAA: C100, 1201734, 'Interview singer Paul Robeson and Mrs Robeson, by Bob Moore', broadcast on Adelaide ABC radio station 5CL on 25 November 1960.

68 'Paul is "great"'.

69 Email from Mary Okello to author, 26 March 2008.

70 Hilary Langford interviewed by Sari Braithwaite, 23 July 2008.

71 Bob Anderson interviewed by Sari Braithwaite, 14 October 2008. The rest of the verse that Bob so warmly remembered from *Sanders of the River* was 'Righter of wrong/ Hater of lies/ Laughed as he fought/ Worked as he played/ As he has taught/ Let it be made'.

72 'Statement issued by Chinese delegation', *Seamen's Journal Special Supplement*, November 1960: 375. 'China trade union delegation gets warm welcome', *Tribune*, 19 October 1960: 10.

73 'Police guard for Robeson', *Sunday Truth* (Brisbane), 16 October 1960: 1, 84.

74 'Paul Robeson inspired all', *Maritime Worker*, 33:20 (2 November 1960): 7.

75 Phil O'Brien and Bernie Dowling, *Towards Peace: A Worker's Journey* (Social History Publishing Enterprise, 1992).

76 Wally Stubbings interviewed by Sari Braithwaite, 14 October 2008.

77 See also Lesley Synge, 'Wal Stubbings', in Bob Boughton et al. (eds), *Comrades! Lives of Australian Communists* (Search Foundation, 2020): 274–9.

78 Jackie Huggins and Rita Cynthia Huggins, *Auntie Rita* (Aboriginal Studies Press, 1994).

79 Elaine Darling, *They Spoke Out Pretty Good: Politics and Gender in the Brisbane Aboriginal Rights Movement, 1959–1962* (Janoan Media Exchange, 1999).

80 At some point, perhaps at the cocktail party, Paul had also met Valerie Mald, a singer, actor and active member of the CPA who had performed in *Reedy River*.

Her obituary in the *Courier-Mail* says that Robeson recorded her singing Australian songs and took the tapes back to the US: 'Singer committed to the communist cause', *Courier-Mail*, 8 January 2004.

81 Mary Okello interviewed by Sari Braithwaite, 25 July 2008.
82 Connie Healy interviewed by Sari Braithwaite, 25 July 2008.
83 'Paul is "great"'.
84 'Variety plus by Robeson'.
85 W Lovelock, 'Robeson greatly to taste', *Courier-Mail*, 17 October 1960: 10.
86 Warren A Bebbington, 'William Lovelock (1899–1986)', *ADB* website, 2012.
87 'Sundry Shows: Paul Robeson in Brisbane', *The Bulletin*, 26 October 1960: 23.

Chapter 6: 'Captivated by Paul Robeson'

1 'Paul Robeson arrives in New Zealand', *People's Voice*, 19 October 1960: 1, describes those present as 'a crowd of Māoris and Pakehas, workers and students, peace-fighters and progressives'.
2 'Big crowd meets Paul Robeson', *New Zealand Herald*, 17 October 1960: 3. There is a photo of Paul and Mrs KG Bidois pressing their noses together.
3 Barbara Ransby, *Eslanda* (Yale University Press, 2013): 252.
4 'Big crowd meets Paul Robeson'; 'Robeson welcomed in New Zealand', *The Age*, 17 October 1960: 3.
5 'Strong man of music: Robeson aims at middlebrow', *Auckland Star*, 17 October 1960: n.p.
6 'Paul Robeson sings in his hotel room', *Evening Post* (Wellington), 20 October 1960: n.p.
7 Their letters are now held in the Moorland-Spingarn Research Center, Howard University. At the time of writing (December 2023), there was no public access to them.
8 'Paul Robeson sings in his hotel room'.
9 LCMS, '"Ol' Man River" triumphed', *New Zealand Herald*, 19 October 1960: 3.
10 Ibid.
11 Desmond Mahoney, 'Robeson as artist stands alone', *Auckland Star*, 19 October 1960: n.p., copy in NLNZ: Rona Bailey Papers, Folder 4.
12 'Captivated by Paul Robeson', *The Dominion*, 21 October 1960: n.p., copy in NLNZ: Rona Bailey Papers, Folder 4.
13 Owen Jensen, 'Paul Robeson is a truly great artist', *Evening Post* (Wellington), 21 October 1960: 13.
14 Ibid. See also 'Captivated by Paul Robeson'; John Mansfield Thomson, 'Jensen, Arthur Owen', *DNZB* website, 2000.
15 Mahoney, 'Robeson as artist stands alone'.
16 Martin Duberman, *Paul Robeson* (New Press, 1989): 467; Grant Olwage, 'Paul Robeson's microphone voice and the technologies of easy singing', *Technology and Culture*, 49:4 (October 2018): 823–5.

17 Olwage, ibid.: 827, 842.
18 Letter from Bettina Bradbury to author, 23 February 2023.
19 Notice in *The Press* (Christchurch), 22 October 1960: 1.
20 Quoted in Carl Blackmun, 'One struggle: Paul Robeson in Australia and New Zealand, 1960', *Labour History Project Newsletter*, 47 (2009): 29.
21 Cited in Grant Olwage, *Paul Robeson's Voices* (Oxford University Press, 2024): 162, 309, n. 139.
22 Honours List, *New Zealand Gazette*, 13 August 1959: 1107.
23 'General News: Negro singers', *The Press* (Christchurch), 8 August 1960: 12.
24 CFB, 'Audience deeply moved by Paul Robeson', *The Press* (Christchurch), 26 October: 17.
25 'Man—dig that crazy Macbeth-type blues!', *Auckland Star*, 1 November 1960: 3, copy in NLNZ: Rona Bailey Papers, Folder 4. Gillespie's and Vaughan's performances were to be in Wellington on 31 October and Auckland on 1 November. See NLNZ: [Music programmes and other ephemera of octavo size for jazz concerts, 1960–1969], Eph-A-MUSIC-Jazz-1960s, concert programme.
26 'International Jazz Festival: It will be cool, man, cool', *Australian Women's Weekly*, 2 November 1960: 21.
27 Penny Von Eschen, *Race Against Empire* (Cornell University Press, 1997): 178.
28 Carl T Towan, 'Has Paul Robeson betrayed the Negro?', *Ebony*, 12 (October 1957): 33, quoted in Von Eschen, ibid.: 180.
29 'Inside Paul Robeson', *The Listener*, 11 November 1960: 6–7.
30 Paul Callan, 'The mighty Robeson puts his audience happily at ease', *Auckland Star*, 31 October 1960: 16. See also 'Robeson enthrals full crowd', *New Zealand Herald*, 31 October 1960: n.p.
31 'Dunedin Town Hall', *Wikipedia*, 30 July 2024.
32 KG, 'Inimitable singer charms capacity Town Hall crowd', *Otago Daily Times*, 3 November 1960: 2.
33 Ralph Vaughan Williams, *The Making of Music* (Cornell University Press, 1955); William Pencak, 'Paul Robeson and classical music', *Pennsylvania History*, 66:1 (1999): 88.
34 'Strong man of music'.
35 'Paul Robeson sings in his hotel room'.
36 Photograph of Paul and Eslanda in Christchurch in *The Press* (Christchurch), 24 October 1960: 12.
37 'Paul Robeson arrives in Christchurch', ibid.: 15.
38 'Marx still suits him', *New Zealand Herald*, 18 October 1960: 3; 'Paul Robeson explains his philosophy', *The Press* (Christchurch), 18 October 1960: 19.
39 'Paul Robeson arrives in Christchurch'.
40 'Strong man of music'.
41 'Paul Robeson arrives in Christchurch'. Although this report had no byline, a recording of it in the Australian NFSA names the interviewer as James

Homes. See NFSA: 'Paul Robeson: Interviewed by James Homes' (228315) [sound recording].
42 NLNZ: Rona Bailey Papers, Eric Beardsley to Bailey, 10 April 1997.
43 'Paul Robeson arrives in Christchurch'.
44 NFSA: 'Paul Robeson: Interviewed by James Homes'. Christchurch radio station 3YA broadcast an interview with Paul on 27 October 1960; see 'Broadcasting Programmes', *The Press* (Christchurch), 27 October 1960: 8.
45 Andrew Mason, 'Holcroft, Montague Harry', *DNZB* website, 2000; 'Inside Paul Robeson', *The Listener*, 11 November 1960: 6–7.
46 Olwage, 'Paul Robeson's microphone voice': 846.
47 'A voice to charm you', *Weekly News*, 26 October 1960. Clipping in NLNZ: Rona Bailey Papers, Folder 4.
48 'Marx still suits him'; 'Paul Robeson explains his philosophy'.
49 FBI: Paul Robeson, Sr, Part 26 of 31, FBIHQ File 100-12304, Section 19: 43–4, *FBI Vault* website.
50 For an example of a standard interview, in which Paul talks about his World War II battlefields tour, singing in Black churches during the period of his banishment, his political education in the United Kingdom and the influence of the Welsh miners, see 'UK responsible for his views claims Robeson', *Christchurch Star*, 24 October 1960: n.p.
51 'Strong man of music'.
52 Noel Holmes, '"Chaka" now—not "Sanders"', *Auckland Star*, 18 October 1960: 44.
53 Duberman, *Paul Robeson*: 5.
54 'Inside Paul Robeson'.

Chapter 7: New Zealanders Meet the Robesons

1 'Harper, Sir Arthur Grant: Biography 1971', *Knowledge Bank: Hawke's Bay Digital Archives Trust* website, n.d. (originally published in *Who's Who in New Zealand*, 10th edn (AH & AW Reed, 1971).
2 Switzer Hudson, 'Anderton, William Theophilus', *DNZB* website, 2000.
3 Martin Duberman, *Paul Robeson* (New Press, 1989): 739, n. 62.
4 'Women's contribution to world peace', *The Press* (Christchurch), 28 October 1960: 2.
5 See 'Paul Robeson arrives in New Zealand', *People's Voice*, 19 October 1960: 1.
6 RH Brookes, 'The CPNZ and the Sino-Soviet split', *Political Science*, 17:2 (1965): 21.
7 Elsie Locke, *Peace People* (Hazard Press, 1992): 155, 164.
8 NLNZ: O'Connor Material.
9 'Distinguished visitor at opera rehearsal', *The Dominion* (Wellington), 22 October 1960, in NLNZ: Munro, Donald George Alfred, 1913–2012: Papers, MS-Group-0606, *Don Pasquale*—Scrapbook of newscuttings (83-011-17). Thank you to Doug Munro for providing me with this information and image.

10 Peter Franks, 'Bailey, Chip', *DNZB* website, 2000. See also Cybèle Locke, 'The New Zealand Northern Drivers' Union: Trade union anti-racism work, 1937–80', *Labour History*, 120 (May 2021): 21–47.
11 'Paul Robeson arrives in Christchurch'.
12 See Cybèle Locke, 'Dancing for the revolution: Rona Bailey, New Zealand artist activist (1914–2005)', in F de Haan (ed.), *The Palgrave Handbook of Communist Women Activists Around the World* (Springer Nature, 2023); Peter Franks, 'Bailey, Rona', *DNZB* website, 2018.
13 Harold Winston Rhodes, *New Zealand and the Soviet Union: An Historical Account of the New Zealand USSR Society* (NZ-USSR Society, 1979): 52, 56–7.
14 NLNZ: Rona Bailey Papers, Folder 4, Bailey, 'Paul Robeson saga 1947 and 1960'.
15 Ibid., Bailey, 'Paul and Eslanda Robeson's visit to New Zealand in October 1960', 8 July 1997.
16 Locke, 'The New Zealand Northern Drivers' Union': 23.
17 NLNZ: Rona Bailey Papers, Bailey to Mark Rogovin, 21 April 1998.
18 John Thornley, 'Paul Robeson in the Union Workshops New Zealand 1960', *Music in the Air*, Summer 1997: 22.
19 'Paul Robeson talks to wharfies', *People's Voice*, 2 November 1960: 1.
20 Bailey, 'Paul and Eslanda Robeson's visit to New Zealand in October 1960'.
21 Ted Thompson, speaking on Marie Russell (presenter), 'Remembering Paul Robeson' (12 April 1998) [radio program], *Spectrum*, RNZ, Wellington (replayed on 27 February 2015).
22 Ken Douglas, in 'Remembering Paul Robeson'.
23 Ciaran Doolin, '"Bugger the contract, I'll sing!" Paul Robeson in New Zealand', *The Maritimes*, Autumn 2015: 27.
24 Bailey, 'Paul and Eslanda Robeson's visit to New Zealand in October 1960'.
25 David Dowling, 'Mason, Bruce Edward George', *DNZB* website, 2000.
26 Rhodes, *New Zealand and the Soviet Union*: 57; *New Zealand China Friendship Society 40 Years On* (New Zealand China Friendship Society, 1990).
27 NLNZ: 'Langley, Frank Lloyd, 1900–1965' (catalogue entry).
28 Nicola Barnett, 'Efford, Lincoln Arthur Winstone', *DNZB* website, 2000. He had long suffered from a severe illness and would die eighteen months later.
29 Information supplied by Brent Efford, who is researching his family's history.
30 Brent Efford informs me that the WEA Centre is still going strong as a centre of activism in Christchurch, and its main room—the Lincoln Efford Hall—is the venue for the Lincoln Efford Memorial Lecture held every year in his father's memory.
31 Photo of Addington Railway Workshops meeting, *The Press* (Christchurch), 27 October 1960: 7.
32 NLNZ: 'Paul Robeson sings and talks to Lincoln Efford and other workers at Railway Workshops, Addington, tape one' [audio recording], OHT7-0225, April 1960; Russell, in 'Remembering Paul Robeson'.

33 Collins, on Russell, in 'Remembering Paul Robeson'.
34 Later, Flora and her husband, Nat, would support the CPNZ and the NZ Peace Council in following the Chinese line de-emphasising the threat from nuclear weapons. Later still, well after the Robesons' visit, when the NZ party abandoned Maoism, Flora and her husband left the CPNZ. See 'Flora Gould', *Struggle: A Marxist Approach to Aotearoa/New Zealand*, September 2006: 19.
35 *New Zealand Herald*, 3 November 1960, clipping in NLNZ: Rona Bailey Papers, Folder 4; Duberman, *Paul Robeson*: 739, n. 62.
36 STHA: Hannah Middleton Papers, Correspondence Folder, Rona Bailey to Middleton, 13 March 1998.
37 Merrilyn Hope, 'Paul Robeson in New Zealand', *WordPress.com*, 16 July 2014 (originally published on merrilynhope.com on 31 October 2010).
38 Jenny Carlyon and Diana Morrow, *Urban Village: The Story of Ponsonby, Freeman's Bay and St Mary's Bay* (Random House, 2008): 97–8.
39 Michael Bassett, 'Airey, William Thomas Goodwin', *DNZB* website, 1998.
40 Willis Airey, 'A New Zealander on tour', *Bulletin of the World Council of Peace*, 15 February 1959: 20.
41 John Shennan, 'Ford, Robert Preston', *Abraham Lincoln Brigade Archives* website, n.d.
42 Mark Derby, 'Refugees from McCarthyism in New Zealand: The story of Bob and Augusta Ford', *The Volunteer*, 30 August 2023. See also Mark Derby (ed.), *Kiwi Compañeros: New Zealand and the Spanish Civil War* (Canterbury University Press, 2009): 115–17.
43 Derby, 'Refugees from McCarthyism in New Zealand'.
44 See Anne Else, 'New York, New York—cheesecake, that is', *Something Else to Eat* [blog], 17 December 2016.
45 Lin Johnson, *Māori and the Anti-Apartheid Movement: Generating a Space to Oppose Domestic Racism 1959–1985* (MA thesis, Massey University, 2007): 24.
46 Ibid.: 27–8.
47 Ibid.: 39.
48 Ibid.: 45–6.
49 Ibid.: 47.
50 Richard Thompson, 'Community conflict in New Zealand: A case study', *Race*, 3:1 (1961): 35.
51 NLNZ: 'Paul Robeson sings and talks to Lincoln Efford and other workers at Railway Workshops'.
52 'Tribute to Paul Robeson: Unionists and Māoris', *People's Voice*, 2 November 1960: 8.
53 'Traditional Māori welcome for famous Negro singer', *The Press* (Christchurch), 17 October 1960: 12.
54 'Big crowd meets Paul Robeson'.

55 'Paul Robeson sings in his hotel room'.
56 Carlyon and Morrow, *Urban Village*: 248.
57 Chris Bourke, *Blue Smoke: The Lost Dawn of New Zealand Popular Music, 1918–1964* (Auckland University Press, 2010): 252.
58 'Tribute to Paul Robeson', *People's Voice*.
59 Garry Hooker, 'Paikea, Tāpiana Paraire', *DNZB* website, 2000.
60 'Melbourne Cup interested Paul Robeson', *Evening Star* (Dunedin edn), 2 November 1960.
61 'Letters', *Otago Daily Times*, 1 November 2023.
62 Ibid., 2 November 2023.
63 '"New Zealand is marvellous I want to return to its warmth", says Robeson', *People's Voice*, 9 November 1960: 1, reprinted in Philip S Foner (ed.), *Paul Robeson Speaks: Writings, Speeches, Interviews, 1918–1974* (Brunner/Mazel, 1978): 467–8.
64 Henrik Gurkow in interview with Paul Robeson, 'My plans: Fight for freedom', *Neue Zeit* (New Times), 27 April 1961, trans. and included in Kenneth O'Reilly, *Black Americans: The FBI Files* (Carroll & Graf, 1994): 378–9.
65 NLNZ: Rona Bailey Papers, Folder 5, typescript of speech on 7 April 1998, Paul Robeson birthday celebrations evening held by the Trade Union History Project in Wellington.

Chapter 8: 'I'm a good union man'

1 'From a *Times* correspondent', *Canberra Times*, 9 November 1960: 2.
2 Wendy Charell, *Paul Robeson in Australia* (ABC, 1979) [documentary film], ABC Archives, accession number 165623.
3 Transcript of interview by Robin Hughes with Faith Bandler for the ABC-TV series *Australian Biography*, 25 March 1993; see NFSA: *Faith Bandler: Civil Rights Activist* (403180) [video], Film Australia, 1993.
4 'Enthusiastic listeners', *Daily Telegraph* 5 November 1960: 3. There is archival footage of the meeting in the ABC documentary *Paul Robeson in Australia*.
5 Jensen was an old-style Labor politician from a working-class Catholic background who had joined the ALP when he was sixteen; he became an electrician and later an organiser for the Electrical Trades Union and a delegate to the Sydney Trades and Labor Council. He had been a council member on the Randwick City Council for six years and the Sydney City Council for four, the last three of these as mayor. 'Jensen, Henry Frederick', *City of Sydney Archives* website, n.d.
6 There appears to be no newspaper coverage of this visit, even in *Tribune*, and while ASIO agents recorded Paul's attendance at the WWF Hall that evening, none appear to have been present inside. NAA: ASIO, Robeson vol. 2: 16, 'CPA interest in Paul Robeson', 15 November 1960.
7 *Tribune*, 2 November 1960: 11.
8 Lisa Milner, 'The Wharfies' Film Unit', *Dictionary of Sydney* website, 2014.

9 PM (Paul Mortier), 'Paul Robeson concert was unforgettable', *Tribune*, 9 November 1960: 3.
10 NAA: ASIO, Morrow, William Robert—Volume 5, 1959–61, A6119, 2992: Intercept Report, 7 November 1960.
11 Email from Darrell Dawson to author, 21 February 2008.
12 PM, 'Paul Robeson concert was unforgettable'.
13 Email from Ron Witton to author, 12 August 2014.
14 Email from Chris Hamerton to author, 13 August 2014.
15 Peter McCallum, 'Roger Covell: Herald music critic across four decades', *SMH*, 17 June 2019.
16 Roger Covell, 'Robeson's first Sydney recital', *SMH*, 8 November 1960: 6. The article is signed RC.
17 AW, 'Paul Robeson concert at Town Hall', *SMH*, 14 November 1960: 4.
18 Julian Russell, 'Robeson's thrilling opening', *The Sun*, 8 November 1960: 20.
19 Frank Harris, 'Robeson (62) just keeps rolling on', *Daily Mirror*, 8 November 1960: 20l.
20 Martin Long, 'Impact intense and individual', *Daily Telegraph*, 8 November 1960: 20l.
21 SWK, 'Sundry Shows: Stage and Music: Paul Robeson', *The Bulletin*, 16 November 1960: 23–4.
22 Ibid.
23 'Hirsh Glick', *Music and the Holocaust* website, n.d.
24 Scott Allen Nollen, *Paul Robeson: Film Pioneer* (McFarland & Company, 2010): 176.
25 Alan Knight, 'Sydney Journalists Club remembered' [blog], *Online Journalism*, 29 October 2010.
26 'In New South Wales this week', *Canberra Times*, 9 November 1960: 2.
27 Don Angel, *The Journalists' Club, Sydney: A Fond History* (Journalists' Club, 1985): 94.
28 Jeff Sparrow, *No Way But This* (Scribe, 2017): 1–3.
29 Shana Redmond, *Everything Man* (Duke University Press, 2020): 5–6.
30 NBAC: BWIU, Z534, Box 112, folder 'Overseas Delegations, Press Statements', subfolder 'Robeson Visit' (hereafter NBAC: BWIU, Robeson Visit), copy of letter Pat Clancy to Paul Robeson, 27 October 1960.
31 Bob Evans, 'Paul Robeson: Salute to the voice of freedom', *Good Weekend*, 19 September 1987, reprinted 13 July 2017.
32 The BWIU's assistant national secretary, Ernie Boatswain, had played a role in organising the event; see Evans, 'Paul Robeson: Salute to the voice of freedom'.
33 'Robeson sings there first', *Daily Telegraph*, 10 November 1960: 15; 'Robesons win hearts of Sydney people', *Tribune*, 16 November 1960: 10.
34 Transcript by Sari Braithwaite of recording of Robeson's speech at Paddington Town Hall, 10 November 1960.

35 'Robeson sings there first'; 'Robesons win hearts of Sydney people'.
36 Tom and Audrey McDonald, *Dare to Dream: The Memoirs of Tom and Audrey McDonald* (Audrey and Tom McDonald, 2016): 104.
37 CH7AR: '9/11/1960 Robeson Sydney Opera House', ARCH02-021 (one-minute Channel 7 film clip of Robeson singing 'Ol' Man River').
38 NFSA: 'Paul Robeson: First singer at Opera House' (63163) [video], Cinesound Productions, first shown as part of *Cinesound Review* no. 1516, 17 November 1960 (hereafter NFSA: 'First singer at Opera House'). The version in the NFSA has news narration at the end by Channel 9 newsreader Brian Henderson; TV station Channel 9 was linked to Cinesound Productions.
39 'Flashback: Howard Rubie ACS', *Australian Cinematographer*, 44 (2010): 45.
40 ABC Archives, 'A first performance', accession no. 374206, segment no. NC1765, CV96/220.14. The BWIU, which had organised the event, was able to gain a copy of the news clip from Channel 7, but not from the ABC. See NBAC: BWIU, Robeson Visit, Pat Clancy to Director of News, ATN Channel 7, agreeing to pay for two copies of the film, 2 December 1960, and K Fraser, Director, ABC Television News, to Pat Clancy, Secretary, BWIU, 5 December 1960, refusing his request for a copy of the ABC film.
41 Quoted in 'Robeson sings there first'; comments by Miriam Hampson in *Paul Robeson in Australia*; *Tribune*, 16 November 1960: 10.
42 Transcript by Sari Braithwaite of Robeson's speech at Paddington Town Hall.
43 'American folk singer, Paul Robeson, yesterday gave the first recital at Sydney Opera House', *Canberra Times*, 10 November 1960: 1.
44 'Robeson sings there first'.
45 'Robesons win hearts of Sydney people'.
46 'Paul Robeson welcomed', *Building Worker*, 11:11 (November 1960): 1.
47 NSW Legislative Assembly, *Debates*, 20 October 1998, 'Paul Robeson Exhibition', Mr Thompson (Rockdale), followed by Mr Aquilina (Riverstone).
48 John McCutcheon, 'Live at the barns of Wolf Trap / 1990 & 1991' [video], *YouTube*, 18 April 2019.
49 David Marr, *Barwick* (George Allen & Unwin, 1980): 159.
50 Ralph Gibson, *My Years in the Communist Party* (International Bookshop, 1966): 234–5.
51 'Lord mayor at stopwork', *Maritime Worker*, 3 October 1960: 1; 'ACTU calls national Crimes Act rallies', *Maritime Worker*, 2 November 1960: 1.
52 Marr, *Barwick*: 162.
53 It would succeed in the long run in gaining some changes to the proposed amendments, but not in preventing them altogether.
54 Jim Healy was two weeks older than Paul (he was born on 22 March 1898) and died seven months after this meeting, on 13 July 1961.
55 'Robeson at stopwork', *Maritime Worker*, 16 November 1960: 9.
56 In the finding aid to the Paul and Eslanda Robeson papers at Moorland-Spingarn Research Center, one of the items listed is 'Waltzing Matilda',

Southern Folk Singers Presenting Australian Songs, 45 rpm, Opal. See MSRC Staff, 'Robeson, Paul and Eslanda', Manuscript Division Finding Aids 168, 2015: 142.

57 Ralph Sawyer speaking in *Paul Robeson in Australia*.

58 See 'Posters designed and printed by Ralph Sawyer: History', *Powerhouse Collection* website, n.d.

59 'Paul Robeson talks to Aust. peace lovers', *Seamen's Journal Special Supplement*, November 1960: 372–4; NFSA: *Paul Robeson for Peace* (774600) [sound recording], digitised copy of recording made by NSW Peace Committee (hereafter NFSA: *Paul Robeson for Peace*).

60 WF Burns, 'Paul Robeson never was a "Bosambo"', *Maritime Worker*, 1 December 1960: 4; *SMH*, 11 November 1960: 6.

Chapter 9: Two Television Appearances and a Visit to the Theatre

1 Arita Malik, *Representing Black Britain: Black and Asian Images on Television* (Sage, 2001): 111.

2 Paul Robeson Jnr, *The Undiscovered Paul Robeson: Quest for Freedom* (John Wiley & Sons, 2010): 286.

3 John Schlesinger (director), 'Bert Haanstra/Paul Robeson/HiFi-Fo-Fum' [TV program], *Monitor*, season 2, episode 15, 12 April 1959, BBC, London.

4 Martin Duberman, *Paul Robeson* (New Press, 1989): 481; *Reunion with Robeson* [TV program], 2 November 1959, ITV Granada, England.

5 MrDomin099 Stone, 'Paul Robeson: Rare TV appearance 1960' [video], *YouTube*, 21 February 2021.

6 'Sunday 13 November 1960', *TV Week* (Sydney), 10–16 November 1960: 55.

7 NLNZ: O'Connor Material, Robert Kerridge to Harold Davison, 7 September 1960.

8 For the screening in Sydney, see *SMH*, 6 November 1960: 104.

9 Australian House of Representatives, *Debates*, 24 August 1961, 'Answers to questions: Television programme', Mr Davidson, Postmaster-General.

10 Julia Horne, 'Cecil Robert Quentin (1917–1979)', *ADB* website, 2006 (originally published in 2002).

11 Duberman, *Paul Robeson*: 449, 465; 'Sunday 13 November 1960', *TV Week*.

12 David Hendy, 'History of the BBC: The bombing of Broadcasting House', *BBC* website, n.d.

13 Kylie Andrews, 'Broadcasting inclusion and advocacy: A history of female activism and cross-cultural partnership at the postwar ABC', *Media International Australia*, 174:1 (2020): 99.

14 See Cedric Robinson, *Black Marxism: The Making of the Black Radical Tradition* (Zed, 1983).

15 ABC Archives, 'Spotlight: Paul Robeson', N5292A.

16 Duberman, *Paul Robeson*: 113, 214.

17 *Paul Robeson: Highlights from Porgy and Bess*, HMV 7EGO 8510, vinyl, 45 rpm. The songs were 'Summertime', 'A Woman Is a Sometime Thing', 'It Ain't Necessarily So' and 'It Takes a Long Pull to Get There'.
18 Nan Musgrove, 'Paul Robeson took charge', *Australian Women's Weekly*, 23 November 1960: 62.
19 Robeson Jnr, *The Undiscovered Paul Robeson: Quest for Freedom*: 307.
20 *The Guardian* (Melbourne), 1 December 1960: 3.
21 'Robeson TV personality', *The Age*, 17 November 1960: 28.
22 'Close-Up with Dolly Shot', *TV Week*, 17–23 November 1960: 69.
23 'Spotlight: Attaining equality, 1960' [video], *ABC Education* website, 23 June 2022.
24 Ann Curthoys, 'Television before television', *Continuum: Australian Journal of Media and Culture*, 4:2 (1991): 152–70.
25 Hal Lashwood, 'Australia and television', *Meanjin*, 13:4 (December 1954): 565–69.
26 Joyce Morgan, 'Harold Frances (Hal) Lashwood (1915–1992)', *ADB* website, 2021 (originally published in 2016); 'Adelaide, Perth welcome Robesons', *Tribune*, 7 December 1960: 10.
27 'Hal Lashwood' (research notes), *Australian Variety Theatre Archive* website, 9 May 2018.
28 'Ladies and gentlemen … be seated', *ABC Weekly*, 25 June 1958: 9.
29 Christine Grandy, 'The show is not about race: Custom, screen culture, and *The Black and White Minstrel Show*', *Journal of British Studies* 59: 5 (2020): 874.
30 John Strausbaugh in interview with Sean Illing, 'The complicated, always racist history of blackface', *Vox*, 17 February 2019.
31 Nan Musgrove, 'Christmas treat', *Australian Women's Weekly*, 28 December 1960: 46.
32 'Television topics: Paul Robeson', *The Biz* (Fairfield, NSW), 21 December 1960: 8.
33 NFSA: 'Hal Lashwood's Minstrels' (331469) [video], 15 December 1960 (incorrect label—it should be 24 December 1960).
34 'Television topics', *The Biz*.
35 NFSA: 'Hal Lashwood's Minstrels', quotes at 20:49 and 21:54.
36 Ibid., at 25:33.
37 Ibid., at 26:23.
38 Ibid., at 25:33, 26:23, 27:44, 28:02, 28:19.
39 See, for example, 'Paul Robeson sings and reminisces', *Le Courrier Australien*, 23 December 1960: 5; 'Television topics', *The Biz*.
40 NLNZ: [New Zealand and Australian music programmes collected by Charles Cabot. 1960–1964], Eph-A-CABOT-Music-1960/1964, programme of *The Black and White Minstrel Show*.
41 Stephen Vagg, 'Counterfeit images: A history of blackface on Australian television', *Metro Magazine*, 206 (2020): 96–7.

42 Duberman, *Paul Robeson*.
43 Duberman, ibid. See also Jennifer Wilson, 'When the Harlem Renaissance went to Communist Moscow', *New York Times*, 21 August 2017.
44 Len Fox, *Glimpses of a Century* (Len Fox, 2011): 19.
45 'New Theatre group', *The Age*, 15 June 1939: 13; Geoffrey Hutton, 'Theatre Notes', *The Argus*, 14 July 1939: 4.
46 Lyn Collingwood, 'Sydney New Theatre: The fight for equality', in Lisa Milner (ed.), *The New Theatre: The People, Plays and Politics Behind Australia's Radical Theatre* (Interventions, 2022): 354; see also the lyrics for 'Song for Bridges' at *Protest Song Lyrics* website.
47 *The New Years 1932– : The Plays, People and Events of Six Decades of Sydney's Radical New Theatre* (New Theatre, 1992): 17.
48 Collingwood, 'Sydney New Theatre': 354.
49 She was also the sister of Sam Aarons, who appears in Chapter 14. See 'Person: Miriam Hampson', *New Theatre History*.
50 SLNSW: New Theatre Records 1914–1990, MLMSS 6244 [hereafter New Theatre Records], Box 19, Outward Correspondence, Miriam Hampson to Harry Belafonte, 25 August 1960.
51 Wendy Charell, *Paul Robeson in Australia* (ABC, 1979) [documentary film], ABC Archives, accession number 165623.
52 It was also adapted into a Hollywood film in 1948, a Lux Radio Theatre play in 1950, and a BBC made-for-television film in 1958.
53 SLNSW: New Theatre Records, Box 19, Outward Correspondence, Miriam Hampson to Mr H Hunt, 9 August 1960.
54 SLNSW: New Theatre Records, Box 2, Minutes of Management Committee, 8 November 1960.
55 SLNSW: New Theatre Records, Box 232, Mark McManus, 'Paul Robeson visits us', *Spotlight*, undated but apparently December 1960: 3–4; Margaret Fulton, *I Sang for My Supper: Memories of a Food Writer* (Lansdowne, 1999): 124.
56 Fulton, ibid.
57 Over 200 people attended the performance and stayed for the ceremonial welcome afterwards; see SLNSW: New Theatre Records, Minutes of Management Committee, 15 November 1960.
58 McManus, 'Paul Robeson visits us'.
59 Ibid. See also the report in *Tribune*, 16 November 1960: 11.
60 New Theatre website, 'Our history'.

Chapter 10: 'I wept and wept'

1 MSRC Staff, 'Robeson, Paul and Eslanda', Manuscript Division Finding Aids 168, 2015: 241.
2 Jim Mitchell, 'Adelaide raised roof for Paul', *Maritime Worker*, 15 December 1960: 7.

3 'Robesons win hearts of Sydney people', *Tribune*, 16 November 1960: 10.
4 The charge had arisen in the wake of the killing of a pregnant Pitjantjatjara woman, Fay Iowa, at the Morris Soak town camp in Alice Springs, where Namatjira lived—a killing that was linked to alcohol. Iowa's husband was charged but eventually acquitted. For a detailed account of these events, see Martin Edmond, *Double Lives: Rex Battarbee and Albert Namatjira* (Doctor of Creative Arts thesis, University of Western Sydney, 2013): 287.
5 Julie Wells and Michael F Christie, 'Namatjira and the burden of citizenship', *Australian Historical Studies*, 31:114 (2000): 125.
6 See Joyce D Batty, *Namatjira: Wanderer Between Two Worlds* (Hodder & Stoughton, 1963); Wells and Christie, 'Namatjira and the burden of citizenship'.
7 Grantlee Kieza, 'Acts of faith helped cut through racism', *Courier-Mail*, 28 May 2017; Faith Bandler and Len Fox, *The Time Was Ripe: A History of the Aboriginal-Australian Fellowship (1956–69)* (Alternative Publishing Cooperative Ltd, 1983): 1.
8 Key Aboriginal members included Pearl Gibbs, Bert Groves, Ray Peckham, Charlie Leon and Ken Brindle, while important non-Aboriginal members included Hans Bandler, Muir Holburn, Roland Robinson, Jack and Jean Horner, and Helen Hambly.
9 Heather Goodall, *Invasion to Embassy: Land in Aboriginal Politics in New South Wales, 1770–1972* (Allen & Unwin, 1996): 267.
10 See Marilyn Lake, *Faith: Faith Bandler, Gentle Activist* (Allen & Unwin, 2002).
11 Sandra Le Brun Holmes, *Faces in the Sun: Outback Journeys* (Viking, 1999): 99–100. Frank Hardy later told his biographer that this event took place at his home, but that is contradicted by both Holmes and Faith Bandler, who locate it at the hotel, which is where Paul and Eslanda conducted their meetings. Jenny Hocking, *Frank Hardy: Politics, Literature, Life* (Lothian, 2005): 136.
12 'Four Hiroshima bombs for South Australia', *Tribune*, 22 August 1956: 10.
13 'William Grayden (1920)', *Collaborating for Indigenous Rights* website, n.d.; Richard Broome, *Aboriginal Victorians: A History Since 1800* (Allen & Unwin, 2005): 290–1; Ravi de Costa, *A Higher Authority: Indigenous Transnationalism and Australia* (UNSW Press, 2006): 77.
14 Bain Attwood, *Rights for Aborigines* (Allen & Unwin, 2003): 150.
15 'William Grayden (1920)'.
16 Attwood, *Rights for Aborigines*: 149–51; Sue Taffe, *Black and White Together* (University of Queensland Press, 2005): 34–6.
17 SLNSW: Hannah Middleton Collection, 1918–95, MLMSS 5866/10, Aboriginal-Australian Fellowship, 'Special report and conclusions on interviews with the people of Walgett, NSW, and impressions gained during the visit 6th to 10th September 1957, by Mrs W Garland and Mrs I McIlwraith'. See also Bandler and Fox, *The Time Was Ripe*: 65; and SLNSW:

Aboriginal-Australian Fellowship subject files, 1956–78, MLMSS 4057, Box 16, Walgett file, letter from Irene McIlwraith to the Editor, *Walgett Spectator*, 18 September 1957.

18 Pam McGrath and David Brooks, 'Their darkest hour: The films and photographs of William Grayden and the history of the "Warburton Range controversy" of 1957', *Aboriginal History*, 34 (2010): 131–3.

19 Richard Brennan, 'Cecil William Holmes (1921–1994)', *ADB* website, 2021 (originally published in 2019).

20 Cecil Holmes, 'An Aboriginal film in color is born', *The Age*, 12 November 1960: 19.

21 Michael Hess, 'Black and red: The Pilbara pastoral workers' strike, 1946', *Aboriginal History*, 18:1 (1994): 65–83.

22 Holmes, 'An Aboriginal film in color is born'.

23 Le Brun Holmes, *Faces in the Sun*: 100; Cecil Holmes, *One Man's Way* (Penguin, 1986): 57.

24 Le Brun Holmes, ibid.: 99.

25 Alec Robertson, 'Paul Robeson's advice: Stand with the people', *Tribune*, 23 November 1960: 6.

26 See, for example, Lake, *Faith*: 86; Shane Maloney, 'Faith Bandler and Paul Robeson', *The Monthly*, July 2009.

27 Interview by Robin Hughes with Faith Bandler for the ABC-TV series *Australian Biography*, 25 March 1993; see NFSA: *Faith Bandler: Civil Rights Activist* (403180) [video], Film Australia, 1993. This account is similar to the one Bandler gave in 1978 in Wendy Charell, *Paul Robeson in Australia* (ABC, 1979) [documentary film], ABC Archives, accession number 165623.

28 'Robeson will "fight for our Aborigines"', *Sunday Mirror*, 13 November 1960: 9.

29 NBAC: BWIU, Robeson Visit, circular Bill Morrow and Geoff Anderson, joint secretaries, NSW Peace Committee for International Cooperation and Disarmament, to friends (in this case the BWIU), 19 October 1960.

30 'Robeson will "fight for our Aborigines"'.

31 NAA: ASIO, Robeson vol. 2: 93.

32 Letter from Jack Tarlington to author, undated but sent in 2008, in author's possession.

33 Martin Duberman, *Paul Robeson* (New Press, 1989): 740, n. 64.

34 Jack Horner, 'Lester (Charlie) Leon (1900–1982)', *ADB* website, 2012.

35 NLA: McDonald, Tom, 1926–2022 (interviewee), *Tom McDonald Interviewed by Richard Raxworthy in the Labor Council of New South Wales Oral History Project* [sound recording], 23 August 1994, TRC 3128/8. See also Tom and Audrey McDonald, *Intimate Union: Sharing a Revolutionary Life* (Pluto Press, 1998): 100–1.

36 Bob Evans, 'Paul Robeson: Salute to the voice of freedom', *Good Weekend*, 19 September 1987, reprinted 13 July 2017.

37 'Paul Robeson talks to Aust. peace lovers', *Seamen's Journal Special Supplement*, November 1960: 372–4; NFSA: *Paul Robeson for Peace*.
38 'Paul Robeson talks to Aust. peace lovers': 373.
39 See Paul Robeson, 'Primitives', *New Statesman and Nation*, August 1936, reprinted in Marie Seton, *Paul Robeson* (Dennis Dobson, 1958): 237, 241–2; 'Robeson discovers Africa', *Fighting Talk*, 11:2 (April 1955): 4. See also John Henrik Clarke, 'Paul Robeson: The artist as activist and social thinker', *Présence Africaine*, 107 (3e Trimestre 1978): 223–41.
40 'Robeson will "fight for our Aborigines"'.
41 Eslanda Robeson, 'People are people—we belong to the human race', *Seamen's Journal Special Supplement*, November 1960: 376.
42 'Robeson will "fight for our Aborigines"'; 'Australia has a color problem', *Truth* (Queensland), 13 November 1960: 11; '"I'll fight for the Aborigines"—Paul Robeson', *Northern Territory News*, 15 November 1960: 3.
43 'The dark people', *Current Affairs Bulletin*, 29:4 (25 December 1961): 54.
44 Amanda Harris, *Representing Australian Aboriginal Music and Dance 1930–1970* (Bloomsbury, 2020): 39, 164, n. 59. See 'To see native life: Negro singer here', *The News* (Adelaide), 5 July 1952: 10.
45 Jonathon Bollen and Anne Brewster, 'NADOC and the National Aborigines Day in Sydney, 1957–1967', *Aboriginal History*, 42 (2018): 5.
46 SLNSW: Len Fox Papers, 1852–2001, MLMSS 8085, Box 31, copy of *Fellowship*, 1:3 (May 1960): S1; Katherine Ellinghaus, '"The moment of release": The ideology of protection and the twentieth century assimilation policies of exemption and competency in New South Wales and Oklahoma', *Pacific Historical Review*, 87:1 (2018): 128–49.
47 Susan Greer, *Paying the Rent: A Case Study of Accounting in the Service of Aboriginal Assimilation Policies* (Macquarie University, 2009): 10.
48 SLNSW: Len Fox Papers, MSS 8085, Box 31, Len Fox, 'Aboriginal housing', typescript based on a report given at the Third Annual Conference on Aboriginal Advancement at Newport, Sydney in February 1960: 2. See also Denis Byrne and Maria Nugent, *Mapping Attachment: A Spatial Approach to Aboriginal Post-Contact Heritage* (NSW Department of Environment and Conservation, 2004): 89–90.
49 Byrne and Nugent, ibid.: 89.
50 For a more detailed account, see Ann Curthoys, 'A rent strike at Purfleet: Barbara Curthoys, the Newcastle Trades Hall Council and the strike of 1960–1961', in James Bennett, Nancy Cushing and Erik Eklund (eds), *Radical Newcastle* (NewSouth, 2015): 162–76.
51 Deirdre O'Connell, *Harlem Nights* (Melbourne University Press, 2021): 88–9.
52 Ibid.: 88.
53 *Fellowship*, 1:6 (September 1960): 1.
54 Gary Foley, 'Time to dream', *Tracker*, May 2013. Gary Foley found the film footage many years later under the house of Bill Onus's son Lin Onus, and

characterises it as 'a priceless film record of one of the many African-American entertainers who sought out Aboriginal people when they visited Australia in the 1950s and 1960s'. He suggests that it is also probably 'the first known moving film footage ever shot by an Aboriginal person'.

55 Helen Hambly interviewed by Heather Goodall, 22 August 1989, transcript no. 2: 1/17, in interviewer's possession. Many thanks to Heather Goodall for providing me with a copy. I have been unable to discover any more about Eslanda's visit despite searching the records of the Aborigines Protection Board and others.

56 Audrey Johnson, 'Morrow, William, 1888–1980', *Biographical Dictionary of the Australian Senate* website, n.d. [originally published in 2004]. See Audrey Johnson, *Fly a Rebel Flag* (Penguin, 1986).

57 NBAC: Audrey Johnson Papers, N162-407/1, 'Paul Robeson speaks to Mrs Morrow, who could not meet him, and recites poem by Blake, Little Black Boy', c. 5 minutes.

Chapter 11: Eslanda's Tour

1 NLNZ: Rona Bailey Papers, Bailey, 'Paul and Eslanda Robeson's visit to New Zealand in October 1960', 8 July 1997.

2 Ibid.

3 'Scholar behind the scenes', *West Australian*, 2 December 1960: 27.

4 Graham Hassall, 'The United Nations association of New Zealand: Past, present and future', presentation to the UNANZ Canterbury Branch, 31 March 2014.

5 Barbara Curthoys and Audrey McDonald, *More Than a Hat and Glove Brigade: The Story of the Union of Australian Women* (Union of Australian Women, 1996). Eslanda's lectures in Australia appear to have been organised after she arrived on 12 October. See NAA: ASIO, Communist Party of Australia—Interest in personalities and associations—Aborigines Volume 4, 1960–61, A6122, 1527 (hereafter NAA: ASIO, CPA—Aborigines vol. 4): 144, 'Union of Australian Women'. The report on the welcome at Sydney Airport on 12 October notes that Lurline Simpson invited Eslanda to speak to a UAW luncheon when she returned to Sydney in November, and she agreed.

6 Imaobong Umoren, *Race Women Internationalists* (University of California Press, 2018).

7 'Robeson's wife is a writer', *SMH*, 13 October 1960: 40.

8 'Chemist, student and writer, too', *Courier-Mail*, 15 October 1960: 13.

9 Ibid.

10 'Singer Paul Robeson's wife charming, intelligent', *Otago Daily Times*, 2 November 1960: n.p.

11 Mrs Paul Robeson is anthropologist, writer', *The Sun* (Melbourne), 16 November 1960: n.p. Other reports include 'Singer's wife', *The Age*, 12 November 1960: 7; 'Persuaded husband to stick to singing', *The Dominion*, 20 October 1960: n.p., copy in NLNZ: Rona Bailey Papers, Folder 6.

12 'Chemist, student and writer, too'.
13 'Mrs Robeson is notable too', *New Zealand Herald*, 18 October 1960: 2.
14 'Robeson's wife enjoys her full life', *Evening Post*, 19 October 1960: n.p., copy in NLNZ: Rona Bailey Papers Folder 6.
15 'Paul Robeson's wife is author, anthropologist', *The Press* (Christchurch), 24 October 1960: 2.
16 'Singer's near "flop"—no cowboy song', *The Age*, 16 November 1960: 14. See also 'Mrs Paul Robeson is anthropologist, writer'; 'Scholar behind the scenes'; and Marjorie Stapleton, 'Robeson: Happy giant who loves children', *Australian Women's Weekly*, 2 November 1960: 71.
17 'Robeson's wife enjoys her full life'; 'Singer Paul Robeson's wife charming, intelligent'.
18 'Scholar behind the scenes'.
19 'Singer's near "flop"—no cowboy song'.
20 Connie Healy interviewed by Sari Braithwaite, 25 July 2008.
21 Eslanda was welcomed on arrival in Christchurch by Mr Lewis from the local UNA: 'Paul Robeson arrives in Christchurch', *The Press*, 24 October 1960; 'Mrs Robeson's views on Africa and the UN', *The Press*, 27 October 1960: 19. Eslanda also gave public lectures in Wellington on 22 October and Auckland on 30 October.
22 Barbara Ransby, *Eslanda* (Yale University Press, 2013): 159–78; Annette K Joseph-Gabriel, 'Feminist networks and diasporic practices: Eslanda Robeson's travels in Africa', in Keisha N Blain and Tiffany M Gill (eds), *To Turn the Whole World Over* (University of Illinois Press, 2019): 45–51.
23 I have tried unsuccessfully to track who the Australian representative(s) might have been.
24 Mandy Banton, David Wardrop and Susan Williams, '"Hands off Africa!!"' [blog], *Review of African Political Economy* website, 20 December 2018.
25 Ibid.
26 Ransby, *Eslanda*: 244.
27 'Mrs Robeson's views on Africa and the UN'.
28 NLNZ: 'Woodward, Mary Christina, 1924–2014' (catalogue entry).
29 'Women's contribution to world peace', *The Press* (Christchurch), 28 October 1960: 2.
30 Ransby, *Eslanda*: 198.
31 Ibid.: 197–9. See also Elizabeth B Armstrong, *Bury the Corpse of Colonialism: The Revolutionary Feminist Conference of 1949* (University of California Press, 2023).
32 Ransby, *Eslanda:* 201.
33 'Mrs Robeson's views on Africa and the UN'. In response to questions, she rejected a questioner's comparison of the Congo situation with the presence of China in Tibet and the USSR in Hungary, but avoided discussing the question further: 'I did not come to talk about Hungary; this is a digression, and I will not talk about it.'

34 'Reception for Mrs Robeson', advertisement in *Maritime Worker*, 2 November 1960: 4, noting it would be at Vine House, 535 George Street; 'Robesons win heart of Sydney people', *Tribune*, 16 November 1960: 10.
35 Eslanda Robeson, 'Learning how to live together', *Seamen's Journal Special Supplement*, November 1960: 378.
36 NBAC: Papers of Della and EV Elliott, N343–389: 89, Eslanda Robeson to Eliot V Elliott, 45 Connaught Square, London W2, 31 December 1960.
37 Diane Kirkby, '"Those knights of the pen and pencil": Women journalists and cultural leadership of the women's movement in Australia and the United States', *Labour History* 104 (May 2013): 97.
38 Robeson, 'Learning how to live together': 371.
39 Ibid.: 378.
40 Ibid.: 379.
41 Ibid.: 379, 382.
42 Eslanda Robeson, 'Women's influence needed in all spheres', *Seamen's Journal Special Supplement*: 383. For another account of Eslanda's speech, see 'Learn to live together', *Our Women*, March–May 1961: 2.
43 'The journalist—and the press', *Seamen's Journal Special Supplement*: 384. The report does not make it clear whether the question was asked at the UAW event or elsewhere, but it seems likely it was the same event.
44 SLNSW: Women's International League for Peace and Freedom. NSW Branch, MLMSS 9015, Collection 2, 1960–95, 2004, MLOH 716, Eslanda Robeson radio interview with Tom Jacobs, 10 November 1960.
45 Kevin Perkins, *Dare to Dream: The Life and Times of a Proud Australian* (Golden Wattle Publishers, 2001): 79.
46 Ibid.: 87.
47 On Fridays, *My World*, with Jacobs and the feisty Andrea, ran from 11.30 till noon; see 'Allan Black, part 5', *Australian Old Time Radio* website, n.d. Andrea was not involved in the interview with Eslanda.
48 'Slim for a White Australia', *Daily Telegraph*, 11 November 1960: 11.
49 This interview is on the same cassette as the first interview, which is not noted in the catalogue, thus the reference is SLNSW: Women's International League for Peace and Freedom. NSW Branch, MLMSS 9015, Collection 2, 1960–95, 2004, MLOH 716.
50 Curthoys and McDonald, *More Than a Hat and Glove Brigade*: 71.
51 Valerie Yule, 'Elwyn Aisne Morey (1914–1968)', *ADB website*, 2006 (originally published in 2000).
52 *The Guardian* (Melbourne), 24 November 1960: 8. Morey is incorrectly listed as Evelyn Morey.
53 'Recognise China, says Mrs Robeson', *Tribune*, 30 November 1960: 10.
54 'Mrs Robeson critical of Austral-Asian relations', *The Age*, 22 November 1960, press clipping in NAA: ASIO, Robeson vol. 1: 34.
55 Lloyd Evans, *Australia and the Modern World* (Cheshire, 1956): 1.

56 NAA: ASIO, Robeson vol. 2: 65, 'Visit of Soviet Youth Delegation'; 'Mrs Robeson speaks to SA women', unidentified newspaper, 5 December 1960, clipping in SLNSW: Salmon Family Papers, 1927–86, MLMSS 6105, Box 19 (21). There is also a brief mention in 'Adelaide, Perth welcome Robesons', *Tribune*, 7 December 1960: 10.

57 'Beautiful St Andrews in Wakefield Street, Adelaide City, had a modified second life as Willard Hall until 1970s', *Adelaide AZ* website, n.d.

58 SLSA: SRG 781/60/3: Willard Hall November 1960, 'Photographs selected for 2005 UAW publication', photo of Mrs Eslanda Robeson and UAW executive, Ms Beryl Jury (secretary), Mrs V Howe (president), Mrs J Bell (treasurer).

59 NAA: ASIO, Robeson vol. 2: 72, 'Union of Australian Women', 25 November 1960.

60 SLSA: SRG 781/60/5, Willard Hall November 1960, 'Photographs selected for 2005 UAW publication', photo entitled 'Gifts being presented to Mrs Eslanda Robeson at Willard Hall, November 1960 / Left to right: Val Howe (UAW president), Irene Bell (UAW treasurer), Eslanda Robeson, wife of bass baritone, Paul Robeson, gift presenter, Judy Howe'.

61 NAA: ASIO, Robeson vol. 2: 72, 'Union of Australian Women', 25 November 1960.

62 Val Howe, 'Mrs Robeson speaks for us', *UAW News Sheet*, SA branch, November–December 1960: 3–4. Copy in NAA: ASIO, Robeson vol. 2: 67.

63 SLWA: 'Paul Robeson and Eslanda Robeson: Palace Hotel, Perth, Dec. 1960' [sound recording], 327.172 Rob.

64 SLWA: Union of Australian Women, Western Australia, Papers, 1838A (hereafter SLWA: UAW WA Papers), Box 13, Management Committee Minutes, resolution to invite Eslanda to speak, 31 October 1960.

65 The UAW had also twice hosted Jessie Street, when in Perth as part of her investigations into the conditions of Aboriginal people around Perth and in the north-west, and Ada Bromham, who worked closely with Mary Bennett on matters of Aboriginal rights; see Roma Gilchrist, *Union of Australian Women: A History of the Western Australian Branch* (LJ Fleay, 199?): 86–9.

66 'Adelaide, Perth welcome Robesons'; Julie Lewis, *On Air: The Story of Catherine King and the ABC Women's Session* (Fremantle Arts Centre Press, 1979).

67 Kylie Andrews, *Trailblazing Women of Australian Public Broadcasting, 1945–1975* (Anthem Press, 2022): 14.

68 SLWA: UAW WA Papers, Box 10, Folder 4, General. Letter from Hon. Sec. to Mrs King, 5 December 1950.

69 NAA: ASIO, Robeson vol. 2: 79, 'Union of Australian Women', 5 December 1960.

70 SLWA: Annette Cameron Collection, 1919–1995 (acc. 4765A) (hereafter SLWA: Annette Cameron Collection), Box 26, Folder 7a, Annette Cameron to Martin Duberman, 3 June 1983.

71 NAA: ASIO, Robeson vol. 2: 80, 'Union of Australian Women', 5 December 1960.

72 Ibid.: 79. NAA: ASIO, Broomhall, Joan Volume 1, A6119, 3873: 60/779, 'Union of Australian Women', report dated 5 December 1960.
73 NAA: ASIO, Robeson vol. 2: 81, 'Union of Australian Women', 5 December 1960.
74 'A never to be forgotten event', *News for Everywoman*, December 1960, typed extract, in NAA: ASIO, Union of Australian Women Volume 6, 1956–61, A6122, 1450: 13, copy also in NAA: ASIO, ibid.: 67.

Chapter 12: 'I shook his hand'

1 'News of the Day', *The Age*, 1 November 1960: 2. See also *The Age*, 8 November 1960: 2.
2 *The Age*, 12 November 1960: 7 (Eslanda) and 19 (Paul).
3 Geoffrey Hutton, 'The many-sided career of Paul Robeson', *The Age*, 12 November 1960: 19.
4 Advertisement, *The Age*, 12 November 1960: 64.
5 NFSA: 'First singer at Opera House'.
6 'Robeson: I carry songs, not bombs', *The Sun*, 16 November 1960: 3.
7 CH7AR: '23/11/1960 Robeson Melbourne', HSVXF-015, no sound.
8 'Greeting for Robeson', *The Herald*, 15 November 1960. See also 'Welcome', *The Guardian* (Melbourne), 17 November 1960: 8; NAA: ASIO, Morrow, William Robert—Volume 5, 1959–61, A6119, 2992: 1475.
9 Nick Richardson, *1956: The Year Australia Welcomed the World* (Scribe, 2019): 100, 144, 183.
10 'First interstate TV broadcast of Melbourne Cup', *SMH*, 2 November 1960, reprinted as 'From the Archives, 1960', *SMH*, 1 November 2019.
11 'Melbourne Cup interested Paul Robeson', *New Zealand Evening Star*, 2 November 1960.
12 'Yiddish Melbourne: Statistics', *Australian Centre for Jewish Civilisation* (Monash University) website.
13 Anne Longmire, *St Kilda: The Show Goes On*, vol. 3 (Hudson, 1989): 216.
14 Goldbloom had been expelled from the ALP for standing in the federal election of 1951 as an independent candidate against Labor and for working with communists, but had been readmitted in 1956; Laura Rovetto, *Peace Activism in the Cold War: The Congress for International Cooperation and Disarmament, 1949–1970* (PhD thesis, Victoria University, 2020): 78, n. 304; Sandra Goldbloom Zurbo, *My Father's Shadow* (Monash University Press, 2023): vii.
15 Email from Sandra Goldbloom Zurbo to author, 30 March 2023.
16 'Robeson: I carry songs, not bombs'; Jack Cannon, 'His songs are poetry', *The Herald*, 16 November 1960.
17 'Paul Robeson talks and talks and talks', *The Age*, 16 November 1960: 5.
18 JS Lennie, 'Questions for Paul Robeson', Letters to the Editor, *The Age*, 19 November 1960: 2.
19 Vaughan Greenberg interviewed by Sari Braithwaite, 3 July 2008.

20 FBI: Paul Robeson, Sr, Part 26 of 31, FBIHQ File 100-12304, Section 19: 43–4, *FBI Vault* website.

21 'Margret Roadknight, troubadour', in Meredith Burgmann, *Radicals: Remembering the Sixties* (NewSouth, 2021): 74.

22 Jane Mullett interviewed by Sari Braithwaite, 1 July 2008.

23 Email from Bronwyn Silver to author, 5 August 2008.

24 Email from Les Rosenblatt to author, 22 February 2008.

25 Letter from Ila Marks to author, 3 April 2023.

26 Email from Juliet Flesch to author, 16 February 2024.

27 Email from Jim Falk to author, 29 March 2023.

28 In a rare negative note, Rodney Timinlay thought Robeson less at ease with the classical elements of the programme, such as the two Mussorgsky songs—see Timinlay, 'Robeson added his own verse', *The Herald*, 17 November 1960: 7.

29 Warren Burt, 'Champion of the new tweaked conservative noses', *SMH*, 9 May 2012; Paul Bartrop with Gabrielle Eisen (eds), *The Dunera Affair: A Documentary Resource Book* (Schwartz and Wilkinson with the Jewish Museum of Australia, 1990).

30 Felix Werder, 'Robeson has voice like a 'cello string', *The Age*, 17 November 1960: 5.

31 Felix Werder, 'Paul Robeson is brilliant entertainer' *The Age*, 19 November 1960: 3.

32 Linda Phillips, 'Paul, it was really great', *Sun News-Pictorial*, 17 November 1960: 9

33 Linda Phillips, 'Another gem', *Sun News-Pictorial*, 19 November 1960: 21.

34 Otherwise written as 'Yisgadal v'yiskadash sh'mei rabbaw'. Phillips, 'Another gem'; she was referring here to 'The Mourners' Kaddish' (Yisgadal v'yiskadash sh'mei rabbaw). See also Juliet Flesch, 'Phillips, Linda (1899–2002)', *Australian Women's Register* website, 2018.

35 'Linda Phillips (1899–2002): Represented artist', *Australian Music Centre* website, n.d.

36 'Robeson and Jewish melodies', *Jewish Herald*, 25 November 1960, clipping in NAA: ASIO, Robeson vol. 1, 5033: 33.

37 See also David Blumenthal, 'Observations and reflections on the history and meanings of the Kaddisch', *Judaism*, 50:1 (2001): 35–51.

38 Jonathan Karp, 'Performing Black-Jewish symbiosis: The "Hassidic Chant" of Paul Robeson', *American Jewish History*, 91:1 (2003): 53–81.

39 Ibid.: 72.

40 Ibid.: 56.

41 Ibid.: 65.

42 Ibid.: 73.

43 'He sang and he talked', *The Age*, 19 November 1960: 1.

44 Jim Beggs, *Proud to Be a Wharfie* (Australian Scholarly Publishing, 2014): 108; email from Kerry Greenwood to author, 6 March 2008.

45 The amendments to the *Crimes Act* were discussed in parliament on 15 November and passed on 17 November (*The Age*, 18 November 1960: 12).
46 Beggs, *Proud to Be a Wharfie*: 108.
47 Tas Bull, '4000 stood to cheer Robeson', *Maritime Worker*, 1 December 1960: 4.
48 'John Brown of Harper's Ferry' appeared in *Hobart Town Advertiser*, 30 November 1861: 3 and *SMH*, 23 December 1861: 3, copied in both cases from *New York Independent*, 29 August 1861.
49 Nicole Anae, '"They seemed to recognise us as brethren from a far distant tribe"', *The Historian*, 80:2 (2018): 249, 254.
50 Bull, '4000 stood to cheer Robeson'.
51 Beggs, *Proud to Be a Wharfie*: 108–9.
52 Ibid.: 138.
53 Rovetto, *Peace Activism in the Cold War*: 117.
54 Aldermaston was the English village associated with Britain's nuclear weapons program that from 1958 the Campaign for Nuclear Disarmament used as its starting point for a series of massive protest marches to London.
55 'Paul Robeson speaks', *Peace Action*, December 1960 – January 1961: 5.
56 NAA: ASIO, Robeson vol. 3: 39, 'Reception to Paul Robeson'.
57 NLA: *Norm O'Connor Folklore Collection* [sound recording], 1950–69, recording by O'Connor of 'Paul Robeson speaks in Australia'. I thank Martie Lowenstein for alerting me to this recording, which is uncatalogued at the NLA.
58 NAA: ASIO, Robeson vol. 3: 39, 'Reception to Paul Robeson'.
59 NLA: O'Connor recording of 'Paul Robeson speaks in Australia'.
60 These events had been reported in *The Age*—see 'Louisiana torn by New Orleans integration crisis', 16 November 1960: 5; 'Street clashes as New Orleans race riots spread', 18 November 1960: 1.
61 See 'White mobs violently riot against six-year-old Ruby Bridges integrating elementary school', *Equal Justice Initiative* website, n.d.; Alan Wieder, 'The New Orleans school crisis of 1960: Causes and consequences', *Phylon*, 48:2 (1987): 122–31.
62 NLA: O'Connor recording of 'Paul Robeson speaks in Australia'.
63 *The Guardian*, 1 December 1960: 3.
64 Email from Alan Anderson to author, 21 February 2008.
65 Email from Lorraine Paul to author, 29 March 2023.
66 Email from Jane Mullett to author, 22 February 2008.
67 Barry Hill, 'A letter to my father', in Barry Hill, *Reason and Lovelessness: Essays, Encounters, Reviews 1980–2017* (Monash University Publishing: 2018): 28–9, originally published in *Griffith Review: Re-imagining Australia*, 19 (Autumn, 2008): 195–207.
68 Boris Frankel, *No Country for Idealists: The Making of a Family of Subversives* (Greenmeadows, 2023): 339.
69 'Cleric's tribute to Paul Robeson', *The Age*, 21 November 1960: 10.

70 Rowland S Ward, *The Scots Church, Melbourne: A Story of 175 Years 1838–2013* (Australian Scholarly Publishing, 2014): 160.
71 'Cleric's tribute to Paul Robeson'.
72 Bain Attwood, *Rights for Aborigines* (Allen & Unwin, 2003): 146–60.
73 Richard Broome, 'At the grass roots of white support: Victorian Aboriginal Advancement League branches 1957–1972', *La Trobe Journal*, 85 (May 2010): 141. By the time the Robesons arrived, the League had nineteen branches in Victoria and five in Tasmania: 142.
74 Richard Broome, *Aboriginal Victorians* (Allen and Unwin, 2005): 290–1; Ravi de Costa, *A Higher Authority* (UNSW Press, 2006): 77.
75 See Steve Thomas (director), *Harold* [documentary film], Ronin Films, 1995; Richard Broome, *Fighting Hard: The Victorian Aborigines Advancement League* (Aboriginal Studies Press, 2015): 107.
76 Faith Bandler later commented that after Sydney, Paul had few further opportunities to meet Aboriginal people—see Bandler to Lloyd Davies, 11 May 1983, quoted in Duberman, *Paul Robeson*: 740, n. 64. This seems to have been true in Melbourne and Adelaide, though less so in Perth.
77 NLA: Papers of Gordon Bryant, 1917–1991, MS 8256, Series 11, subseries i, Box 169, Aboriginal Advancement League (Victoria) Annual Report, 1960.

Chapter 13: 'A family party'

1 Johanna McMahon, 'Rare footage of Satchmo rediscovered', *NFSA* website, n.d.
2 'Robeson "touched by destiny"', *The Advertiser*, 12 November 1960: 19.
3 NAA: ASIO, Robeson vol. 2: 97, 'CPA interest in visit of Paul Robeson'.
4 Margaret Kartomi, 'Growing up in a musical Quaker family', in Susan Blackburn (ed.), *Growing Up in Adelaide in the 1950s* (GHR Press, 2012): 298.
5 Martin Duberman, *Paul Robeson* (New Press, 1989): 5.
6 Kartomi, 'Growing up in a musical Quaker family': 298.
7 George Hutchesson and Edna Hutchesson, *Venture in Goodwill: George and Edna Hutchesson's Report on the 1955 World Peace Assembly at Helsinki Finland, the World Congress of Mothers at Lausanne Switzerland and Their Journey to Europe and the Soviet Union* ('SA Farmer', undated); Kartomi, 'Growing up in a musical Quaker family': 306–7.
8 'Cheers, flowers for Robeson', *The News*, 23 November 1960: 34; NAA: ASIO, Robeson vol. 1: 23, 'Paul Robeson, Laurence Brown', and vol. 3: 59, 'Paul Robeson, Laurence Brown'.
9 Ralph Summy, *Australian Peace Movement, 1960 –1967* (MA thesis, University of Sydney, 1971): 67, n. 71. See also Peter Lovibond, 'Obituary: Emeritus Professor Sydney (Syd) Harold Lovibond Hon FAPS', *InPsych*, 39: 5 (October 2017).
10 'Singer arrives', *The Advertiser*, 24 November 1960: 1. This front-page story was accompanied by a large photograph. See also *The Advertiser*, 24, 26 and 28 November and *The News*, 23, 24 and 25 November 1960.

11 JM, 'His voice a gift—and a burden', *The News*, 24 November 1960: 31.
12 Adelaide ABC radio station 5CL broadcast 15 minutes of the 25-minute recorded interview on 25 November at 9.15 p.m. NAA: C100, 1201734, 'Interview singer Paul Robeson and Mrs Robeson, by Bob Moore', broadcast on Adelaide ABC radio station 5CL on 25 November 1960.
13 Margot Kerley, 'Robert Clifton Moore (1932–1979)', *ADB* website, 2006 (originally published in 2000).
14 Duberman, *Paul Robeson*: 486.
15 Ray Polkinghorne, 'Singer keen to see "Rules"', *Advertiser*, 28 November 1960: 18.
16 Unley Museum, 'Did you know the first movie screened at The New Star Theatre in 1928 …' [Facebook status], 2 February 2018.
17 Nadra Penhalurick, 'Robeson shows his magic', *The News*, 25 November 1960: 34.
18 Doug Eason, 'Odd Spot', *The News*, 25 November 1960: 13.
19 John Horner, 'Paul Robeson is everyman', *The Advertiser*, 25 November 1960: 11.
20 See also 'Adelaide, Perth welcome Robesons', *Tribune*, 7 December 1960: 10.
21 John Horner, 'The sincerity of Robeson', *The Advertiser*, 28 November 1960: 16.
22 Brian Nankervis (host), 'Performer and recording artist Kamahl', *Songs & Stories* [podcast], 30 October 2021.
23 *Adelaide Festival of Arts, March 12–26 1960: Souvenir Programme* (Adelaide Festival of Arts Executive Committee, 1960): 41.
24 Andrew Stafford, 'Nature Boy' [interview transcript], *Notes from Pig City* website, 18 May 2021 (interview originally conducted in March 2009).
25 Nankervis, 'Performer and recording artist Kamahl'.
26 SLSA: Oral History Collection, OH 111/7, Side 2, transcript of interview with Arthur Shertock (Catherine Murphy, interviewer), 2 November 1990.
27 'Port men sing with Robeson', *The News*, 25 November 1960: 27.
28 Jim Mitchell, 'Adelaide raised the roof for Paul', *Maritime Worker* 33:22 (15 December 1960): 7.
29 'Watersiders get the works', unidentified newspaper, 26 November 1960, clipping in NAA: ASIO, Robeson vol. 1: 28.
30 NFSA: 'NWS9 News footage. CAN 103. Paul Robeson in Adelaide: SA' (77292) [video], 1960.
31 'Port men sing with Robeson'.
32 Mitchell, 'Adelaide raised the roof for Paul'.
33 NAA: ASIO, Robeson vol. 2: 97, 'CPA interest in visit of Paul Robeson'.
34 Email from Arthur Shertock to author, 11 March 2008.
35 SLSA: JD Somerville Oral History Collection OH 991, Rex Munn interview transcript: 28–30.
36 Mitchell, 'Adelaide raised the roof for Paul'.
37 STHA: Hannah Middleton Papers, Box 1, tape labelled 'Old Man River … Soviet Youth Reception, Australia 1960'.

38 NAA: ASIO, Robeson vol. 3: 63, 'CP of A Norwood Branch'.
39 'Soviet youth group arrives', *Tribune*, 16 November 1960: 12 and 'Soviet youth welcomed in Melbourne', *Tribune*, 23 November 1960: 1. See also photo and story of the Sydney visit in *Friendship* (journal of the Australia-Soviet Friendship Society), 5:1 (Jan/Feb 1961): 3. 'Reds "study more in jobs"', *The News*, 23 November 1960: 9.
40 Email from Shertock to author, 11 March 2008.
41 'SA welcomes Robeson, Soviet youth', *Tribune*, 30 November 1960: 10; 'Adelaide, Perth welcome Robesons'.
42 NAA: ASIO, Robeson vol. 2: 42, 'Visit of Soviet Youth Delegation'.
43 'SA welcomes Robeson, Soviet youth'.
44 STHA: 'Old Man River ... Soviet Youth Reception, Australia 1960'.
45 NAA: ASIO, Robeson vol. 2: 42, 'Visit of Soviet Youth Delegation'.
46 NAA: ASIO, Robeson vol. 3: 61, 'Souvenir Invitation: To Meet the Robesons', 27 November 1960, Community Hall, Belair.
47 NAA: ASIO, ibid.: 57, 'Visit of Paul Robeson'; 'Adelaide, Perth welcome Robesons'.
48 NAA: ASIO, ibid.: 58.
49 NLNZ: New Zealand Federation of Chamber Music Societies: [Music ephemera ... 1960], Eph-A-MUSIC-NZFCMS-1960, Jasek-McStay Duo. Christchurch Chamber Music Society. Civic Theatre, 24 May 1960. Programme. Similar for Wellington, 25 May.
50 NAA: ASIO, Robeson vol. 3: 58, 'Visit of Paul Robeson'.
51 Kartomi, 'Growing up in a musical Quaker family': 302.
52 'Margaret Kartomi wins Australia Indonesia research award', *Music Archive of Monash University* website, 15 March 2018.
53 NAA: ASIO, Robeson vol. 3: 57, 'Visit of Paul Robeson'.
54 Mitchell, 'Adelaide raised roof for Paul'.
55 'His voice a gift—and a burden'.
56 Duberman, *Paul Robeson*: 740, n. 64. See also FBI: Paul Robeson, Sr, Part 26 of 31, FBIHQ File 100-12304, *FBI Vault* website.
57 Val Howe, 'Mrs Robeson speaks for us', *UAW News Sheet*, SA branch, November–December 1960: 3–4.

14 'A kind of farewell':

1 Author interview with Hazel Butorac, Perth, 23 September 2019.
2 See John Docker, *In a Critical Condition* (Penguin, 1984): 30–3; 'Adelaide, Perth welcome Robesons', *Tribune*, 7 December 1960: 10.
3 Nathan Hobby, *The Red Witch: A Biography of Katharine Suzannah Prichard* (Miegunyah Press, 2022): 351.
4 NAA: ASIO, CPA—Aborigines vol. 4, 60/787: 145, 'Union of Australian Women—WA Division—Management Committee Meeting', 29 November 1960.

5 'Adelaide, Perth welcome Robesons'.
6 Martin Duberman, *Paul Robeson* (New Press, 1989): 491.
7 'Lloyd Davies', *AustLit* website, 13 March 2019.
8 SLWA: Annette Cameron Collection, 1919–1995 (acc. 4765A), Box 26, Folder 7a, Annette Cameron to Martin Duberman, 3 June 1983.
9 Email from Margaret Lindley to author, 5 January 2021.
10 Hazel Butorac interview, 23 September 2019.
11 'George H Clutsam', *Australian Variety Theatre Archive* website, n.d. (updated and expanded from: Clay Djubal, *What Oh Tonight*, PhD dissertation, University of Queensland, 2005).
12 Frank Harvey, 'Paul Robeson looks the world over', *West Australian*, 1 December 1960: 12.
13 John Clements Oral History Collection, biographical summary, Murdoch University Library. He was known more formally to ASIO as Harold Godric Clements.
14 Sharon Delmege, 'Allawah Grove Native Settlement: Housing and assimilation', *Aboriginal History*, 39 (2015): 96.
15 Trisha Kotai-Ewers, 'Frederick Bert Vickers (1903–1985)', *ADB* website, 2012.
16 'Promotion of Aboriginal arts', *Beverley Times*, 16 December 1960: 7. Exhibition catalogue entitled *Exhibition of Paintings by a Selection of Aboriginal Artists, 28 November – 9 December 1969*, Dulux Colour Centre, First Floor, NMLA Building, 81 St George's Terrace, Perth—see SLWA: PR10914.
17 Proceeds from the sale of catalogues went to the recently formed WA Association for the Advancement of Coloured People—see SLWA: Doreen Trainor Papers, 8342, Box 1. See also 'Palmyra woman helps Aboriginal artists', *Sunday Times*, 27 November 1960: 21.
18 Correspondence in SLWA: Doreen Trainor Papers, 8342/5, Miscellaneous Correspondence, Folder 2; note especially letter from WAAACP to Secretary, Original Australians Progress Association, 19 August 1960.
19 Stephen Kinnane, *Shadow Lines: The Story of Jessie Argyle and Edward Smith* (Fremantle Arts Centre Press, 2003); Anna Haebich, *Dancing in Shadows: Histories of Noongar Performance* (UWA Press, 2018): 186–209.
20 Haebich, ibid.: 195.
21 Jo Darbyshire, *The Coolbaroo Club, 1947–1960* (catalogue of an exhibition titled, *The Coolbaroo Club and the Coffee Pot: Two Extraordinary Places in 1950s Perth*, held at Perth Town Hall, 20 October – 5 November 2010): 7.
22 Haebich, *Dancing in Shadows*: 197; *Westralian Aborigine*, March–April 1956: 1; Darbyshire, ibid.: 6.
23 Darbyshire, ibid.
24 John Joseph Jones to John Clements, 28 October 1960, copy in NAA: ASIO, Robeson vol. 1: 14 of 105.
25 'Our songs he'd like to keep', *Daily News*, 2 December 1960: 4.

26 'Letter from the West', *Target*, February 1961:14, copy in NAA: ASIO, Robeson vol. 3: 48.
27 Fidelio, 'Unorthodox Paul Robeson in fine form', *West Australian*, 2 December 1960: 12.
28 Email from Margaret Lindley to author, 5 January 2021.
29 Fidelio, 'Unorthodox Paul Robeson in fine form'; Roger Simms, 'Albert Hubert Carl Kornweibel (1892–1980)', *ADB* website, 2006 (originally published in 2000).
30 SLWA: Oral History Project Ref OH 3307, transcript of interview with Colin Hollett, Westrail Workshops [Midland]. Interviewed 1 May 2002 by Simone McGurk, Australian Society for the Study of Labour History (Perth branch).
31 Patrick Bertola and Bobbie Oliver (eds), *The Workshops: A History of the Midland Government Railway Workshops* (UWA Press, 2006).
32 Tony Thomas, 'Memories of a Bolshevik baritone', *Quadrant Online*, 13 September 2016.
33 Ibid. See also the account in R McCracken, 'The workforce cultures', in Bertola and Oliver (eds), *The Workshops*: 206–7.
34 SLWA: Oral History Project, transcript of interview with Colin Hollett.
35 Thomas, 'Memories of a Bolshevik baritone'.
36 'Adelaide, Perth welcome Robesons'.
37 Skye Smith, 'Indigenous apprenticeships at the Workshops', *Papers in Labour History*, 28 (October 2004—'The Midland Railway Workshops Centenary Issue', Bobbie Oliver et al., eds): 31–42.
38 'Ol' Man River', *West Australian*, 3 December 1960: 14.
39 'Adelaide, Perth welcome Robesons'.
40 SLWA: Oral History Project, transcript of interview with Colin Hollett.
41 'Adelaide, Perth welcome Robesons'.
42 NAA: ASIO, Robeson vol. 3: 37, Eslanda Robeson to John Clements, 4 October 1960.
43 NAA: ASIO, Robeson vol. 2: 84, 'Western Australia, Paul Robeson—welcomed at afternoon tea party organised by the Australian Peace Council', 5 December 1960. There is also at NAA: ASIO, ibid.: 91 a shorter version of the report that adds a list of those present.
44 NAA: ASIO, ibid.: 84.
45 Stuart Macintyre, 'Patrick Lawrence (Paddy) Troy (1908–1978)', *ADB* website, 2006 (originally published in 2002).
46 For Sam Aarons' account of his time in Spain, see 'Reminiscences of the Spanish Civil War', *Australian Left Review*, 39 (March 1973): 24–9. This is a posthumous publication of an interview conducted on 23 December 1968.
47 Amira Inglis, *Australians in the Spanish Civil War* (Allen & Unwin, 1987): 140.
48 Mark Aarons, *The Family File* (Black Inc., 2010): 76.
49 NAA: ASIO, Robeson vol. 2: 56, 'Western Australia: Paul Robeson', 16 December 1960.

50 'Address by Paul and Eslanda Robeson', audio recording in John Clements Oral History Collection, Murdoch University. See also a detailed report at ASIO: NAA, ibid.: 59, 'Australian Peace Council (WA Division), visit of Paul and Eslanda Robeson'. Nicola Sacco and Bartolomeo Vanzetti were anarchist Italian immigrants in the United States who were in 1920 convicted of murder during an armed robbery. Despite widespread concern that they had been unfairly tried, they were executed in 1927; their case has long been remembered as one of politically and ethnically inspired injustice. When Clements was speaking, the case of Julius and Ethel Rosenberg, executed in 1953 for spying for the Soviet Union, was widely regarded as a case of judicial injustice. Subsequent evidence suggests that Julius was guilty but Ethel may not have been. Linus Pauling was a Nobel-prize-winning scientist whose involvement in the communist-led peace movement, especially his vocal opposition to nuclear weapons, led him to be denied his passport in 1952 and subject to other government scrutiny.

51 'Address by Paul and Eslanda Robeson', my transcription. There is also a transcription by an ASIO agent in ASIO: NAA, ibid.: 59–61, and an incomplete and often faulty transcription by Tony Thomas in SLWA.

52 Paul's mention of Canada seems to be referring to an incident in 1952 when he was turned away at the border even though no passport was required at that time. Duberman, *Paul Robeson*: 399.

53 'WA radio station censors Robeson', *Tribune*, 21 December 1960: 12.

54 NAA: ASIO, Robeson vol. 3: 30, John Clements, circular letter, 22 December 1960.

55 The distributors were listed as Grand Specialities, Box K808 GPO Perth.

56 'Guide to the papers of James Penberthy: Series 12. Music manuscripts: orchestral, c1941–1990 (Kooree and the Mists)', *Trove* website, 2005.

57 James Penberthy, 'Robeson is beyond criticism', *Sunday Times*, 4 December 1960: 35.

58 NAA: ASIO, Robeson vol. 2: 18, summary report headed 'Paul Robeson'.

59 NAA: ASIO, ibid.: 57, 'Western Australia: Paul Robeson'.

60 'Alan Finger: 1909–1985', in Bob Boughton et al. (eds), *Comrades! Lives of Australian Communists* (Search Foundation, 2020): 87–90.

61 NAA: ASIO, Robeson vol. 2: 53, 'Australian Peace Council'.

62 Hobby, *The Red Witch*: 351.

Chapter 15: 'A symbol of hope for many'

1 Paul Robeson to Clara Rockmore, 6 December 1960, quoted in Martin Duberman, *Paul Robeson* (New Press, 1989): 491.

2 Fryer Library: Collection UQFL30—Bill Morrow Papers, Box 4, folder labelled 'Election dodgers, ARU materials, Peace movement material, letter from Jessie Street to Alf Dickie'; V Drannikov, 'Paul Robeson in Moscow', *Trud*, 2 April 1961. *Trud* was the newspaper of the Russian All-Union Central Council of Trade

Unions. An abridged typescript in English was produced on 8 April 1961, copy stamped by the Australia-Soviet Friendship Society in Phillip Street in Sydney.

3 Henrik Gurkow in interview with Paul Robeson, 'My plans: Fight for freedom', *Neue Zeit* (New Times), 27 April 1961, trans. and included in Kenneth O'Reilly, *Black Americans* (Carroll & Graf, 1994): 378–9.

4 Duberman, *Paul Robeson*: 490.

5 'Peace', *The Bulletin*, 11 November 1961: 11.

6 NAA: ASIO, Robeson vol. 2: 35, 'CP of A interest in native affairs', 19 January 1961.

7 NAA: ASIO, Robeson vol. 1: 58, typed extract from *News for Everywoman*.

8 NAA: ASIO, Robeson vol. 3: 30, John Clements, circular letter to Peace Council members, 22 December 1960.

9 NFSA: *Paul Robeson for Peace*; advertisement for the record in *Peace Action*, October 1962: 16.

10 NLNZ: Paul Robeson's message to Mrs Morrow and songs by Unity Artists of New Zealand, MSD10-0988 (disc marked 'AUSTAS Record and Radio Centre, Sydney, 1960').

11 NAA: ASIO, Robeson vol. 2: 41, 'CP of A Fremantle Branch Meeting', 12 December 1960.

12 'Aborigines demand nothing less than full rights', *Tribune*, 22 February 1961: 7.

13 NAA: ASIO, CPA—Aborigines vol. 4: 22, 26, 27.

14 Ibid.: 30–3.

15 Anderson attracted considerable ASIO surveillance—see his file at NAA: ASIO, Anderson, Robert Vincent Volume 1, A6119, 3693. There are four other files, not yet digitised.

16 'Bob Anderson interviewed by Robin Sullivan and Rodney Sullivan', *Queensland Speaks* website, 12 December 2013.

17 NAA: ASIO, CPA—Aborigines vol. 4: 107–9.

18 The ASIO agent records the name as Ruth Page Corby.

19 NAA: ASIO, Robeson vol. 3: 51, 'Union of Australian Women', 26 February 1961.

20 Jessie Street to Eslanda Robeson, Tweed Heads South, 16 April 1961. There are copies of the letter in SLNSW: Faith Bandler Papers, Collection 3, c.1938–c.2001, MLMSS 10400, Box 1 (7), and in Correspondence 2300–2397, February–August 1961, in Series 1, Correspondence 1951–1975, Council for Aboriginal Rights, MS 12913, State Library Victoria.

21 Barbara Ransby outlines several book projects that Eslanda had at this time but was unable to complete for medical reasons, in *Eslanda* (Yale University Press, 2013): 256.

22 Duberman, *Paul Robeson*: 497.

23 Drannikov, 'Paul Robeson in Moscow'.

24 Gurkow in interview with Robeson, 'My plans: Fight for freedom'.

25 Duberman, *Paul Robeson*: 491.

26 Paul Robeson to Betty Bateman, 7 November 1961, cited in Gerald Horne, *Paul Robeson* (Pluto Press, 2016): 184.
27 Duberman, *Paul Robeson*: 438.
28 Ibid.: 499.
29 NLNZ: O'Connor Material, Eslanda to Shirley O'Connor, 12 January 1962.
30 *The Guardian* (Melbourne), 5 April 1962: n.p.
31 NAA: ASIO, Robeson vol. 3: 18, '"Paul Robeson" Evening', 26 February 1963.
32 *Building Worker*, 16:3 (April 1963): 7.
33 Grant Olwage, *Paul Robeson's Voices* (Oxford University Press, 2023): 154.
34 Ibid.: 308, n. 138.
35 Ibid.: 156, quoting Elizabeth Perkins to Paul Robeson, undated, Victoria, in MSRC Robeson Collection.
36 Ibid.: 158, quoting Mona Frame to Paul Robeson, 27 March 1963, in MSRC Robeson Collection.
37 Paul's return to the US was reported in the *SMH*, which noted that he planned 'to retire from entertainment and to devote his remaining years to the struggle for civil rights in America'. 'Paul Robeson returns to America', *SMH*, 24 December 1963: 1.
38 Ransby, *Eslanda*: 256–9.
39 Ibid.: 269–70.
40 'Remembrances of Eslanda', *Freedomways*, 6 (1966): 341.
41 'Eslanda Robeson dead', *Tribune*, 9 February 1966: 9.
42 Ann Curthoys, *Freedom Ride: A Freedom Rider Remembers* (Allen & Unwin, 2002): 42–5.
43 Garry Raffaelo, 'New look Christmas message', *Canberra Times*, 5 November 1964: 21.
44 John Howard, 'One of the great entertainers', *Canberra Times*, 9 February 1965: 12. The program screened on 7 February 1965.
45 'What to stay home for', *Canberra Times*, 1 February 1965: 13. Author's memory.
46 'Famous Negro bass dies', *Evening Post*, 24 January 1976. Clipping in NLNZ: Rona Bailey Papers, Folder 6.
47 'Robeson was first star', *Courier-Mail*, 25 January 1976: 4.
48 'Paul Robeson: He was a champion of the Negro cause and singer extraordinary', *Courier-Mail*, 26 January 1976: 5. See also 'Curtain drops for Paul Robeson', *SMH*, 26 January 1976: 5.
49 'Paul Robeson', *Tribune*, 28 January 1976: 7.
50 Advertisement, 'Paul Robeson—the life of a coloured man', *Tribune*, 11 August 1976: 11.
51 'Paul Robeson ... "the universal man"', *Anti-War Forum*, April 1976, copy in UMA: Papers of Sam Goldbloom, 2003.0002, Box 3, Folder 18. The article was reprinted from *Black News Service*, 1 (23 February 1976).
52 UMA: Consolidated Records of Congress for International Co-operation and Disarmament, 1979.0152, Box 45, Series 2, File 30.

53 Ralph Gibson, *One Woman's Life: A Memoir of Dorothy Gibson* (Hale & Iremonger, 1980): 114.

54 Shana Redmond, *Everything Man* (Duke University Press, 2020): 8.

55 Peter Luck (presenter) (1979), 'Great works' [TV program], *This Fabulous Century*, episode 36, Seven Network, Sydney.

56 Saul J Turell (director), *Paul Robeson: Tribute to an Artist* [motion picture], Janus Films, New York, 1979.

57 NFSA: 'First singer at Opera House'.

58 *Queensland Community Arts News*, 1 (March 1987): 1; Nancy Wills, *Robeson* (Gem Publications, 1987): 22–3. See also 'How deep the bells came to ring' (an extract from Wills, *Robeson*), *Tribune*, 1 April 1987: 8.

59 NLA: Nancy Wills Oral History Transcript. Wills was in Canberra for the performance of *Deep Bells Ring* and was interviewed on 17 and 18 September 1987.

60 'BWIU presents *Deep Bells Ring: The Life and Songs of Paul Robeson*, written by Nancy Wills, April 1–11, 1987, Princess Theatre', programme, in author's possession.

61 'Robeson recalled in hard hats', *Courier-Mail*, 26 March 1987: n.p.

62 'Roadknight rings the bells', *Courier-Mail*, 18 March 1987: n.p.

63 'BWIU presents *Deep Bells Ring*', programme: 2. See also NLA: O'Neill, Errol (interviewee), *Errol O'Neill Interviewed by Wendy Lowenstein for the Communists and the Left in the Arts and Community Oral History Project* [sound recording], 6 July 1995, TRC 3111/35.

64 Wills, *Robeson*, contains the full script. See review by John Harris in the *Daily Sun* (Brisbane), 6 June 1987: 22.

65 The first workplace lunchtime concert was held on 25 March at the Myer Centre construction site in Queen Street, Brisbane, followed by theatre performances from 1 to 11 April 1987 at the Princess Theatre; see 'Deep Bells Ring', *AusStage* website, n.d.

66 'Robeson recalled in hard hats'; Nancy Wills and Mark Roberts, 'BWIU's theatrical triumph', *Tribune*, 8 April 1987: 5.

67 'Tunes and times of Robeson', *Daily Sun* (Brisbane), 28 March 1987: n.p.; John Harris, 'Robeson story a powerful work', *Daily Sun*, 4 April 1987: n.p.; Peta Koch, 'Show has the ring of success', *Courier-Mail*, 2 April 1987: n.p.; Melissa Finlay, 'Workers applaud an insight into the past', *Queensland Times* (Ipswich), 8 April 1987: n.p.

68 The revived version played at the Schonell Theatre at the University of Queensland in Brisbane on 2–5 September 1987. 'Show rings bell for Nancy', *Courier-Mail*, 3 September 1987: n.p.

69 Sue Gough, 'A powerful tribute to Robeson the legend', *The Australian*, 3 April 1987: n.p. See also Kerry McGee, 'A night out for the soul: The uplifting life of Paul Robeson', *Time Off*, 9 April 1987: n.p.

70 Barry Oakley, 'A conviction that rings with political myopia', *Times on Sunday*, 12 April 1987: n.p.

71 Ann Nugent, 'The deep bells ring hollow in a didactic production', *Canberra Times*, 14 September 1987: 17. See also Karen Middleton, 'Deep Bells Ring', *Canberra Times*, 10 September 1987, *Good Times* supplement: 1–2.
72 Angela Bennie, 'Robeson the man still elusive', *The Australian*, 25 September 1987: 9. See also Andrew Harris, 'The ole man of politics comes to the workers again', *SMH*, 15 September 1987: n.p; Bob Evans, 'Paul Robeson: Salute to the voice of freedom', *Good Weekend*, 19 September 1987, reprinted 13 July 2017: 71–4.
73 The Queensland towns tour lasted from 15 February to 12 March 1988. The Melbourne performances were from 24 March to 2 April 1988, reviewed by Leonard Radic, 'The bells still ring for Robeson', *The Age*, 25 March 1988: 14.
74 'Andy Rashleigh: Personal details', *IMDb* website, n.d.; 'Robeson Song of Freedom', *Theatricalia* website, n.d.
75 Simei-Barton had directed *Feiva/Favour* by New Guinea playwright John Kolia and subsequently *The Nine Night* by Caribbean writer Edgar Nkosi White.
76 Auckland Central City Library, Theatre—Pacific Theatre collection, 'Robeson: Song of Freedom' programme. In the programme, the producers thank Rona Bailey for 'support and encouragement'.
77 Redmond, *Everything Man*: 16. Considerable material on the worldwide celebration is held in the Paul Robeson Centennial Project records at Columbia College Chicago.
78 Hannah Middleton wrote to ABC Classic FM on 3 October 1997 praising their program and informing them of the work of the committee—STHA: Hannah Middleton Papers, Correspondence Folder.
79 'Paul Robeson's Ashanti chief's stool: An update', *Sydney Trades Press*, November 2021: 1–4.
80 SLNSW: Hannah Middleton Collection, 69758 (catalogue entry).
81 NLNZ: Rona Bailey Papers, correspondence from April 1997 onwards concerning the acquisition of photographs from the tour for an exhibition.
82 STHA: Hannah Middleton Papers, Correspondence Folder, Ken Douglas to Rona Bailey, Trade Union History Project, 4 March 1998, copy attached to letter from Bailey to Middleton, 9 March 1998.
83 STHA: ibid., Rona Bailey to Middleton, 16 March 1998.
84 Peter Franks, 'Report on the TUHP celebration', *TUHP Newsletter*, 22 (June 1998): 5–6.
85 NLNZ: Rona Bailey Papers, Folder 5, typescript of speech on 7 April 1998, Paul Robeson birthday celebrations evening held by the Trade Union History Project in Wellington.
86 NLNZ: Rona Bailey Papers, audiotape titled 'Robeson Centennial—Speeches', typed unsigned note to Bailey listing the speeches and songs.
87 NLNZ, Rona Bailey Papers, copy of Franks, 'Report on the TUHP celebration': 4.
88 Ibid. lists 'Voice of the People', *New Zealand Listener*, 11 April 1998; 'US discovering a forgotten hero', *Evening Post*, 4 April 1998; and several shorter articles.

89 Franks, 'Report on the TUHP celebration'.
90 Marie Russell (presenter), 'Remembering Paul Robeson' (12 April 1998) [radio program], *Spectrum*, RNZ, Wellington (replayed on 27 February 2015).
91 STHA: Hannah Middleton Papers, Correspondence Folder, circular letter from Middleton to various, dated August 1997, seeking to form a Paul Robeson 100th Birthday Committee in Sydney.
92 STHA: ibid., letterhead on letters sent by Middleton during May 1998.
93 'RSVP', Letters to the Editor, *SMH*, 18 December 1987.
94 STHA: Hannah Middleton Papers, Correspondence Folder, Middleton to John Coombs, 10 October 1997.
95 Ibid., Middleton to Barbara Tiernan, 20 August 1997.
96 Ibid., Roadknight to Middleton, 21 September 1997.
97 Ibid., Evan Williams, Secretary, NSW Ministry of the Arts to John Davis, Australian Music Centre, 23 February 1998.
98 Australian House of Representatives, *Debates*, 30 March 1998, 'Paul Robeson: Centenary of birth', Mr Robert Brown (Charlton).
99 Queensland Legislative Assembly, *Debates*, 21 April 1998, 'Ministerial Statement: Mr M Miller', Hon. NKW Wilson (Mulgrave).
100 Amy Egan, 'Rolling along with Robeson', *Daily Telegraph*, 3 April 1998. Middleton wrote to the cast of the international revival of *Show Boat* inviting them to attend the exhibition and concert; STHA: Hannah Middleton Papers, Correspondence Folder, Middleton to Walter van Nieuwkuyk, Show Boat, 31 March 1998.
101 STHA: ibid., Middleton, 'Paul Robeson Centenary Exhibition'.
102 University of Chicago, 'Paul Robeson Centennial Celebration … Major centennial events and exhibitions: Pacific Rim, Sydney, Australia': 1, describes the exhibition.
103 Demand was such that the record had been reissued in 1965—see 'Available once more', *Peace Action*, October 1965: 16. A digitised version is held by the NFSA (see NFSA: *Paul Robeson for Peace*).
104 When Paul Robeson died, 'AK' (possibly Bert Keesing of the Australia-Soviet Friendship Society) wrote in *Tribune* (28 January 1976: 7): 'Many of us still carefully preserve the LP record made of one of these meetings, held in Paddington Town Hall, Sydney.' Ernie Boatswain of the BWIU says in an interview in 1997 that he still has a scratchy old 78 recording of the event as a memento; Evans, 'Paul Robeson: Salute to the voice of freedom'. At least two copies of this record, converted to tape, were given to the 100th Birthday Celebration Committee in Sydney in 1998; STHA: Hannah Middleton Papers, cassette tape labelled 'Robeson at Paddington … Message of Peace' (20 February 1950).
105 STHA: Hannah Middleton Papers, Correspondence Folder, Roadknight to Middleton, 21 September 1997.
106 Email from Middleton to author, 16 August 2023.

107 STHA: Hannah Middleton Papers, Correspondence Folder, Evan Williams, Secretary, NSW Ministry of the Arts to John Davis, Australian Music Centre, 31 March 1998.
108 Ibid., Middleton, 'Paul Robeson Centenary Exhibition'.
109 Ibid., Bob Brown, MHR, to Hannah Middleton, 24 April 1998.
110 University of Chicago, 'Paul Robeson Centennial Celebration ... Major Centennial Events and Exhibitions': 1, 2. See copy of the advertising flyer in STHA: Hannah Middleton Papers, Misc. 5, Middleton to Pat O'Shane, 12 March 1998. The Melbourne concert was on 19 April and the Adelaide concert on 10 September. See 'Paying tribute to "old man" Robeson', *Pulse*, cutting from Adelaide newspaper, in NLNZ: Rona Bailey Papers.
111 The exhibition, facilitated by local resident Don Mudie, was opened by the mayor, Peter Black, at the Napredak Club, and Hannah spoke—'Robeson exhibition for a special man', *Barrier Daily Truth*, 4 September 1998: 5. The exhibition opened on 5 September.
112 NSW Legislative Assembly, *Debates*, 20 October 1998, 'Paul Robeson Exhibition', Mr Thompson (Rockdale), followed by Mr Aquilina (Riverstone).
113 Ron Banks, 'Revisiting Robeson', *West Australian*, 30 October 2004: 9.
114 Midland Redevelopment Authority, *A Tribute to Paul Robeson*, 27 November 2004, concert programme.
115 'Theatre—Kevin Maynor', Auckland Central City Library, theatre programme: 3.
116 Seven performances from 20 February to 1 March in Wellington at the NZ Fringe and twelve from 4 to 15 March 2015 at the Adelaide Fringe Festival. See Wellington Quakers, 'Quaker theatre outing, Paul Robeson at the Fringe Festival, 22 February 2015' [Facebook event].
117 Redmond, *Everything Man*: 61–2.
118 For example, see event at Toorak Uniting Church in Melbourne in 2015, 'Tribute to Paul Robeson', *Eventfinda* website; and another at the Anglican Church of St Peters in Adelaide in 2019—see Mal Byrne, 'The life and songs of Paul Robeson (Adelaide Fringe Festival)', *Limelight: Music, Arts & Culture*, 13 March 2019.
119 'The men who built the Opera House', *Building Worker Special Supplement*, September 1973: 1, 3, 5. The supplement had a photo of Paul at the construction site on the front cover.
120 CH7AR: '22/9/1987, Paul Robeson', ATNC1-984.
121 Mahir Ali, 'Big voice of the left Paul Robeson resounds to this day', *The Australian*, 9 November 2010: 16.
122 Helen Pitt, 'Sixty years on, opera singer pays tribute to Paul Robeson', *SMH*, 9 November 2020: n.p.
123 Sandra Goldbloom Zurbo, *My Father's Shadow*: 215; Phillip Adams (host), 'Life as Samuel Goldbloom's daughter', *Late Night Live* [podcast], 4 September 2023.
124 Berenice Nyland interviewed by Sari Braithwaite, Melbourne, 3 July 2008.

Index

THE MIEGUNYAH PRESS
This book was designed and typeset by Cannon Typesetting
The text was set in 11¾pt Whitman
with 15 points of leading
The text is printed on 80 gsm woodfree
This book was edited by Katie Purvis